William Wickes

A Treatise on the Accentuation of the 21 so Called Prose Books of the Old Testament

William Wickes

A Treatise on the Accentuation of the 21 so Called Prose Books of the Old Testament

ISBN/EAN: 9783744696579

Printed in Europe, USA, Canada, Australia, Japan

Cover: Foto ©Lupo / pixelio.de

More available books at **www.hansebooks.com**

טעמי כ״א ספרים

A TREATISE ON THE ACCENTUATION

OF THE TWENTY-ONE SO-CALLED

PROSE BOOKS OF THE OLD TESTAMENT

WITH A FACSIMILE OF A PAGE OF THE CODEX ASSIGNED TO
BEN-ASHER IN ALEPPO

BY

WILLIAM WICKES, D.D.

Oxford
AT THE CLARENDON PRESS
1887

[*All rights reserved*]

PREFACE.

THE present Treatise aims at explaining the accentuation of the so-called Prose Books—twenty-one in number, according to Jewish reckoning[1]—of the Hebrew Bible. The favourable reception given to my Work טעמי אמ״ת, on the accentuation of the three Poetical Books (Psalms, Proverbs, and Job), has encouraged me to proceed further, and complete the investigation which I then commenced.

I have been asked why, contrary to the usual practice, I *began* with the accentuation of the three Books. My answer is that the subject seemed to me to stand in special need of careful examination[2]. There was besides this advantage in taking the three Books first, that owing to their comparatively small compass, it was more easy to examine them exhaustively and so to arrive at the general principles underlying their accentuation. Those principles once established had then only to be applied, with the necessary modifications, to the twenty-one Books.

I have endeavoured to carry out with thoroughness the task I had undertaken, and have not intentionally allowed difficulties in the accentuation to pass unnoticed. My plan has been, either, by a process of induction, to bring such instances under a general rule; or to furnish a special explanation of them, partly in the course of the Work, and more particularly in the Notes collected in Appendix I. Of course, I have not been concerned to *defend*

---

[1] The two Books of 1 and 2 Samuel, 1 and 2 Kings, and 1 and 2 Chronicles are counted respectively as one. The same is the case with Ezra and Nehemiah. The ten Minor Prophets are also taken together to make one book. In this calculation the beginning and the end of Job (i. 1–iii. 1 and xlii. 7–17) are not taken into account, which however are pointed according to the same system.— It is to be observed that Jewish writers know nothing of the distinction between Prose and Poetical Books; they speak simply of the twenty-one and three Books.

[2] I hope that it is no breach of confidence on my part, when I state that the late Prof. Ewald told me that, whilst he had no doubt that he had furnished the true explanation of the prose accentuation, he was not so satisfied in regard to the poetical.

the accentuation in all cases. It is enough if we can trace the principles on which the accentuators proceeded, or the interpretation which in particular instances led to the accentuation employed.

I have found it necessary often to propose a correction of the *textus receptus;* but have very rarely done so without manuscript authority. The labour of collating MSS. in our great English collections and the Libraries of the Continent, for a text of such extent as that of the Old Testament, has been very considerable, and one which no previous writer on the accents has thought of undertaking. Yet, without a correct text, what hope can there be of establishing any rules on a satisfactory basis?

One Codex, which is in the Synagogue at Aleppo, and which I have been able to consult, although only indirectly, has the reputation of having come from the hand of Ben-Asher himself, and of having been, on that account, always regarded as a model copy for fixing the readings of the Sacred Text. Its claim to the exceptional importance thus assigned to it I have considered in the pages immediately following.

I have once more to express my obligations to my friend Dr. Baer, for the valuable assistance he has willingly rendered me. His familiar acquaintance with the Massora—a department of study in which he ranks *facile princeps* [1]—has been of special service to me.

W. WICKES.

81, WOODSTOCK ROAD, OXFORD,
May, 1887.

---

[1] I have the pleasure of informing scholars, that there is at length a prospect of a complete and correct edition of the Massora. The firm Romm in Wilna (already favourably known through a splendid edition of the Babylonian Talmud lately brought out by them) have in hand a new edition of the so-called Great Rabbinical Bible (מקרא גדול), to which Dr. Baer has undertaken to furnish the Massora. The arrangement adopted will be the same as in Jacob ben-Chayyim's edition, with this exception, that wherever a word occurs *for the first time,* there all that is Massoretic in regard to it will be given; so that, by the help of a Concordance, any particular rubric will be readily traced. I may add that the first part of Dr. Baer's manuscript is already in the printers' hands.

MSS. CONSULTED FOR THE PRESENT WORK.

I. BIBLE MSS.

Codex in the Synagogue at Aleppo—containing the whole text, the punctuation of which is assigned in an epigraph[1] to the famous Aaron ben-Asher (beginning of the 10th century). M. Isidore Loeb, Secretary of L'Alliance Israélite, well known from his learned contributions to the Revue des Études Juives, was good enough to procure for me, through his correspondent at Aleppo, some of the accentual readings of this Codex.

As it is of no little importance for us to know whether such a model codex[2] really exists, to which we might refer for the correction of the *textus receptus*[3], I think it necessary to say a few words on the subject of the epigraph above referred to.—Jacob Sappir, who (in his Work, אבן ספיר, vol. i. p. 12^b) was the first to furnish a copy of this epigraph, which he obtained through a friend at Aleppo, accepted it as genuine, and was followed by Graetz (Monatsch. für Gesch. und Wiss. des Judenthums, 1871, p. 6, 1887, p. 30), and by Strack (Prol. crit., pp. 44–46). My reasons for arriving at an opposite conclusion are briefly the following:—

1. *The character of writing* of the Codex. M. Loeb succeeded in obtaining for me a photograph of a page of the same (Gen. xxvi. 34–xxvii. 30),—a copy of which serves as Frontispiece to the present Work[4]. Although this copy has not been quite so successfully executed as I could have wished, it is sufficiently clear to enable adepts to form a judgment as to the approximate date of the writing. I venture to give my own opinion, which is that the MS. presents a specimen of

---

[1] Copied Dikd. hat., p. xxii. inf.

[2] Ben-Asher was (as is well known) the normative authority for fixing the text as we now have it.

[3] For fixing the *accentuation* such a Codex would be invaluable. My remarks on it therefore will be seen not to be out of place.

[4] The photograph and the copy are both much reduced in size. The height of each column of writing (without the Massora) is in the original 23 cm., and average breadth 6 cm. The size of each page is therefore somewhat smaller than that of Codex Babylonicus. The MS. is of parchment equally smooth (*très poli*, I am told) on both sides.

calligraphy, not in keeping with the early period to which it is assigned. Really old MSS., provided with Massora—as Codex Babylonicus (of the date of Ben-Asher, A. D. 916) and Erfurt 3 (a facsimile of which will appear in Stade's Geschichte Israel's, vol. i)—have a plainer and less finished appearance, and the characters are of a coarser type. I would draw attention, in particular, to the artificial arrangement by which a separate Massoretic rubric of two lines and no more is introduced above and below each column.—It is not, however, on the graphical peculiarities that I lay the main stress.

2. The conclusive proof is to be found in the fact that the punctuation is, in many instances, *at variance with Ben-Asher's known practice* and the rules laid down by the Palestinian Massoretes.

It will be observed that *Métheg generally fails*, e. g. יַעֲקֹב (often; only once, col. 3, l. 7, וְיַעֲקֹב); אָנֹכִי (col. 2, l. 3, although אָנֹכִי, col. 2, l. 6 from below); קִלְלָתְךָ (col. 2, l. 8); הָאַתָּה (col. 3, l. 3); וַאֲבָרְכָה (col. 1, l. 21); &c. Now although this is constantly the case in Spanish and even Oriental MSS.[5], we should not expect such an irregularity in a model text marked by the careful hand of the Master himself (הַמְלַמֵּד הַגָּדוֹל, as he is termed), particularly when we bear in mind that it is just on the use of Métheg that his controversy with his rival, Ben-Naphtali, mainly turns. Still less should we be prepared for the *false introduction of Métheg*, as in קַח־לִי (col. 1, l. 5 from below) and וַיִּשְׁתַּחַו (col. 3, l. 6 from below),—the latter Ben-Naphtali's pointing[6], and expressly condemned in Dikd. hat. § 30, אִם הַקִּיף תְּפוּל הַמַּעְיָא. Moreover, קִלְלָתְךָ (col. 2, l. 8) is Ben-Naphtali's vocalization, whereas Ben-Asher would have pointed קִלֲלָתְךָ[7].

---

[5] It is the *light* Métheg that generally fails; *heavy* Métheg is as generally introduced, and so in this page, אֶת־יַעֲקֹב, וְיִתֶּן־לְךָ, וַיְבָרֲכֵהוּ. On the failure of Métheg, comp. Man. du Lect., p. 98, ובמקצת ספרים כותבין הגעיה ובמקצת אין כותבין אלא סומכין על דעת הקורא.

[6] Cf. the examples brought together by Baer, Gen., p. 82, note 1.

[7] See the list of Variations between Ben-Asher and Ben-Naphtali in Baer's Gen., p. 84.

We may also be surprised at not finding the Parasha (col. 1, l. 3) marked in the margin, for it was expressly to note these divisions that Maimonides (see יד החזקה, ספר תורה, c. viii, § 4) consulted a text written and pointed by Ben-Asher.—N. B. The ס (col. 1, l. 3, margin) does not stand for סתומה, as the same sign (col. 3, l. 20) shews, but for סדר. Many punctators, who took no notice of the Parashas, were in the habit of marking in this way the Palestinian Sidras, as may be seen in Ox. 10, 2326; Br. Mus. Or. 2201.

So much from the page before us. Other proofs are not wanting. Sappir informs us (ibid., p. 12) that he sent from Jerusalem a list of words, which he had found variously written in texts (as to punctuation, *scriptio plena* and *def.*, &c.), to a distinguished Jewish scholar in Aleppo, with the request that he would examine the Codex and note for him how these words were written in it. This was done, and subsequently Sappir published in the Jewish periodical, לבנון (I. pp. 31, 32), some of these various readings, from which I select the following: יְהִי אוֹר (Gen. i. 3)[8]; הָאִוָּה (iv. 23)[9]; בֵּית אֵל (xii. 8, two words)[10]; כְּסִיָה (Ex. xvii. 16, one word)[11]; all contrary to Ben-Asher's rules or the Palestinian Massora, and which therefore could not have been so written by Ben-Asher himself. I also sent a list of passages, which I wished compared on account of the accentuation, and M. Loeb's correspondent volunteered the information that וְאִיֶּנּוּ (Qoh. vi. 2) is so pointed with Gaya, and יִבְחַר (ix. 4) so vocalized, for יְבָחַר; both mistakes which we may be sure would never have been made by Ben-Asher.

From these few test-passages we may conclude that the statement, assigning this Codex to Ben-Asher, is a *fabrication*,—merely introduced to enhance the value of the same,—and that the whole long epigraph, with its list of Qaraite names (shewing it to be of Qaraite origin), &c., is untrustworthy and undeserving of serious notice. How many other epigraphs to Jewish texts would, when carefully tested, have to be rejected, notably that of the Cambridge Codex 12, which makes a Spanish MS., unquestionably younger than the one we have been considering, written in the year 856[12]!

Attached to the Aleppo Codex is what the Jews call a קונטרס (a copy of which M. Loeb also procured for me). This farrago of grammatical and Massoretic rules has been sufficiently described in Dikd. hat., Pref., pp. xxi–xxiii, from a copy obtained by the Qaraite,

---

[8] So Ben-Naphtali. Cf. Baer, Gen., p. 74; Ginsb. Mas. ח, § 589.

[9] So Ben-Naphtali. Cf. Baer, Gen., p. 82, note 7; Pss. 1880, p. 138, note 6.

[10] So the Orientals. See Cod. Bab. passim. Comp. also Baer, Gen., p. 76, where the Palestinian Massora is quoted.

[11] So the Orientals. See Cod. Bab., Massora magna to Is. xxxvi. 12; and comp. the Palestinian Massora,—as given by Norzi, ad loc., or Ginsb. Mas. א, § 238,—which requires כֶּס יָה to be written as *two words*.

[12] I have myself no doubt, from personal inspection, that the Codex B. 19ᵃ, in the Imperial Library at St. Petersburg, dated 1009, is much younger, although the editors of the Catalogue accept the date.

A. Firkowitsch, when at Aleppo [13]. It contains the list of Paseqs, to which I refer, p. 121 note.

Bab. Codex prophetarum posteriorum Petropolitanus Babylonicus (A. D. 916), the text marked with the so-called Babylonian punctuation, photo-lithographed, under the editorship of Dr. Strack, 1875.

Ber. MSS. in the Royal Library, Berlin. The numbers given are those of the printed catalogue.

MSS. in the British Museum,—cited according to the press-marks Add., Harl., and Or., e.g. Add. 21161; Harl. 1528; Or. 4709. The reader will please notice that I have not thought it necessary to prefix *Br. Mus.* to these marks.

De R. De Rossi's MSS., now in the Royal Library, Parma. See De Rossi's printed catalogue.

Erf. The Erfurt MSS. 1-4, described by Lagarde in his Symmicta, p. 133 ff. (These MSS. are now in the Royal Library, Berlin.)

Hm. MSS. in the Town Library, Hamburg. The numbers are those of the printed catalogue.

K. When I had no printed catalogue to refer to, as in the case of the smaller Libraries, I have given the numbers according to Kennicott's list.

Ox. MSS. in the Bodleian Library, Oxford. See printed catalogue.
Par. MSS. in the National Library, Paris. See printed catalogue.
Vi. MSS. in the Imperial Library, Vienna.

II. MSS. on the Accents of the Twenty-one Books.

1. Ambrosian Library, Milan, A. 186. This MS. consists of two quite distinct parts: *a.* The first and larger part (18 pp.) is headed זה הוא תוכן עזרא, a name which occurs again just before the list of the accents, זה מן העתק תוכן עזרא. A cursory examination shewed me that this part is (as far as it goes) identical with the epitome of הורית הקורא, edited by Mercerus (Paris, 1565) under the title of ספר טעמי המקרא [14], and

---

[13] In this copy, however, a section has been dropped at the end of both Parts of the קונטרס, and three others introduced (§§ 22, 23, 24, ibid., p. xxiii) which are not in the original. That Firkowitsch was in the habit of falsifying texts that passed through his hands is well known. Were the Qaraites δεὶ ψεῦσται ?

[14] How far the two texts agree I am not able to state, for I had not Mercerus' edition with me when examining this MS.

assigned by him (on the authority of the Paris MS.) and by all scholars since,—falsely, as I believe I have shewn, טעמי אמ״ח, pp. 104-5,—to R. Jehuda ben-Bil'am. This conclusion of mine seems to receive the fullest confirmation from the title above given. For I would ask Jewish scholars whether it may not be taken for certain that the *name of the author* is given in the double-entendre which it conveys? Ezra was the name not only of the great סופר, but of a distinguished scribe whose copy of the Tora is constantly quoted, under the name of ספר עזרא, as of authority [15]. Such an experienced scribe we may well suppose to have been competent to treat of דקדוק המקרא בנקודיה ובטעמיה (as the subject of the Work is described in the introductory words). Another discovery we make is that the proper title of the epitome of הורית הקורא is תּוֹכָן עֶזְרָא, 'Ezra's arrangement' [16]. But it would seem that it was only a fragment of this Work that lay before the copyist, for at the section on the accent יתיב he suddenly breaks off, and adds matter of his own. β. At this point we read in the margin: מכאן והלאן היא העתק דייקות מת׳ מנחם ברבי [שלמה] דרך קצרה העלה על אבן בחן [17]. Unfortunately what follows (6½ pp.), mostly about the accents, is marked by blunders, and of no value. Whatever Menachem's other acquirements he was evidently no accentuologist.

2. That part of חִבּוּר הַקּוֹנִים—written by Simson the punctator (circa 1230)—which refers to our subject. Simson does little else

---

[15] See e.g. Lonzano, Ôr Tora, on Gen. iv. 13; vii. 11; ix. 29; etc.; Ox. Cat. 2543; Ginsb. Mas. i. p. 611 (*bis*), iii. p. 25. Meïri (קרית ספר, Part I, 8ᵇ) states that in his time (end of the 13th century) ספר עזרא was in Toledo, and was consulted, as a standard authority, for its readings.

[16] I beg my readers to observe that this is the *earliest* notice we have of the Work assigned to Ben-Bil'am, and as being nearer to the source, is more likely to be correct. Moreover as the copyist, himself a grammarian by profession (see note following), lived within a few years of Ben-Bil'am, we may take it for granted that he would have known, and would have stated, the fact, if the author had been really Ben-Bil'am.

[17] With this agrees the statement at the end of the Part about the accents: ותשלם מערנחם העתק ספר אבן בחן, אך אני מנחם אצלתי לי עיקר חנוחם דרך קצרה וישרה. Menachem, therefore, himself condensed and copied this Part from his larger Work, אבן בחן,—'ein grammatisch-lexicalisch-hermeneutisches Werk' (not a mere Lexicon, as is generally supposed), as Dr. Perles, who has examined the unique MS. of it in the Munich Library, informs me. (Comp. Steinschneider, Hebr. Bibliographie, pp. 38 ff. and 131-4.) In this MS. the sections (שערים) about the accents are wanting.—It may be added that the treatise in the Ambrosian Library was originally attached (as the epigraph states) to a copy of the twenty-four Books, made also by Menachem, in the year 1145.

than copy the treatise assigned to Ben-Bil'am. Of this Work—sometimes called Simsonî, from its author—there are three copies known, one in the Br. Mus. (Or. 1016), one in the University Library, Leipzig (Or. 102ᵃ), and one in De Rossi's Library, Parma (389)[18].

3. Ber. 118 (Heb. Cat.) contains (*a*) some rules for the accents, more or less fragmentary—in part by Samuel, the grammarian and punctator[19]—full of mistakes and quite worthless. (β) A poem (otherwise known[20]) in forty-five verses on the accents of the twenty-one Books, by R. Tam. Written in a crabbed fantastic style, it merely gives in a condensed form Ben-Bil'am's well-known rules for the *servi*, and is altogether undeserving of notice. (γ) A poem in ninety verses by Joseph ben-Qalonymos (circa 1240), on the same subject, to which the same remarks apply[21].

4. Prefixed to the Bible-text, Par. 5, is a treatise on the accents of the twenty-one Books, by Zalman the punctator[22]. He twice quotes הוריות הקורא by name, and gives the same title to his own treatise. It contains nothing of consequence.

5. Ox. 2512, a grammatical treatise in Arabic (brought from Yemen), containing at the end rules for the accents, the most interesting part of which I give, pp. 13, 14.

---

[18] Any one who is curious to know something more of this work may consult Hupfeld, *Commentatio de antiquioribus apud Judæos accentuum scriptoribus*, Partic. II, p. 11 ff. (Halle, 1846).

[19] How little he understood of the rudiments of his craft I found out when examining a MS. pointed by him (A. D. 1260), in the Library of St. John's College, Cambridge.

[20] Brought out in Kobak's Jeshurun, v. p. 126 ff.

[21] A poem on the accents of the three Books by the same author has been recently edited by Dr. Berliner (Berlin, 1886). But it is lost labour to publish such a work. Moreover, the editor's part has been very negligently performed. Both text and commentary are made in his hands to express arrant nonsense. And yet the publication is intended 'die jüdische Literatur zu bereichern!' (Pref. p. 5.)

[22] Not to be confounded with Jequthiel (Zunz, Zur Geschichte und Literatur, p. 115), for I found that his rule about Paseq after Shalshéleth is opposed to Jequthiel's remarks, Gen. xix. 16. He is doubtless the punctator (not named by Zunz), who is quoted in Br. Mus. Add. 9403 (section on ש), יסוד ר' זלמן הנקדן מרומנבורק.—The Paris MS., to which this treatise is prefixed, is dated 1298; and Zalman may have lived about this time, for as he is not named in other works on the accents, he would seem to have been a late punctator.

THE PRINCIPAL PRINTED TEXTS

QUOTED IN THE PRESENT WORK.

Bomb. 1. 1st Rabbinical Bible, printed by Bomberg, Venice, 1518.
Bomb. 2. 2nd Rabbinical Bible, printed by Bomberg, Venice, 1525.
Jabl. Heb. Bible edited by D. E. Jablonski, Berlin, 1699.
Mich. Heb. Bible edited by J. H. Michaelis, Halle, 1720. This ed. is valuable to the student because of the various accentual readings, taken from the Erfurt MSS.
Baer. Edd. of Genesis (Leipzig, 1869), Isaiah (1872), Ezekiel (1884), Minor Prophets (1878), Five Megillôth (1886), and Daniel, Ezra, and Nehemiah (1882), by this distinguished Massoretic scholar. I strongly recommend my readers to procure these carefully prepared texts for themselves, as I have rarely thought it necessary to take notice of errors, which Baer had already corrected.
Dikd. hat. ספר דקדוקי הטעמים לרבי אהרן בן משה בן אשר עם מסורות עתיקות אחרות, edited by S. Baer and H. L. Strack (Leipzig, 1879). This Work contains, with other matter, the rules assigned to Ben-Asher on the accents, the oldest notices that we have on the subject.
Ben-Bil. The epitome of הוֹרָיַת הַקּוֹרֵא, 'Instruction for the reader,' edited by Mercerus (see p. vi), and assigned by him to R. Jehuda ben-Bil'am. My references are to the copious extracts in Heidenheim's משפטי הטעמים (see below). Occasionally I have quoted the Ox. MS. (1465) [23]. The proper title of this Work I have given above, p. xi.
Chayyug. I quote from Nutt's ed. of ספר הנקוד, pp. 126–9. This part of the Work is not, however, by Chayyug himself (see Nutt's remarks, p. xii).
עֵט סוֹפֵר, 'Pen of the Scribe,' by David Qimchi. The text has been

---

[23] The original הורית הקורא is not known to exist, with the exception of a fragment on the accentuation of the three Books printed in Ginsb. Mas. iii. p. 43 ff., § 246*, from a MS. (Or. 2375) in the British Museum. (The second section, however, with the same no. 246* has nothing to do with it, but comes from quite a different source.) Comp. my remarks in טעמי אמ"ת, pp. 103–5.

carelessly copied and carelessly edited by B. Goldberg [21] (Lyck, 1864). The part relating to the accents is fragmentary and of little importance.

Moses the punctator [25], reputed author of דַּרְכֵי הַנִּקּוּד וְהַנְּגִינוֹת. I quote Frensdorff's edition (Hannover, 1847). The שער הנגינות in this Work is almost entirely from Ben-Bil'am.

Jequthiel, author of עֵין הַקּוֹרֵא [26], an orthographical commentary,— mostly in regard to vowels and accents,—on the Pentateuch; published by Heidenheim, in his edition of the Pentateuch entitled מאור עינים (Rödelheim, 1818).

Man. du Lect. Manuel du Lecteur,—a name given by J. Derenbourg to a compendium of grammar and massora, edited by him (Paris, 1871), from a Yemen MS. now in the Bodleian Library (1505). The proper title is [27] מחברת התינאן, 'The Bible-treatise.' (It is strange that Derenbourg has neither used nor explained this name.) This or some similar Work constantly appears as a Preface or Introduction in Yemen Bible Codd.

Mishp. hat. משפטי הטעמים, a useful compilation from the works of early Jewish writers on the accents of the twenty-one Books, by Wolf Heidenheim (Rödelheim, 1808), with his own comments.

(Other known Works, such as Norzi's מנחת שי, the Massoretic compilation אכלה ואכלה, and Die Massora magna (the two latter edited by Frensdorff), do not need particular notice. Nothing is to be learned from El. Levita's טוב טעם, Arqivolti's ערוגת הבושם, and the Works of Jewish writers on the Accents, other than those named above. Even from Christian accentuologists, as Wasmuth, Ouseel, Spitzner, and Ewald, I have derived little or no help.)

---

[24] Thus, the very first words, הא לך, are given as המלך, and in p. לב, שופר נשוא, 'the elevated Sh.,' is made שופר בשוא, 'Sh. with Sh'va.'

[25] The fullest notice about this writer will be found in Histoire Littéraire de la France, xxvii. p. 484 ff.

[26] On the work and its author, see Zunz, Zur Geschichte und Literatur, p. 115.

[27] لِيجَان is pl. of تَاج, 'crown,' a name given to the Tora or Bible (תנ״ך) as the 'crown' of Books. See אבן ספיר, p. 12ᵇ, note.

CONTENTS.

CHAP.		PAGE
I.	Introductory. The origin and design of the accentuation	1
II.	The division, names, and signs of the accents	9
III.	The dichotomy. General principles of division	29
IV.	Syntactical dichotomy	44
V.	Silluq	61
VI.	Athnach	69
VII.	Zaqeph	75
VIII.	S'gôlta	85
IX.	Ṭiphcha	89
X.	R'bhia	93
XI.	Pashṭa, T'bhîr, and Zarqa	99
XII.	Géresh, Pazer, and Great T'lisha	112
XIII.	L'garmeh	119
XIV.	Paseq	120
APPENDIX I.	Notes on difficult passages	130
„ II.	On the so-called Babylonian system of accentuation	142
INDEX I.	Subjects	151
„ II.	Hebrew technical terms	153
„ III.	Scripture passages	153

ERRATA AND ADDENDA.

Page 16, note 25, *add* a third example of סיחסא, from Cod. Bab. p. 181[a]
- " 23, l. 7, *point* מְנַעְנֵעַ
- " 41, note 22, *for* Is. ix. 8 *read* Is. ix. 6[b]
- " 51, l. 1, *point* אֲרוֹן
- " 70, l. 21, אֶת־הָאָרֶץ, *dele* Meţheg
- " 88, l. 21, *dele* 'Even Ben-Asher's famous Codex &c.'
- " 129, note 28, *for* 2 Ki. xxv. 2 *read* 2 Ki. xxv. 4

CHAPTER I.

INTRODUCTION [1].

THE Hebrew accentuation is essentially a musical system. The accents are *musical signs*—originally designed to represent and preserve a particular mode of cantillation or musical declamation, which was in use for the public reading of the Old Testament text at the time of their introduction, and which had been handed down by tradition from much earlier times [2]. That the signs introduced failed to answer their purpose, and that

---

[1] I may be permitted to refer to my previous treatise, chap. I, for some general remarks, which I do not think it necessary to repeat here.

[2] From the testimony of the Talmud, we are able to trace the practice of such a system to the first centuries of the Christian era, and it may have been much older. Thus the statements on the subject in Megilla 32ᵃ and Nedarim 37ᵇ are given in the names of R. Jochanan and Rab (who lived towards the middle of the third century), and that in Berakhoth 62ᵃ on R. 'Aqiba's authority (which brings us close to the beginning of the second century). Besides these, which may be regarded as historical notices, we have the tradition (Megilla 3ᵃ) that the system was in use even in Ezra's time. Nor is this tradition (as it seems to me) to be altogether rejected. It requires only to be rightly interpreted. The method of musical recitation may well have been one of the institutions established under the second temple, *and soon after Ezra's time*, for the more formal and solemn conduct of public worship. Originally introduced by the Sopherim, Ezra's immediate successors, as a kind of סִימָן לַתּוֹרָה — distinguishing the public reading of the Law, fixing its sense, and serving as a help to the memory in retaining its precepts—it may afterwards have been applied to the other Sacred Books. From the Temple it would pass into the Synagogue. And perhaps Christ Himself made use of it, when reading from the prophet Isaiah (Luke iv. 17 ff.).

(On the activity of these early סופרים, and the influence their *dicta* and the rules they laid down exercised, see Graetz, Geschichte, ii. 2, p. 180 ff. That they regulated the arrangements for public worship seems certain, ibid., p. 190. Their work was creative, and left its mark behind it.)

it is quite uncertain how far the modern chanting of the Jews—whether Oriental, Ashkenazic, or Sephardic[3]—represents the original melodies, is on various accounts to be regretted. For—independently of the interest attaching to the earliest development of sacred music—if these melodies had been preserved, we should be able to understand the reasons of various musical changes, of which we have to take account, but for the introduction of which we can at present only offer conjectures.

One marked peculiarity of the system could not, however, so long as the signs were accurately preserved, be lost. From the first, the aim had been so to arrange the musical declamation, as to give suitable expression to the *meaning* of the Sacred Text. For this purpose, the *logical* pauses of the verse were duly marked—and that according to their gradation—by pausal melodies[4], later by the accentual signs that represented those melodies; and where no logical pause occurred in a clause, the *syntactical* relation of the words to one another and to the whole clause was indicated by suitable melodies—partly pausal, partly conjunctive—and their corresponding signs. In this way, the originators of the system, and the accentuators who aimed at stereotyping their work, sought to draw out the sense and impress it on the minds of both reader and hearers. It need hardly be added that it is this, their *interpunctional* character, which constitutes for us the chief value of the accents.

Generally speaking, the logical and syntactical division has been carefully carried out, in the way just indicated. And so far we have before us a system of interpunction, which, for

---

[3] For the differences between these several modes, comp. Fétis, Histoire Générale de la Musique, i. p. 445 ff. The character of the cantillation seems to have been influenced by the style of music of the particular nation in which the Jews were settled.

[4] These are the פסקי טעמים or פיסוק ט׳ of the Talmud (e.g. Megilla 3ᵃ, Nedarim 37ᵃ), which, before the introduction of the *signs*, could only be learned from oral instruction and continued practice. Hence we read of professional teachers, who received their fee (שכר פסקי טעמים, Nedarim, l.c.) for giving instruction in this branch.

minuteness and accuracy, leaves nothing to be desired,—a system whose only fault is that it errs on the side of excessive minuteness and apparent striving after accuracy. But it is not always so. When we come to examine the text carefully, we meet with many exceptions. We find words joined by the accents, which ought, according to rule, to be separated; and separated, which ought to be joined; moreover, pausal accents out of their place, a greater where a less is due and *vice versa*.

Such irregularities (if we are so to term them) cannot be ignored. What then are we to say to them? Are we, on account of them, to reject the whole system, as unreliable for the discrimination of the sense? or are we to try and find some explanation of them, so that we may make due allowance, in every case, for disturbances as they occur? Unquestionably, the latter is the true scientific course; nor till we have failed in discovering the necessary explanation, have we any right to condemn what it may turn out we did not understand.

One main object of the present work is to attempt to remove these stumbling-blocks in the way of accepting the accentual system of the twenty-one Books—the same task which I took in hand for the three Books. And the explanation proposed will be virtually the same.

I. In many instances, the accentuation of our texts is *false*, and has to be corrected by the testimony of MSS. Yet I do not know a single writer on the accents, who has been at the pains of seeking to remove this source of error.

II. The *predominance* of the *musical element* must be recognised. This was plainly evident in the examination of the three Books, and must be accepted, though it does not shew itself in so marked a manner, for the twenty-one Books. But then all such exceptional cases come under rule, and need occasion no difficulty. Given certain conditions, the exception must, or at least may, follow. Cases of *transformation* come under this head; and where the musical division ceases, as it often does before the minor pausal accents, there the logical or (what is more common in such cases) the syntactical division necessarily ceases also [5].

III. The well-known law of *parallelismus membrorum*—by no means confined to the poetical, or even the prophetical parts—frequently leads to an irregular division of the text.

IV. The accentuators did not hesitate to make the strict rules for logical (or syntactical) division give way, when they wished to express *emphasis*, or otherwise give effect to the reading. Undoubtedly they were right in principle; although, as we have here to do with questions of taste, we may not always agree with them.

The irregularities here briefly alluded to will of course come fully under review in the sequel.

We start then on the supposition that the accentuation does *not* furnish a perfect system of interpunction. Still, if (as I hope to be able to shew) we can trace and make allowance for disturbing causes, we shall be able to accept it as a reliable guide to the exegesis of the text. Even with what may seem to us its shortcomings [6] and superfluities, it fixes the sense in a far more effective and satisfactory way than our modern system of punctuation [7].

I conclude this chapter with a few remarks on a subject of some interest, about which much has been written, viz. the *date* of the introduction of the accentual signs [8].

---

[5] I do not find in the accentual division of the twenty-one Books that *musical equilibrium* was much regarded. Rhythmical effect was much more studied.

[6] Among which may be mentioned that owing to the purely musical character of the signs employed, it was not possible to mark the interrogation, exclamation, parenthesis, &c.

[7] This has often struck me in comparing the Hebrew text with modern translations, even those few that are careful and accurate in their punctuation.

[8] The student must be warned against statements to be found in the works of some modern scholars, Graetz, Delitzsch, and others, assigning the invention of the Babylonian signs to a certain Moses the punctator, in the sixth century, and that of the Palestinian to two Qaraites, Mocha and his son Moses, at the end of the eighth century. These scholars were misled by certain forgeries and pretended discoveries of the well-known literary impostor, Abraham Firkowitsch, which have been since exposed by Harkavy (Mem. de l'Acad. Imp. des Sciences de St. Pet., xxiv. 8 ff.) and Strack (Luth. Zeitsch., 1875, p. 619).

INTRODUCTION. 5

The silence of the Talmud on the subject of the punctuation, and Jerome's express testimony [9] that it was not found in the texts of his day, have long since satisfied scholars that it cannot have been *earlier* than the fifth century [10]. The following considerations will (I think) shew that it could not have been *later* than the seventh century. (We have thus a sufficient interval for any stages of development, through which it may have passed.) Direct historical notices on the subject fail, as is well known, altogether.

1. We find that in the latter half of the ninth century as little was known about the origin of the punctuation as in the present day. All that Mar Natronaï II, Gaon (A.D. 859–869), can say about it is: לא נתן נקוד בסיני כי החכמים ציינוהו לסימן [11]; whilst Ben-Asher (who completed the Massoretic Work on which his father had been engaged at the close of the same century [12], and who may be considered to give his father's views) more distinctly, but erroneously, assigns it to the Prophets, Sopherim, and wise men, who, with Ezra at their head, were supposed to have constituted the Great Synagogue [13]. It is clear that a system, the origin of which was lost in obscurity at the end of the ninth century, was of *much older date*.

---

[9] Jerome's testimony refers indeed to the vowel-signs (see his Comm. on Is. xxvi. 14; Jer. ix. 21; Hos. xi. 10, &c.). As to the accents (in our sense of the term) he is significantly silent; so in his Preface to Isaiah he states that he has introduced divisions of *his own* into the text (*interpretationem novam novo scribendi genere distinximus*), but makes no reference to division by the accents, Athnach &c., shewing that they were not before him. Indeed, the vocalization and accentuation were no doubt introduced at the same time. Where the one failed, so did the other.

[10] See Bleek's Einleitung, 3rd ed., § 330.

[11] Graetz, Geschichte, 2nd ed., v. p. 502.

[12] Dikd. hat., p. xvi, 1.

[13] Ibid., § 16 and passim. The notion that Ezra was the author and inventor of the signs for the vowels and accents, due to a false interpretation of a passage in the Talmud, Megilla 3ᵃ (see Man. du Lect., p. 53), was generally accepted by the Jews in the middle ages (Buxtorf, De punctorum origine, p. 313). Some Rabbinical authorities indeed maintained that the punctuation was revealed to Moses on Sinai (ibid., p. 312); whilst others went so far as to make it coeval with the language itself, and communicated to Adam in Paradise (ibid., p. 305).

To these testimonies may be added those of Nissi ben-Noach (A.D. 840) and Mar Ṣemach ben-Chayyim, Gaon (889–896), who both refer to well-known differences in the matter of punctuation between the two great Schools of the East and West [14]. Now who does not see that a considerable space of time must have elapsed for those differences to have developed themselves and to have become formally tabulated? We are thus brought to the same conclusion that the punctuation was *much older than the ninth century*.

2. The above-named famous Aaron ben-Asher, who has the credit of having finally fixed the punctuation as we have it in our texts, was the last of a distinguished family of Massoretes and punctators, whose genealogy we are able to trace through several members up to the latter half of the eighth century [15]. There seems no reason to question the correctness of this genealogical table, when we bear in mind the care which the Jews

---

Elias Levita, himself a Jew, in his Massoreth ha-massoreth (1538), was the first to refute systematically these false notions, and to lay down correct views on the subject. (On the controversy to which this epoch-making work gave rise, and which lasted, off and on, for a century and a half,—the chief disputants being the Buxtorfs, father and son, as the assailants, and Ludovicus Cappellus as the defender, of El. Levita's views,—see an interesting pamphlet by Dr. Schneidermann, Die Controverse des L. Cappellus mit den Buxtorfen, Leipzig, 1879, or Bleek's Einleitung, 3rd ed., § 329.)

[14] The former recommends the student to make himself acquainted with the peculiarities of the Babylonian system: לאלף נקודות ומשרתות ופסוק טעמים וחסרות ויתרות לאנשי שנער (quoted in Pinsker's Liqqute Qadmonioth, p. מא). The latter alludes to the variations which the written texts of his time exhibited: במקראות שהם כתובים וקבועים יש שנוי בחם בין בבל לארץ ישראל בחסרות ויתרות ובפתוחות וסתומות ובפסקי הטעמים ובמסורות ובחתוך הפסוקים (end of ספר אלדד).

[15] See Dikd. hat., p. 79 above: (1) his father, Moses, who wrote in the year 895 a Cod. of the Prophets, still preserved in the Qaraite Synagogue in Cairo; (2) Asher ben-Moses; (3) Moses ben-Nehemiah; (4) Nehemiah; (5) Asher הזקן הגדול.—From Nos. 1 to 5 we may well allow a period of 120 years, which will bring us to A.D. 775.

From about 750 to 920 must have been a time of special activity in elaborating rules and fixing all the details of the vocalization and accentuation, for we have two lists (in which many of the names are *the same*, and which therefore confirm one another) of distinguished punctators, who flourished in this period. (Dikd. hat., pp. 78, 79.)

have always exercised in such matters. It follows that the punctuation must have been *older than the middle of the eighth century.*

3. A difficulty has indeed been started, which, however, when examined, only confirms the view above expressed as to the date of the first introduction of the punctuation. It has been argued that because a book like Sepher Jeṣîra, assigned to the eighth century, contains no allusion to the vowel-signs or accents,— although from the subjects of which it treats, such allusion was to be expected,—therefore they were not known at that time [16]. But the *argumentum ex silentio* will not apply here. The silence may be explained from the simple circumstance that pointed texts were at the time in question regarded as an *innovation.* They had still to overcome the prejudices of learned doctors and scribes who, when compiling works that dealt with early tradition, ignored them altogether. We know that the pointing of the text of the Qorân had to encounter, in the same way, at the first, objections and opposition (see Nöldeke, Geschichte des Qorân's, p. 309). Among peoples imbued with such conservative tendencies as those of the East, changes which affected their Sacred Books could be only gradually introduced. Let us suppose the eighth century to have been such a period of transition, and the difficulties broached by scholars disappear. If, however, the punctuation was at this time regarded with

---

[16] See, e. g. Derenbourg in Revue Critique, 1879, p. 455. When, however, he asserts that in the post-talmudic Tract Sopherim no trace can be found of graphical signs, for the indication of the vowels or accents, few scholars will agree with him. The best printed texts and most MSS. name *Athnach* and *Soph Pasuq* in xiii. § 1; and in iii. § 7, ספר פסקו או שניקד ראשי פסוקים שבו אל יקרא בו, the term פסקו most naturally refers to the 'accentual divisions.' (Comp. the parallel passage in M. Sepharim, i. § 4, ספר המנוקד לא יקרא בו, where מנוקד indicates both the vocalization and accentuation.) Zunz, in his Gottesdienstliche Vorträge, p. 264, draws attention to the absence of all allusion to the punctuation in the Midrash on Canticles, at the word נקדות, chap. i. 11, and in the Hagada of the Gaonic period generally, and finds therein a proof of the late origin of the same. But such conclusions prove too much. We *know* (see above) that it was in use in the Gaonic period.

suspicion as an *innovation*, the seventh century and most probably the latter part of that century must have been the date of its introduction[17]. I pointed out in my former treatise, p. 1, that this date suits otherwise well, as it was that at which the Syriac and Greek Churches had perfected (or nearly so) their systems of interpunction and musical notation. The Arabs copied somewhat later for the Qorân the examples thus set them.

By whom and under what circumstances these graphical signs were introduced into the Hebrew text, we have no evidence to assist us in deciding. It may have been that the leading signs were first employed for the instruction of children in school. Even in the time of the Talmud, the case of children was considered, and the reading of the text made more easy for them[18]. And among the Arabs, pointed texts of the Qorân were allowed for school-teaching by authorities who forbad the use of them for public reading[19]. But on such points we are never likely to advance beyond mere conjecture.

---

[17] I mean in anything like a *complete* form. Up to this time, it would have been following a course of gradual development.

[18] In Megilla 22ᵃ R. Chananya says: לא החיר לי לפסוק אלא לחינוקות של בית רבן, i.e. 'I was not allowed to break up a Bible-verse, except in the instruction of school-children.'

[19] Nöldeke, l. c. p. 310.

CHAPTER II.

ON THE DIVISION, NAMES, SIGNS, ETC. OF THE ACCENTS.

The name טְעָמִים, 'meanings' commonly given to the accents (and κατ' ἐξοχήν to the *pausal* accents), refers to their function as indicators of the *sense* of the text[1]. The Arabic-speaking Jews employed another name, having reference to their *musical value*, أَلْحَان, 'melodies, modulations.' A corresponding Hebrew name נְגִינוֹת is used by later Rabbinical writers.

The accents may be divided into two classes, according to their *pausal* (disjunctive), or *non-pausal* (conjunctive) character[2]. In using these terms, however, we must be careful to remember that they apply, strictly speaking, only to the *melody*. (It has been already pointed out that the musical division does not always correspond to the interpunctional.) Jewish grammarians indeed generally distinguish otherwise. By what was with them a favourite figure of speech, they commonly term the pausal accents מְלָכִים or שָׂרִים, as dominating the verse, in regard to both the melody and the sense; whilst the other accents as subordinated to them, and only able to stand when a pausal accent follows, are called מְשָׁרְתִים, *servi*[3]. The latter is a useful *terminus technicus*, and may be retained.

---

[1] This name is first found in the Talmud, which more than once draws special attention to the *logical* importance of the accents. It must be remembered, however, that the Talmud knew nothing of the *signs* (which had not, at the time of its composition, been introduced into the text). If, therefore, we render the term טעמים, as used in the Talmud, by 'accents,' we must understand the melodies, and specially the *pausal melodies*, which determined the meaning. These melodies were afterwards represented by the *signs*. (Some scholars seem to forget that the *system* was precisely the same, before and after the introduction of the signs.)

[2] Comp. the terms מפסיקים, מחברים, &c., occasionally used by Rabb. writers for these two classes, טעמי אמ"ה, p. 10 inf.

[3] So the seven Vowels, which were regarded as dominating the pronunciation,

The following list gives the signs and names of the accents in common use, according to the Palestinian (or Tiberian) system[4]:—

I. PAUSAL OR DISJUNCTIVE ACCENTS (מְלָכִים)[5].

1. ֔ Silluq (סִלּוּק), as in . . . . . . דָּבָֽר
2. ֑ Athnach (אַתְנָח), as in . . . . . . דָּבָ֑ר
3. ֒ S'gôlta (סְגוֹלְתָּא), postpositive, as in . . דָּבָ֒ר
   ֓ Shalshéleth (שַׁלְשֶׁלֶת), as in . . . דָּבָ֓ר
4. ֕ Great Zaqeph (זָקֵף גָּדוֹל), as in . . . דָּבָ֕ר
   ֔ Little Zaqeph (זָקֵף קָטוֹן), as in . . . דָּבָ֔ר
5. ֖ Tiphcha (טִפְחָא), as in . . . . . דָּבָ֖ר
6. ֗ R'bhîa (רְבִיעַ), as in . . . . . . דָּבָ֗ר
7. ֘ Zarqa (זַרְקָא), postpositive, as in . . . דָּבָ֘ר
8. ֙ Pashṭa (פַּשְׁטָא), postpositive, as in . . . דָּבָ֙ר
   ֚ Y'thîbh (יְתִיב), prepositive, as in . . . מֶ֚לֶךְ
9. ֛ T'bhîr (תְּבִיר), as in . . . . . . דָּבָ֛ר

---

are often called מלכים, the משרתים in this case being the half-vowels, which can only stand when a full vowel follows (עמ׳ סופר, p. 4). We may also compare the אותיות משרתות, 'servile letters,' each of which has its נגיד ושר (Dikd. hat., p. 4 inf.) in the stem-word.

[4] There is another system of accentuation—the so-called Babylonian—agreeing in some respects with, but differing in others from, the Palestinian, and known to us chiefly by a MS. of the Prophets in the Imperial Library at St. Petersburg. In my opinion, this system is not only younger than, but completely dependent on, the Palestinian. I propose therefore to confine our attention, for the present, to the latter, and to give, in an Appendix, the particulars in which the other differs from it.

[5] The orthodox number of the מלכים is twelve—(S'gôlta and Shalshéleth were not counted, as we shall see further on)—answering, according to Rabbinical fancy, to the twelve signs of the Zodiac. So even Aben-Ezra, Sachoth 2ᵇ, הצמים שנים עשר כנגד חלקי גלגל המזלות. On the other hand, the seven vowels were the seven planets (ibid.). Vowels and accents together were supposed to lighten up, like the heavenly bodies, what would have been otherwise dark and perplexing.

NAMES, SIGNS, ETC. OF THE ACCENTS.

10. ֜ Géresh (גֶּרֶשׁ), as in . . . . . דָּבָר

֞ Gersháyim, or Double Géresh (גֵּרְשַׁיִם)[6], as in . דָּבָּר

11. ֡ Pazer (פָּזֵר), as in . . . . . דָּבָר

֟ Great Pazer (קַרְנֵי פָרָה or פָּזֵר גָּדוֹל), as in . דָּבָר

12. ֠ Great T'lisha (תְּלִישָׁא גְדוֹלָה), *prepositive*, as in דָּבָר

13. ׀ ֣ L'garmeh (לְגַרְמֵיהּ), as in . . . . . דָּבָר׀

II. Non-pausal or Conjunctive Accents (מְשָׁרְתִים).

1. ֣ Munach (מוּנָח), as in . . . . . דָּבָר

2. ֤ M'huppakh (מְהֻפָּךְ), as in . . . . . דָּבָר

3. ֥ Mer'kha (מֵירְכָא), as in . . . . . דָּבָר

֦ Double Mer'kha (מֵירְכָא כְפוּלָה), as in . . דָּבָר

4. ֧ Darga (דַּרְגָּא), as in . . . . . דָּבָר

5. ֨ Azla (אַזְלָא), as in . . . . . דָּבָּר

6. ֩ Little T'lisha (תְּלִישָׁא קְטַנָּה), *postpositive*, as in דָּבָר

7. ֪ Galgal (גַּלְגַּל), as in . . . . . דָּבָר

[8. ֤ Mây'la (מָאיְלָא), as in . . . . [לְהֵחָלוּ

The *notation* (signs) given in the above list may be regarded as original[7]. The *names* are in some cases Aramaic, in others

---

(The Jews were not alone in indulging in such fancies. The Greeks compared the seven notes of the lyre to the seven planets, the twenty-eight sounds to the twenty-eight days of the month, &c. See Chappell's History of Music, pp. 30, 52.)

[6] So written and pronounced. The regular form would of course be גֵּרְשַׁיִם, like קַרְנַיִם, &c.

[7] Certainly not derived from the Syriac, as Ewald (Abhandlungen, p. 130) seems to assert. If in one or two minor points a resemblance can be traced, it is purely accidental.

In some leather Tora-rolls, brought from Yemen, and now in the British Museum (Or. 1451, 1452, 1453, 1457), there is indeed what seems at first sight an approximation to the *Syriac system*. A point (not in ink, but marked by an

Hebrew. The meanings of the same may be traced (see below) to their figure, their position, their pausal and above all their musical value.

The signs fall generally on the *tone-syllable*. This (as is well-known) is a subsidiary purpose served by the accentuation. When therefore, in the case of a prepositive or postpositive accent, the tone does not fall on the first or last syllable respectively, the accent is bound to be *repeated* on the tone-syllable. With Pashṭa the rule is carried out, e. g. הַמֶּ֨לֶךְ֙ תֹּ֣הוּ [8]; but with S'gôlta, Zarqa, and the two T'lishas, it is very irregularly observed, in both Codd. [9] and printed Texts. Jequthiel, indeed, in his carefully prepared text (עֵין הקורא) and Baer in his editions repeat the accent, e. g. הַמֶּ֣לֶךְ֮, הַמֶּ֣לֶךְ֒, הַמֶּ֣לֶךְ֓, and הַמֶּ֣לֶךְ֔. A Codex, like Par. 1, that regularly does so, is very rare indeed.—For the reasons which led to the omission of the second sign, see the remarks on the several accents.

It is to be observed that every word in the text has its proper melody assigned to it, and is provided with either a disjunctive or conjunctive accent. The only exception is in the case of two or more words, joined by the hyphen, called Maqqeph, which are treated as a single word. Thus כָּל־אַפְסֵי־אָֽרֶץ (Is. lii. 10) has only one accent, not three.

The character of the accentuation is (as has been stated) pre-eminently musical. We should expect therefore a classification of the accents based on their *musical* value. And this has been

---

instrument, that left a small circular indentation) to the *left hand* of the word, marks the close of the verse, and one *under* the word the position of Athnach. Moreover, a diacritic point is placed *over* the word, to ensure the proper pronunciation, in the cases of אֵת (אֶת), כֹּל (כָּל), and הוּא (הִיא). Thus

∘בְּרֵאשִׁית בָּרָא אֱלֹהִים אֵת הַשָּׁמַיִם וְאֵת הָאָֽרֶץ (Gen. i. 1).

But these points are apparently of *modern* date (later than the writing), and can hardly be due to the influence of the old Syriac notation. (In Or. 1453, 1457 the attempt has been made, more or less, to erase them.)

[8] Many Codd. omit the second Pashṭa (found in Baer's and other texts) in forms like גֹּ֨ה (Gen. viii. 13); שֹׁ֨מֵעַ (Judg. xi. 10); וַיָּ֨בֹךְ (2 Sam. iii. 32); אָמְרָ֨ה (Is. xlvii. 10). So too it is unnecessary to point, with Heidenheim and Baer, אָ֨שֶׁר, בְּלִ֨ל (Gen. vi. 22; vii. 2).

[9] Even those which lay claim to exceptional correctness, as De R. 413, which professes to have been copied from the famous Cod. Hillel!. Comp. Man. du Lect., p. 92, l. 13, where it is taken for granted that S'gôlta, Zarqa, &c. are *not* repeated.

attempted in some earlier treatises [10], but in terms so brief and enigmatical that no one has yet succeeded in deciphering and explaining them. The difficulty has in a great measure arisen from scholars not having had before them the original Arabic *termini technici*, which the Hebrew terms but imperfectly represent. This deficiency I am able to supply from an Arabic treatise on the accents in the Bodleian Library [11], by the help of which we can arrive at a sufficiently clear idea of what the old grammarians meant. They divided then the מלכים under three heads:—

I. Those which were chanted with the *highest* tone [12], Pazer, T'lisha, and Géresh. As these accents often *lead off* the melody, the highest notes were suitably enough assigned to them. In this class we must further include Shalshéleth [13], a very rare accent, which (as we shall see further on) belonged to the same musical category as Pazer.

II. Those which were chanted *high* [14], viz. Zarqa [S'gôlta],

---

[10] See Ben-Bil. in Mishp. hat., p. 8, and Chayyug, p. 128.

[11] Ox. 2512. The same treatise is found in Or. 2349 and Par. 1327. These MSS. are all from Yemen.

[12] Of this division, Ben-Bil., p. 8, says simply ירים הקול ויעלהו. The author of Man. du Lect., p. 90, who styles it דרך גובה, describes it in the same way, and adds, by way of illustration, that when two or three Pazers occur in the same verse 'the voice of the reader is elevated, so as to be heard afar off' (יגבה קול הקוראים וישמע עד למרחוק). In Ox. 2512, p. 13, we have the original Arabic *terminus technicus*, الْإِعْلَان, which is thus explained: معنى الاعلان هو انك ترفع الصوت وتعلنه [sic] الى فوق بقوّة. The proper meaning of اعلان is 'a making (or being) known.' (Hence Chayyug, p. 128, has derived his strange name of ידיעה for this division.) It came then to signify 'a publishing abroad, making (the voice) heard aloud,' and in this latter sense was used as synonymous with رفع الصوت, 'lifting up of the voice' (comp. Sa'adia's rendering of Is. xlii. 2, 11, and Abu'l-walid s.v. נשא). We have therefore no proper distinction between the terms used for the first and second divisions. Only *conventionally* can الاعلان have signified a higher and more powerful elevation of the voice than الرفع.

[13] As Ox. 2512 also distinctly states: סלסלה من هذا القسم.

[14] Ben-Bil. and Chayyug call this division עלוי, Man. du Lect., p. 75, דרך רום. The Arabic name agrees, الرَّفْع. All that Ox. 2512 says of it is that it is intermediate between I and III: معنى الرفع ان يكون متوسّط بين الاعلان والوضع.

R'bhîa, L'garmeh, T'bhîr. These accents constantly occupy in practice an intermediate position between those of I and III, and so had an intermediate melody (comp. note 14). Even T'bhîr was made a *high* note, in antithesis to the fall of the voice with Ṭiphcha, which always follows.

III. We pass on, in natural order, to the *low*, which were at the same time *sustained*, tones [15], represented by Pashṭa, Zaqeph, Ṭiphcha, Athnach, and Silluq. The voice dropped and proceeded in measured tones, on approaching the two great pauses in the middle and at the end of the verse, and also the pauses next in magnitude to them marked by Zaqeph. (This last rule is indeed contrary to what we should have expected, for Zaqeph and its foretone Pashṭa seem from form and position *high* notes [16].) When however the word, on which any of these accents falls, is Mil'el, we are told [17] that the melody changed and that they were chanted with a *high* note (the voice dropping however again, I presume, with the last syllable). The *arsis* in such cases explains the change in the melody.

The author of Man. du Lect. (p. 75) informs us that the משרתים, *servi*, admit of being divided in the same way, but no particulars are given.

One error Jewish grammarians avoided. They did not attempt to classify the מלכים according to their supposed *interpunctional*

---

[15] Ben-Bil. calls this division מונח, Chayyug העמדה, Man. du Lect., pp. 75 and 93, דרך נצב and דרך שחייה. The Arabic name is الوضع. The term שחייה shews that the tones were '*low*.' The other names are synonymous, and indicate steady '*sustained*' tones. Comp. Man. du Lect., p. 96: ענין נצב שיישב את הנעימה לא ינביהנה בקולו, ולא ירימנה בגרונו, ולא ישפילנה בהגיונו, אלא יישבנה במתק לשונו. Ox. 2512 agrees: معنى الوضع هو ان تحط (*dolce*) الذى هم عليها ولا تعلن الصوت بها ولا ترفعه بل تضعه وضعا ساكنا.

[16] If we were to transfer these accents to Class II, and bring T'bhîr into Class III, we might suppose that all was in order. But we know too little of the musical value of the accents to be able to dogmatize.

[17] See Ben-Bil., and more fully Man. du Lect., p. 97 sup. In the latter passage, however, two of the quotations are falsely accented. For Gen. i. 1, take 2 Chr. ii. 11; and for Ex. i. 2, Gen. xxxv. 23.

value. On the other hand, early Christian writers on the accents aimed at establishing on this basis a kind of hierarchy, consisting of *Imperatores, Reges, Duces, Comites*, &c. Strange indeed is it to find this fanciful and misleading distinction (long ago rejected by Spitzner) still retained in so standard a Work as Gesenius' Heb. Gr., p. 52. Athnach and Silluq are both made *Imperatores*, although (as will be seen hereafter) the former is as much subordinated to the latter, as Zaqeph is to Athnach. Nor can Ṭiphcha (as in the early editions) be properly placed in the same class with Zaqeph, &c. (The present editor has indeed avoided the last-named error, but only to fall into a more serious one. He has actually reckoned R'bhia among the *Reges*, whilst Ṭiphcha follows only as a *Dux !* And this mistake has already begun to circulate as current coin, see Curtiss, Outlines of Heb. Gr., p. 20, and König, Lehrgebäude der Hebr. Sprache, p. 76.) The few pages devoted to the accentuation in this otherwise correct and useful Work sadly need revision.

REMARKS ON THE SEVERAL ACCENTS [18].

The variety of names assigned to some of the accents will perhaps appear surprising to the student. They are doubtless to be mainly accounted for, as having originated in different schools, or under the influence of this or that distinguished teacher. Occasionally, perhaps, we may trace the fancy of some unimportant punctator,—the names he proposed not being found elsewhere than in the list he drew up. It is with the least important accents that the greatest liberties have been taken. The names of the leading accents, Silluq, Athnach, Zaqeph, &c. were left for the most part undisturbed. After all, any modern Dictionary of Music will shew almost as great a variety

---

[18] In these remarks, I quote not only printed lists, but lists found in the following MSS.: Ox. 2512 (already described); Vat. 475 (? 14th century); De R. 333 (dated 1392), 1016 (? 14th century), and 1262 (dated 1454). The Arabic list, Pet. 123 (? 16th century), has been printed in Pinsker's Einleitung &c., pp. 42–43.

I also refer occasionally to the *Zarqa-lists*, so named from the accent with which they all commence. Three such lists are current, differing slightly from one another, and named after the communities in which they are in use,—ספרדי (Spanish), איטליאני (Italian), and אשכנזי (German). The date of their introduction is uncertain, but they can hardly be older than the 14th century, for no writer on the accents alludes to them, and they are very rare in manuscript. Perhaps they were originally intended for popular use, for giving instruction to children in school,—a purpose which they still serve,—&c. Accurate they are not. Any one who is curious to see them will find them in Norzi's Bible, i. p. 135^b, after the Megilloth. As given in Bartolocci's Biblioth. magna rabbin., iv. 441–442, they are full of mistakes.

of names for many notes, particularly for musical figures, graces, &c., such as were more or less in use in the Hebrew cantillation [19].

I have quoted several times Villoteau's description of the musical value of the accents [20]. A distinguished musician, he took great pains to ascertain and reproduce correctly the melodies in use in the synagogues of Egypt. These Oriental melodies seem to me sometimes really to represent the true character of the accents.

DISJUNCTIVES. I. 1. The terms סִלּוּק and סוֹף פָּסוּק: are indifferently used for the final accent of the verse. The former, which means 'cessation,' 'close,' i.e. of the melody, is the name of the stroke (inclining often in Codd. slightly to the left [21]) placed under the tone-syllable of the word. The latter term indicates properly the two points (or small strokes) which separate the verses from one another [22]. Evidently, these points served as the main guide for the reader. In Yemen Codd. the stroke under the tone-syllable is often wanting altogether [23].

2. אֶתְנַחְתָּא, אַתְנַחְתָּא, or אַתְנָח. An Aramaic name, derived from the Aphel of נָח, secondary form of נוּחַ [24], and properly signifying 'a causing to rest' (comp. אַפְטָרָה, אַזְכָּרָה, &c.). Another name of very rare occurrence is סְחֻפָא (so written in Codd.), which means 'a turning over.' This name properly belongs, as it seems to me, to the Babylonian system, in which Tiphcha is represented by ֽ, and Athnach following by the same sign *turned over*, ֿ [25]. For an explanation of the form see טעמי אמ"ת, p. 15.

3. סְגוֹלְתָּא, סְגוֹלָה, or סְגוֹל, so named from its similarity to the vowel-sign S'gôl [26]. The three points have, however, a meaning of

---

[19] Heidenheim (Mishp. hat., p. 5ᵇ) has given various names of the accents, but has mixed together those of the three and twenty-one Books, and copied, without scruple, blunders of Qalonymos and El. Levita.

[20] In the great Work, Description de l'Egypte, État moderne, vol. i. p. 838 ff.

[21] As the Arabic treatise, Ox. 2512, says, in describing Silluq : هو شكل عصا واقف يميل الى اليسار قليلا.

[22] Sometimes, as in Or. 1467, 1477, 2363, and Ox. 2484 (all Yemen Codd.), a *single* point (or stroke) is used, as in Syriac.

[23] As in Or. 1469, 1473, 1477, 2366; Ox. 2484; Par. 1325, &c.

[24] The part. of this form, מתנח, occurs in the Talmud, Erubin 53ᵃ.

[25] Full as our Massora is, the name occurs but *once*, in the mas. parva to Lev. xviii. 15; whereas, in the scanty remains that have come down to us of the Oriental Massora, it has already been found twice, in Cod. Bab. mas. parva to Hos. xiii. 12, and in a rubric given in Ginsb. Mas., iii. p. 246. (In the list at the end of Bomb. 1, the word is misprinted סכפא.) The very name Sichpha (a strange form) may have been intended as a play on the word Tiphcha.

[26] Hence called by Hadassi (Sepher ha-eshkol, p. 61) סגול העליון.

their own, being intended to indicate that S'gôlta was (relatively) a greater pausal accent than Zaqeph with its *two* points, as Zaqeph, in its turn, was greater than R'bhîa with only *one* point. A probably older name, which is intimated in Cod. Bab. and is used by Chayyug (p. 127) and retained in the Italian Zarqa-list, is שָׁרֵי, 'encamping,' 'halting for rest [27],' by which the greater pause made by S'gôlta was indicated. Rabbinical writers have also another name, הָרוֹדֵף לְזַרְקָא, due to their fanciful notion that, as S'gôlta always 'follows Zarqa,' it was not entitled to rank as a separate and independent accent [28]. Ben-Asher's strange name קְבֵלָה, meaning 'What is over-against' (Zarqa), conveys the same idea (Dikd. hat., p. 18).

This accent was made *postpositive* (according to the grammarians [29]) for clearness' sake, that its points might not be mixed up with the others that appear above the word, as they would have been, e. g. in שְׁלֹמֹה, יְהוֹשֻׁעַ. For the same reason doubtless it was but seldom *repeated*, when the word is Mil'el.

4. 'שַׁלְשֶׁלֶת, 'Chain [30].' A very rare accent, occurring only seven times in the twenty-one Books [31]. The sign (which was supposed to represent a hanging chain [32]) and the name both point to the melody, which is described as a double-trill [33], with its *chain* of notes; or as two notes connected by an *ascending chain* of sounds [34]. The former melody suits better the descriptive terms applied to this accent in the Massora and elsewhere [35].—The Paseq, which accompanies it (Mas. to

---

[27] Comp. חוּנָה used for Athnach, טעמי אמ"ח, p. 14. Or שָׁרֵי may mean *dissolvens, separans*, like the Syriac accent, ܫܳܪܶܐ (Duval, Gr. Syr., p. 154).

[28] See Mishp. hat., p. 36ᵃ below. 'Olev'yored in the three Books is treated in the same way.

[29] Comp. Mishp. hat., p. 38ᵇ.

[30] Sometimes the form סלסלה is used (e. g. in Pet. 123) = سِلْسِلَة. In Dikd. hat., § 16ᵃ, the name is רָתָק, in Vat. 475 רִתּוּק, comp. Is. xl. 19.

[31] As it occurs so seldom it was not counted entitled to a place among the מלכים (see Mishp. hat., p. 7).

[32] צורתו כשלשלת ברול (Zalman the punctator in Par. 5).

[33] Comp. El. Levita's description of it as sung by the Ashkenazim of his day: 4 § ,טוב טעם) יש לו קול יותר גבוה מכל המלכים עד שמנגנים אותו כשני פורים). (For Pazer as a trill, see p. 21.)

[34] According to the Oriental mode, see Villoteau, p. 838.

[35] מַרְעִים, 'reverberating' (Mas. to Lev. viii. 23; Dikd. hat., p. 18 below); מַרְעִיד, 'making to tremble' (Ox. 41; Par. 4; St. Pet. Cat., p. 85); פַרְפָא, 'agitating, shaking' the voice (De R. 861; comp. Ginsb. Mas. ש, § 235),—terms all suiting its character as a *tremolo* or trill.

Lev. viii. 23), was introduced for the sake of conformity with the pausal Shalshéleth of the three Books[36].

5. זָקֵף, זַקְפָא. Doubtless derived its name from the 'upright' finger employed, in the teaching of the cantillation, to mark it. Comp. Ben-Asher (Dikd. hat., p. 18), מיוחד באצבע זקף. Why *two points*—instead of an upright line, as we should have expected—were chosen as its sign, has been explained under S'gôlta. But the upright line was not lost sight of, as we shall see immediately.

Zaqeph is an accent of very frequent occurrence,—four or more often appearing in one verse,—and probably on this account was subjected (more than any other accent) to various musical modifications, with the view of varying the recurring melody. Thus we have the simple sign of two points, ד׳ קָטֹן or ד׳ סְתָם, with a simpler melody; and a double sign, made up of the two points and the upright line named above,—a double Zaqeph[37],—with a fuller, stronger tone. This form of the accent is known as ד׳ גָּדוֹל. (We must not, however, be misled by the names, and suppose that ד׳ גָּדוֹל represents a *greater pausal* accent than ד׳ קָטֹן (see e.g. Gen. ii. 9[b]). The difference is simply musical[38].) The rules—which have never yet been clearly made out—for the employment of the one or other of these accents will follow in due course; as also the explanation of the other musical modifications to which Zaqeph's word is subject.

6. טִפְחָא means 'handbreadth.' The name refers, as I conjecture, to the 'outspread hand,' the manual sign employed for this accent. (Unfortunately but few of these signs have been described to us by those who knew them.) Another name, in equally common use, is מַרְכָא, 'laboring, toiling,' which can only mean a 'slow, heavy' melody, *lento*. Tarcha, as immediately preceding the cadence at Athnach and Silluq, may well have been of this character. Before Silluq it had also the special name (an intimation that the melody varied slightly from that before Athnach) דְּחִי, 'thrust back,' in allusion to the backward inclination of the sign[39], in contrast to Silluq.

7. רְבִיעַ, an Aramaic word, = 'resting.' The name may refer to the *pause*, or the character of the *melody*, 'resting,' 'sustained' (see

---

[36] But it was quite unnecessary, and fails in many old Codd., as Add. 21161; De R. 10, 226; K. 154. Comp. Jequthiel's note to Gen. xix. 16.

[37] So we have a double Géresh and a double Mer'kha.

[38] Comp. Man. du Lect., p. 96: הוקף נחלק לשנים סעם יקרא וקף קטון וסעם יקרא וקף גדול ווה לפי נעימות המלה.

[39] As in the list at the end of Bomb. 1 (copied in Ginsb. Mas. i. p. 658). So Mây'la, which has the same inclination, is called דְּחוּיָה. In Pet. 123 we have the Arabic name رَاجِع, 'thrusting back' the sign.

טַעֲמֵי אמ"ח, p. 15)⁴⁰. The shape of the accent, as laid down by grammarians⁴¹, and *found in all Codd.*, is an ordinary *point*, like Chôlem or Chîreq. I mention this, because some scholars still cling to the notion that R. had its name from its *square* shape (רָבִיעַ=רְבִיעַ). But this form, where found in printed texts, has been simply due to the same mistaken notion on the part of the editors.

8. זַרְקָא̇ or צִנּוֹרִי̇. Jewish writers on the accents derive the name זרקא from זרק, 'to sprinkle, scatter.' It may be taken to refer to the character of the melody, which is further symbolized by the *form* of the accent⁴². Comp. Villoteau, p. 838: 'Les sons semblent *se répandre et s'étendre, en tournoyant.*' The form would then represent what is called in music 'a turn.' Originally it was so ↷, whence the name צִנּוֹרִי, 'hook-like⁴³.' This form is still common in Codd. But as there was not always room for this upright sign between the lines, it was made recumbent, and delineated with a free hand assumed the shape which appears in our printed texts.

Zarqa was made *postpositive* for the sake of conformity with its position in the three Books; and as it is in these Books seldom *repeated*, when the word is Mil'el (lest it should be confounded with Ṣinnorith), so punctators rarely repeat it in the twenty-one Books.

9. פַּשְׁטָא̇ or פָּ֒שֵׁט, 'extending,' 'stretching out in length.' The name may be most simply explained, as referring to the melody, 'indique qu'on doit *étendre et prolonger* la voix *sur le même ton*' (Villoteau, p. 840). So the Orientals chant this accent. The sign is properly a straight line inclined to the left, made *postpositive*, to distinguish it from Azla, with the same form.

When Pashṭa would come on a monosyllable, or a dissyllable which is Mil'el, and no servus precedes, it is changed into יְ֚תִיב⁴⁴,—an accent of

---

⁴⁰ Here and there in lists (e.g. in Chayyug, p. 129) the name רְבִיעִי is found. This change of the original name, if not a corruption, may have been due to the (incorrect) notion that R. marks the *fourth* pausal division of the verse after Silluq, Athnach, and Zaqeph.

⁴¹ As, for instance, by Aben-Ezra (צחות, p. 1), צורת החולם נקודה למעלה בסוף המלה, שלא יתערב עם הנקודה הנקראת רביע.

⁴² On further consideration, this explanation appears to me more probable than that which I proposed in טעמי אמ"ח, p. 16.

⁴³ For צִינוֹרָא, 'hook,' comp. Levy, Neuhebr. W. B.—Menachem ben Salomo (in his work אבן בוחן) describes Zarqa (כצין אגמון, this word being understood by Rabb. writers in the sense of 'hook,' and in Or. 2349 I found: زرقا وهو شكل صِنَّارَة, 'is in the form of a hook.'

⁴⁴ A fine musical distinction, not without parallel, as we shall see further on. But it is surprising that the *same* signs should have been chosen for Azla and M'huppach, the servi of Pashṭa, as for Pashṭa itself and Y'thibh. As might have been expected, no little confusion has been the result. Pashṭa has been confounded in texts with Azla, and M'huppach with Y'thibh.

the same *disjunctive* value, but differing in form and melody; thus
מִי becomes מֶי (Gen. iii. 11), אֵלֶּה, אֵלֶּה (vi. 9). This new accent was
made *prepositive*, in order to distinguish it from the conjunctive accent
M'huppach with the same form, e.g. אֵלֶּה and אֵלֶּה, נַעַר and נַעַר[45].
Its own *disjunctive* character was indicated by the name given it, יָתִיב,
'resting, pause.'

(Different schools did not, however, all agree in the above nomenclature. Some grammarians make יָתִיב the generic name, and understand by it generally Pashṭa, distinguishing when necessary between
יָתִיב פַּשְׁטָא and יָתִיב מַהְפָּךְ. With others the distinction is between
מִלְמַעְלָה י׳ and מִלְמַטָּה י׳, or between יָתִיב *simplex*, and מוּקְדָּם י׳ [46].—
Y'thibh is also known as שׁוֹפָר יָתִיב [47]. Chayyug (p. 129) speaks of it
as שׁופר הפוך אשר הוא מוכרת, i.e. 'which is disjoined.' Rashi (on
Deut. xi. 30) has the name מַשְׁפֵּל, 'making low,' and Pet. 123 כַּאֲרָכָה,
perhaps 'enveloping,' because standing outside the vowel.)

10. תְּבִיר or תַּבְרָא (=Heb. שֶׁבֶר). The name is derived from the
melody, which was a *broken* note, a series of broken tones in one
measure (as it is sung in the present day). Hence T'bhir is described as מַשְׁבִּיר הַתֵּיבָה (Man. du Lect., p. 72). The *form*—as made
up of R'bhia and Mer'kha—represents it as an intermediate accent,
neither so strong as the former, nor so weak as the latter (R'bhia,
T'bhir, Mer'kha, is the frequent order in the full melody preceding
Ṭiphcha).

11. גְּרִישׁ, פֶּרֶשׁ, *expulsio*. This accent was one of the highest notes
(see p. 13), and required a strong 'expulsion' of the voice to produce
it. It was also known as טָרֶף, טַרְפָא, being a *trill* like Pazer [48].
Another very common name is טָרֶס, טָרִים, 'bar [49],' derived from the

---

[45] It may be noted that, where there is no vowel under the first letter,
M'huppach is (in carefully pointed Codd.) placed under the *middle* of the letter,
Y'thibh more to the *right*, e.g. כֹּל and כָּל, קָדֹשׁ and קָדֹשׁ.

Moses the punctator tells us (דרכי הנקוד, p. 27) that Y'thibh was also distinguished by being *smaller* in size, which is false (as any Codex will shew).
Equally so is his statement that the melody was the *same* as that of Pashṭa, for
then there would have been no change in the sign.

[46] For these different names, see Mishp. hat., 32ª, 35ᵇ; Man. du Lect., pp. 77, 94.

[47] Mishp. hat., 37ª.

[48] See note 35 and Dikd. hat., p. 17 note. In De R. 1262, Géresh and Pazer
are both described as מרעישות, 'making (the voice) tremble.'

[49] See Fleischer's note in Levy's Neuhebr. W. B., ii. p. 211. So Ab'ul-walīd,
Lexicon, p. 113, uses ترس for Heb. בריח. Chayyug (p. 128) has the form תרים,
which is more correct, in view of the derivation.

form (properly a straight line) and indicating the *disjunctive* character of this accent. So we use 'bar' of a dividing line in music.

גֵּרֶשׁ and גֵּרְשַׁיִם, 'Double Gérésh,' (called ג׳ קטן and ג׳ גדול respectively in Ox. 2512, p. 18), differed musically, and in the rules for their employment. Their *disjunctive* value is the same.

12. פָּזֵר, פָּזְרָא, derives its name from its melody, מגביה וחוזר ובלשון מתפזר (Dikd. hat., p. 18). It was a *trill*, but of a more pronounced character than Gérésh. Like Gérésh it occurs with a twofold melody and two different signs, known as Great and Little Pazer. The original sign of the former, still preserved in many Codd., was no doubt פָּזֵר גָּדוֹל, in which we may see a representation of the manual sign used for this accent, '*two fingers turned upwards*' (Man. du Lect., p. 108). Sometimes in Codd. Little Pazer differs only in being *smaller*, but generally there is a slight alteration in the form as well, thus : פֹּזֵר, פֹּזֵר. The original meaning of the sign was after a time lost sight of, and many variations of form were introduced.

By a poor figure of speech Great Pazer was commonly known as קַרְנֵי פָרָה, 'cow-horns;' in Man. du Lect., p. 91, it is likened to the *antennae* of the locust, כקרני חגבים; and in Pet. 123 it is مِقْرَاض, 'a pair of scissors.' This accent, from its rare occurrence (it is found only sixteen times), attracted the attention of the punctators, who amused themselves with giving it various ornamental forms, one of which is that which appears in printed texts and is made to resemble two T'lishas,—a misleading representation, for Pazer had no connection (as far as we know) with T'lisha. The Mas. parva to Ezek. xlviii. 21, which describes Great Pazer with its servus Galgal as אופן ועגלה, 'wheel and waggon,' was doubtless due to this form.

Little Pazer—sometimes called פ׳ סְתָם—is the ordinary Pazer of our texts, and is of very frequent occurrence.

13. תְּלִישָׁא or תַּלְשָׁא. Like Gérésh and Pazer, a musical term (from the root תָּלַשׁ, 'to pluck out, draw out with effort') indicating that this accent 'drew out' the voice with a marked effort and impulse. (It was one of the highest notes, p. 13.) The sign is properly a small circle[50], which seems to have been intended to symbolize the melody[51]. From this circular form was derived another name, תַּרְסָא, 'shield[52].'

---

[50] دَائِرَة صَغِيرَة, Ox. 2512, and so it is marked in Cod. Bab. and Yemen Codd.

[51] Comp. Villoteau, p. 842, who after giving the melody as he had heard it in the East, adds: 'Il faut arracher la voix avec force du fond de la poitrine, et étendre les sons, en faisant *un petit circuit*.'

[52] הרסא = חריס, but I have found no other example of this form. The name חרים was avoided, as being too like to שרים, No. 11. For 'round as a shield,' comp. Dozy, s.v. ترس.

T'lisha had, like Géresh and Pazer, with which it is so often associated, a twofold melody, distinguished as תְּלִישָׁא גְדוֹלָה and תְּלִישָׁא קְטַנָּה; but here the weaker melody is a *conjunctive*. The sign of the former is *prepositive* and sometimes called in consequence ת׳ יָמִין, that of the latter *postpositive*, ת׳ שְׂמֹאל. Grammarians tell us that they were so placed, that they might not be confounded with the circular sign ֯, marked over words which are the object of a Massoretic note[53]. For the same reason punctators rarely *repeat* the sign.

14. מוּנָח לְגַרְמֵיהּ[54], i.e. לְגַרְמֵיהּ ׀. The name L'garmeh means 'for or by itself, independent' = disjunctive, and was chosen to designate a particular *disjunctive* melody—which must originally have resembled Munach—in contrast to the *conjunctive* Munach, with or without Paseq following. With Paseq, the signs are the same. How the one was distinguished from the other in practice we shall see further on. But it was clearly a mistake to employ the *same signs* for two distinct accentual values,—a mistake that has been avoided in the Babylonian system. (Such mistakes are sure to lead to confusion, and the present instance forms no exception, as any one who has consulted the Paseq-lists will have observed.)

The melody of L. must have been 'drawn out' in comparison with that of the simple Munach, as we gather from the name נֶגֶד, נְגִדָא, *protractio*, assigned to this accent in Dikd. hat., p. 17 (see Baer's note), and elsewhere.

II. 1. Of the CONJUNCTIVES, the most important, owing to their frequent occurrence, are those belonging to the Shophar-class, so named as the sign was meant to represent the שׁוֹפָר, 'trumpet,' which is still employed by the Jews in their religious observances. This musical instrument, the only one in use since the destruction of the second temple, could hardly have been passed over, in choosing the signs and names for the musical notes.

Early writers on the accents distinguish as follows:—

a. שׁוֹפָר מוּנָח or שׁוֹפָר מְיֻשָּׁב[55], representing a 'sustained' note. (The name Munach does not refer, as is generally supposed, to the position under the word, but to the melody.)

---

[53] Man. du Lect., p. 92.

[54] We must not call it פסק לגרמיה, as Qimchi does (עם סופ, p. ל), and above all not מונח לפני לגרמיה, as in the printed Mas. to Ex. xxx. 13 (although Frensdorff has copied without scruple); לפני is a clerical error. Parallel to our Munach L., are the Azla L. and M'huppach L. of the three Books.

[55] The name מיושב is regularly used in Man. du Lect. for Munach (it is also found in Chayyug, p. 128), and is thus explained, p. 87: לשון מיושב שהמלה תצא בו בנעימה מיושבת לא למעלה ולא למטה. Corresponding names in עם סופר, p. ל, and Ox. 2512, p. 18, are שׁ׳ מַעֲמָד and שׁ׳ עוֹמֵד. The Arabic name is שׁ׳ נָחַת = שׁוֹפָר وَفْع.

b. שׁ׳ נָשׂוּא (נָשׂוּאי) or שׁ׳ מוּרָם, שׁוֹפָר עִלּוּי, had, as its names imply, an 'ascending' tone [56].

c. שׁוֹפָר מְבַרְבֵּל or שׁ׳ בַּרְבְּלָא, an *ornamental* note, whence its name, in reference to 1 Chr. xv. 27 and Dan. iii. 21. Its only use was to vary the melody before Zaqeph. The musical character was a 'broken' note (answering to the שׁ׳ שָׁבוּר of the three Books), as the names שׁ׳ מְנַעְנֵעַ and שׁ׳ קַלְקֵל (so pointed) shew. That it was also a 'descending' note appears from another name, שׁ׳ נָחִית [57].

The שׁוֹפָר therefore, according to its position before this or that disjunctive accent, had a 'sustained,' an 'ascending' or a 'descending' melody; and thus (speaking roughly) one may say that the three Shophars are explained. Precise rules are laid down for their respective employment, which will be referred to hereafter.

But why (it has been asked) three such different melodies with *one and the same sign*? I think I can explain. These three Shophar-intonations were meant to correspond to the three notes (or trumpet-calls) appointed to be sounded on the Shophar upon the great Festival of the New Year [58]. Not that the musical value was the same. But the *threefold* distinction in the one case suggested the same distinction for the other. We have the *Shophar with three notes* in both cases.

The *single sign* employed, however, gradually led to the obliteration of the distinction so carefully laid down; and though a variety of names (including some of those given above) came into use, they had a common signification, and pointed to *one* accent (instead of to three) [59]. Such names are שׁ׳ הוֹלֵךְ, שׁ׳ יָשָׁר, שׁ׳ גָּדוֹל, κατ᾽ ἐξοχήν, שׁוֹפָר, שׁ׳ עִלּוּי, מוּנַח, (these three last names in contrast to שׁ׳ מְהֻפָּךְ), and lastly—most inappropriate of all—גַּלְגַּל [60]. As the musical division has no meaning

---

[56] For these names, see Mishp. hat., 6ᵇ; Man. du Lect., p. 87; Chayyug, p. 128; and עמ סופר, p. לב. (Here for נשוא the editor has carelessly printed, twice over, בשוא!) The Arabic name is شׁ׳ رَفْع.

[57] For the above names, see Mishp. hat., 11 and 13; Man. du Lect., pp. 103, 108; Chayyug, l.c., and עמ סופר, l.c. (קַלְקֵל is Infinitive-form of קִלְקֵל, Ezek. xxi. 26). The Arabic name was borrowed from the Hebrew. Ben-Bil. (Ox. MS.) says of this accent that it was chanted בהכרעה והניעה, 'with an emphatic agitation' (of the voice).

[58] Viz. הקיעה, יבבות (or שברים), and תרועה. See Mishna at the end of ראש השנה. The New Year is the only occasion on which the Shophar is so used, and to the present day much is made of this part of the Festival ceremonies.

[59] And so in the chanting of the present day, there is but *one* melody in use.

[60] One or other of these names will be found in the list printed in Ginsb. Mas., i. p. 658, in עמ סופר, p. ל, in the several Zarqa-lists, &c. But how are we to explain the strange name גַּלְגַּל, 'wheel,' found in some texts of the Italian Zarqa-list (whence Norzi has borrowed it, e.g. in his note to Gen. i. 3)? A form of

for us, we too may be content with one name and may accept that which has become established by long use, viz. Munach, although the proper signification of the term no longer applies.

d. מְהֻפָּךְ ,שׁוֹפָר הָפוּךְ, or מַהְפָּךְ, so named from its form. It was an 'inverted' Shophar [61]. As compared with Munach its use was limited, for it occurs only before Pashṭa. Its musical value is described (Dikd. hat., p. 19) יורד ועולה וגם מתעלה; so that we might also term it מְהֻפָּךְ in regard to its melody [62].

2. (מֵרְכָא). מַאֲרְכָא ,מַאֲרִיךְ or מֵירְכָא. These names are all from the same root ארך, (מֵירְכָא like מֵימְרָא and מֵיכְלָא), and indicate the accent as 'prolonging' the modulation. It had a *long* tone [63], which was at the same time, as the Massora and all writers on the accents describe it, a *descending* tone [64]. In MSS. it is generally represented as a *straight* line, turned more or less to the left, but in some made perpendicular.

[It may be noted that the term מאריך is often used in the Massora and elsewhere not only for the accent Mer'kha, but for Gaya = Métheg as well. And even the *signs* are not always kept distinct in Codd. Hence an excuse may be found for our printed texts, which constantly mark the (euphonic) Métheg at the end of a word as *Mer'kha*, פַּדֶּנָה (Gen. xxviii. 5) for פַּדֶּנָה; וַתִּוָּשַׁע (Is. lxiii. 5) for וַתִּוָּשַׁע, &c. Another occasional use of מאריך in the Massora is to indicate the *opposite to*

Munach occurs occasionally in Codd. with the angle rounded off ־֢, and it must have appeared to some punctator—one of the class, whose restless ingenuity was wholly occupied with such trifles—that here was an opening for a new name, after the analogy of Galgal, No. 6. The name has, however (as far as I have noticed), been adopted only by Norzi.

If we find any of the names above given, loosely used in the Massora (MS. or printed), we must not suppose that the genuine Massora sanctioned them. Both copyists and editors have introduced the modern names familiar to them.

[61] עומר כקרן הסוך (Man. du Lect., p. 73). Comp. the נון הסוכה, Mas. to Num. xi. 1.

[62] By Chayyug, p. 127, this accent is called מקף, fully שופר הסוך מקף (Ox. 2512, p. 18). The meaning is 'conjunctive' (comp. Dikd. hat., § 30, and Ginsb. Mas. ש, § 235), in opposition to the disjunctive Y'thibh with the same form. An extraordinary name occurs in Pet. 123, הליל צגיר, i.e. هلال صغير, 'small new moon.' *Mutatis mutandis*, the explanation is the same as for Gilgal above.

[63] מחוברת לאחותה בארוכה (Dikd. hat., p. 19), 'joined to its partner with a *long* tone.' And so Ben-Bil. (Ox. MS.) המלה שמאריכה. Another explanation is '*long-stroke*' in contrast to Shophar, but the other meanings of the term (given above) shew that this explanation is not the true one.

[64] Comp. Mas. to Num. xxxvi. 3 (נָחַת); Dikd. hat., § 21; Mishp. hat., p. 16; Man. du Lect., p. 97 below, &c. Hence in Pet. 123, the double name of مَاد, 'lengthening,' and هَابِط, 'descending.'

REMARKS ON THE ACCENTS. 25

Maqqeph, thus: על ח׳ מאריבין בטעם בספרא (Mas. to Lev. i. 11), i.e. 'eight instances in Lev. lengthen out the particle עַל with an *accent*' (instead of contracting it with Maqqeph). Comp. Mas. parva to Esth. ii. 5. As these instances affect the accentuation, it seemed necessary to allude to them.]

Mer'kha appears in a few instances *doubled*, and is termed מֵירְכָא כְפוּלָה, or תְּרֵין חוּטְרִין, 'two rods or strokes.' As the servus of T'bhir always precedes, this Double Mer'kha was regarded as a reduced or impoverished T'bhir, whence the fanciful name given to it of הַמִּסְכֵּן, *pauper, tenuis* [65]. Qimchi (Mikhlol 89ᵃ) goes so far as to say that its *melody* was like T'bhir's. But his authority on such a point is not of much weight.

3. דַּרְגָּא is also termed שַׁלְשֶׁלֶת and שִׁישְׁלָא (سلسل) [66]. These latter names seem to indicate a certain relationship with the disjunctive Shalshéleth. And in some old Codd., as De R. 10 and K. 154, the sign for Darga is precisely the *same* as that for Shalshéleth, as also it is described in Dikd. hat., p. 19, and Man. du Lect., p. 76. But the Shalshéleth-sign stands, as we have seen, p. 17, for *a trill*. Such then would seem to have been the musical value of Darga. The name דרנא had also probably this meaning. Comp. درج, *he chanted, or sang, in a trilling or quavering manner* (Lane). Of course, the trill or quaver must have been feeble, in comparison with that of Shalshéleth [67]. The sign in common use, and the modern melody of a descending scale running through the octave, represent דַּרְגָּא in its ordinary meaning of *scala*.

4. אָזֵל, אַזְלָא, i.e. 'going on,' not pausing in the melody, = conjunctive (in contrast to Pashṭa, disjunctive, with the same sign) [68]. Other names for this accent are מַקֵּל, 'rod,' 'stroke' (comp. l. 7 above), and אֶשֶׁל, 'cord,' 'line.' When associated with Géresh, it is frequently termed קַדְמָא, Géresh then, by a strange confusion of terms, being known as אַוְלָא [69]; or the two are described by the Massoretic formula אָזֵל וְאָתֵי. The melody is an *ascending* one, לעולם עולה (Dikd. hat., p. 19).

---

[65] Dikd. hat., p. 18. Baer indeed explains the term of *Silluq*. But this is a mistake; for Ox. 2512, p. 15ᵇ, expressly names the Double Mer'kha in תַּעֲשֶׂה (Ex. v. 15) משכן. The description also, given in Dikd. hat., l. c., exactly suits this accent.

[66] Chayyug, p. 128 below; Man. du Lect., p. 76; Dikd. hat., § 19. The ignorant Qalonymos gives a further name שׁוֹשַׁר גלגל, which is quite false (the name belongs to another accent, see p. 23). Yet he is followed by El. Levita, Heidenheim, Ewald, and others.

[67] It ought also to have a corresponding name, ש׳ קְטַנָּה, as in De R. 1262.

[68] So David ben Abraham (10th century) in his Dictionary (Journal Asiatique, 1862, p. 77 note) uses הוֹלֵךְ, 'joined on,' as opposed to מוּבְדָּת, 'separated.'

[69] קַדְמָא וְאַוְלָא, as it were 'the leader and the goer on' with the melody. The

5. תְּלִישָׁא קְטַנָּה [70]. See Remarks under תְּלִישָׁא above, p. 22. The melody of Little T'lisha must have been similar to that of Great T'lisha, although of course feebler. Ben-Naphtali apparently treated this accent as a *disjunctive* (comp. חלופי הנקוד to Gen. xix. 17 and Baer's note), and so the modern Ashkenazic Jews give a certain *pausal* value to Little T'lisha, as in chanting וַיִּסָּר בַּיּוֹם הַהוּא אֶת־הַתְּיָשִׁים (Gen. xxx. 35). Bad taste indeed!

6. גַּלְגַּל, 'wheel.' Although this accent occurs only sixteen times (always immediately before Great Pazer) punctators exercised their ingenuity in devising for it a number of names and even forms. Its original circular form may be gathered from the name 'wheel.' Under this form it was also called עֲגוּלָה, 'round,' and תְּלִישָׁא קְטַנָּה or ת׳ זְעִירָה [71], being like a small T'lisha. With the circle incomplete [72], it became יָרֵחַ בֶּן יוֹמוֹ [73], 'the moon a day old.' Other forms of Galgal, beside that found in printed texts, are ⸗ and a small Têth, answering to similar forms, on a larger scale, of Great Pazer. The original melody probably resembled that of Little T'lisha.

7. דְּחִיָּה, נְטוּיָה, or מָאיְלָא [74]. Names given to Ṭiphcha, when in the same word with Athnach or Silluq. (It occurs only fifteen or sixteen times [75].) The character of Ṭiphcha was changed, hence a new name was given to it. But somewhat of the melody of Ṭiphcha must have been retained in the chanting, for we find the same subordinate accents as before Ṭiphcha,—and Zaqeph preceding, which requires for

---

expression is found in Chayyug, p. 127, in the printed Mas. (e. g. to Ex. iv. 11), in the Italian Zarqa-list, &c., and is commonly used by the Jews in the present day. The two accents may come together in the *same* word, and are then called in Pet. 123 طَارْفَتَين, as if they were both Géresh! see p. 20.

[70] In the list, Chayyug, p. 128, this accent is actually called תלישא רבא! to distinguish it from Galgal, which is there termed תלישא זעירא (see No. 6 above). What we call Great T'lisha has the simple name תלשא. One sees there is no end to the vagaries of schools and punctators in these trivial matters!

[71] As in Chayyug, p. 128; Man. du Lect., p. 76 below; Ox. 2512, p. 10.

[72] So the Massoretic circle and the Arabic Ǵezm are sometimes complete, sometimes incomplete in MSS.

[73] As in Mas. magna to Ezek. xlviii. 21, the Zarqa-lists, &c. In Pet. 123 this name is changed to هِلَال كَبِير, 'the great new moon,' because Galgal had to be contrasted with M'huppach, 'the small new moon' (see note 62).

[74] For these several names, see Mishp. hat., p. 6ᵇ; Dikd. hat., p. 19 and note; Chayyug, p. 128; and Man. du Lect., p. 73.

These names are also given to an accent of the same form (but different character) in the three Books, see טעמי אמ״ה, p. 19.

[75] Properly speaking, it does not belong to our list (of Conjunctives). I have however inserted it, as all Rabbinical writers on the accents, and even the Massora, number it among the משרתים (*servi*).

the melody Ṭiphcha following. The name מָאיְלָא (the one now in common use) must have been first employed by the grammarians, who wrote in Arabic, for it is مَآئِلَة, i.e. 'inclined[76].' The Hebrew names have the same signification. In Dikd. hat., p. 17, the name is מתחה, 'extending,' scil. the melody of the word in which it occurs.

(The term מָאיְלָא is also found in a rare Mas. printed in Bomb. 2 at Gen. xxx. 16 and elsewhere. It is there used for the *Mer'kha preceding Zarqa*. But such a use is opposed to the testimony of early writers on the accents, who expressly state that Mây'la occurs *only* before Athnach and Silluq. The Mas., in this form, is undoubtedly false[77].)

Were we able to trace the development of the graphical representation of the accentual melodies, we should probably find that it was, at first, confined to Athnach and Soph Pasuq[78]; and that it was only *gradually* that the other signs, of which we have just treated, came into use.

The first step towards a musical arrangement of the text was the breaking it up into a number of 'sections,' פְּסוּקִים—verses, as we call them—of varying length, according as the sense or the requirements of the cantillation suggested. Each section or verse was then treated as an independent whole; and, whatever its connection in sense with the verse preceding or the verse following, had its musical division assigned to it, quite irrespectively of them[79]. These verses we must accept, as (with rare exceptions) common to all texts[80]. Their number is counted and fixed by the Massora for each Book.

---

[76] Comp. the use of the word, as it is found in Ox. 2512, p. 10, in the description of Mer'kha: هو عصا تحت الكلمة مَآئِل الى اليسار.

[77] It may perhaps be traced to a *single* MS. For Moses the punctator (דרכי הנקוד, p. 27), after quoting it at length, adds וה נמצא בספר אסטמיא אחר. This quotation seems then to have passed into other works, as Simson's חבור הקונים, and was copied *verbatim* by Jacob ben-Chayyim in the Mas. to Gen. xxx. 16. Perhaps the original form of the Mas. was י״ח מילין מאריכין בין אולא לורקא וגו׳.

[78] Many extant Codd. do not (as is well known) go beyond this simple division.

[79] Hence it is often called in the Talmud קְרָא (e.g. Qiddushin 30ᵃ) and מִקְרָא (Yoma 52ᵃ), properly 'portion to be read' (chanted), 'lection.'

[80] It was not always so. For a long time there were considerable differences between the various schools, a reminiscence of which is found in the *Pisqas*

The verses, like all the other divisions, were marked off for the *cantillation*[81]. They necessarily vary in length; but the general rule is to avoid *too short* or *too long* verses. Hence a short period is often attached to a longer one preceding or following (Gen. i. 10; v. 1; xxxvii. 2; xxxix. 6), and two short periods are constantly brought together into one verse (i. 5, 8; xlvii. 31). On the other hand, when the period runs on to any length, it is broken up into two or more verses. So the protasis may be separated from the apodosis (Ex. ix. 2, 3; Deut. xxx. 17, 18); a compound subject or object kept apart from the verb (Num. xxxi. 22; Neh. x. 29); a speech extended through any number of verses (Gen. xii. 1–3; xxiv. 34–49); details of every kind marked off in groups—often small, for distinctness of enunciation—(Gen. x. 11–18; Ex. xxxv. 10–19; Deut. xi. 2–6; Jer. xxv. 17–26; &c.) The division, it must be allowed, shews freedom enough, as when we find the apodosis in the same verse with the *last part* of the protasis (Gen. xxiv. 44; 2 Sam. xi. 21; 1 Ki. x. 5; Ezek. xviii. 9); or a shorter period in the same verse with the *last part* of a long period preceding (Gen. i. 18; xiv. 20; l. 17; Ex. xii. 27; Jer. xi. 5; li. 64). In such cases, the division which seemed most convenient for the cantillation was adopted. The musical principle admitted,—and due allowance made for divisions, designed to emphasize, or otherwise give effect to the reading,—we shall not often have occasion to find fault with the verses as marked off. The above remarks refer particularly to the *prose* portions of the text. For the *poetical*, the parallelism of the members sufficed generally to fix the limits of the verse.

The rules for the division of the *verse itself* must now engage our attention.

---

marked in our text (for the list of which see Baer's note on Hos. i. 2). These Pisqas, always coming after Athnach, indicate that some authorities made *two* verses, where our Massoretic text has only *one*. The latest treatise on the differences named is by Graetz in the Monatschrift für Geschichte und Wissenschaft des Judenthums, 1885, p. 97 ff. But the learned professor has not succeeded in throwing any fresh light on a very obscure and perplexing subject.

[81] The verses, once fixed, would furnish suitable portions for separate reading, when a translation of the text was to be given at the same time. So in the Mishna, Megilla iv. 4, the translator is directed to render verse by verse in the reading of the Tora. But I cannot consider (with Vitringa and Hupfeld) that the verses owed their origin to the necessity of providing for the translation *small divisions in the sense* which the congregation could easily follow. The Mishna, l. c., appointed *three* verses of the Prophets to be read together, before the translation was given.

CHAPTER III.

THE DICHOTOMY. GENERAL.

EVERY verse, however short, was divided, for the purpose of chanting, into *two* parts. This is what Christian writers on the accents have termed the DICHOTOMY of the verse. The accent employed to mark the division is generally Athnach, but in some cases other accents are allowable, or are even necessary from the influence of musical laws.

The further division was on the same principle. Each half-verse constituted by the main dichotomy—if of sufficient length—was divided by a *minor* dichotomy. And the parts thus formed were subjected to the same process, which was continued, as long as the condition just named, of there being a sufficient number of words in the clause, was fulfilled. We thus arrive at the law of the CONTINUOUS DICHOTOMY, the simple principle that regulates the division of the verse. It is sufficient at present to lay down the general law. The conditions for its application cannot be stated as simply as for the three Books. It will depend on the particular accent, whose clause has to be divided, whether three or even more words can stand without the dichotomy. But the law must be accepted. It constitutes one of the marked and distinguishing features of the system of Hebrew accentuation [1].

We naturally ask, what was the purpose designed by this remarkable process of division and minute sub-division? No doubt it served to mark the logical and syntactical interpunction. But the logical use will account only very partially for its introduction; and even for the syntactical, it was not needed to anything like the extent to which it was applied. Some

---

[1] Jewish writers on the accents had no more idea of this law than they had of many of the chief grammatical rules. Its discovery is due to the unwearied diligence, with which the study of the accents was pursued by Christian scholars of the 17th century.

other explanation therefore is necessary. And there can be no question that the object aimed at, was that which is the essential characteristic of the accentuation,—*musical effect*. The result of the continuous dichotomy was a succession of pausal melodies (more or fewer) fixed by rule, which, with the conjunctive melodies dependent on them, gave the cantillation of the verse. It was a peculiar system, but one that must have answered its purpose. Certainly it secured fulness and variety for the melody. How far it corresponded to our modern notions of a melodious result, we have no sufficient means of determining, inasmuch as we are but imperfectly acquainted with the musical value of the accents, and not at all with the changes which they doubtless underwent, according to their relative position.

As for the *origin* of the system, it seems to me that it may have been as follows. We may well suppose that a musical recitation was early employed for the *poetical* parts of the Tora, as the שִׁירוֹת, Ex. xv and Deut. xxxii. Such parts would, from their very character, be the first to claim it. We may further consider that the musical divisions as we now have them were first established for these pieces. For how does the matter stand with them? The dichotomy — resulting from *parallelismus membrorum*—is the reigning principle of division, and shews itself not only in the bisection of the verse, but often in that of the subordinate parts as well. This *formal* dichotomy necessarily supplied (as far as it went) the basis for the *musical*, and from its constant recurrence seems to have suggested to the originators of the accentual system a guiding principle for the musical division *in general*. We note that in the poetical pieces, it did not need frequent application. It is not often that the subdivision is carried beyond the *second* minor dichotomy. The continuous dichotomy shews itself therefore here in a simple form.

When now it was determined to introduce a musical recitation for the *prose* parts, there was, according to the above hypothesis, a model already provided. True, in these parts there is, generally speaking, no *formal* dichotomy to serve as a basis for the *musical*. But this could form no objection, for there are even in the poetical pieces verses that read as simple prose, e. g. Ex. xv. 18, Deut. xxxii. 19, and yet have the dichotomy applied to them. The model then was accepted, and the principle of the continuous dichotomy adopted for the prose reading. Here, owing to the long verses often marked off, its application became more extended and much more complicated.

One drawback was involved in its adoption. Two or more *equal* pauses, in succession, cannot be represented as such. *Subordination* (variously carried out) necessarily takes place [2]. No doubt the accentuators would have been often glad to mark the equal pauses by accents of equal disjunctive value, if the law which they had laid down for themselves would have permitted it, as in Gen. xlix. 31; Josh. vii. 14[b]; Is. iii. 24; lxvi. 3; &c. In certain cases, indeed, the same accent is *repeated* in the division of the clause; but, from the very nature of the continuous dichotomy, *it loses in disjunctive value* each time of repetition. Instances are Zaqeph repeated (often more than once) in Silluq's clause, R'bhia in Zaqeph's clause, &c.

The question how the *position* of the dichotomy (main or minor) was fixed, has been already answered. It is found, where the main *logical* pause of the clause, or the rules for *syntactical* division require it. But, as has been pointed out, pp. 3, 4, there are many notable exceptions. I would here only once more remind the reader that we have to do with a system of *public recitation*, the main object of which (like that of all effective delivery) was to bring out and impress upon the minds of the hearers the full meaning of the Sacred Text. And I would add that unless we are prepared to recognise the utmost freedom in the application of the dichotomy, we shall never be able to explain to ourselves the accentual division. In the higher style, where *parallelism* is found, the same freedom necessarily prevails.

I purpose, in the present chapter, to consider certain *general* principles of division, which will, in my opinion, account for the most noticeable instances of deviation from rule, just referred

---

[2] So *abiit, evasit, erupit*, could not, when turned into (accented) Hebrew, be separated by *equal pauses*. Comp. וַיִּבְרַח וַיִּמָּלֵט ׃ (וַיֵּלֶךְ נִיבְרַח וַיִּמָּלֵט (1 Sam. xix. 12).

to. In the next chapter, I shall lay down the laws for *syntactical* division.

I. We often see a tendency to delay the dichotomy, till the main statement of the verse or clause has been set before the reader,—what follows the dichotomy serving to supplement, explain, qualify, &c. the *last part* of what precedes it. Looked at from the rhetorical point of view, such a division is often effective enough, although it may come in the middle of a subordinate clause, or may cut in two the apodosis. There is nothing peculiar in it, for we often adopt it in our own interpunction. (In the examples given, the vertical line marks the position of the dichotomy):

'For God doth know that, in the day ye eat thereof, then your eyes shall be opened, | and ye shall be as gods, knowing good and evil' (Gen. iii. 5).

'And Jehovah God said unto the serpent, Because thou hast done this, cursed art thou above all cattle and above every beast of the field; | upon thy belly shalt thou go, and dust shalt thou eat all the days of thy life' (iii. 14).

'Are we not counted of him strangers? for he hath sold us, | and hath also quite devoured our money' (xxxi. 15).

'When thou comest into thy neighbour's vineyard, then thou mayest eat grapes thy fill at thine own pleasure; | but thou shalt not put any in thy vessel' (Deut. xxiii. 25).

'Jehoshaphat made ships of Tarshish to go to Ophir for gold. But none went; | for the ships were broken at Ezion-geber' (1 Ki. xxii. 49).

Further examples are unnecessary.

II. *Emphasis* is distinctly marked:

'In the beginning *God created* | the heavens and the earth' (Gen. i. 1. Comp. Ex. xx. 11).

'Thy sons and thy daughters shall be given unto another people, *and thine eyes shall see it* | and fail with longing for them all the day' (Deut. xxviii. 32).

'And the king of Israel said unto Jehoshaphat, There is yet one man by whom we may enquire of Jehovah; *but I hate him,* | for he doth not prophesy good concerning me, but evil' (1 Ki. xxii. 8).

'Who gave Jacob for a spoil, and Israel to the robbers? *Did not Jehovah?*' | [emphatic pause[3]]; 'He against whom we have sinned, &c.' (Is. xlii. 24).

'If any stir up strife, it is *not* | *of me*' (liv. 15)[4].

'*No peace,* | saith Jehovah, for the wicked' (xlviii. 22; lvii. 21).

---

[3] I cannot agree with Delitzsch's remark: *Das Athnach ist an unrechter Stelle.* Comp. Athnach before אשר, Jer. xli. 2[b].

[4] Luzzatto is completely puzzled by the accentuation, as other commentators would no doubt have been, if they had noticed it.

Such examples are common enough. Had they been wanting, we might well have questioned the taste of the accentuators. What calls for remark is the lengths to which they went in carrying out this principle of division. In their desire to mark the emphasis, they did not scruple to pass over the most prominent logical pauses. (These pauses were indeed marked by musical pauses, but the *main musical pause* was reserved for the emphasis.) In no other way can we explain the division in such cases as the following:

'And it came to pass at the end of two months that she returned to her father, *who did with her according to his vow which he had vowed;*' | [pause for effect at these solemn words [5], on which the whole narrative hinges]; 'and she had not known a man. So it became a custom in Israel' (Judg. xi. 39) [6].

'Therefore thus saith the Lord Jehovah, Behold, I have founded in Zion a *stone*,' | [the Messiah] [7], 'a tried stone, a precious corner-stone of sure foundation: he that believeth shall not make haste' (Is. xxviii. 16).

'Then said Jehovah unto me, What seest thou, Jeremiah? and I said, *Figs;* | the good figs, very good; and the bad, very bad, &c.' (Jer. xxiv. 3).

'Then this Daniel *distinguished himself above the presidents and satraps*,' | [an emphasis not altogether unsuitable in view of the narrative following], 'because an excellent spirit was in him; and the king thought to set him over the whole realm' (Dan. vi. 4).

Other examples will occur in the sequel.

Occasionally (it must be allowed) the accentuators have been led into fanciful extremes by the Midrash-teaching of the Schools. Thus in Gen. i. 21 the Athnach is with הַתַּנִּינִם הַגְּדֹלִים, instead of at its proper place before וַיִּבְרָא אֱלֹהִים כִּי־טוֹב. And why? Because these wonderful creatures, about which Jewish fable has so much to relate [8], were counted to have nothing in common with the other creatures named. They were beings *per se*, and are put *by themselves* at the beginning of the verse! In Gen. xxxv. 10 the Athnach rests on

---

[5] Josephus, Targum, and Rabb. Comm. generally, suppose that Jephthah really offered up his daughter, in fulfilment of his vow.

[6] Comp. Judg. iv. 21, where Athnach is properly due at וְהוּא־נִרְדָּם, but has been transposed for the sake of emphasis and effect. The attention was to be fixed on the details of Jael's heroic act, culminating in the words וַתִּצְנַח בָּאָרֶץ.

[7] So Rashi explains. Raymund Martini, in Pugio Fidei, ii. 5. 2, quotes the Targum as also rendering אבן by מלך המשיח. So far he is right that the מלך חקיף of the Targum evidently points to the Messiah (comp. 1 Pet. ii. 6).

[8] See e.g. Rashi, *ad loc.*, and Levy, Neuhebr. W. B. s.v. לויתן.

שִׁמְךָ יַעֲקֹב, to intimate that the patriarch, though he had a new name given him, was not (like Abraham) to lose the old one. The words are made emphatic: '*Thy name is, and shall be, Jacob!*'[9] In 2 Chr. ii. 13 the accentuators have abandoned the obvious accentuation, in order that they might emphasize the lesson that a son is bound to follow his father's occupation and to support his mother, when left a widow![10] Such instances are however rare. That a few occur is not surprising, when we bear in mind the influence that Haggadic teaching has always exercised among the Jews.

III. *a*. It is on the same principle that the introductory part of the verse, although logically requiring the main accent (Athnach) after it, is constantly passed over, that this accent may be introduced where the weight of meaning of the passage seems to lie[11]. Observe the division in the following instances:

'There I will meet with thee, and I will speak with thee, from above the mercy-seat, from between the two cherubim which are upon the ark of the testimony, | all that I will command thee to the children of Israel' (Ex. xxv. 22).

'And Moses wrote all the words of Jehovah; and rose up early in the morning, and builded an altar under the mount, | and twelve pillars, according to the twelve tribes of Israel' (Ex. xxiv. 4). [The accentuation draws attention to the altar and the twelve representative pillars. They were to be noted from their connection with the Covenant, the ratification of which is the grand subject of the narrative.]

'Yet it pleased Jehovah to bruise him,—He hath put him to grief: when Thou shalt make his soul an offering for sin, he shall see his seed, he shall prolong his days, | and the pleasure of Jehovah shall prosper in his hand' (Is. liii. 10). [It is on the *glorious results* of the sufferings of 'the servant of Jehovah' that the accentuation dwells.]

'And he said, Naked came I out of my mother's womb, and naked shall I return thither: Jehovah gave, and Jehovah hath taken away; | blessed be the name of Jehovah' (Job i. 21).

And so even in short and simple sentences like the following:

'And Abraham stretched forth his hand, and took the knife | to slay his son' (Gen. xxii. 10).

'Then these men assembled, and found Daniel | making petition and supplication before his God' (Dan. vi. 12).

---

[9] Comp. Berakhoth 13ᵃ. So R. El'azar in the Midrash (Ox. 2338) insists, ויאמר אלהים שמך יעקב שמך יעקב מכל מקום.

[10] See Qimchi on the passage.

[11] Hence often where הִנֵּה precedes the second clause, e.g. in Lev. xiii. 5, &c.; Num. xvii. 7; 1 Sam. xx. 2; xxx. 16; 2 Ki. vi. 25; Ezek. x. 1; Amos vii. 7.

THE DICHOTOMY.

Where the reader sees at once that the pause comes in just where it is most telling.

This free mode of division, adopted for the sake of effect and impressiveness in the reading, is not to be regarded as exceptional, but is found everywhere. It is, however, so different from our own ideas of interpunction, that I append some other examples, which the student may examine for himself: Gen. xxxiv. 7; Ex. iii. 12; xii. 23; Num. xx. 13; Deut. iii. 11; 1 Sam. xiv. 27; 2 Sam. xii. 4; Is. xxvii. 13; Jer. ii. 23; Ezek. xxxix. 13; Qoh. vii. 2; ix. 12 [12].

The above are all instances of division by Athnach; but of course the same principle applies to the division of the half-verse or any section of the same, e.g. Is. xxxvii. 9^b; Jer. xxvi. 12^b; Mal. iii. 3^a.

β. Particularly noteworthy is the way in which the words that introduce a speech—or anything similar, as a command, decree, oath, covenant, &c.—are treated. They constantly occupy a *subordinate position*, as far as the accents are concerned. The clause containing *the speech itself, the command*, &c., is counted the more important, and receives the main accentuation. In short, the division is made (as above) just as if the introductory words were absent, e.g. [13]

'And God said, Let there be a firmament in the midst of the waters, | and let it divide the waters from the waters' (Gen. i. 6).

'And Jehovah said to him, Therefore whosoever slayeth Cain, | vengeance shall be taken sevenfold' (iv. 15).

'And Moses said to the children of Israel, See, Jehovah hath called by name | Bezalel, the son of Uri, &c.' (Ex. xxxv. 30).

'The Lord Jehovah hath sworn by His holiness, that lo! the days shall come

---

[12] He may also compare Gen. vi. 9; xi. 10; xxxvii. 2; where we do not find Athnach with the superscriptions, as we should have expected, but the clause following is divided, just as if the superscriptions were absent.

[13] There is no real difficulty here; we divide often in the same way: 'And they said, Nay; but we will abide in the street all night' (Gen. xix. 2). 'And Lot said unto them, Oh, not so, my lord: behold now, thy servant &c.' (xix. 18, 19). Only the accentuators go farther than we do, subordinating the words in question to a syntactical, as well as logical, division (see examples in text).

upon you, | that they shall take you away with hooks, and your residue with fish-hooks' (Amos iv. 2).

'And he commanded to destroy | all the wise men of Babylon' (Dan. ii. 12).

'Thou, O king, hast made a decree, that every man that shall hear the sound of the cornet, ... and all kinds of music, | shall fall down and worship the golden image' (iii. 10).

Such cases occur in every page.

γ. What is next to be noticed is that α and β may be combined, or β may be repeated; in other words, we may have a *compound* procemium consisting of two (or even more) members, each of which will be subordinated, directly or indirectly, to the same main division of the speech, &c., marked by Athnach or some other leading accent. The position of this accent is indicated, as before, in the following examples:

'And Jacob awaked out of his sleep, and said, Surely Jehovah is in this place; | and I knew it not' (Gen. xxviii. 16)[14].

'And he told it to his father and to his brethren; and his father rebuked him, and said unto him, What is this dream that thou hast dreamed? | Shall I and thy mother and thy brethren indeed come to bow down ourselves to thee to the earth?' (xxxvii. 10).

'Go and say to Hezekiah, Thus saith Jehovah, the God of David thy father, I have heard thy prayer, I have seen thy tears: | behold, I will add unto thy days fifteen years' (Is. xxxviii. 5)[14].

'From the uttermost part of the earth have we heard songs, "Glory for the righteous!" But I said, I pine away, I pine away, woe is me! | the treacherous dealers have dealt treacherously; yea, the treacherous dealers have dealt very treacherously' (xxiv. 16).

'And she conceived again, and bare a daughter. And He said unto him, Call her name Lo-ruchamah: | for I will no more have mercy on the house of Israel, that I should in any wise pardon them' (Hos. i. 6).

Other examples are Gen. i. 28; viii. 21; xxi. 17; xlvii. 29; Ex. x. 3; xxxii. 13; 2 Ki. i. 6; v. 15; Is. xlvii. 8; lix. 21; Jer. xlii. 20.

The student, when he has become familiar with the rules for the accentuation, may examine these examples for himself. He will observe that the several procemial members are *variously subordinated,*

---

[14] Our interpunction is here the same. And so in Gen. xxxvii. 32; 2 Sam. iv. 8; Is. vi. 7; xlvii. 8; lxii. 11; Jer. xxxviii. 25; Job i. 16; and many other passages. (See the Revised Version.)

sometimes the first to the second, sometimes all to Athnach, &c. The accentuators chose the musical pauses, which seemed to them suitable, nor is there generally any cause to find fault with their selection.

δ. Lastly, among prœmial expressions are to be reckoned וְהָיָה and וַיְהִי, in the sense of 'coming to pass,' which are usually subordinated by the accents to the first word or words of the clause which they introduce: וְהָיָה כָל־מֹצְאִי ׀ יַהַרְגֵנִי (Gen. iv. 14); וְהָיָה הוּא ׀ יִהְיֶה־לְּךָ לְפֶה (Ex. iv. 16; comp. Gen. xxiv. 15); וַיְהִי כִּשְׁמֹעַ חִירָם ׀ אֶת־דִּבְרֵי שְׁלֹמֹה (1 Ki. v. 21); וַיְהִי בִשְׁלֹשִׁים וָשֶׁבַע ׀ שָׁנָה (2 Ki. xxv. 27). The merely *formal* character of these introductory words suffices to account for their subordinate position.

IV. In contrast to the *prœmium*, are the cases where an *appendage* is made to the clause, without affecting the division of the same. (Here the proper logical divison would have been immediately *before* the appendage.) Such cases are not so numerous as the prœmial instances. They may be divided into three classes:

a. Those in which there is a close connection in *sense* between the concluding member of the clause and the appendage. Thus in Gen. i. 16, וְאֵת הַכּוֹכָבִים is not preceded by Athnach, but is joined on by the accents to the part of the clause describing the 'lesser light,' because the stars were appointed *with the moon* to lighten up the night [15]. In iii. 19 the accentual division is: 'In the sweat of thy face shalt thou eat bread, ׀ till thou return unto the ground, for out of *it* thou wast taken;' and in iv. 25: 'God hath appointed me another seed ׀ in place of Abel, because Cain *slew him*.' Comp. xxxiv. 7 end; xlix. 10; Lev. xiii. 6 end; Deut. xvi. 3[b]; Judg. vi. 21[b] (see Bertheau); 1 Ki. xx. 12[b]; Is. xxxviii. 16; lv. 5; lxvi. 13; 1 Chr. xvi. 33 (as Ps. xcvi. 13).

β. The second class embraces certain recurrent phrases, which

---

[15] Comp. Jer. xxxi. 35: 'Thus saith Jehovah, who giveth the sun for a light by day, and the ordinances *of the moon and stars for a light by night*.'

are occasionally attached to the end of the verse, without affecting the regular division preceding, as נְאֻם יְהוָֹה, אָמַר יְהוָֹה and cognate expressions, Is. i. 20; xvii. 6; Jer. xlviii. 43; Ezek. v. 15; xv. 8; xxx. 12; Amos i. 15; &c. So אֲנִי יְהוָֹה, Lev. xix. 10; xxi. 12; xxii. 2, 3; xxvi. 45; and יְהוָֹה שְׁמוֹ, Jer. xxxi. 35; xxxiii. 2; Amos v. 8; ix. 6.

γ. The third class relates to the peculiar division often found before לֵאמֹר, e.g. וַיְצַו יְהוָֹה אֱלֹהִים ׀ עַל־הָאָדָם לֵאמֹר (Gen. ii. 16); בַּיּוֹם הַהוּא כָּרַת יְהוָֹה אֶת־אַבְרָם ׀ בְּרִית לֵאמֹר (xv. 18); וַיֻּכּוּ שֹׁטְרֵי בְּנֵי יִשְׂרָאֵל ׀ אֲשֶׁר־שָׂמוּ עֲלֵהֶם נֹגְשֵׂי פַרְעֹה לֵאמֹר (Ex. v. 14); וַיְהִי דְבַר־יְהוָֹה אֶל־יִרְמְיָהוּ שֵׁנִית ׀ וְהוּא עוֹדֶנּוּ עָצוּר בַּחֲצַר הַמַּטָּרָה לֵאמֹר (Jer. xxxiii. 1). In these examples the clauses have been divided, just as if לֵאמֹר were not present, with the consequence that לֵאמֹר and the word (or words) between it and the main dichotomy preceding are brought together in a very awkward way. And so in numberless other passages. The object of the division seems to have been purely *musical*, to introduce more variety into the chanting than would have been possible if the division had been always on the word immediately preceding לֵאמֹר, and to secure a fuller melody for *long* sentences (e. g. 2 Sam. vii. 7; Jer. xliv. 15). From the frequent occurrence of לֵאמֹר with Athnach and Silluq, it is here that the monotony would have been most felt; and here the above division is most common. With the other accents, it is frequently neglected [16].

V. It is important to notice the influence which *parallelism* has on the division of the verse. This main ornament of the Hebrew style [17] characterizes all the poetical and (to a great

---

[16] Thus in Genesis, it occurs only twice (xlii. 37; xlv. 16), as far as I have observed, out of some thirty examples.

[17] But not confined to Hebrew, for it is found equally in old Egyptian and Assyrian compositions.

extent) the prophetical parts of the twenty-one Books. It is also found in the simply narrative portions, for a poetic colouring often shews itself even there. The most conspicuous instances are where it is marked by the main dichotomy, but it appears hardly less frequently in the minor divisions of the verse.

For the different kinds of parallelism, I may be allowed to refer to my remarks in טעמי אמ״ת, pp. 24–28.

The most common form in which it appears is that of *partial* parallelism,—with or without addition, thus:

a. Without addition, e. g.

'In blessing I will bless thee, and in multiplying I will multiply thy seed as the stars of heaven, | and as the sand which is upon the sea-shore' (Gen. xxii. 17).

'Your new moons and your appointed feasts my soul hateth; they are a burden upon me, | I am weary of bearing them' (Is. i. 14).

'Like as many were astonished at thee,—his visage was so marred more than man, | and his form more than the sons of men' (lii. 14).

'They are waxen fat, they shine: yea, they overpass the deeds of wickedness; they plead not the cause, the cause of the fatherless, that they should prosper; | and the right of the needy do they not judge' (Jer. v. 28)[18].

In these and similar cases, the main idea of the verse (or clause) is first given, and then follows an echo (as it were) of the *last* part of the same. The logical division is disregarded. No less is this the case, in many of the instances of parallelism

β. With addition, e. g.

'But the multitude of thy foes shall be like small dust, | and the multitude of the terrible ones as chaff that passeth away: and it shall be at an instant suddenly' (Is. xxix. 5).

'For Jehovah is our judge, Jehovah is our lawgiver, | Jehovah is our king; He will save us' (xxxiii. 22).

'I will bring the blind by a way that they know not; in paths that they know not will I lead them: | I will make darkness light before them, and crooked places straight. These are the things which I will do and not forbear' (xlii. 16).

'Sing, O barren, thou that hast not borne; | break forth into singing and cry aloud, thou that hast not travailed with child: for more are the children of the desolate than the children of the married wife, saith Jehovah' (liv. 1).

---

[18] For the sake of beginners, I add a few more examples: Gen. xlix. 27; Is. xxx. 10; xli. 20; Jer. i. 10 (antithetic); Hos. vi. 1; Amos v. 11; ix. 14; Nah. iii. 7.

'Go up to Lebanon, and cry; and lift up thy voice in Bashan; | and cry from Abarim: for all thy lovers are destroyed' (Jer. xxii. 20)[19].

I have noted a few instances of what has been termed *progressive* parallelism, e.g.

'Therefore the abundance they have gotten | and their store—over the poplar-brook shall they carry them' (Is. xv. 7).

'The meadows by the Nile, by the brink of the Nile, | and all that is sown by the Nile,—shall become dry, be driven away, and be no more' (xix. 7).

'A thousand at the rebuke of one, | at the rebuke of five,—shall ye flee' (xxx. 17).

'Yea, from of old men have not heard, nor perceived by the ear, | eye hath not seen,—a God beside Thee, who worketh &c.' (lxiv. 3).

This kind of parallelism is more common in the three Books.

VI. In cases of *specification*, we often find the proper logical or syntactical division—particularly the latter—neglected, and the main musical pause introduced *between the details* or *particulars given*. Distinctness of enunciation, and emphasis (where necessary), were thus secured. The pause was introduced where it seemed likely to be most effective. Thus the *logical* division is disregarded:

'And Moses said, With our young and with our old will we go, | with our sons and with our daughters, with our flocks and with our herds will we go; for we must hold a feast unto Jehovah' (Ex. x. 9).

'I have sent among you the pestilence after the manner of Egypt; I have slain with the sword your young men, and given your horses into captivity, | and I have made the stink of your camp to come up even into your nostrils: yet have ye not returned unto Me, saith Jehovah' (Amos iv. 10)[20].

Comp. Gen. xlii. 36[b]; Lev. xxii. 13[a]; Is. xliv. 12; Jer. xlii. 14; Ezek. xiv. 7 (not 4); Amos vi. 2; Ob. 11.

Syntactical clauses are treated in the same way, and subject, object, &c. are cut in two—or members that belong together, separated—by the dichotomy. (A logical pause may occur in the verse or not.)

---

[19] I give a few additional examples: Is. ii. 12; v. 29; viii. 10; x. 15; xiii. 4; lii. 1; lvii. 6; Ezek. xvi. 45; Joel i. 12.

[20] It is interesting to compare with this verse, vv. 6, 8, 9, 11, all with the same refrain. The details in these verses are not so numerous, hence the division is *regular*.

THE DICHOTOMY.   41

'In the selfsame day entered Noah, and Shem and Ham and Japheth the sons of Noah, | and Noah's wife, and the three wives of his sons with them, into the ark' (Gen. vii. 13).

'And Isaac was forty years old, when he took Rebekah, the daughter of Bethuel the Aramean of Paddan-aram, | the sister of Laban the Aramean, to be his wife' (xxv. 20).

'And every man, with whom was found blue and purple and scarlet, and fine linen, and goats' hair, | and rams' skins dyed red, and sealskins, brought them' (Ex. xxxv. 23).

'And ye shall offer a burnt-offering unto Jehovah, two young bullocks and one ram, | and seven he-lambs of the first year; they shall be unto you without blemish' (Num. xxviii. 19; comp. 11^b).

'And I will set a sign among them, and I will send such as escape of them unto the nations,—to Tarshish, Pul and Lud that draw the bow, to Tubal and Javan, | to the isles afar off, that have not heard My fame, neither have seen My glory,— and they shall declare My glory among the nations' (Is. lxvi. 19).

Perhaps the most notable instances of this mode of division are the following:

'And Jehovah said unto Moses, Speak unto Aaron thy brother, that he come not at all times *into the holy place within the veil,* | *before the mercy-seat which is upon the ark,* that he die not; for I will appear in the cloud upon the mercy-seat' (Lev. xvi. 2). [Specification with emphasis [21].]

'And thou shalt say in thy heart, Who hath borne me these? seeing I was bereaved and barren, | an exile and outcast; and these, who hath brought them up? Behold, I was left alone; these, where were they?' (Is. xlix. 21). [The grouping of the words, though forced, is not without effect.]

Comp. Gen. xxxiv. 28; Ex. xxvii. 19; Deut. xi. 6; Josh. vi. 21; 2 Ki. x. 5^a; Jer. xli. 3; Ezek. xxvii. 27; Esth. ix. 26; Ezra iv. 17 [22].

---

[21] It appears to me a mistake to suppose, with Luzzatto, Malbim, and Geiger (whom Dillmann follows), that the Athnach here rests on a fanciful interpretation given in the name of R. Jehuda, Menachoth 27^b. Had this interpretation indeed represented the traditional and generally accepted view of the passage, we might have allowed that the accentuation had been influenced by it. But, so far from this being the case, it was *opposed* to the recognised teaching (note רבנן חברו וגו׳ l. c.). Nor is it found in the Versions or in any Rabbinical Commentary. In short, there is nothing to shew that it was anything more than the extravagant conceit of a single Rabbi, who perhaps imagined that he had the accentuation on his side. (Geiger, Jüdische Zeitschrift, ii. p. 30, has certainly not succeeded in establishing his point that R. Jehuda's view was that held by the *Pharisees*.)

[22] Gen. xii. 8 and Is. ix. 8 seem to belong under this head. In the former passage, the details are so accented as to draw special attention to the *place* which Abraham chose for pitching his tent and solemnizing the worship of Jehovah. In the latter, it is the *last* of the details that is marked off, but that is an important one.

It is not often that this prominent division occurs, where only *two* objects are specified, or *two* particulars given:

'The bread of his God, both of the most holy, | and of the holy, shall he eat' (Lev. xxi. 22).

'And the holy oblation | and the sanctuary of the house shall be in its midst' (Ezek. xlviii. 21ᵇ).

'For three transgressions of Damascus | and for four, I will not turn it away' (Amos i. 3; comp. 6, 9, &c.).

(Such instances answer to the progressive parallelism of p. 40.) See further, Gen. vi. 9ª (two adjectives); Deut. ix. 28; 1 Ki. vii. 7ª, 36ª; Ezek. xlv. 11; Qoh. iii. 17ᵇ; 1 Chr. vi. 34; xxix. 4.

Other modes of dealing with specification present no difficulty. The several details are usually marked with accents in regular *crescendo* order,—a *climax ascendens*,—or are formed into pairs or groups, which are treated in the same way. For examples, see Gen. xii. 5; xv. 9; Josh. xi. 16; Is. iii. 24; lxvi. 3; Qoh. ix. 11ª: and comp. the rules for the division of the verbal clause, p. 49.

Where specification runs on in *successive verses*, the same principle of distinct enunciation is observable. For instance, when strings of names occur, we constantly find them broken up into *short* verses. See Gen. x. 15 ff.; Is. iii. 18 ff.; Ezra vii. 1 ff.; 1 Chr. viii. 14 ff.; &c.

VII. The *parenthesis* may be indicated in various ways.

It may occupy a separate verse (or verses), as in Deut. ii. 10-12; iii. 9, 11; Jer. xxxix. 1, 2.

Or it may occur in the *middle* or at the *end* of the verse, when the rule is to mark it off with the accent *next greater than that which precedes it* (with Athnach or Silluq after Zaqeph, with Zaqeph or Ṭiphcha after R'bhîa, &c.). The principle of the rule is evident [23].

'If they sin against Thee' [R'bhîa],—'for there is no man that sinneth not' [Zaqeph],—'and Thou be angry with them, &c.' (1 Ki. viii. 46).

'Now Pashchur the son of Immer the priest heard' [Zaqeph],—'and he was chief officer in the house of Jehovah' [Athnach],—'Jeremiah prophesying these things' (Jer. xx. 1).

---

[23] It is very rarely indeed that this rule fails. Ex. xxx. 13ᵇ is an unimportant exception. In Ezek. xxxiii. 33 the accentuators perhaps supplied יאמרו, as the LXX ἐροῦσιν. A strange mistake occurs in 1 Ki. xi. 26. For צרופה point צרועה, with Ox. 1, 7, 10, &c.

So the scruples of the accentuators led them to mark a parenthesis in the well-known passage:

'And the lamp of God was not yet gone out' [Zaqeph],—'and Samuel was asleep [24]' [Athnach]—'in the temple of Jehovah' (1 Sam. iii. 3).

For other examples, see Gen. xix. 20[b]; Deut. iii. 19; 2 Sam. xiv. 26; xxi. 2; Jer. xli. 9; Amos vi. 14; 2 Chr. xxxii. 9.

The above are the usual modes of marking the parenthesis. Variations are infrequent. Sometimes the clause is broken up into parts, each of which is treated successively as above, e. g.

'Like as many were astonished at thee' [Zaqeph],—'his visage was so marred more than man' [Athnach], 'and his form more than the sons of men' [Silluq],—'so &c.' (Is. lii. 14, 15).

'And the sons of Reuben, the first-born of Israel' [Zarqa],—'for he was the first-born' [S'gôlta]; 'but forasmuch as he defiled his father's couch, his birthright was given unto the sons of Joseph' [Athnach]; 'and the genealogy is not to be reckoned after the birthright' [Silluq] (1 Chr. v. 1). The parenthesis in this case, from its length and many details, passes on into the next verse.

Comp. 1 Ki. xii. 2 (2 Chr. x. 2); Esth. ii. 12; 1 Chr. viii. 13.

Sometimes again, where verses are closely connected in sense and construction,—as 1 Ki. xviii. 3, 4; 2 Ki. ix. 14, 15; 2 Chr. v. 11, 12,—the parenthesis occupies the last half of one verse, and is then continued in the next[25]; or it may occur even at the *beginning* of the verse, as in 1 Ki. viii. 42; ix. 11 (but this is unusual).

In the course of the present chapter, the most frequent and most important cases of irregular division have been considered. My aim has been, by the comparison of a sufficient number of examples, to shew that a *principle* underlies the deviation in each case. An explanation thus determined can hardly (I venture to think) be called in question.

---

[24] Rabb. Comm. supply בִּמְקוֹמוֹ (see verse 2), or something similar, after שֹׁכֵב.

[25] There is nothing peculiar in this, for other constructions are treated in the same way, in the verse-division. It must, however, be allowed that the arrangement in Judg. xx. 27, 28 is awkward in the extreme.

CHAPTER IV.

ON SYNTACTICAL DICHOTOMY.

The most frequent, although for us the least important, instances of the application of the dichotomy come under this head. In almost every verse—owing to the minute subdivisions which the continuous dichotomy introduces—we meet with cases where the *syntactical* relation of the words to one another, and to the whole clause of which they form a part, alone decides its position. And it is not always easy to see on what principle the dichotomy in such cases is made. It is therefore necessary to consider somewhat at length what *the relation is between syntax and the accentual division.*

We should not expect the dichotomy to intervene where only *two* words come together, either as forming an independent clause, or as simply left together in the course of the accentual division. Occasionally indeed (as we shall see) under the influence of musical laws, or in cases where a distinct or emphatic enunciation was desired, separation takes place even here. But the rule is *to keep two words united*. Concepts therefore—as subject and predicate, adverb and verb,—which are kept apart in longer clauses, are here constantly brought together, thus: יְהוָה מַלְכֵּנוּ יְהוָה הוֹדִיעֵנִי (Is. xxxiii. 22); (Jer. xi. 18); בַּעֲלָטָה וְיֵצֵא (Ezek. xii. 12); עַל־מִשְׁמַרְתִּי אֶעֱמֹדָה (Hab. ii. 1). And as words united by Maqqeph are regarded (for accentual purposes) as constituting a single word, we meet with such combinations as וְהָיָה־אִישׁ כְּמַחֲבֵא־רוּחַ (Is. xxxii. 2); תִּפְתַּח־אֶרֶץ וְיִפְרוּ־יֶשַׁע (xlv. 8).

But in sentences consisting of three or more words, the dichotomy is more or less regularly introduced. Here the first step is to notice which of the component parts of a grammatical clause—subject, object, verb, &c.—precedes [1].

---

[1] In this chapter, where it is necessary to distinguish the main from a minor dichotomy, I mark the former by d 1, and the latter by d 2, d 3, &c.

SYNTACTICAL DICHOTOMY.

I. The SUBJECT may precede, and—from its independent position[2]—is generally marked off by the main dichotomy: וְאַבְרָהָם ׀ הָיוֹ יִהְיֶה ׀ וְהָאָרֶץ ׀ הָיְתָה תֹהוּ וָבֹהוּ (Gen. i. 2); הָאִשָּׁה אֲשֶׁר נָתַתָּה עִמָּדִי ׀ הִוא ׀ (xviii. 18); לְגוֹי גָּדוֹל וְעָצוּם נָתְנָה־לִּי מִן־הָעֵץ וָאֹכֵל (iii. 12). The subject may be common to two clauses, as in וְצֹאנִי ׀ מִרְמַס רַגְלֵיכֶם תִּרְעֶינָה ׀ וּמִרְפַּשׂ רַגְלֵיכֶם תִּשְׁתֶּינָה (Ezek. xxxiv. 19).

The usual exceptions come under the following heads:

1. The *personal* and *other pronouns* are not always considered important enough to stand by themselves, thus: אֲנִי אַגִּיד ׀ צִדְקָתֵךְ (Is. lvii. 12); comp. הוּא (Gen. ii. 11); אַתָּה (vi. 21); זֶה (v. 1); אֵלֶּה (xxxvi. 14); אֲשֶׁר (xiv. 20); מִי (Num. xxiii. 10); &c.[3]

The same may be said of the indefinite אִישׁ, אָדָם, 'one, any one' (Qoh. vi. 2; ix. 15[b]), and the distributive אִישׁ, 'each, every one' (Lev. xix. 3).

2. When the clause, which the subject introduces, consists of two parts, the first syntactically complete in itself, the second a supplemental appendage (a *Zusatz*, to use a German term, which exactly expresses the construction), consisting generally of a preposition with its government or an adverbial expression, the main dichotomy may be placed at the end of the first part[4]. The subject will then either have no disjunctive accent, or be marked with a minor dichotomy. The following examples will explain what I mean: וְשָׂרָה שֹׁמַעַת ׀ פֶּתַח הָאֹהֶל (Gen. xviii. 10); הָאֵל מָעוּזִּי ׀ חָיִל ׀ יְהוָה יִמְלֹךְ ׀ לְעֹלָם וָעֶד (Ex. xv. 18); וּמַתְנַי חֲגָרִים ׀ בְּכֹחָם אוֹפָן (2 Sam. xxii. 33); (Dan. x. 5). Or the minor dichotomy appears: וְהַנָּחָשׁ ׀ הָיָה עָרוּם ׀ מִכֹּל חַיַּת הַשָּׂדֶה (Gen. iii. 1); וַיהוָה ׀ בֵּרַךְ אֶת־אֲדֹנִי ׀ מְאֹד (xxiv. 35). Such cases are very common[5].

Instances of a *double* Zusatz are found, as in וְאַנְשֵׁי סְדֹם ׀ רָעִים ׀ וְחַטָּאִים ׀ לַיהוָה מְאֹד (Gen. xiii. 13), and 2 Chr. xxix. 34[b], but are rare.

---

[2] See Gesenius' Gr., § 144.

[3] Of course, in such cases, the minor dichotomy is due, if the length of the part of the clause before the main dichotomy requires it, e. g. אָנֹכִי ׀ יוֹצֵר עֲלֵיכֶם ׀ רָעָה (Jer. xviii. 11).

[4] The *Zusatz* answers to the supplemental clause in the logical division, p. 32.

[5] It being understood that the division is quite optional. Hence Codd. frequently vary. Thus we have וְרוּחַ יְהוָה and וְרוּחַ יְהֹוָה (1 Sam. xvi. 14); וַהֲשִׁשָּׁן and וְהַשָּׁשָׁן (Zech. iii. 2); הָרָצִים and הָרָצִים (Esth. iii. 15). Even the same verse sometimes shews a different division, as Gen. xxxi. 25[b]; Josh. vi. 9.

3. Sometimes, notwithstanding the position of the subject at the head of the clause, the main tone or emphasis lies—or was considered by the accentuators to lie—further on in the clause. In such cases they did not hesitate to transfer the main dichotomy accordingly,—the subject being marked, where necessary, by a *minor* dichotomy,—e. g. יְהֹוָה^{d2}| הִפְגִּיעַ בּוֹ ^{d1}| אֵת אֲשֶׁר דִּבֶּר בְּיַד עֲבָדוֹ אֵלִיָּהוּ יְהֹוָה עָשָׂה (2 Ki. x. 10); הָאֱמִים^{d2}| כִּי הַחַיִּים^{d1}| יוֹדְעִים שֶׁיָּמֻתוּ (Qoh. ix. 5); אֶת עֲוֹן כֻּלָּנוּ (Is. liii. 6); לְפָנִים^{d1}| יָשְׁבוּ בָהּ (Deut. ii. 10); וְצַדִּיק בֶּאֱמוּנָתוֹ | יִחְיֶה⁶ (Hab. ii. 4). Comp. Gen. xix. 24; Num. xv. 13; Josh. ix. 3; 1 Sam. v. 1; Is. iii. 1; viii. 7; lxiv. 3^{b 7}.

4. Lastly, we cannot but expect to find the subject occupying an inferior position, when its verb governs a clause introduced by כִּי (אֲשֶׁר) or an Infinitive with לְ. Such clauses are often of considerable length, and it would manifestly have been awkward in the extreme to mark off always the subject at the commencement. The rule, therefore, is to make the main dichotomy immediately precede these clauses (just as we, in reading, make a slight pause before them), e. g. יְהֹוָה^{d2}| צִוָּה וְאָבִיו וְאִמּוֹ^{d2}| לֹא יָדְעוּ^{d1}| אֶת־מֹשֶׁה^{d1}| לָתֶת־לָנוּ נַחֲלָה בְּתוֹךְ אַחֵינוּ (Josh. xvii. 4); כִּי מֵיְהוָה הִיא (Judg. xiv. 4). (Corresponding instances with the *object*, II, or an *adverbial expression*, III, at the head of the clause, are, I believe, very rare. I mention, therefore, here the only ones I have noted: 1 Ki. xvii. 4^b; 2 Chr. xxviii. 10, 13.)

II. The OBJECT may precede, and as its position at the head of the clause implies a distinct emphasis, it is marked off by the main dichotomy: אַךְ־בָּשָׂר | בְּנַפְשׁוֹ דָמוֹ לֹא תֹאכֵלוּ (Gen. ix. 4);

---

[6] Much has been written on the accentuation of this passage. Unquestionably it may stand as in our texts, comp. Ezek. xiv. 14^b; Dan. ii. 25^a. But it is to be noted that the great majority of Codd. (I have not noticed a single exception) *point regularly* וְצַדִּיק | בֶּאֱמוּנָתוֹ יִחְיֶה.

[7] That variations occur in Codd. is no more than we should expect. Thus, we have עַמִּי and עַמִּי (Jer. viii. 7); וְעַרְמֹנִים and וְעַרְמֹנִים (Ezek. xxxi. 8); סַלְקָא and סַלְקָא (Dan. v. 12); וַיהוָה and וַיהוָה (2 Chr. xviii. 22), with a different tone or emphasis according to the taste of the punctators. In a few unimportant instances the division is quite arbitrary. Thus in Gen. x. 8, 13, 15, 24 *bis*, the subject is regularly marked off before יָלַד; then in verse 26 comes an instance to the contrary, וְיָקְטָן יָלַד | אֶת־אַלְמוֹדָד. Comp. 1 Chr. iv. 2, where there is a change in the *same* verse, (in verse 8 point וְקוֹץ with Codd.) We have here such a variation of tone as a reader in the present day might adopt, without assigning to it any particular meaning. (So when the object or an adv. expression precedes, Neh. iii. 6; Gen. x. 25.)

הֵמֵת לְיָרָבְעָם בָּעִיר | יֹאכְלוּ (xxi. 6); צָחַק | עָשָׂה לִי אֱלֹהִים
הַכְּלָבִים (1 Ki. xiv. 11).

The exceptions follow the same lines as with the subject, but are *far fewer* in number. The accentuators rightly felt that the emphatic position of the *object* was to be as little disturbed as possible.

1. Thus under the head of the *pronouns*, I have noted only זֶה (אֵלֶּה), זֶה יִתְּנוּ | כָּל־הָעֹבֵר עַל־הַפְּקֻדִים : and מָה, אֲשֶׁר, without the dichotomy
מָה אֲדֹנִי | (Ex. xxx. 13); אֵלֶּה עָשָׂה | בְּנָיָהוּ בֶן־יְהוֹיָדָע (2 Sam. xxiii. 22); | אֲשֶׁר־בָּרָא אֱלֹהִים (Gen. ii. 3); and with מְדַבֵּר אֶל־עַבְדּוֹ (Josh. v. 14); the minor dichotomy אֲשֶׁר | יְהוָה אֱלֹהֶיךָ | נֹתֵן לְךָ (Deut. xix. 10).

2. The *Zusatz*, however, is freely used, on the same principle as with the subject: וְאֶת־דָּמוֹ יִשְׁפֹּךְ | אֶל־יְסוֹד מִזְבַּח הָעֹלָה (Lev. iv. 25); וְאֶת־נַפְלֻתּוֹ תָקְעוּ | בֵּית דָּנוֹן (Ezek. xxxiii. 7); צֹפֶה נְתַתִּיךָ | לְבֵית יִשְׂרָאֵל (1 Chr. x. 10); or with the minor dichotomy on the object: כִּי־אֹתוֹ | אָהֵב דָּבָר | שָׁלַח אֲדֹנִי | בְּיַעֲקֹב (Is. ix. 7). אֲבִיהֶם | מִכָּל־אֶחָיו (Gen. xxxvii. 4);

3. In only a few other cases has the emphasis, due on the object, been *moved further on* in the clause, e.g. אִשָּׁה אֶל־אֲחֹתָהּ | לֹא תִקָּח (Lev. xviii. 18); חָטְאוּ יִשָּׂא | הָאִישׁ הַהוּא (Num. ix. 13); שְׁעָרֵךְ כִּי־עֲנָבִים בְּפִיהֶם | הֵמָּה עֹשִׂים (Jer. xviii. 13); עָשְׂתָה מְאֹד | בְּתוּלַת יִשְׂרָאֵל (Ezek. xxxiii. 31); יַיִן לֹא־יִשְׁתּוּ | כָּל־בֹּהֵן (xliv. 21). In Jer. ix. 7[b]; x. 13[b] (li. 16) texts vary.

III. ADVERBS, and PREPOSITIONS with their government, at the beginning of the clause, are also generally marked off by the main dichotomy, e.g. וּלְאָדָם | לֹא־מָצָא עֵזֶר כְּנֶגְדּוֹ (Gen. ii. 20); מֵהָעוֹף לְמִינֵהוּ (Jer. vi. 26); פִּתְאֹם | יָבֹא הַשֹּׁדֵד עָלֵינוּ וּמִן־הַבְּהֵמָה לְמִינָהּ מִכֹּל רֶמֶשׂ הָאֲדָמָה לְמִינֵהוּ | שְׁנַיִם מִכֹּל יָבֹאוּ אֵלֶיךָ לְהַחֲיוֹת (Gen. vi. 20).

The exceptions run for the most part parallel to those with the subject and object.

1. Prepositions with *pronominal suffix*, or with the independent *pronouns*, often occupy an inferior position: מֵהֶם תִּקְנוּ | עֶבֶד וְאָמָה אַחֲרָיו הֶחָזִיק [a] | מֵאֲשֶׁר יִשְׁאֲבוּן | הַנְּעָרִים (Ruth ii. 9); (Lev. xxv. 44); אַחֲרֵי מִי יָצָא | מֶלֶךְ יִשְׂרָאֵל (1 Sam. xxiv. 15); נְחֶמְיָה בָּן־עַזְבּוּק (Neh. iii. 16).

---

[a] So עַל־יָרוֹ, עַל־יָדָם, verses 2, 4, &c., 'beside him (them).'

עַמּוֹ ²ᵈהָרֽאוּבֵנִי וְהַגָּדִי | ¹ᵈלָקְחוּ נַחֲלָתָם (Judg. vi. 15); בַּמָּה אוֹשִׁיעַ | אֶת־יִשְׂרָאֵל (Josh. xiii. 8).

2. Instances with the *Zusatz* are common enough: בְּעֶצֶב תֹּאכֲלֶנָּה | וּלְאָבְרָם הֵיטִיב | בַּעֲבוּרָהּ (xii. 16). And with כֹּל יְמֵי חַיֶּיךָ (Gen. iii. 17); ²ᵈלַמּוֹעֵד | ¹ᵈאָשׁוּב אֵלֶיךָ | כָּעֵת חַיָּה (xviii. 14). The double Zusatz is found in Lev. xxiv. 4, לִפְנֵי יְהוָֹה תָּמִיד, and Deut. xxix. 14, עִמָּנוּ הַיּוֹם.

3. As with the subject and object, the main dichotomy is at times *moved forward* in the clause to where the chief stress or emphasis seems to rest, e.g. בְּרֵאשִׁית | ²ᵈבָּרָא אֱלֹהִים | ¹ᵈאֵת הַשָּׁמַיִם וְאֵת הָאָרֶץ (Gen. i. 1); וּפְתָאֹם יָבוֹא אֶל־ | בַּשֵּׁבֶט | ²ᵈיַכּוּ עַל־הַלֶּחִי | ¹ᵈאֵת שֹׁפֵט יִשְׂרָאֵל (Mic. iv. 14); הֵיכָלוֹ | הָאָדוֹן | אֲשֶׁר־אַתֶּם מְבַקְשִׁים (Mal. iii. 1).

4. Sometimes *two* adverbial expressions are found together at the head of the clause,—answering to the double Zusatz at the close,— e.g. עַל־שֻׁלְחַן הַמֶּלֶךְ תָּמִיד (2 Sam. ix. 13); לְפָנִים בְּיִשְׂרָאֵל (1 Sam. ix. 9); בַּיּוֹם הַשְּׁבִיעִי כְּטוֹב לֵב־הַמֶּלֶךְ בַּיָּיִן (Esth. i. 10). Comp. Cant. iii. 1; Dan. ii. 19; iii. 8; 1 Chr. xii. 37.

5. Lastly, the rule for the dichotomy is often relaxed in the case of the common and less important adverbs, as עַל־כֵּן, לָכֵן, אוּלַי, אוֹ, אַף, אֵיךְ, אַחֲרֵי־כֵן, מַדּוּעַ, עוֹד, עַתָּה, שָׁם, &c. Such cases are very common, see אוּלַי in Gen. xviii. 24; אַחֲרֵי־כֵן, xxiii. 19, &c.[9] To them may be added the frequently recurring adverbial expressions, בָּעֵת הַהִיא, בַּיּוֹם הַהוּא (Is. ii. 20; xxxix. 1, &c.), and בְּיָמָיו (2 Ki. xxiv. 1).

IV. The VOCATIVE, at the beginning of the clause, is generally marked off by the dichotomy: אֲדֹנָי יְהוִֹה | בַּמָּה אֵדַע כִּי אִירָשֶׁנָּה (Gen. xv. 8). But when a *long* clause follows, it is almost necessarily subordinated to a part of the same, as in Gen. xviii. 3; Deut. iii. 24; Ezek. xliv. 5; 1 Chr. xxix. 16; &c.

[If it be asked, how, when we have marked off the subject, object, &c., we are to proceed with the division of the rest of the clause, the answer is very simple. We start *de novo* with the members remaining, always supposing there are at least three words left to be divided. If the subject is succeeded by the

---

[9] In these minor matters Codd. often vary. Sometimes the Massora fixes the accentuation, as Gersháyim in לָכֵן (Jer. vii. 32); and T'bhir in וְעַתָּה (Mic. iv. 11).

object, or the object by the subject, &c., we have simply to proceed as before, and mark off this second member by a *minor* dichotomy, e. g. הֵמָּה ׀ בָּנַיִךְ וּבְנוֹתַיִךְ ׀ יִקָּחוּ (Ezek. xxiii. 25); כָּלָה וְנֶחֱרָצָה ׀ (2 Ki. v. 13); דָּבָר גָּדוֹל ׀ הַנָּבִיא ׀ דִּבֶּר אֵלֶיךָ אֲדֹנָי יְהֹוִה צְבָאוֹת ׀ עֹשֶׂה ׀ בְּקֶרֶב כָּל־הָאָרֶץ (Is. x. 23, where the three last words are treated as a verbal clause); עַל מְאוּרַת צִפְעוֹנִי ׀ גָּמוּל ׀ יָדוֹ הָדָה (xi. 8); and so on. But in most cases *the verb* succeeds, and we then divide according to Rule V, immediately following.]

V. With the VERB[10], the division is quite different. Here the weight of the clause lies at the *end;* and the *last member* is first separated by the dichotomy, then the second from the end, and so on till we reach the verb: הוֹצִיא יְהוָֹה ׀ אֶת־בְּנֵי יִשְׂרָאֵל ׀ מֵאֶרֶץ מִצְרַיִם ׀ עַל־צִבְאֹתָם (Ex. xii. 51); וַיִּקֶן ׀ אֶת־ חֶלְקַת הַשָּׂדֶה ׀ אֲשֶׁר נָטָה־שָׁם אָהֳלוֹ ׀ מִיַּד בְּנֵי־חֲמוֹר אֲבִי שְׁכֶם ׀ בְּמֵאָה קְשִׂיטָה (Gen. xxxiii. 19)[11].

The student may find for himself examples in every page.

Variations from this simple rule are the following:

1. The several parts of a compound member are constantly treated by the accentuation as *separate* members, e. g. וְנָתַתִּי לְךָ ׀ וּלְזַרְעֲךָ אַחֲרֶיךָ ׀ אֵת אֶרֶץ מְגֻרֶיךָ ׀ אֵת כָּל־אֶרֶץ כְּנַעַן ׀ לַאֲחֻזַּת עוֹלָם (Gen. xvii. 8); כֹּה־אָמַר יְהוָה ׀ אֱלֹהֵי צְבָאוֹת ׀ אֲדֹנָי (Amos v. 16).

Or else they are grouped in various ways: וַיִּתֶּן־לוֹ ׀ צֹאן וּבָקָר ׀ וְכֶסֶף וַיִּקְרָא שְׁמוֹ ׀ פֶּלֶא ׀ זָהָב ׀ וַעֲבָדִים וּשְׁפָחוֹת וּגְמַלִּים וַחֲמֹרִים (Gen. xxiv. 35); יוֹעֵץ ׀ אֵל גִּבּוֹר ׀ אֲבִי־עַד שַׂר־שָׁלוֹם (Is. ix. 5).

---

[10] Participles, infinitives, and verbal adjectives come, so far as they have verbal government, under the category of the verb.

With הֵן (הִנֵּה, אֵין, עוֹד, יֵשׁ), the verbal idea is often *implied* (see Gesenius' Gr., § 100. 5), Gen. xxii. 13; xxiv. 23; xxviii. 17; xxxi. 14.

[11] The vocative is generally made a *separate* member, e. g. in Judg. v. 31; Mic. vi. 8; but sometimes not, when the suffix of the 2nd pers. precedes, as in Is. viii. 8; x. 22; or even *follows*, Is. xiv. 31; Mic. ii. 12.

2. On the other hand, adverbial expressions or prepositions with their government—homogeneous members, be it observed—are sometimes *kept together* by the accentuation [12], e. g. וַתִּתֵּן אֹתָהּ | לְאַבְרָם אִישָׁהּ
וַיִּקְרָא | מַלְאַךְ יְהוָֹה | אֶל־אַבְרָהָם | שֵׁנִית מִן־הַשָּׁמָיִם לוֹ לְאִשָּׁה (Gen. xvi. 3);
(xxii. 15); וַיַּעַל אֵלִיָּהוּ | בַּסְעָרָה הַשָּׁמָיִם (2 Ki. ii. 11; comp. ver. 1). Other examples are Ex. ii. 5; xxv. 30; Lev. xiv. 27 (not 16); Num. xiv. 37; Josh. xxi. 8; Is. xl. 2 end; Jer. xxxvi. 10; Qoh. ii. 15; 1 Chr. xxiii. 31.

3. Some *anomalous* cases occur, which may almost all be explained by the desire to *emphasize* the part of the clause, to which the dichotomy has, contrary to rule, been transferred. It is enough to trace the principle which guided the accentuators. We are not bound always to agree with them.

(a) Thus, when the verb which introduces the clause, receives its nearer definition through another verb, governing an accusative, adverbial expression, &c., and this accusative or adverbial expression is placed *before* the verb on which it depends, they considered that a certain emphasis was intended, and pointed accordingly: אֲשֶׁר לֹא־נִפְתָּה
הַמַּעֲמִיקִים מֵיְהוָה | לַסְתִּר עֵצָה | כַּפִּי־רַגְלְךָ | הַגֵּד עַל־הָאָרֶץ (Deut. xxviii. 56);
וְלֹא־אָבוּ (Is. xxix. 15); [13] הֲלוֹא־שְׁמַעְתָּ לְמֵרָחוֹק | אוֹתָהּ עָשִׂיתִי (xxxvii. 26);
לָא־חָשְׁחִין אֲנַחְנָא עַל־דְּנָה | פִּתְגָם לַהֲתָבוּתָךְ (xlii. 24); בְּדָרְכַיִן | הַלּוּךְ (Dan. iii. 16); לָא־כָהֲלִין פְּשַׁר־מִלְּתָא | לְהַחֲוָיָה (v. 15; comp. vv. 8, 16 [14], and iv. 15). And so in 2 Sam. xv. 20; xxi. 4; Qoh. viii. 3; Esth. ii. 9; Dan. vi. 5; Ezra iv. 22; 2 Chr. xxxi. 7, 10.

(β) In the following passages the accentuators have placed the dichotomy even at the *status constructus* [15], as a measure of emphasis seemed to be due there: [16] וְהוּא שֹׁכֵן בְּאֵלֹנֵי | מַמְרֵא הָאֱמֹרִי (Gen. xiv. 13);

---

[12] Particularly at the *end* of the clause, like the double Zusatz at the end of the nominal clause. It is but rarely (as far as I have observed) that the expressions referred to come together in the *middle* of the clause, as in 1 Ki. xi. 36; 2 Ki. xvii. 13; Is. xxix. 4.

[13] Here Luzzatto and Delitzsch have both misapprehended the accentuation, which, it must be allowed, is ambiguous.

[14] The change Baer makes (see his note) is therefore quite unnecessary.

[15] Such a free division is not without parallel in our own chanting, as in the Te Deum: 'Heaven and earth are full of the majesty | of Thy glory,' of which we might make a verbal clause in Heb., with the dichotomy at the st. const.:

מָלְאוּ הַשָּׁמַיִם וְהָאָרֶץ הוֹד | כְּבוֹדֶךָ

[16] That Abraham should be dwelling at *such* a place was a circumstance worthy of observation! The Midrash has something to say on the point.

(Ex. וְעָשׂוּ אֲרוֹן | עֲצֵי שִׁטִּים (xl. 3); וַיִּתֵּן אֹתָם בְּמִשְׁמַר | בֵּית שַׂר הַטַּבָּחִים[17] xxv. 10; similar vv. 13, 31; xxxvi. 31; xxxvii. 4; xxxix. 25). The further instances I have noticed are Ex. xxxii. 22; Num. vi. 5[b]; Deut. xiv. 6; xxxiii. 24[b]; Judg. iv. 5; Is. xxviii. 4; Jer. xix. 1; Esth. vi. 1[18].

(γ) A few other isolated cases shew divergence. Thus we have וַיִּשְׁמַע יְהוָה אֱלֹהִים | גַּן בְּעֶדֶן (Gen. ii. 8), to avoid the awkward junction of אֱלֹהִים | גַּן בְּעֶדֶן. In Gen. xxx. 7, 10, 12 the maids of *Leah* and *Rachel* are carefully distinguished. In Num. xxvii. 16 אִישׁ is kept apart from the Divine titles. In 1 Sam. xxv. 8[b]; 1 Ki. i. 45; Jer. xxxiv. 6; xxxviii. 11; Ezek. xxvi. 7; Nah. ii. 1[b]; Cant. vii. 7; Lam. iii. 50; and 2 Chr. xxvi. 15, it is not difficult to see that a certain emphasis was designed, and is, in most cases, appropriate enough. They are none of them passages of any importance.

The above are the only exceptions I have observed. Others may, perhaps, be found. Against them are to be set the thousands of instances, in which the *rule for the division of the verbal clause is carried out*.

VI. In nominal sentences, when *the predicate precedes*, the division is the same as with the verb, e.g. טוֹב | תִּתִּי אֹתָהּ רִאשׁוֹן הוּא | לָךְ | מִתִּתִּי אֹתָהּ לְאִישׁ אַחֵר (Gen. xxix. 19); כִּי־קָרוֹב אֵלֶיךָ | הַדָּבָר | לָכֶם | לְחָדְשֵׁי הַשָּׁנָה (Ex. xii. 2); מְאֹד (Deut. xxx. 14).

Only when הָיָה follows, the dichotomy comes not on it, but on the predicate (which is indeed in the accusative): עֶבֶד כִּי אֹהֵב | הָיָה חִירָם לְדָוִד (Gen. ix. 25); עֲבָדִים | יִהְיֶה לְאֶחָיו (1 Ki. v. 15).

---

[17] The place is to be noted. All Joseph's future history depends on their having been sent *there!* Once introduced, this division is repeated in verse 7 and xli. 10. We might be tempted to point בְּמִשְׁמָר with Qāmeṣ, as in xlii. 17, and then all would be regular; but this would be contrary to the Massora, which requires Pathach, בְּמִשְׁמַר ג׳ פתחין.

[18] One might be inclined to explain some of these cases by a reference to rhythm, or equilibrium in the section of the clause, but such explanations will not apply, for the simple reason that in other similar instances, and those the great majority, these influences do not make themselves felt, but the division is according to the *rule* for the verbal clause. See Gen. iii. 24[b]; Judg. viii. 5[b]; 1 Ki. xi. 27[b]; Jer. xxxviii. 6; 1 Chr. xvi. 10[b]; &c.

An occasional exception is indeed found, as in לֹא־טוֹב ׀ הֱיוֹת הָאָדָם ׀ לְבַדּוֹ (Gen. ii. 18); בְּד־שֶׁבַע שָׁנִים ׀ יְהוֹאָשׁ בְּמָלְכוֹ (2 Ki. xii. 1; and similar passages); יוֹבֵל הִיא ׀ תִּהְיֶה לָכֶם (Lev. xxv. 10); עַבְדְּךָ אָנִי ׀ רַמָּלֶךְ ׀ אֶהְיֶה (2 Sam. xv. 34); and נָכוֹן יִהְיֶה ׀ הַר בֵּית־יְהוָה (Is. ii. 2); the explanations of which will readily suggest themselves. In Jer. iv. 27ª, texts vary.

VII. Lastly, the CONJUNCTIONS, as גַּם, אַף, אִם, אוֹ, אֲשֶׁר, אַיִן, בַּל, לֹא, the NEGATIVES, as פֶּן, עַד, לְמַעַן, לוּ, כִּי, יַעַן, עַל כִּי, כִּי אִם, בִּלְתִּי, בְּלִי, and forms compounded from them, as עַד־בִּלְתִּי, אִם לֹא, כִּי לֹא, &c., need not detain us. They are, from their character, generally *joined*, either by a conjunctive accent or Maqqeph, to the word following. It is unnecessary to give examples, as they may be found in every page.

But, sometimes on musical grounds, sometimes with a view to emphasis, even these unimportant words, which have so little claim to an independent position, are found marked with a pausal accent, thus: אִם (Gen. iv. 7); אֲשֶׁר (xi. 7); גַּם (xxxii. 21); כִּי (ii. 17; and often); יַעַן (Is. vii. 5; and often); לֹא (Gen. ii. 25); אַל־נָא (xviii. 30); אִם־לֹא (Ezek. xxxiv. 8; Baer rightly); לֹא כִּי (1 Ki. xi. 22; and often); but לֹא כִּי (iii. 22, 23; Is. xxx. 16); &c. These two last examples shew that the punctators are not always consistent, even where we should expect them to be so. And so in Codd. there is, in these trifling points, frequent variation, thus in לוֹא־קָרַעְתָּ שָׁמַיִם (Is. lxiii. 19) some have לוּא, others לוֹא; in Mic. vi. 5 we find לְמַעַן and לְמַעַן, &c. Sometimes the Massora comes in and *fixes* the accentuation, as כִּי כ"נ בט' ; וְאִם ב' בט' ; יַעַן ג' בטעם; &c.

The INTERJECTIONS are used in the same way, e. g. הִנֵּה, הֵן (Gen. iii. 22; xxvii. 42ᵇ)[19]; הוֹי (Is. xvii. 12; xviii. 1); הָבָה (Ex. i. 10).

Thus far we have had to do with the division of the *clause* into its several members, but there is a further point that requires consideration, and that is, the division, in certain cases, of the *members themselves*. Every member of a clause—subject, object, &c.—will be either

---

[19] רָאֹה and רְאוּ, as in Gen. xxvii. 27; Ex. xxxv. 30; Deut. i. 8; ii. 31, may take the place of הִנֵּה.

SYNTACTICAL DICHOTOMY. 53

simple, consisting of one word, or *compound*, consisting of two or more words. And such compound members introduce a new element into the dichotomy of the verse, about which it is necessary to say a few words.

1. Two Nouns in *apposition* are generally kept together by the accentuation, as אֶת־חַוָּה אִשְׁתּוֹ, הַמֶּלֶךְ דָּוִד, יְהוָֹה אֱלֹהִים (Gen. iv. 1), &c.

But where emphasis or distinctness of enunciation seems to require it, the dichotomy—and even the main dichotomy of the clause—may come between, e. g. שָׁלוֹם ׀ הִנְנִי נֹתֵן לוֹ אֶת־בְּרִיתִי (Num. xxv. 12); נָתַן יְהוָֹה אֶת־אֹיְבֵיכֶם ׀ אֶת־מוֹאָב ׀ בְּיֶדְכֶם (Zech. iii. 8); צֶמַח ׀ מֵבִיא אֶת־עַבְדִּי (Judg. iii. 28). And so the emphatic pronoun may be separated from the noun, הוּא ׀ וְעָבַד הַלֵּוִי (Num. xviii. 23).

The cases, in which more than two nouns come in apposition, or instead of the noun we have a nominal expression consisting of several words, present no difficulty. The subdivision of such expressions will be according to the general rules for the dichotomy, see Gen. xxiii. 16; Num. xvi. 2; 1 Ki. xi. 36ᵇ; Amos v. 16.

2. So two Nouns, *in the same construction and joined by* ו, are constantly kept together by the accentuation, as בַּיּוֹם וּבַלַּיְלָה (Gen. i. 18); עָפָר וָאֵפֶר (xviii. 27); גָּדוֹל וְכָבֵד (l. 10), &c.

But for the reasons above given, they may be separated by the dichotomy, e. g. וָבֹהוּ ׀ הָיְתָה תֹהוּ (i. 2); וּדְבָשׁ ׀ אֶרֶץ זָבַת חָלָב (Ex. iii. 8); וַיִּזְעַק (Is. i. 13); לֹא־אוּכַל אָוֶן ׀ וַעֲצָרָה (Judg. vii. 20); וְלִגְדְעוֹן ׀ חֶרֶב לַיהוָֹה (Esth. iv. 1); וָטֹפַח ׀ שֵׁשׁ־אַמּוֹת בָּאַמָּה (Ezek. xl. 5); וּמָרָה ׀ זְעָקָה גְדוֹלָה.

Examples, where several nouns come together, or where the nominal expression consists of several words (see remark above), are Deut. xxix. 7; Is. xxvii. 1; xxx. 30; xxxvii. 12²⁰.

3. The substantive may be *qualified* in various ways, either by another substantive in apposition, or by an adjective, relative or adverbial expression following. In these several cases (as we have seen with the apposition²¹), the substantive may be *separated* from the qualifying expression by the main (or a minor) dichotomy. Somewhat more of weight generally attaches to the latter in consequence. Thus

(*a*) Substantive and adjective: מְאֹד ׀ וַיָּהֲפֹךְ יְהוָֹה רוּחַ־יָם ׀ חָזָק (Ex. x. 19); דָּוָה ׀ וְאֶרְאֶה אֶת־אֲדֹנָי יֹשֵׁב (Lev. xx. 18); אִשָּׁה ׀ אֲשֶׁר־יִשְׁכַּב אֶת־אִשָּׁה; וְאֵיךְ תָּשִׁיב אֶת־פְּנֵי פַחַת אַחַד עַבְדֵי אֲדֹנִי ׀ עַל־כִּסֵּא ׀ רָם וְנִשָּׂא (Is. vi. 1); הַקְּטַנִּים (xxxvi. 9). And so the demonstrative זֶה (אֵלֶּה) often stands

---

²⁰ Sometimes the nouns appear ἀσυνδέτως, as עֵץ (Gen. i. 11, not 12).

²¹ In reality, the adjective and relative are to be regarded as *in apposition*, see Ewald, §§ 293 a, 364 c; Stade, § 176; and even the adv. expression, when we can supply אשר before it (see note 23), is equally *in apposition*.

outside the rest of the clause: לְיִרְאָה אֶת־הַשֵּׁם הַנִּכְבָּד וְהַנּוֹרָא | הַזֶּה (Deut. xxviii. 58); יְהוָה אֱלֹהֶיךָ נֹתֵן לְךָ אֶת־הָאָרֶץ הַטּוֹבָה | הַזֹּאת (ix. 6); סוּרוּ נָא מֵעַל אָהֳלֵי הָאֲנָשִׁים הָרְשָׁעִים | הָאֵלֶּה (Num. xvi. 26).

(β) *Substantive and relative*. Here it is not so much the *separation* of the relative clause from the substantive, to which attention has to be drawn (for in our own interpunction such separation is common enough), as the character of the dichotomy,—the *main*, where we look for a minor,—e.g. לְמַעַן תִּחְיוּן וּרְבִיתֶם | וּבָאתֶם וִירִשְׁתֶּם אֶת־הָאָרֶץ | אֲשֶׁר־נִשְׁבַּע מִפְּנֵי רָעָתָם אֲשֶׁר עָשׂוּ לְהַכְעִסֵנִי | לָלֶכֶת | יְהוָה לַאֲבֹתֵיכֶם (Deut. viii. 1); לְקַטֵּר לַעֲבֹד לֵאלֹהִים אֲחֵרִים | אֲשֶׁר לֹא יְדָעוּם הֵמָּה אַתֶּם וַאֲבֹתֵיכֶם (Jer. xliv. 3). For the relative, we may have the participle: הַמִּתְהַפֶּכֶת | אֶת לַהַט הַחֶרֶב (Gen. iii. 24); בְּאֵר לַחַי | רֹאִי (xxiv. 62); וַעֲשִׂיתָם צַלְמֵי עַפְלֵיכֶם וְצַלְמֵי עַכְבְּרֵיכֶם | הַמַּשְׁחִיתִם אֶת־הָאָרֶץ (1 Sam. vi. 5).

Often the relative conjunction is *understood*: וַיִּבְעַר בְּיַעֲקֹב כְּאֵשׁ לֶהָבָה | אָכְלָה סָבִיב (Lam. ii. 3); גַּם־אַתְּ אַף־בְּדָם בְּרִיתֵךְ שִׁלַּחְתִּי אֲסִירַיִךְ מִבּוֹר אֵין מַיִם בּוֹ (Zech. ix. 11).

Obs. Sometimes, for emphasis' sake, the dichotomy appears in the *middle* of the relative clause, e.g. הַדָּבָר אֲשֶׁר חָזָה | יְשַׁעְיָהוּ בֶּן־אָמוֹץ (Is. ii. 1. The weight of the clause does not rest on הדבר, but on the *contents* of the same, *a vision of Isaiah*[22]); לֹא | אֹרַח (אשר) בְּרַגְלָיו יָבוֹא (xli. 3, בְּרַגְלָיו emphatic); הַמָּקוֹם אֲשֶׁר יָדַע | כִּי אַנְשֵׁי־חַיִל שָׁם (2 Sam. xi. 16, 'the place where he *knew*' &c.). Comp. Deut. i. 31, 39; xi. 2, 7; xxviii. 69; xxxiii. 1; Judg. xviii. 10[b]; xx. 15[b].

(γ) *Adverbs*, and *prepositions* with their government, are constantly employed to qualify a noun (subst. or adj.), and are joined to it by the accents; but frequently they appear with the dichotomy preceding, e.g. לָרָשׁ | וַיִּשְׂמֵם כֶּעָפָר (2 Ki. xiii. 7); מֵרָחוֹק | וְנָשָׂא־נֵס לַגּוֹיִם (Is. v. 26; comp. Joel iv. 12); כִּי־עָשׂוּ בְנֵי־יְהוּדָה | מִיַּעַר (Jer. v. 6); עַל־כֵּן הֵפַם אָרֶיחַ | בְּעֵינַי | הָרַע (vii. 30); וַיהוָה נָתַן בְּיָדָם חַיִל | לָרֹב מְאֹד (2 Chr. xxiv. 24). Comp. לְמַלְכֵי יִשְׂרָאֵל (1 Ki. xiv. 19) and לֶאֱלִישָׁע (2 Ki. v. 9)[23]. An extreme case is בְּעֵדָה | וַיֵּשְׁבוּ אֵלָיו אַהֲרֹן וְכָל־הַנְּשִׂיאִים (Ex. xxxiv. 31).

---

[22] The first verses of Hos., Joel, Mic., Hab., and Zeph. are similarly divided. (Comp. Jer. li. 59.) On the other hand, in מַשָּׂא בָּבֶל | אֲשֶׁר חָזָה יְשַׁעְיָהוּ בֶּן־אָמוֹץ (Is. xiii. 1), the weight of the clause comes on the *first* words.

[23] We may often in such expressions supply אשר. Comp. Lev. iv. 7 and 18 (לִפְנֵי); Num. xxvi. 63[b] and xxxi. 12[b] (עַל); 1 Sam. xxvi. 1[b] and 3 (do.); Is. xxxvi. 2[b] and 2 Ki. xviii. 17[b] (בְּ); where it fails in the first, but is given in the second of the verses quoted.

SYNTACTICAL DICHOTOMY.

4. The connection between a noun in *status constructus* and the genitive following is closer than that in any of the cases already considered, yet even here, under certain circumstances, the dichotomy intervenes,—as when the word in st. constr. is followed by *two or more* others, which together express the genitive relation, e. g. | עֵץ אָבִי | יֹשֵׁב אֹהֶל וּמִקְנֶה (Gen. ii. 9); | דְּמֵי אָחִיד | קוֹל (iv. 10); הַדַּעַת טוֹב וָרָע (iv. 20); | אֲשֶׁר יִשְׁכֹּן הֶעָנָן עַל־הַמִּשְׁכָּן | כָּל־יְמֵי (Num. ix. 18); | חָבַשׁ | בְּיוֹם יְהוָה אֶת־שֶׁבֶר עַמּוֹ (Is. xxx. 26)[24].

When several nouns follow one another in st. constr., they are marked off (as far as is necessary) in succession: אֶת־יְמֵי | שְׁנֵי ᵈ²חַיֵּי ᵈ¹אֲבֹתַי (Gen. xlvii. 9); אֶת־רוּחַ ᵈ² | כָּל ᵈ¹ | שְׁאֵרִית הָעָם (Hag. i. 14); | שְׁאוֹן ᵈ² | קוֹל ᵈ¹ מַמְלְכוֹת גּוֹיִם (Is. xiii. 4).

The following variations occur: (*a*) In the case last-named, the dichotomy sometimes comes after the *second* noun, particularly when the two first nouns form together a *compound* idea, e. g. | עֲטֶרֶת גֵּאוּת שִׁכֹּרֵי אֶפְרַיִם (Is. xxviii. 1); | בְּכִי תַחֲנוּנַי | בְּנֵי יִשְׂרָאֵל (Jer. iii. 21); אֹהֶל | מוֹעֵד | הָאֱלֹהִים (2 Chr. i. 3)[25]. In Is. xxi. 17 *five* nouns are brought together in st. constr., and the dichotomy comes, suitably enough, after the *third*: שְׁאָר מִסְפַּר־קֶשֶׁת | גִּבּוֹרֵי בְנֵי־קֵדָר.

(β) The small and frequently recurring words אֵת and כֹּל, regarded as in st. constr., are often marked off by the dichotomy (Gen. i. 25; ii. 20). So also the prepositions, as אַחֲרֵי, אַחַר (v. 4; xv. 1); בֵּין (xiii. 7); עַד (xii. 6); עַל (viii. 4); עִם (xxxi. 32); לִפְנֵי (xli. 46); בַּעֲבוּר (xxvi. 24); &c. But these words are all more commonly joined by Maqqeph or a conjunctive accent to the word following, or are marked by a minor dichotomy, (see text passim) according to the taste of the punctators. (Codd. in consequence vary greatly. Where some place R'bhia or Zaqeph, others have Maqqeph, &c.)

Other small words of frequent occurrence, treated in the same way, are בֶּן and בַּת (Gen. vii. 6; xvii. 17); אָב (xvii. 5[b]); בֵּית (1 Ki. x. 21); דְּבַר (Deut. xxii. 24); יוֹם (Gen. ii. 4; Is. lviii. 5); יְמֵי (Deut. xxxiv. 8[b]; Judg. xviii. 31); עֵת (Mic. v. 2); and יַד (Jer. xxii. 25).

5. Correlative expressions, formed by בֵּין—וּבֵין, בְּ—וּבְ, כְּ—כְּ, &c., are sometimes kept together and sometimes separated by the accents.

---

[21] The relative דִּי, which often expresses the genitive relation in Chaldee, leads to another division. See Dan. vi. 17, 25; Ezra iv. 15; v. 13, 16; vii. 21[b]. In reality this particle is in *apposition* (comp. Philippi, Status constructus, p. 114), and the division is to be explained accordingly.

[25] Gen. l. 17; Ex. xxviii. 11; Num. iii. 36; 2 Sam. xxiii. 20[b]; Is. x. 12[b]; xxviii. 1[b], 16[b]; 1 Chr. xxiii. 28[b], may be compared. Sometimes *emphasis* may have influenced the division, as in Is. xxxvi. 9.

Equilibrium of the parts of the clause will generally decide. Thus we have וַיַּבְדֵּל בֵּין (Gen. i. 4), but וַיַּבְדֵּל אֱלֹהִים | בֵּין הָאוֹר וּבֵין הַחֹשֶׁךְ הַמַּיִם אֲשֶׁר מִתַּחַת לָרָקִיעַ | וּבֵין הַמַּיִם אֲשֶׁר מֵעַל לָרָקִיעַ (ver. 7). Verses 6, 14, 18 are like the former, but xiii. 7; xx. 1, like the latter. (In Num. xvii. 13 texts vary.) And so בְּדָוִד וּבַפִּיר are joined in 1 Sam. xix. 10, but separated in xviii. 11. In Gen. xviii. 25 we have וְהָיָה כַצַּדִּיק | כָּרָשָׁע, but necessarily כַּקָּטֹן כַּגָּדֹל | תִּשְׁמָעוּן (Deut. i. 17).

It is the same with the contrasted prepositions מִן—אֶל, מִן—עַד, מִן—לְ, which are, according to the taste of the punctators, kept together, as in Gen. xiii. 3; xv. 18; Ex. xxviii. 28; or separated, as in Gen. xxv. 18; Num. xxxiii. 49; Jos. xiii. 5.

6. The VERB.—(α) Two verbs, in the same construction, are joined by the accents: וַיִּקֹּד וַיִּשְׁתָּחוּ | לְאַפָּיו (Num. xxii. 31); אֶת־מִי | דָּאַגְתְּ וַתִּירְאִי (Is. lvii. 11).

Yet, not unfrequently, particularly if emphasis is to be marked, the dichotomy comes between: הֲלֹא יִמְצְאוּ | יְחַלְּקוּ שָׁלָל (Judg. v. 30); אֶת־קִבְעַת כּוֹס הַתַּרְעֵלָה שָׁתִית | מָצִית (Is. xxxvii. 23); אֶת־מִי חֵרַפְתָּ | וְגִדַּפְתָּ (li. 17). Comp. Is. lxii. 7; Jer. vi. 27[b]; vii. 29[b]; Jon. iii. 9; and with three verbs, Is. xxxvii. 37; Esth. iii. 13.

(β) The *inf. abs.* is generally joined to the *verb. fin.*, as in הַרְבָּה אַרְבֶּה | עִצְּבוֹנֵךְ (Gen. iii. 16); הָשֵׁב תְּשִׁיבֶנּוּ | לוֹ (Ex. xxiii. 4).

(γ) When two verbs are connected to form one idea[26], this connection is constantly marked by the accents: וַיֹּאסֶף לָלֶדֶת | אֶת־אָחִיו (Gen. iv. 2); שׁוּב קַח־לְךָ | מְגִלָּה אַחֶרֶת (Jer. xxxvi. 28); אַל־תִּרְבּוּ (Is. xxx. 9); &c. לֹא־אָבוּ שְׁמוֹעַ | תּוֹרַת יְהוָה (1 Sam. ii. 3); תְּדַבְּרוּ | גְבֹהָה Or the first verb receives the *minor* dichotomy: אַתָּה הַחִלּוֹתָ֖ לְהַרְאוֹת אֶת־עַבְדְּךָ֧ | אֶת־גָּדְלְךָ (Deut. iii. 24).

We may also note the cases where the first verb is merely *introductory* to the other, which is the main verb of the clause, e.g. בֹּא וּרְאֵה | אֶת־הַתּוֹעֵבוֹת (Gen. xxxvii. 14); לֶךְ־נָא רְאֵה | אֶת־שְׁלוֹם אַחֶיךָ (Ex. ix. 19); שְׁלַח הָעֵז | אֶת־מִקְנְךָ (Ezek. viii. 9); וְצָא הָעָם הָרָעוֹת (xvi. 4). And so יָרַד (Gen. xviii. 21); וְלָקְטוּ | דְּבַר־יוֹם בְּיוֹמוֹ עָמַד (Num. ix. 8); קָרַב (Deut. v. 24); סָבַב (Cant. ii. 17); קָם (Jer. i. 17); שָׁמַע (Deut. xxxiv. 9; Jer. xxxv. 10); and many other verbs[27].

---

[26] In the sense laid down in Ges. Gr., § 142.

[27] Of the verbs used in this way בָּא and הָלַךְ are particularly common. These verbs sometimes *follow* the main verb in a complemental sense, and are still joined to it by the accents: אֶתְרַעֲבוֹן בְּתֵיכֶם | קְחוּ וָלֵכוּ (Gen. xlii. 33). Comp. Ex. xvii. 5; Deut. xii. 26; 1 Sam. xxx. 22.

SYNTACTICAL DICHOTOMY.

In conclusion, I have once more to draw attention to the peculiar use of the ZUSATZ. We have already had many instances of this construction. It remains only to mention that, like the apposition, relative, &c., it often belongs syntactically only to the *last part* of the clause, or division of the verse, preceding. Note how we divide sometimes, in chanting, in the same way:

'As it was in the beginning, is now, and ever shall be | world without end.'

Examples are:

'And they heard the voice of Jehovah God, walking in the garden | at the cool of the day' (Gen. iii. 8).

'And he shall dip them and the living bird in the blood of the bird that was killed | over the running water' (Lev. xiv. 6).

'And they took his land in possession, and the land of Og king of Bashan, the two kings of the Amorites, which were beyond Jordan | toward the sun-rising' (Deut. iv. 47, comp. 49).

'Wilt thou keep silence, and afflict us | very sore?' (Is. lxiv. 11).

Comp. Gen. xxii. 4; xxxviii. 12^b; xlix. 29^b; Lev. xxvii. 18^a; Deut. xi. 28^b; Is. lxi. 10^b; Mic. ii. 8; Ezra vi. 21 [28].

Of course, we may have one Zusatz duly marked off, and then another following:

'These are the commandments and the judgments, which Jehovah commanded, by the hand of Moses, |$^{d\ 2}$ unto the children of Israel, |$^{d\ 1}$ in the plains of Moab by the Jordan of Jericho' (Num. xxxvi. 13).

What is irregular is the *double Zusatz*, e. g.

'These are the statutes, ... which Jehovah made between Him and the children of Israel, | in Mount Sinai, by the hand of Moses' (Lev. xxvi. 46) [29].

It is observable that the relative, or a term in apposition, may take the place of one member of the double Zusatz. (This is possible, inasmuch as the relative, apposition, and Zusatz appear under the *same conditions*, at the end of the clause.) Comp. Deut. iv. 40^b, with the Zusatz כל־הימים, and xxviii. 52^a with בכל־ארצך, both after the relative. In this way Is. ii. 20^b may be explained, without having recourse to the Rabbinical rendering to account for the accentuation. A somewhat similar case is Gen. i. 11: 'Fruit-tree bearing fruit after its kind, | in which is the seed thereof, upon the earth,' where על־הארץ

---

[28] Sometimes it is the second accusative, which we express by a preposition, that serves as Zusatz, as in Gen. xlix. 25, after בְּרָךְ; and Num. xxii. 18 after מְלֹא.

[29] So virtually Is. lxiii. 13: 'Who led them through the depths, | like the horse on the plain, without stumbling.' And so Gen. xiii. 10^b may be explained.

does not refer to the relative clause [30], but to the clause preceding the dichotomy.—An instance of Zusatz+Apposition is found in Deut. xxvi. 15[b].

Having completed the examination of the principles on which the division—logical and syntactical—proceeds, we are now prepared to enter on the analysis of the verse and its component parts. It will (I think) be found that we have already mastered the chief difficulties of our investigation. Henceforth our main task will be to *observe the accents*, that are employed to mark the necessary divisions. The rules above laid down will be applied at every step, and I shall not consider it necessary to draw the reader's attention to their particular application, but shall take it for granted that he has made himself familiar with them in a general way, so as to be able readily to refer to them for the explanation of any particular case. Beside the above rules, we shall find that musical and rhythmical laws have to be taken into account.

Perhaps before I leave this, the preparatory part of my work, it may be well to remind the student that the accents employed to mark the various divisions of the verse, have no *fixed* interpunctional value. We could not say that one answers *per se* to our comma, another to our semicolon, and so on; for they simply note *musical* divisions, which are bound to appear whatever the logical or grammatical construction of the verse may be. Hence Athnach, for instance, may represent at one time the fullest logical, and at another the feeblest syntactical pause; and hence too the same clause will be marked by quite different accents, as it varies its position in the verse. (See e.g. Jos. vii. 14[b]; 1 Ki. vii. 21[b].) The point which the student must bear in mind is that the interpunctional value of the accents is *relative*, not absolute.

---

[30] At least, no one (I presume) will accept Dillmann's explanation: *In welcher sein Same* [ist zur Fortpflanzung!] *auf der Erde.*

SYNTACTICAL DICHOTOMY. 59

Corrigenda [31]

(in accordance with the rules laid down in this chapter).

1. The *casus absolutus* (p. 45) must be marked off in
נָבִיא פַּח יָקוֹשׁ עַל־כָּל־דְּרָכָיו (Hos. ix. 8), with Ox. 1, 5, 6, 7, &c. 'As for the prophet—the snare of the fowler is on all his ways.'

2. The accentual arrangement of the *verbal clause* (p. 49) has to be corrected in the following passages:

תִּהְיֶה זֹאת אוֹת (Jos. iv. 6), with Par. 9; Hm. 3. T'bhir is evidently due at זֹאת.

הֲבָא־עוֹד הֲלֹם אִישׁ (1 Sam. x. 22), with Ox. 16; Erf. 1, 2, 3.

וַתִּהְיֶיןָ נָם־שְׁתֵּיהֶן לוֹ לְנָשִׁים: (xxv. 43), with Ox. 16, 72, 75, &c. T'bhir is again out of place in our texts.

וַתְּהִי־שָׁם הַמַּגֵּפָה גְדוֹלָה (2 Sam. xviii. 7), with Add. 11657; Ber. 2. Géresh is properly due (as we shall afterwards see) at הַמַּגֵּפָה, but has been transformed.

לֹא בָא־כֵן עֲצֵי אַלְמֻגִּים (1 Ki. x. 12), with Ox. 1, 6, 8, &c.

וַיָּשֶׁב אֶת־הַצֵּל בַּמַּעֲלוֹת אֲשֶׁר יָרְדָה בְּמַעֲלוֹת אָחָז אֲחֹרַנִּית (2 Ki. xx. 11), with Or. 2091; Par. 30; Ber. 32; and so Is. xxxviii. 8. The pointing of our texts, הַצֵּל, makes the shadow to have already gone down backwards, *before* the sign was performed!

הוֹלִיךְ גּוֹלָה מִירוּשָׁלַ͏ִם בָּבֶלָה: (xxiv. 15), with Ox. 1, 7, 10, &c.

וְהִצִּיתוּ אֶת־הָעִיר הַזֹּאת בָּאֵשׁ (Jer. xxxii. 29), with Ox. 1, 5, 6, &c.

וְעָטָה אֶת־אֶרֶץ מִצְרַיִם כַּאֲשֶׁר־יַעְטֶה הָרֹעֶה אֶת־בִּגְדוֹ (xliii. 12). R'bhia is absolutely necessary here, and is supplied by Add. 15252; Par. 30; Ber. 32; De R. 942.

לָשֵׂאת מַעְשַׂר הַחֹמֶר הַבַּת (Ezek. xlv. 11), with Ox. 2421; Harl. 5498; Or. 2091; Vi. 2, &c.

וָאֹמַר אֶל־הַמַּלְאָךְ הַדֹּבֵר בִּי (Zech. ii. 2), with Ox. 1, 4, 9, &c.

וַיִּבְחַר יְהֹוָה אֱלֹהֵי־יִשְׂרָאֵל בִּי מִכֹּל בֵּית־אָבִי (1 Chr. xxviii. 4), Harl. 1528; Hm. 16; and De R. 384, have rightly Munach, instead of the Pazer of our texts. Here the dichotomy due before בִּי ought properly to have been marked with Paseq.

---

[31] I have not thought it necessary to give the minor accentual variations in the Codd. quoted, where the principle of division is the same.

3. With the *nominal predicate* (p. 51) at the head of the clause, we must point in the following passages thus :

שֶׁמֶן מִשְׁחַת־קֹדֶשׁ יִהְיֶה זֶה לִי (Ex. xxx. 31), with Ox. 6, 18, 20, &c.

וְעָמַק אֵין־מַרְאֶהָ מִן־הָעוֹר (Lev. xiii. 4), with Ox. 18; Add. 4709; Erf. 1.

כִּי־אִישׁ גָּדוֹל הוּא מְאֹד׃ (2 Sam. xix. 33), with Ox. 68, 76.

4. The accentuation in the case of a few *compound members* (p. 53 ff.) needs correcting, as follows :

בַּעַל הַחֲלֹמוֹת הַלָּזֶה (Gen. xxxvii. 19), with Ox. 2436; Par. 4.

וּפָרְשׂוּ בֶּגֶד כְּלִיל תְּכֵלֶת (Num. iv. 6), with K. 251; De R. 2. Comp. Ex. xxviii. 31.

כִּימֵי הַפֻּרִים הַמְאָרִים (v. 19), with Add. 15252; De R. 384. Comp. ver. 18 end.

רֹאשׁ אֲבוֹת בֵּית־אָב (xxv. 15), with Ox. 3, 6, 8; Erff. 1–4.

הַנַּעַר הַמַּחֲזִיק בְּיָדוֹ (Judg. xvi. 26), with all Codd.

אֶבֶן־שְׁלֵמָה מַסָּע (1 Ki. vi. 7), with all Codd.

עַתָּה־זֶה (1 Ki. xvii. 24), with Ox. 76; Ber. 2; and עַתָּה זֶה (2 Ki. v. 22), with K. 187; De R. 440. The two adverbs cannot be separated as in our texts.

אֵת כָּל־הָרָעָה אֲשֶׁר עָשָׂה יִשְׁמָעֵאל בֶּן־נְתַנְיָה׃ (Jer. xli. 11), with Ox. 5, 72, &c.

דֶּרֶךְ הֵנָּה פְנֵיהֶם (Jer. l. 5), with Ox. 13, 72. See also Rashi and Qimchi.

בַּאֲשֶׁר לְמִי (Jon. i. 8), with Ox. 4, 7; like בְּשֶׁלְּמִי, ver. 7.

כְּנָבְרִים בּוֹסִים בְּטִיט חוּצוֹת (Zech. x. 5), with Ox. 4, 6, 7, &c.

וִימֵי הַפֻּרִים הָאֵלֶּה [32] (Esth. ix. 28), with Ox. 51; Harl. 5506.

וְרַבִּים מִיְּשֵׁנֵי אַדְמַת־עָפָר (Dan. xii. 2), with Ox. 1, 5, 7.

In these trifling matters, I have been often satisfied, when I have found *two* Codd. supporting the obviously necessary correction. The instances shew how even the best editors have failed to master, or at least to observe, the simplest rules of the accentuation.

Other similar instances will doubtless be found, which have escaped my notice, and which will all have to be corrected in the same way, unless (as is sometimes the case) they should admit of explanation, from the application of some special rule.

---

[32] הָאֵלֶּה qualifies not הַפֻּרִים, as in texts, but יָמִים, see the first words of the verse.

CHAPTER V.

SILLUQ.

SILLUQ's clause is to be considered as embracing the *whole* verse[1].

The verse itself is of varying length. It may contain only *two* words. But such cases are exceedingly rare. The only examples are Gen. xlvi. 23; Ex. xx. 13-15 (Deut. v. 17); and Num. xxvi. 11. Here Ṭiphcha appears as *musical foretone* to Silluq in the first word, e. g. לֹא תִרְצָח׃.

Where *three* or *more* words occur in the verse, we have, first of all, to observe the rules for the *main division* of the same. The following cases will occur:

I. The main dichotomy—fixed by the rules we have already laid down—may come on the *first* word before Silluq, and will be marked by Ṭiphcha or Athnach.

1. Ṭiphcha is by far the more common (perhaps for the sake of the musical foretone), whether the verse be long or short, e.g. וַיְהִי בָאַרְבַּע ;(Gen. ii. 1) וַיְכֻלּוּ הַשָּׁמַיִם וְהָאָרֶץ וְכָל־צְבָאָם עֶשְׂרֵה שָׁנָה לַמֶּלֶךְ חִזְקִיָּהוּ עָלָה סַנְחֵרִיב מֶלֶךְ־אַשּׁוּר עַל כָּל־עָרֵי יְהוּדָה הַבְּצֻרוֹת וַיִּתְפְּשֵׂם (Is. xxxvi. 1)[2].

With *only three* words in the verse,—as in Gen. xxvi. 6; Ex. xxviii. 13[3]; Num. vi. 24,—Ṭiphcha is always used.

2. Athnach occurs occasionally, and more particularly in cases

---

[1] So Pasûqa's clause is treated in Syriac. Comp. Bar-Zu'bî (ed. Martin), p. 4.

[2] Other examples of long verses with Ṭiphcha are Num. ix. 1; Deut. v. 23; vi. 22; Jos. xiii. 16; Jer. viii. 1; xiii. 13; xxix. 2; lii. 18; Ezek. xli. 17; Neh. v. 17; 1 Chr. xxviii. 1; 2 Chr. xx. 22; xxiv. 9; xxxiv. 20.

Ṭiphcha, as the main divider of the verse, constantly *lengthens* the short vowel, as Athnach would have done: פֶּסַח (Num. ix. 2); יְרוּשָׁלָ͏ִם (Jer. viii. 1; xiii. 13); אֶפְרָיִם (Hos. iv. 17); חָיִל (1 Chr. xxviii. 1).

[3] The Massora to this passage cites fourteen such verses in the Tora, ten of which come under this head.

of a *marked logical pause*, e. g. וַיֹּ֣אמֶר אֱלֹהִ֔ים יְהִי־א֖וֹר וַיְהִי־אֽוֹר (Gen. i. 3); וַתָּבֹ֣אנָה אֶל־קִרְבֶּ֗נָה וְלֹ֤א נוֹדַע֙ כִּי־בָ֣אוּ אֶל־קִרְבֶּ֔נָה (xli. 21). Comp. v. 5; xlii. 20; Ex. xxiii. 23; Num. x. 28; Ezek. vii. 21; Hag. ii. 5. Such instances, with Athnach on the first word, are the only ones in which the foretone fails before Silluq.

II. With the main dichotomy on the *second* word before Silluq, the same accents are employed to mark it. But Athnach is here the more common (the foretone Tiphcha following on the first word). Examples are, with Tiphcha: וַיְהִי־עֶ֥רֶב וַיְהִי־בֹ֖קֶר י֥וֹם שְׁלִישִֽׁי (Gen. i. 13); יְהוָ֥ה יִמְלֹ֖ךְ לְעֹלָ֥ם וָעֶֽד (Ex. xv. 18); שִׁמְע֣וּ אֶת־הַדָּבָ֗ר אֲשֶׁ֨ר דִּבֶּ֧ר יְהוָ֛ה עֲלֵיכֶ֖ם בֵּ֥ית יִשְׂרָאֵֽל (Jer. x. 1); and with Athnach: וַיִּתֵּ֥ן אֹתָ֛ם אֱלֹהִ֖ים בִּרְקִ֣יעַ הַשָּׁמָ֑יִם לְהָאִ֖יר עַל־הָאָֽרֶץ (Gen. i. 17); וּבַחֹ֤דֶשׁ הַשֵּׁנִי֙ בְּשִׁבְעָ֣ה וְעֶשְׂרִ֣ים י֔וֹם לַחֹ֖דֶשׁ יָבְשָׁ֥ה הָאָֽרֶץ (viii. 14).

We have to notice a further variation. When Silluq's word, or the word preceding it, is *long*[4], Zaqeph is admissible instead of Tiphcha, and is indeed generally preferred, for the sake of the rhythmical cadence at the close of the verse (Tiphcha, as before, marking the foretone on the first word), e. g. וַיִּשְׁתַּ֖חוּ אַבְרָהָ֛ם לִפְנֵ֥י עַם־הָאָֽרֶץ (Gen. xxiii. 12); וַיִּשְׁמַ֥ע מֹשֶׁ֖ה וַיִּיטַ֥ב

---

[4] A *long* word is technically one that has two or more vowels before the tone-syllable, or if only one vowel, that vowel must be *long*, followed by Métheg and Sh'va. In the latter case, the Sh'va may be *mobile*, as in קָֽסְל֔וּ, אָֽהֲבָ֔ה, or *quiescens*, as in בְּיִתָ֔אֵל, בָּתִּ֔ים.

With *two short* words following, Tiphcha is bound to appear. See the list of names of the spies, Num. xiii. 4 ff., where the only instance in which Tiphcha stands is of this kind, ver. 8. Or comp. 1 Chr. xi. 27–47, where vv. 35 and 42 alone have Tiphcha and for the same reason. Some few exceptions indeed occur, as לְק֗וֹץ לְנֶ֥פֶשׁ תִּדְרְשֶׁ֖נּוּ (Lam. iii. 25); and (where Zaqeph marks a minor dichotomy) in Ex. xxxiii. 1; Is. xlviii. 4; lxii. 6; Ezra vi. 12. But these are only the exceptions that prove the rule; for the rule is carried out in hundreds, if not thousands, of instances. Jer. v. 30 is pointed with Athnach in Ox. 1, 7.

אַחֲרֵי־כֵן פָּתַח אִיּוֹב֙ אֶת־פִּ֔יהוּ וַיְקַלֵּ֖ל (Lev. x. 20); בְּעֵינָ֑יו אֶת־יוֹמֽוֹ (Job iii. 1). Tiphcha, however, not unfrequently retains its place, as in בַּיהוָ֧ה יִצְדְּק֛וּ וְיִֽתְהַלְל֖וּ כָּל־זֶ֥רַע יִשְׂרָאֵֽל (Is. xlv. 25).

As under I, when the verse consists of *only three* words, Tiphcha (Zaqeph) can alone be employed. See Gen. xliii. 1; Lev. xi. 14; Num. i. 6, 9; Is. ii. 18.

How entirely *optional*, in other cases, the use of Tiphcha (Zaqeph) or Athnach was, may be seen from a comparison of 2 Sam. xxii. 2 ff. and 1 Chr. xvi. 8 ff. We have here the prose accentuation applied to certain Psalms (2 Sam. xxii gives us Ps. xviii, and 1 Chr. xvi parts of Pss. cv, xcvi, and cvi). Now these Psalms are similar in their build, consisting mainly of short verses, with from five to seven words in each. Yet we find that wherever the choice lay between Tiphcha (Zaqeph) on the one hand and Athnach on the other—as when the main dichotomy is on the second word (the case before us), or on the third and fourth (see III following)—the accentuators invariably decided in 2 Sam. xxii for the latter (Athnach), and in 1 Chr. xvi as invariably for the former. Comp. e. g. 2 Sam. xxii. 4, 23, 47, with 1 Chr. xvi. 9, 11, 31. The matter is not without interest, although no one, as far as I am aware, has taken any notice of it. For we have here a manifest attempt (as far as it goes) to provide different modes of chanting for different Psalms. And what is more, it can hardly be doubted that we have in 2 Sam. xxii and 1 Chr. xvi the *original* melodies of certain Psalms as they were chanted *before* the poetical accentuation was introduced (see טעמי אמ״ת, pp. 8, 9)[5].

III. With the main dichotomy on the *third* or *fourth* word, either Athnach or Zaqeph[6] may be employed to mark it, but the former is much the more common,—particularly on the *fourth*

---

[5] The musical division carried out in 2 Sam. xxii is found (with little or no variation) in other poetical pieces, such as Gen. xlix; Ex. xv; Deut. xxxii and xxxiii; &c. Lam. iii and v (with their short verses) are alone divided as 1 Chr. xvi. But it is interesting to notice that the Oriental text had this division for the whole of Job (see a specimen prefixed to Baer's edition), and without doubt for Proverbs also, and at least a part of the Psalms.

[6] Zaqeph occurs mostly in *short* verses, and is particularly common in the few words that *head an address*, as Ex. xii. 1; xx. 1; xxi. 1; Lev. xiii. 1; xv. 1; Is. vii. 10; viii. 5; Jer. vii. 1; and in *lists of names, numbers*, &c., as Josh. xii. 9–24; Ruth iv. 18–22; Ezra ii. 3 ff.; 1 Chr. xi. 27–47; xxv. 10–31. Sometimes texts vary, as in 2 Sam. i. 27; xxiii. 39; where Athnach is better. In 1 Chr. xviii. 12, many Codd. have Zaqeph.

word. The farther back the main division is removed from Silluq, the greater is the tendency to employ Athnach to mark it. We can understand that, by this weightier accent, the balance of the melody was better marked and sustained. So with the main dichotomy on the *fifth* word and further, Athnach *alone* can be employed [7]. For examples under this head, see below.

The accents that mark the *main dichotomy* of the verse have now been determined. The verse has been divided into (what we may call) its two halves; and the next question is how the accentual division of each of these halves is to be carried out. With the first we are not at present concerned. It is under the government of Tiphcha, Zaqeph, or Athnach; and the rules for its division cannot be settled, till we come to treat of these accents respectively. But the last half is still under Silluq's control, and its subdivision must now engage our attention.

When the main dichotomy comes on the first or second word before Silluq (I and II), it is clear that no further division is possible. But when it comes on the third or any further word (III), such division is not only possible but necessary.

For Silluq's clause is subject, in all its parts, to the strict rule of the dichotomy, viz. that wherever three or more words come together, the dichotomy is to be introduced. Now under III, there will be at least three, and there may be many more words, in the last half of the verse. The *minor dichotomy* therefore cannot fail. Its musical notation will be necessarily Tiphcha, if it come on the first word, and Tiphcha (Zaqeph) on the second.

---

[7] The rule that Athnach *alone can stand on the fifth word and further*, is strictly carried out. Hence the Zaqeph in Qoh. iii. 3, 4, 6-8, is changed into Athnach in vv. 2 and 5. I have noted only two trifling exceptions to the rule, in Ezra ii. 35 (repeated Neh. vii. 38) and Neh. vii. 17, where, for uniformity with the headings in the long list before and after, Zaqeph has been retained. Other exceptions in our texts must be corrected, as Zaqeph on the *fifth* word, Cant. vi. 12 (where עֲמִּי־נָדִיב must be written as one word, see Baer's note), and 1 Chr. xxiii. 12 (point קְהָת, with Ox. 5, 9, 11). Zaqeph occurs on the *sixth* word in 1 Chr. vii. 13 (corr. נַחֲלִי, with Ox. 4, 5, 9) and 2 Chr. i. 18 (point שְׁלֹמֹה, with ditto); and on the *seventh* word in Is. xl. 5 (corr. יְהוָה, with Baer).

On the third word or further it will be Zaqeph. In this last case a further subdivision will be necessary.

The following examples of the various cases that arise will make these remarks clear [8]:

I. *a*. With Athnach, as main divider of the verse, on the *third* or *fourth* word: וַיִּקְרָא יְהֹוָה אֱלֹהִים אֶל־הָאָדָם וַיֹּאמֶר לוֹ אַיֶּכָּה (Gen. iii. 9); וַיֹּאמְרוּ הַכְזוֹנָה יַעֲשֶׂה אֶת־אֲחוֹתֵנוּ (xxxiv. 31);

וַיְצַו יְהֹוָה אֱלֹהִים עַל־הָאָדָם לֵאמֹר מִכֹּל עֵץ־הַגָּן אָכֹל תֹּאכֵל (ii. 16); וְעַתָּה יוֹשֵׁב יְרוּשָׁלַ͏ִם וְאִישׁ יְהוּדָה שִׁפְטוּ־נָא בֵּינִי

וּבֵין כַּרְמִי (Is. v. 3). The last is the only case in which a second minor dichotomy is due.

β. With Zaqeph, in place of Athnach, on the third or fourth word: יִשָּׂא יְהֹוָה ׀ פָּנָיו אֵלֶיךָ וְיָשֵׂם לְךָ שָׁלוֹם (Num. vi. 26); אַךְ־ (Qoh. i. 4); דּוֹר הֹלֵךְ וְדוֹר בָּא וְהָאָרֶץ לְעוֹלָם עֹמָדֶת לֹא יָדַעְתִּי נַפְשִׁי (Gen. ix. 4); בָּשָׂר בְּנַפְשׁוֹ דָמוֹ לֹא תֹאכֵלוּ בֵּהּ בְּלֵילְיָא קְטִיל (Cant. vi. 12); שָׂמַתְנִי מַרְכְּבוֹת עַמִּי־נָדִיב בֵּלְאשַׁצַּר מַלְכָּא כַשְׂדָּאָה (Dan. v. 30).

In the two last instances, Zaqeph has been *repeated*, to mark the minor dichotomy. Such cases are, however, not common, and occur only in the later Books. Athnach with Zaqeph following was preferred to two Zaqephs.

II. With Athnach, as main divider of the verse, on the *fifth word or further*.

1. Here, as above, there may be only *one* minor dichotomy,— marked by Tiphcha on the first word, or Tiphcha (Zaqeph) on the second: וַיְהִי מִקֵּץ יָמִים וַיָּבֵא קַיִן מִפְּרִי הָאֲדָמָה מִנְחָה לַיהֹוָה (Gen. iv. 3); וַיַּעַשׂ נֹחַ כְּכֹל אֲשֶׁר צִוָּה אֹתוֹ אֱלֹהִים כֵּן

---

[8] The student will notice in the examples given the logical and syntactical grounds for marking off the several dichotomies. He will observe that Zaqeph is often *repeated*, and will see that, from the very principle of the dichotomy, the first Zaqeph must have a greater disjunctive value than the second, the second than the third, &c.

וְאֶל־קַיִן וְאֶל־מִנְחָתוֹ לֹא שָׁעָה וַיִּחַר לְקַיִן מְאֹד (vi. 22); עָשָׂה
וַיִּפְּלוּ פָנָיו (iv. 5).

2. There may be *two* minor dichotomies, the first of which will be marked by Zaqeph, the second as under 1: אִמְרִי־נָא
אֲחֹתִי אָתְּ לְמַעַן יִיטַב־לִי בַעֲבוּרֵךְ וְחָיְתָה נַפְשִׁי בִּגְלָלֵךְ
(xv. 8); וַיֹּאמֶר אֲדֹנָי יְהֹוָה בַּמָּה אֵדַע כִּי אִירָשֶׁנָּה (xii. 13);
חָזוּת קָשָׁה הֻגַּד־לִי הַבּוֹגֵד ׀ בּוֹגֵד וְהַשּׁוֹדֵד ׀ שׁוֹדֵד עֲלִי עֵילָם
צוּרִי מָדַי כָּל־אַנְחָתָה הִשְׁבַּתִּי (Is. xxi. 2).

3. There may be *three* minor dichotomies, the first two of which will be marked by Zaqeph, the third as under 1: וְהָאָדָם
יָדַע אֶת־חַוָּה אִשְׁתּוֹ וַתַּהַר וַתֵּלֶד אֶת־קַיִן וַתֹּאמֶר קָנִיתִי
אִישׁ אֶת־יְהֹוָה (Gen. iv. 1); וַתֹּסֶף לָלֶדֶת אֶת־אָחִיו אֶת־הָבֶל
וְאִם־כֹּה (iv. 2); וַיְהִי־הֶבֶל רֹעֵה צֹאן וְקַיִן הָיָה עֹבֵד אֲדָמָה
יֹאמַר לֹא חָפַצְתִּי בָּךְ הִנְנִי יַעֲשֶׂה־לִּי כַּאֲשֶׁר טוֹב בְּעֵינָיו
(2 Sam. xv. 26).

4. *Four* minor dichotomies are also frequent enough, the three first marked by Zaqeph, the fourth as under 1: וַיֹּאמֶר דָּוִיד
לִשְׁלֹמֹה בְנִי אֲנִי הָיָה עִם־לְבָבִי לִבְנוֹת בַּיִת לְשֵׁם יְהֹוָה
אֱלֹהָי (1 Chr. xxii. 7). Comp. Gen. iii. 1; xxvii. 42; xliv. 16; Deut. xv. 4; 1 Ki. xvi. 34; Is. xxiv. 2; Ezek. xxvii. 3.

5. Of *five* minor dichotomies I have found only two certain instances in our texts, 2 Sam. xvii. 9 and 2 Ki. i. 3 [9].

We have now completed the analysis of Silluq's clause, and have traced the application of the law of the *continuous dichotomy*, on which the whole fabric of the accentuation rests. Scholars

---

[9] Ben-Bil. (Mishp. hat. 9ᵃ), and other writers on the accents, do not allow even these instances.—Four Zaqephs are found in Judg. xiii. 8; but here we have an early misprint (Bomb. 2), which has been preserved in our texts: שָׁלְחָהּ is impossible after Gersháyim, and must be changed to שְׁלָחָהּ (R'bhia).—In 2 Ki. xvii. 34 most Codd. I have examined (Ox. 1, 5, 7, 8, &c.) have עֹשִׂים (R'bhia).

still hesitate about accepting this law. But it is hoped that no one, who has carefully examined the examples above given, will any longer doubt its operation. It remains to be seen whether it will equally explain the phenomena that occur with the other accents.

Servus of Silluq

is always Mer'kha. Silluq has never more than one servus.

In five passages [10] the Palestinian authorities have introduced Tiphcha (in place of Métheg) into the *same word* with Silluq: לְהֵחַלּ֑וֹ (Lev. xxi. 4); לְדֹרֹתֵיכֶ֑ם (Num. xv. 21); [11] וְקִוֵּיתִי־ל֑וֹ (Is. viii. 17); מִמַּצֵּבוֹתֵיהֶ֑ם (Hos. xi. 6); and וְהָאֶשְׁתָּאֻלִ֑י (1 Chr. ii. 53). As the notions that led them to mark these few words with an anomalous accentuation have not been handed down to us, conjectures on the subject seem to me useless.—It is to be noted that in the first four cases Athnach immediately precedes, in the last Zaqeph.

Grammarians call the accent here a *servus*, and give it the name מָאיְלָא (see p. 26).

Corrigenda.

Zaqeph fails, or has been wrongly introduced, in the following passages (which must be corrected, as we should correct cases of false interpunction in a modern text):

וְקָ֣מוּ נְדָרֶ֗יהָ וֶאֱסָרֶ֛הָ אֲשֶׁר־אָסְרָ֥ה עַל־נַפְשָׁ֖הּ יָקֻֽמוּ (Num. xxx. 8), as in vv. 5 and 12. And so Ox. 13 and Harl. 1528 point.

וְלוֹ־תִהְיֶ֣ה לְאִשָּׁ֗ה תַּ֚חַת אֲשֶׁ֣ר עִנָּ֔הּ לֹא־יוּכַ֥ל שַׁלְּחָ֖הּ כָּל־יָמָֽיו (Deut. xxii. 29), with Ox. 3, 8; Erf. 1, 3.

ק֥וּם בָּרָ֖ק וּֽשֲׁבֵ֣ה שֶׁבְיְךָ֑ בֶּן־אֲבִינֹֽעַם (Judg. v. 12), with Ox. 16, 36, 2437; Harl. 5706.

וַיְנַתֵּ֣ק אֶת־הַיְתָרִ֗ים כַּאֲשֶׁ֨ר יִנָּתֵ֤ק פְּתִיל־הַנְּעֹ֙רֶת֙ בַּהֲרִיח֣וֹ אֵ֔שׁ וְלֹ֥א נוֹדַ֖ע כֹּחֽוֹ (Judg. xvi. 9), with Ox. 6, 7, 15; Erf. 3.

בְּשׁ֣וּב הַכֹּ֔ל הָאִ֕ישׁ אֲשֶׁר־אַתָּ֣ה מְבַקֵּ֑שׁ כָּל־הָעָ֖ם יִהְיֶ֥ה שָׁלֽוֹם (2 Sam. xvii. 3), with Ox. 1, 13, 68, 72.

וַיְקַנְא֣וּ אֹת֔וֹ מִכֹּ֖ל אֲשֶׁ֣ר עָשׂ֣וּ אֲבֹתָ֑ם בְּחַטֹּאתָ֖ם אֲשֶׁ֥ר חָטָֽאוּ (1 Ki. xiv. 22), with all Ox. Codd. I have examined, and others.

---

[10] Enumerated in the Mas. to Lev. xxi. 4.

[11] Cod. Bab. has וְקִוֵּיתִי לוֹ (no doubt the Oriental pointing), and this is correct. Maqqeph is out of place here. In Hos. xi. 6 the Palestinian accentuation has found its way into this text, as is not unfrequently the case.

וּנְתַתִּים לְזַעֲוָה לְכֹל מַמְלְכוֹת הָאָרֶץ לְאָלָה וּלְשַׁמָּה וְלִשְׁרֵקָה וְלִחֲרָפָּה בְּכָל־הַגּוֹיִם אֲשֶׁר־הִדַּחְתִּים שָׁם (Jer. xxix. 18), Zaqeph for R'bhia on הָאָרֶץ, with Ox. 13, 72; Harl. 5498, 5722; &c.[12]

אָמַר יְהוָֹה אֱלֹהֵי־צְבָאוֹת שְׁמוֹ (Amos v. 27), with Ox. 17; Vi. 5; the only two Codd. I have found that point according to the sense.

עוֹר בְּעַד־עוֹר וְכֹל אֲשֶׁר לָאִישׁ יִתֵּן בְּעַד נַפְשׁוֹ (Job ii. 4), with Ox. 4, 5, 19; Bomb. 1; &c.

הֲגַם כְּתוּבִים עַל דִּבְרֵי חוֹזָי (2 Chr. xxxiii. 19). R'bhia, as in texts, is impossible.

Further, nothing is more common in Codd. and printed texts than the interchange of Tiphcha and Mer'kha before Silluq. These accents must be brought into their proper places in the following instances:

בֵּית אֵל בְּרִית (Judg. ix. 46, 'the house of El-berith'), with Ox. 6, 7, 8, &c.; not as in texts, בֵּית אֵל בְּרִית, a mispunctuation, which has led in some Codd. to the writing of בֵּיתְאֵל as one word!

וַיַּלְכֵּד יוֹנָתָן וְשָׁאוּל וְהָעָם יָצָאוּ (1 Sam. xiv. 41), with all Ox. Codd. The pointing of our texts makes nonsense.

וְעֵינֶיךָ עַל־רָמִים תַּשְׁפִּיל (2 Sam. xxii. 28), with Ox. 1, 5, 6, 7.

אַתָּה וּשְׁאָר יָשׁוּב בְּנֶךָ (Is. vii. 3), with Ox. 12, 17, 78.

וְקִיר עֵרָה מָגֵן (xxii. 6), with Ox. 1, 4, 9, 12; Cod. Bab.; &c.

וּכְכַרְמֶל בַּיָּם יָבוֹא (Jer. xlvi. 18), with Ox. 7, 19, 2436; Hm. 10; &c.

נָתַן שְׁאוֹן קוֹלָם (li. 55), with Ox. 9, 70, 2324; Cod. Bab.; &c.

אֶת־יְהוָֹה עָזְבוּ לִשְׁמֹר (Hos. iv. 10), with Ox. 17, 75, 76, 78; Bomb. 1; &c.

חֲמִשָּׁה רָאשִׁים כֻּלָּם (1 Chr. vii. 3), with Ox. 4, 7, 11; Erf. 3; &c. 'Five; all of them chief men.'

Baer has already corrected Gen. xxii. 1; Is. xxviii. 17; xxix. 4; Ezek. iii. 14; viii. 3; &c. On the same principle as the correction in Ezek. viii. 3, we must point in ver. 5, סֵמֶל הַקִּנְאָה הַזֶּה בַּבִּאָה׃.

---

[12] But Harl. 5498 is the only one that has the subordinate accents right.

CHAPTER VI.

ATHNACH.

THE rules for Athnach's clause are so similar to those for Silluq's, that there is but one point that will detain us, in considering them.

Athnach may stand *alone*, at the beginning of the verse, e.g. וַיֹּאמְרוּ (Gen. xxxiv. 31); וְצֹאנִי (Ezek. xxxiv. 19).

When there are only *two* words in the clause, Tiphcha must appear as foretone to Athnach : וַיְגָרֶשׁ אֶת־הָאָדָם (Gen. iii. 24).

When there are *three* or *more* words:

I. The main dichotomy, if on the *first* word before Athnach, is marked by Tiphcha : וַיִּבֶן יְהֹוָה (i. 3); וַיֹּאמֶר אֱלֹהִים יְהִי־אוֹר (ii. 22). אֱלֹהִים ׀ אֶת־הַצֵּלָע אֲשֶׁר־לָקַח מִן־הָאָדָם לְאִשָּׁה

II. If on the *second* word, also by Tiphcha : וַיִּתֵּן אֹתָם אֱלֹהִים בִּרְקִיעַ הַשָּׁמַיִם (i. 17); וַיהֹוָה פָּקַד אֶת־שָׂרָה כַּאֲשֶׁר אָמָר (xxi. 1); for which Zaqeph may be substituted, under the same conditions as before Silluq (p. 62)[1] : יִקָּווּ הַמַּיִם מִתַּחַת הַשָּׁמַיִם וְהָיוּ לִמְאוֹרֹת בִּרְקִיעַ (i. 9); אֶל־מָקוֹם אֶחָד וְתֵרָאֶה הַיַּבָּשָׁה וַיֵּרָא אֵלָיו יְהֹוָה בְּאֵלֹנֵי (i. 15); הַשָּׁמַיִם לְהָאִיר עַל־הָאָרֶץ מַמְרֵא (xviii. 1).

III. If on the *third* word, by Zaqeph—the minor dichotomy being marked as before Silluq (p. 65),—e.g. וַיַּעַשׂ אֱלֹהִים אֶת־שְׁנֵי וְהָאָרֶץ הָיְתָה תֹהוּ וָבֹהוּ וְחֹשֶׁךְ (i. 16); הַמְּאֹרֹת הַגְּדֹלִים וְאֶעֶשְׂךָ לְגוֹי גָּדוֹל וַאֲבָרֶכְךָ וַאֲגַדְּלָה שְׁמֶךָ (i. 2); עַל־פְּנֵי תְהוֹם (xii. 2).

---

[1] Tiphcha may indeed remain with one or both of the words following *long*, as in Gen. ii. 6; iv. 16; vii. 9. But with *both words short*, Zaqeph is of unusual occurrence. Among the few instances I have noted are Gen. xxv. 3; xxxvi. 32; Is. xxxvii. 27; Hos. ii. 18. Comp. p. 62, note.

Exceptions. In a few instances, where the first and second words are both monosyllables, *Tiphcha* marks the main dichotomy on the third word: וַיַּרְא שַׂר־הָאוֹפִים כִּי טוֹב פָּתָר (Gen. xl. 16); and so in Ex. iii. 4; xii. 39; Num. xxii. 36; 1 Sam. xxviii. 13; 1 Ki. xxi. 16; Is. xlviii. 11; lx. 1; Amos iii. 8 [2]. Here, for the first time, as far as we have gone, the strict rule for the dichotomy gives way.

IV. If on the *fourth* word or *further*, by Zaqeph or S'gôlta,—the former being more common when the main dichotomy is *near to* Athnach, the latter when it is *farther removed from* Athnach. The minor dichotomies are marked as after Athnach in Silluq's clause (pp. 65, 66).

1. Examples of *one* minor dichotomy are: וַיֹּאמֶר אֱלֹהִים חָזוֹן יְשַׁעְיָהוּ בֶן־אָמוֹץ אֲשֶׁר (Gen. i. 6); יְהִי רָקִיעַ בְּתוֹךְ הַמָּיִם חָזָה עַל־יְהוּדָה וִירוּשָׁלִָם (Is. i. 1); וַיְבָרֶךְ אֹתָם אֱלֹהִים וַיֹּאמֶר לָהֶם אֱלֹהִים פְּרוּ וּרְבוּ וּמִלְאוּ אֶת־הָאָרֶץ וְכִבְשֻׁהָ (Gen. i. 28).

2. Examples of *two* and *three* minor dichotomies are: וַתִּפָּקַחְנָה וַיֵּצְאוּ אֶת־אֲשֶׁר (iii. 7); עֵינֵי שְׁנֵיהֶם וַיֵּדְעוּ כִּי עֵירֻמִּם הֵם עַל־בֵּיתוֹ לֵאמֹר מָלֵא אֶת־אַמְתְּחֹת הָאֲנָשִׁים אֹכֶל כַּאֲשֶׁר וַיִּירָא יְהוָה אֶל־אַבְרָם וַיֹּאמֶר לְזַרְעֲךָ (xliv. 1); יוּכְלוּן שְׂאֵת וַיַּעַשׂ אֱלֹהִים אֶת־הָרָקִיעַ (xii. 7); אֶתֵּן אֶת־הָאָרֶץ הַזֹּאת וַיַּבְדֵּל בֵּין הַמַּיִם אֲשֶׁר מִתַּחַת לָרָקִיעַ וּבֵין הַמַּיִם אֲשֶׁר מֵעַל לָרָקִיעַ (i. 7).

With S'gôlta there are a few instances of *four* minor dichotomies, as in Num. xvi. 28; Jer. lii. 30; and two of *five*, 2 Ki. i. 6; Ezek. xlviii. 10 [3].

Exceptions. A few, like those given above, occur, in which Tiphcha marks the last minor dichotomy on the *third* word, e. g. וַיֹּאמֶר אֵלַי בֶּן־אָדָם הֲרֹאֶה אַתָּה מָה הֵם עֹשִׂים (Ezek. viii. 6); and so in 1 Sam. xvii. 39; 2 Sam. xii. 19; 1 Ki. ii. 37; 2 Ki. i. 4; xi. 1; Is. liv. 4; lix. 16.

---

[2] Codd. however vary, often joining these small words with Maqqeph.
[3] In 2 Chr. viii. 13, *Zaqeph* has four minor dichotomies following, but many Codd. (Ox. 4, 5, 9, 11, &c.) point here R'bhia instead of the first Zaqeph. I have not noticed any other instance.

On the Relation of S'gôlta to Athnach.

It has been up to the present day a moot point, whether S'gôlta is to be regarded as a main disjunctive, coordinate with Athnach, or as a subordinate in Athnach's clause. The following considerations will shew, I believe, beyond doubt, that the latter is the case:

1. Under the law of the continuous dichotomy, two *coordinate* accents are impossible. S'gôlta must be either a greater, or a less disjunctive than Athnach. But who will say that it is a *greater*?

2. *The Massora treats it as Zaqeph.* Thus the Mas. magna to Is. xiv. 9 gives a list of fourteen passages, which have אֶרֶץ with Zaqeph and Qāmeṣ [4]. But if we examine these passages, we find that two (Is. li. 13 and Jer. xxxi. 8) are pointed not with Zaqeph, but *S'gôlta*. Again in the Mas. magna to Neh. ix. 6 we are told that לְבַדֶּךָ occurs three times with Zaqeph, yet in this very passage it has not Zaqeph but *S'gôlta* [5]. In chap. viii I shall have occasion to quote another Massora, in which Shalshéleth (the name given to S'gôlta, when on the first word of the verse) is also spoken of as Zaqeph. It is strange that these Massoras have never been turned to account, or even noticed, by any writer on the accents (Jewish or Christian). Either the Massoretic text must be shewn to be corrupt in the several rubrics quoted [6], or we must allow that the early Massoretes, by putting S'gôlta under the general category of Zaqeph, regarded it as *subordinated to Athnach*, in just the same way as Zaqeph is.

3. S'gôlta frequently stands where Zaqeph might with equal propriety have stood. Hence the two are found to *interchange* in Codd. Take, for instance, Dan. iii. 15 (where we have one of the longest Athnach-clauses in the whole text). Here some Codd. point with S'gôlta, others with Zaqeph; and so little disturbance does the substitution occasion that the whole long series of subordinate accents

---

[4] One instance is Ps. xliv. 4 with R'bhîa (Great). Properly the Palestinian Massoretes, when they introduced their system for the three Books, ought to have dropped this example from their list. But they did not venture to alter the old Massora, and left their readers to understand that Great R'bhîa before 'Olev'-yored is the same as Zaqeph before Athnach. We may take it for granted that the original accentuation was

כִּי לֹא בְחָרְבָּם יָרְשׁוּ־אָרֶץ וּזְרוֹעָם לֹא־הוֹשִׁיעָה לָּמוֹ וגו׳

[5] Ginsb. Mas., ב, §622c, may also be compared, where שָׁכָב (1 Sam. iii. 9) comes in a similar list.

[6] I am aware that the word וזקף fails in some MSS. for the first two of the Massoras quoted, but it is found in others, and among them some of the oldest (as Cod. Bab. and Add. 21161). *Its absence is easily accounted for.* The third Mas. did not admit (as we shall see) of being so readily altered by punctators and copyists.

preceding passes over from the one to the other without a break, save that the Zarqa immediately preceding S'gôlta, has to be changed to Pashṭa before Zaqeph. We learn from this example (see also p. 86) that the rules for the division of Zaqeph's and S'gôlta's clauses are *the same*, a further proof of the relationship between these two accents.

4. The chief logical pause in the verse, when S'gôlta and Athnach occur together, is regularly marked by Athnach, shewing that S'gôlta was regarded as *subordinated* to it, e.g.

'And he blessed them that day, saying [*S'gôlta*], In thee shall Israel bless, saying, God make thee as Ephraim and as Manasseh [Athnach]. And he set Ephraim before Manasseh' (Gen. xlviii. 20).

'At that time Jehovah spake by Isaiah, the son of Amoz, saying [*S'gôlta*], Go and loose the sackcloth from off thy loins, and put thy shoe from off thy foot [Athnach]. And he did so, going naked and barefoot' (Is. xx. 2).

Comp. Gen. i. 7; xxiv. 7; xxxvi. 6; l. 5; Ex. xx. 24; Lev. xxii. 13; Num. iv. 15; Deut. ix. 4; 2 Ki. xxiii. 4; Jer. xxviii. 11.

S'gôlta may indeed sometimes *appear* to be independent of Athnach, but all such cases admit of ready explanation from the rules laid down in chaps. iii and iv, for the logical and syntactical division of the verse. Many of the examples there given are instances of S'gôlta.

5. It is surprising that those who insist on S'gôlta's being *par dignitate* with Athnach, have not noticed the lack of *pausal forms* with it. It has them indeed occasionally, but *in the proportion in which Zaqeph, not Athnach, has them*. Comp. סַף with סָף (Ex. xii. 22); פֶּרַח with פָּרַח (xxv. 33); יְרוּשָׁלַ͏ִם (2 Sam. xx. 3) with יְרוּשָׁלָ͏ִם (v. 14); &c.

Other reasons might be adduced. I take it, however, for granted that they are unnecessary.

But if we are to accept S'gôlta as a substitute for, and representative of Zaqeph, it may be asked: What is the difference between the two? and why could not Zaqeph always have stood, where we now have S'gôlta? The difference is simply *musical*. The *melody* of S'gôlta was quite distinct from that of Zaqeph; and its introduction into Athnach's clause is an indication of that love for *musical variety*, which is one of the marked characteristics of the accentual system. It has a Zaqeph *parvus* and a Zaqeph *magnus* (differing only musically), and S'gôlta was a Zaqeph *major* or *maximus*, with a fuller and weightier melody, which served better to mark and emphasize the main pause in the longer clauses in which it usually occurs.

We are thus led to consider the musical laws which regulate the appearance of S'gôlta. It can come only *once* in the verse, and then always marks the place of the main dichotomy in Athnach's clause. It may, therefore, have Zaqeph after, but never before it. Its proper place is *at a distance* from Athnach. For the ninth word, and further, it is almost exclusively employed [7]. It is found, indeed, nearer to Athnach, but the nearer it comes, the less frequent—in comparison with Zaqeph—is its occurrence, till on the fifth word (where Zaqeph is as common as possible) it occurs but seldom, and on the fourth but twice [8]. These musical phenomena we can register, but not explain. We see only that here, as elsewhere, the accentuators allowed themselves the utmost liberty within the limits assigned by the melody.

Servi of Athnach.

One servus is 'Illûy [9], or as we term it Munach; which is repeated, in the few passages in which there are two servi.

In יְדִידְיָה (2 Sam. xii. 25) and שַׁעַמְהָם (1 Chr. v. 20), both compound words, the servus has taken the place of Métheg in the same word with Athnach [10].

In ten or eleven passages the Palestinian [11] accentuation has introduced Tiphcha into the same word with Athnach. They are: וַיֵּצֵא־נֹחַ (Gen. viii. 18); בְּשִׁבְעֹתֵיכֶם (Num. xxviii. 26); וּבָאתָ־שָּׁמָּה (2 Ki. ix. 2); מַאְפֵּלְיָה (Jer. ii. 31); קִפְדָּה־בָא (Ezek. vii. 25); לְאוֹפַנִּים (x. 13); וּבָאוּ־שָׁמָּה (xi. 18); וַתֹּאמַרְנָה־לָּהּ (Ru. i. 10); לְכִלְאָ־בֵּהּ (Dan. iv. 9, 18); וַיִּשְׁבְּרוּ־בָהּ (2 Chr. xx. 8). See Mas. magna to 2 Chr. xx. 8. It is there stated that there was a difference of opinion (פלוגתא) about Ezek. x. 13. Hence many authorities (Jequthiel on Num. xxviii. 26; Qimchi on Ezek. xi. 18; Man. du Lect., p. 103; &c.) number only ten.

It is vain to attempt to assign reasons for the anomalous accentuation in the above passages [12]. See the remark under Silluq, p. 67.

Grammarians make the accent here a *servus*, and name it מָאיְלָא (see p. 26); but that it is really Tiphcha is clear from its having the servus of Tiphcha in Jer. ii. 31 (where most Codd. give also the subordinate disjunctive T'bhîr, אָם), and from Zaqeph immediately preceding in Num. xxviii. 26.

---

[7] Zaqeph occurs but rarely on the ninth word, and still more rarely (some five or six times) on the tenth. Beyond the tenth word it is not found, except in a few corrupt passages, which I have corrected. On the eighth word Zaqeph and S'gôlta are about equally common, but on the seventh, and still more on the sixth word, the preponderance of Zaqeph is very marked.

[8] Deut. iii. 19 and 1 Chr. vi. 62.   [9] Mishp. hat. 12.

[10] Baer has rightly dropped the servus in Hos. vii. 15.

[11] Cod. Bab. (which represents the Oriental punctuation) has no trace of this accentuation. In Jer. ii. 31 it has Munach instead;. and in Ezek. vii. 25; xi. 18, Maqqeph fails.

[12] To mark still more the anomaly in Dan. iv. 9, 18, some few punctators and Ben-Bil. (Mishp. hat. 11) have given the previous word the impossible accent Azla, and so Baer has edited. But the great majority of Codd. point regularly with Mer'kha, as in Jer. ii. 31.

Corrigenda.

In a few verses Athnach has been wrongly placed. It is clear that we must point:

וּלְרוּחַ מִשְׁפָּט לַיּוֹשֵׁב עַל־הַמִּשְׁפָּט (Is. xxviii. 6), with Add. 4708; K. 533; De R. 196; Hm. 9.

וּמַכְתִּי אֲנוּשָׁה מֵאֲנָה הֵרָפֵא (Jer. xv. 18), with Ox. 7; Vi. 5; K. 182; Hm. 16.

אִם־יִמָּלְאוּ הֶעָבִים גֶּשֶׁם עַל־הָאָרֶץ יָרִיקוּ וְאִם־יִפּוֹל עֵץ בַּדָּרוֹם וְאִם בַּצָּפוֹן מְקוֹם שֶׁיִּפּוֹל הָעֵץ שָׁם יְהוּא: (Qoh. xi. 3). But I have found only one Codex, De R. 10 (old), which accents correctly.

Zaqeph fails, or has been falsely introduced, in some passages, which must be corrected as follows:

וְלֹא־יִמְכְּרוּ מִמֶּנּוּ וְלֹא יָמֵר וְלֹא יַעֲבִיר רֵאשִׁית הָאָרֶץ (Ezek. xlviii. 14), with Ox. 9, 12, 69; Erf. 1; &c.[13]

כִּי־מִי אֲשֶׁר יְחֻבַּר אֶל כָּל־הַחַיִּים יֵשׁ בִּטָּחוֹן (Qoh. ix. 4). So the old Codex., De R. 10 (see above), rightly points.

וַתִּגְנֹב אֹתוֹ מִתּוֹךְ בְּנֵי־הַמֶּלֶךְ הַמּוּמָתִים (2 Chr. xxii. 11). See 2 Ki. xi. 2. אֹתוֹ can never stand.

וַיְנַתְּצוּ לְפָנָיו אֵת מִזְבְּחוֹת הַבְּעָלִים (xxxiv. 4). The correction is equally necessary, with Ox. 1, 7, 9, &c.

The only objection to וַיֹּאמֶר (Gen. xxvii. 36; 1 Sam. xx. 29) is that Zaqeph is too far removed from Athnach. This the Massoretes saw, and appointed Pazer instead (Mas. to 2 Sam. xxiii. 17). For the same reason we must point וַיִּקָּבְצוּ הַמִּצְפָּתָה (1 Sam. vii. 6), with all Codd. that I have examined.

Early misprints, carefully preserved by subsequent editors, are אִתַּי בֶּן־רִיבַי מִגִּבְעַת בְּנֵי בִנְיָמִן (1 Sam. xi. 5); וַיֹּאמֶר שָׁאוּל מַה־לָּעָם כִּי יִבְכּוּ (1 Chr. xi. 31); מִן־בְּנֵי שִׁמְעוֹן גִּבּוֹרֵי חַיִל לַצָּבָא (xii. 25). One would have thought that the veriest tyro in the accentuation would have seen that Zaqeph alone can stand in these cases.

Many mistakes have been already corrected in Baer's texts, e.g. Gen. i. 11; Is. xxviii. 21; Esth. vii. 8.

---

[13] So it is better to point לֹא יַחֲלִיפֶנּוּ (Lev. xxvii. 10), with Erf. 1, 2, 4; Jequthiel, &c.

CHAPTER VII.

ZAQEPH

appears under two forms, Great and Little Zaqeph (p. 18). Great Zaqeph always stands *alone*.

In the present chapter we have to determine the rules for the division of Little Zaqeph's clause, which I shall call simply Zaqeph.

There may be *two* words (and no more) in Zaqeph's clause.

The rule for the foretone, as it shews itself before the leading accents, Silluq, Athnach, and S'gôlta, begins here to give way. It is only when Zaqeph's word is *long*[1], that the foretone Pashṭa[2] appears; otherwise, the servus (Munach) is employed. Contrast, for instance: וַיֹּאמֶר אַבְרָהָם (Gen. xxi. 24) and וַיֹּאמֶר (6); וְרִבְקָה אָמְרָה (xxvii. 5) and אַבְרָם (xv. 3); בְּזֹאת תֵּדְעוּן (Ex. vii. 17) and וּבְזֹאת תֵּדְעוּ (Num. xvi. 28); וָאֶבְחַר בְּדָוִד (2 Chr. vi. 6ª) and וָאֶבְחַר בִּירוּשָׁלִַם (6ᵇ). The musical principle that underlies these variations is not difficult to apprehend.

The rule for Munach is strictly carried out[3]; whereas that for Pashṭa is occasionally relaxed. Small words — particles, pronouns, and nouns in st. constr. — are sometimes found with Munach, instead of Pashṭa, as הִיא (Gen. ii. 13); לֹא (iii. 1); מִי (vii. 10); כִּי (xxi. 16; and often); בְּנֵי (Num. i. 28, 42; &c.); זֶה (Jer. xxxviii. 21); וְקוֹל (Ezek. xxvi. 13); אֲשֶׁר (2 Chr. xxx. 7); &c. Even longer words of frequent occurrence are joined in the same way, as וַיְחִי (Gen. v. 15); לְמַטֵּה (Num. xiii. 7, 9, 14; &c.); וְאַתָּה בֶן־אָדָם (Ezek. xxi. 19; xxxiii. 7[4]; &c.). But

---

[1] The technical meaning of a *long* word has been already explained, p. 62 note.
[2] It is understood that, when speaking of Pashṭa, I include Y'thîbh.
[3] The few exceptional cases in our texts may be all corrected by the testimony of Codd.: אֲרָיָן וְאֶת־אָהֳלִיבָמָה בַּת־עֲנָה (Gen. xxxvi. 2); וְאָדְרְכֶם בְּאַפִּי (Is. lxiii. 3); הֶעְשִׂיבֵי שִׂמְחִי (x. 8); וַיָּבֹאוּ פְלִשְׁתִּים (1 Chr. i. 43); בֶּלַע בֶּן־בְּעוֹר (Dan. v. 8); עָלָיו (xxv. 17). Baer has already corrected Is. xl. 6; lxvi. 24; Ezek. ix. 10; Hab. iii. 8. Other instances I have not noticed.
[4] See the Mas. parva to this passage, which fixes Munach.

all such forms occur also regularly pointed. So that here a certain license was allowed, and the punctators were at liberty in these unimportant matters to decide for themselves[5].

It is *only* when there are *two* words (and no more) in Zaqeph's clause that the above rules apply.

When there are more than two words, the following cases will occur:

I. The main dichotomy may come on the *first* word before Zaqeph, and will always be marked by Pashṭa[6], e.g. וַיִּקְרָ֨א לָא֤וֹר ׀ יוֹם֙ (iv. 7). הֲל֣וֹא אִם־תֵּיטִיב֮ שְׂאֵת֒ אֱלֹהִ֑ים (Gen. i. 5); See text passim.

II. The main dichotomy may come on the *second* word before Zaqeph,

1. And will still be most frequently marked by Pashṭa (with servus following): וַיַּ֣רְא אֱלֹהִים֙ אֶת־כָּל־אֲשֶׁ֣ר עָשָׂ֔ה (i. 31); וַיִּקַּ֣ח בֶּן־בָּקָ֗ר (ii. 10); לָ֤מָּה חָרָה֙ לָ֔ךְ (iv. 6); וְנָהָר֙ יֹצֵ֣א מֵעֵ֔דֶן (xviii. 7). רַ֣ךְ וָטוֹב֙ וַיִּתֵּ֣ן אֶל־הַנַּ֔עַר

2. But R'bhia is admissible (and is common enough), *if one of the following words be long*[7]. (Pashṭa will then appear on the intermediate word.) E.g. וַיַּ֣עַשׂ אֱלֹהִים֙ אֶת־חַיַּ֣ת הָאָ֔רֶץ (i. 25); שְׁלֹ֧שׁ מֵא֛וֹת אַמָּ֖ה אֹ֣רֶךְ וְאֶת־הַבְּהֵמָה֙ לְמִינָ֔הּ לְמִינָ֗הּ

---

[5] But this license in small matters is no justification for the mistakes of our texts in such passages as Lev. viii. 27; xiv. 52; Jos. xxi. 16; 1 Sam. x.18b; 2 Sam. xvii. 5; 2 Ki. i. 3b; Jer. xvii. 3; xxii. 23; Esth. ix. 25; Dan. i. 13; 1 Chr. xxiii. 19; xxv. 11, 13, 16; 2 Chr. xxviii. 3b; xxxiv. 14; all of which must be corrected with the concurrence of Codd.

[6] In Jer. xxvii. 9 we have in all our texts R'bhia! Point the second וְאַל with Pashṭa (so all Ox. Codd.) in accordance with II. 2. In Joel iv. 7 מֵעֵינָם must have (with correct texts) Zaqeph instead of R'bhia.

[7] The condition that Zaqeph's word, or that preceding, must be *long*, for R'bhia to appear, is carefully observed. Hence we may have R'bhia in בָּנֶ֗יךָ אִם־יִשְׁמְר֣וּ אֶת־דַּרְכָּם֙ לָלֶ֤כֶת בְּתוֹרָתִ֔י (2 Chr. vi. 16), because Zaqeph's word is long; but in אִם־יִשְׁמְר֨וּ בָנֶ֜יךָ אֶת־דַּרְכָּ֗ם לָלֶ֤כֶת לְפָנַי֙ (1 Ki. viii. 25), where both words are *short*, Pashṭa alone can be used. I have noticed only one exception: אֲשֶׁ֧ר אֲמָרְתִּ֛י אֶתְכֶ֖ן לְעֹלָ֑ם (Ex. xxxii. 13), comp. p. 62 note. In Lev. xxvi. 25 I point נָקָם, with Erf. 1, 3; Ox. 6, 16; and in Num. xxi. 6 אֵת, with Jequthiel, Norzi, &c.

וַיַּשְׁכֵּם אַבְרָהָם בַּבֹּקֶר וַיַּחֲבֹשׁ אֶת־חֲמֹרוֹ (vi. 15); הַתֵּבָה (xxii. 3); וַיֹּאמֶר הִשָּׁבְעָה לִּי (xlvii. 31).

We have here simply *musical variation*. Hence we may have the *same* expression pointed either way, with the full rhythmical cadence or not, e. g. אָבִי הִכְבִּיד אֶת־עֻלְּכֶם (2 Chr. x. 14) and אָבִי הִכְבִּיד אֶת־עֻלְּכֶם (1 Ki. xii. 14). This varying rhythmical cadence (though no one has observed the fact) runs through a great part of the accentual system. It is found with all the leading accents. We have already traced it before Athnach and Silluq; and shall notice it afterwards before S'gôlta and Tiphcha. (With R'bhia and the minor disjunctives it fails.)

III. The main dichotomy may come on the *third* word from Zaqeph.

1. R'bhia is usually employed and is very common. (Of course, Pashta must follow on the first or second word.) וְהָאָרֶץ הָיְתָה תֹהוּ וָבֹהוּ (Gen. i. 2); וַיִּקְרָא הָאָדָם שֵׁמוֹת לְכָל־הַבְּהֵמָה (ii. 20); וְהִשְׁמִיעַ יְהוָה אֶת־הוֹד קוֹלוֹ וְנַחַת וּלְעוֹף הַשָּׁמַיִם זְרוֹעוֹ יַרְאֶה (Is. xxx. 30).

2. Pashta is comparatively rare (although more frequent than Tiphcha on the third word before Athnach). Here the strict rule for the dichotomy again gives way: הָאִשָּׁה אֲשֶׁר נָתַתָּה עִמָּדִי (Gen. iii. 12); וַיְדַבֵּר יְהוָה אֶל־מֹשֶׁה לֵךְ עֲלֵה מִזֶּה (Ex. xxxiii. 1); לָכֵן הִנֵּה יָמִים בָּאִים (Jer. li. 47)[8]. In the same way, it is only occasionally that Pashta marks a *minor* dichotomy on the third word, under the heads following.

IV. But, when the main dichotomy comes on the *fourth* word or further, it is always marked by R'bhia. Here several cases arise:

1. There may be only *one* minor dichotomy, occurring on the first, second, or third word, and necessarily marked by Pashta[9]:

---

[8] The two words following Pashta are generally such as might be, and in Codd. often are, joined by Maqqeph. In four cases out of five, the first of them is אֲשֶׁר. It is to be observed that two servi cannot stand before Zaqeph, *without Pashta preceding.* Hence correct Ezek. xvi. 23 אוֹי אוֹי לָךְ (with Ox. 1, 13; Erf. 3).

[9] Unless R'bhia takes the place of Pashta on the second word, in accordance with II. 2, e. g. Judg. xiv. 19.

וַיֹּאמֶר אֱלֹהִים יִקָּווּ הַמַּיִם מִתַּחַת הַשָּׁמַיִם אֶל־מָקוֹם אֶחָד
וְלֹא הָיִית כְּעַבְדִּי דָוִד אֲשֶׁר שָׁמַר מִצְוֺתַי וַאֲשֶׁר (Gen. i. 9);
וַיְדַבְּרוּ אֵלָיו אֵת (1 Ki. xiv. 8); הָלַךְ אַחֲרַי בְּכָל־לְבָבוֹ
כָּל־דִּבְרֵי יוֹסֵף אֲשֶׁר דִּבֶּר אֲלֵהֶם (Gen. xlv. 27).

2. There may be *two* or *more* minor dichotomies, requiring to be marked between R'bhîa and Zaqeph. Such cases necessitate the *repetition* of R'bhîa—just as Zaqeph itself is *repeated*, for the like purpose, before Silluq and Athnach—and that as often as is needful, till we come to the last dichotomy, accented as above.
Thus we have *two* R'bhîas in אָנָה ׀ אֲנַחְנוּ עֹלִים אַחֵינוּ הֵמַסּוּ אֶת־לְבָבֵנוּ לֵאמֹר עַם גָּדוֹל וָרָם מִמֶּנּוּ (Deut. i. 28); וַנִּסַּע מֵחֹרֵב וַנֵּלֶךְ אֵת כָּל־הַמִּדְבָּר הַגָּדוֹל וְהַנּוֹרָא הַהוּא אֲשֶׁר רְאִיתֶם דֶּרֶךְ הַר הָאֱמֹרִי (i. 19); וַיֹּאמֶר יַעַן אֲשֶׁר עָבְרוּ הַגּוֹי הַזֶּה אֶת־בְּרִיתִי אֲשֶׁר צִוִּיתִי אֶת־אֲבוֹתָם (Judg. ii. 20); and *three* R'bhîas in 1 Ki. iii. 11 and 1 Chr. xiii. 2.

But this rule undergoes modification. It is a musical law that when R'bhîa is to be repeated, *there must be three words or more* (i. e. a sufficient melody) *between the two R'bhîas*[10]. Where this is not the case, the second R'bhîa is *transformed*, and Pashṭa

---

[10] The rule is simple enough, and should not have given so much trouble to accentuologists. Luzzatto (Torath emeth, p. 63 ff.) sets to work to *count the syllables* between the two R'bhîas. But this is mere trifling, and leads to no result; as he himself would have found out, if he had examined a sufficient number of examples. The fact is, there is here, as elsewhere, common ground, on which the two accents meet. Thus, whilst in the great majority of cases, where only *three* words intervene, Pashṭa takes the place of R'bhîa, in some twenty instances R'bhîa maintains its position (see Lev. xxii. 3; Deut. i. 28; iv. 9, 19; xvii. 8; Jer. iv. 30; &c.). On the other hand, R'bhîa is far more common where *four* words come between, and Pashṭa appears only in Deut. iii. 21; 2 Sam. ix. 7; Jer. xxiv. 8ᵇ; xxxviii. 12; 2 Chr. i. 11. When there are *less than three* words, Pashṭa alone can be employed. Hence Judg. xv. 14 must be corrected by introducing the Munach-melody אֲשֶׁר (with Ox. and Erff. Codd.); and Pashṭa must come for R'bhîa in Jer. xix. 13ᵇ and 2 Chr. xxx. 6ᵇ. When there are *more than four* words, R'bhîa must stand. 1 Ki. xiv. 21 (2 Chr. xii. 13) therefore needs

put in its stead. Thus, with two R'bhias due: בַּיּוֹם הַזֶּה
(נִבְקְעוּ) נִבְקְעוּ כָּל־מַעְיְנוֹת תְּהוֹם רַבָּה (Gen. vii. 11, not
וַיֹּאמֶר אֵלָיו הָאֱלֹהִים בַּחֲלֹם גַּם אָנֹכִי יָדַעְתִּי כִּי בְתָם־לְבָבְךָ
עָשִׂיתָ זֹּאת (xx. 6, not יָדַעְתִּי). Comp. iii. 22; xxx. 15ᵇ; Is. i.
7ᵇ; iii. 16, 24; Jer. xx. 3ᵇ; Ezek. x. 1; &c. Examples of this
transformation are (as we should expect) much more numerous
than those in which R'bhia remains.

Three R'bhias are often due, but in only two passages (given
above) do they all stand. Either the two first are found, the
third being changed to Pashṭa: וַיַּעֲלוּ אֵלֶיהָ סַרְנֵי פְלִשְׁתִּים
וַיֹּאמְרוּ לָהּ פַּתִּי אוֹתוֹ וּרְאִי בַּמֶּה כֹּחוֹ גָדוֹל (Judg. xvi. 5);
וַתִּבָּקַע הָעִיר וְכָל־אַנְשֵׁי הַמִּלְחָמָה יִבְרְחוּ וַיֵּצְאוּ מֵהָעִיר לַיְלָה
דֶּרֶךְ שַׁעַר בֵּין־הַחֹמֹתַיִם אֲשֶׁר עַל־גַּן הַמֶּלֶךְ (Jer. lii. 7). Or,
the *second* R'bhia is changed into Pashṭa, the *third* always
maintaining its position ¹¹, e.g. וַיַּעַן יִצְחָק וַיֹּאמֶר לְעֵשָׂו הֵן

---

correction, and we must either point שָׁם (Ox. 7, 68), or מִפָּל־ with Maqqeph (Ox.
13, 16, 72, &c.).

Does any one ask: What is the difference between counting the words and
counting the syllables? I answer: A certain number of *words* means a certain
melody, which makes all the difference in the world.

¹¹ We come then to the curious result that Pashṭa (as the representative of the
R'bhia, which it has displaced) is a *greater disjunctive* than the R'bhia which
follows. Had the *second* and *third* R'bhias been *both* changed into Pashṭa, we
should have had, with the foretone to Silluq, *three* Pashṭas following one
another, which would doubtless have been unmusical. (This concurrence is
condemned by all Jewish writers on the accents.) Hence the first of three
Pashṭas in 1 Ki. viii. 25 (2 Chr. vi. 16) must be corrected to Azla, לַעֲבָדְּךָ.
Y'thibh and two Pashṭas are as bad. Correct יַעַן (2 Ki. x. 30) and לְכָל־עַמָּא
(Ezra vii. 25).

Two Pashṭas often come together. But then the first is always due to transformation, and *R'bhia must precede*. Observe how וַיָּבֹאוּ וַיַּעַמְדוּ בִּתְעָלַת הַבְּרֵכָה
הָעֶלְיוֹנָה (2 Ki. xviii. 17) becomes changed into וַיַּעֲמֹד בִּתְעָלַת (Is. xxxvi. 2),
when וַיָּבֹאוּ is dropped. Hence such careless mistakes as occur in Cant. i. 16
(point הִנְּךָ with Azla); Ezra vi. 8ᵇ (point מִלְּפָא); 1 Chr. vi. 17 לִפְנֵי with Azla);
1 Chr. xxi. 17ᵇ (אֱלֹהַי); 23 וַיֹּאמֶר with Azla); 2 Chr. vi. 13ᵇ (צָלְיוֹ); and xvi. 12
(שִׂגְדֹּנָם), must be at once corrected.

(Gen. xxvii. 37); גְּבִיר שַׂמְתִּיו לָךְ וְאֶת־כָּל־אֶחָיו נָתַתִּי לוֹ לַעֲבָדִים

(Ex. xxxii. 1); וַיִּקָּהֵל הָעָם עַל־אַהֲרֹן וַיֹּאמְרוּ אֵלָיו קוּם ׀ עֲשֵׂה־לָנוּ

עַמִּי זְכָר־נָא אֱלֹהִים אֲשֶׁר יֵלְכוּ לְפָנֵינוּ

(Mic. vi. 5) [13]. מַה־יָּעַץ בָּלָק מֶלֶךְ מוֹאָב [12]

There are but three examples, where R'bhîa is due *four* times, viz. 2 Sam. xiv. 7; 1 Ki. ii. 24; 1 Chr. xiii. 2; and only one, with R'bhîa due *five* times, Ezra vii. 25.

Servi of Zaqeph.

Great Zaqeph has no servus.

Little Zaqeph may have *one* or *two* servi, both of which will be Munachs (as we term them). Properly, as all careful writers on the accents lay down [14], the servus, when there is only *one*, is M'kharbel (p. 23), if it comes on the *first* letter of the word, as רֵעַ; and 'Illûy, if it comes on any other letter, as וְרֵעַ. With *two* servi, the first is always M'kharbel, the second 'Illûy.

Rules for Munach and M'thîga in the same word with Little Zaqeph; and for Great Zaqeph [15].

We have once more to deal with musical variations (see p. 18).

1. If Zaqeph stands without its servus (Munach) in the previous word, this servus may take the place of Métheg [16] in the same word

---

[12] In this example note how the R'bhîas and Pashṭas come from syntactical division in *successive* words. So also in 1 Sam. v. 8; Zech. iv. 12; &c.

[13] Of the many examples that come under this head, fully a third are falsely pointed in our texts. See Corrigenda. In 1 Chr. v. 21, the first R'bhîa, on which the whole chain of the accentuation depends, has been changed to T'lisha! and yet none of our modern editors has thought of correcting.

[14] See e. g. Ben-Bil. Mishp. hat. 13.

[15] For these rules, I have found nothing satisfactory in any treatise on the Accents. Heidenheim, in Mishp. hat. 13, 14, is inaccurate and incomplete. His texts shew that he had no clear ideas on the subject.

[16] It is understood, the *light* Métheg, for the heavy Métheg (Ga'ya) does not admit of such substitution. Hence Munach cannot come in לְוַרְעָם (Ex. xxxii. 13) or אֶת־הַחֲלָיִם (Num. viii. 6). On the distinction between the two Méthegs, and the rules for their employment, see Baer in Merx' Archiv, i. pp. 57 ff. and 194 ff., or Ges., Heb. Gr., § 16. 2.

with Zaqeph, only not on the *first letter*[17], e. g. אֶל־הָאִשָּׁה (Gen. iii. 1, but הָאִשָּׁה, ver. 13); וַיֵּרְעוּ (iii. 7); וַיֹּאמְרוּ (xviii. 5); וְנִחַלְתָּ֫ (Deut. ix. 26); מִנַּאֲקָתָם (Judg. ii. 18); בַּלֵּיחִי (Is. xxvi. 14)[18].

EXCEPTIONS. Forms like וַיַּעֲשׂוּ (Deut. xxxiv. 9), and וְנֶחְטָּא (Is. lxiv. 4), retain the Métheg[19]. (It would seem that the short vowels, Pathach and S'gôl, so near to the tone, have not strength enough for the accent.) On the other hand, in מִמָּחֳרָת (Gen. xix. 34, and often); אֶל־נָעֳמִי (Ruth iv. 14), owing to the notion of Jewish grammarians that the Qāmeṣ is long[20], Munach appears.

When the foretone Pashṭa comes in the word immediately preceding, no further musical change is introduced, but when Zaqeph's word stands *alone*, and Munach (according to the rule just given) is not admissible, one or other of the following changes takes place:

2. If there is a closed syllable in the word, separated by one or more others—or, at least, by vocal Sh'va—from the tone-syllable, an emphatic intonation (a *high* tone, as the position of its sign above the word implies) was introduced, serving as a forebeat (*Vorschlag*) to Zaqeph, in the absence of the foretone. It was known as מְתִיגָה[21], being like an upper Métheg (comp. the use of the term in the accentuation

---

[17] See Chayyug, p. 127, l. 28, and Qimchi, טעם סופר, p. לב, l. 16. The musical reader may perhaps see the reason for this restriction. Ordinary texts indeed often place the servus under the *first* letter, and even the Mas. parva is wrong at 2 Ki. ii. 11, אֱלֹיָּהוּ ב' בטעם.

[18] Our texts, of course, need constant correction. They omit the Munach where it is due, introduce it when it stands already in the previous word, &c. Even the Massoretes have not always been as correct as we should have expected. Thus, at מִפְּנֵיהָאֵל (Gen. xxxv. 16) we have the rubric: ג' בטעם שופר, when there are really *six* instances that require to be so pointed, viz. Gen. xxxv. 16; Jos. viii. 17; 1 Ki. xii. 32 (*bis*); xiii. 4; Am. vii. 13. (In the last passage, Baer's correction cannot stand. It is against the syntactical division and Codd.) And again, in the Mas. finalis, p. 17, בתרי טעמי ג', הַבָּתִּים, to the three examples given we must add a fourth, 2 Chr. xxxiv. 11.

[19] This punctuation for the derivatives of עָשָׂה is fixed by the Mas. fin., p. 51 (comp. Dikd. hat., § 35). Analogy decides for the kindred forms. Codd. and printed texts have, however, constantly Munach in such forms. Hence has arisen a false Mas. given at Num. xxvi. 44 (more fully by Jequthiel at ver. 17), which assigns the following accentuation to לְרַעֲבָן, ver. 40.

[20] See Preface to Baer's edition of Job, p. vi.

[21] Mishp. hat. 13[b]. It would further appear that it was in reality a kind of Métheg (i. e. heavy Métheg = Ga'ya), the difference being that it gave a more marked *musical* expression to the syllable than Ga'ya would have done (Ben-Naphtali has Ga'ya. We thus see that it is only in syllables that admit of Ga'ya, that

of the three Books, טעמי אמ״ת, p. 70). Properly, like Munach, it is *non-initial*, yet the tendency is to place it (on musical grounds) as near to the beginning of the word as possible, and under certain conditions it is found on the *first* letter. The following examples exhibit it in its ordinary position: וְאַבְרָהָם (Gen. xviii. 18); וְהִתְקַדִּשְׁתֶּם (Lev. xx. 7); וְכָל־יִשְׂרָאֵל (Deut. xiii. 12); הַנַּסְתָּרֹת (xxix. 28); וְאֶתְּנָה (Gen. xxxiv. 12); שְׁמָר־לְךָ (Ex. xxxiv. 11) [22].

Initial M'thiga is due to *transposition*:

(a) In forms like אֶת־עָרְלְךָ (Deut. iii. 24); וַיְפַשְּׂחוּ (1 Ki. xviii. 26); וַיִּשְׁמְעוּ (Ezra iv. 1), &c., M'thiga is transposed to the first syllable, to cancel the Ga'ya (לבטול הגעיא as Jewish grammarians express it [23]) which is due there [24]. Ga'ya and M'thiga, from the similarity of their character (see note 21), could not come together.

(β) But Ben-Asher and his school went further. If Ga'ya was only *admissible* in certain forms, on the first syllable, they equally transposed to it the M'thiga, which we should have expected to find on the second syllable. So I explain such cases as וּבְחַטֹּאותָיו (1 Ki. xv. 34); וּפְקֻדָּתָם (Is. xv. 7); וּדְבַר־יְהוָה (2 Ki. xx. 4); and אֶל־הַמָּקוֹם (Gen. xix. 27); מִן־הַשָּׂדֶה (Lev. xxv. 12); אֶת־הַדְּבָרִים (Ex. xxxiv. 1) [25]. It is only in the above forms that I have found this transposition.

---

this sign can appear). The musical value we learn from Ben-Bil.'s statement, l. c., that M'thiga comes before Zaqeph, לתיקון הנגינה, 'for the right ordering of the melody;' and in the present day it has a distinct melody assigned to it in the chanting (although whether it is correctly rendered is another question). The old grammarians had however no idea of any musical relationship between it and Pashṭa or Azla, which it resembles in form.

The sign has a variety of names. The most common is מקל, 'stroke.' Grammarians, who wrote in Arabic, term it هَمْز (see טעמי אמ״ת, p. 112, and Ginsb. iii. p. 51) from همز, *impulit*, in reference to the impulse of the voice in the intonation. Hence doubtless the name דרבן, 'goad,' = مهماز (Man. du Lect., p. 77 infra). Qimchi (עט סופר, p. לב) calls it מראה מקום, 'indicator,' and by a name taken from the form, פשט קטן, 'little Pashṭa.' The name in modern use, Qadma = Azla, is similarly derived and equally incorrect.

[22] It will not be expected that I should point out the mistakes of our texts. The matter is not of sufficient importance. Even Baer is not always consistent.

[23] See e. g. Mishp. hat. 14ᵃ supra.

[24] That this is Ben-Asher's pointing may be seen from the חלופים to Lev. xxv. 37; Deut. iii. 24. On the rule for Ga'ya in the examples given, see Merx' Archiv, i. p. 197.

[25] Comp. Ben-Asher's pointing in the חלופים to Deut. x. 2. That Ga'ya is admissible, although irregular, in such cases, may be seen from examples cited in Mishp. hat. 58ᵃ, and by Baer in Merx' Archiv, i. p. 201. Ben-Naphtali has it always.

3. When Zaqeph stands *alone, and neither Munach nor M'thiga is admissible* (according to rules 1 and 2) *in its word*, it takes the form and melody of GREAT ZAQEPH, e. g. וְעֵ֔ץ (Gen. ii. 9); וַיֹּ֕אמֶר (iii. 10); וְחֵרִשֹׁ֔ת (v. 6); וַאֲבִימֶ֔לֶךְ (xx. 4); הַכּוּזָ֔נָה (xxxiv. 31); וַיְדַעְתֶּ֔ם (Ex. xvi. 6); וַיַּעֲבֹ֔ר (Gen. xxxii. 23); בְּבָעֲשׁ֔וֹ (1 Ki. xv. 30); וְלַעֲשׂ֔וֹת (2 Chr. vii. 17); מֵאַחֲרֵ֔י (xxxiv. 33).

Punctators and editors (even the best) exhibit the utmost confusion in the employment of this accent, pointing the *same form*, and frequently even the *same word*, sometimes with Little, sometimes with Great Zaqeph! And yet the rule above given is simple enough. It will be necessary therefore to correct such instances as [26] וְלִהַבְדִּ֔יל (Gen. i. 18); וְיַעֲקֹ֔ב (xxxi. 47); הָאֲזֹרָ֔ח (Lev. xvi. 29); אַל־תַּעֲלִ֔י (Num. xiv. 42); וַיֵּעָ֔נוּ (Josh. i. 16); וַיַּעֲשׂ֔וּ (2 Sam. xxi. 14); וּבְנֻ֔הַ (Is. i. 30); לְמַעֲנִ֔י (xxxvii. 35); וַיְמַהֲרוּ (lix. 7); וְרָאִ֔יתָ וְקָרָ֔אתָ (Jer. li. 61); אַל־יֵרְע֔וֹ (Jon. iii. 7); in all of which, and other similar examples, *Great Zaqeph must appear*.

Corrigenda in Zaqeph's clause.

1. Where three R'bhias are due, and the second has been transformed to Pashṭa, punctators—misled by the usual consecution of R'bhia, Pashṭa, and Zaqeph—have frequently changed the third R'bhia into Zaqeph, and this false accentuation has passed into our texts. Thus R'bhia must be restored to its rights[27] in הַתּוֹרָ֗ה (Josh. i. 7), with Ox. 1, 5, 7, 8;—הָאָ֗רֶץ (Judg. ii. 1), Ox. 10, 2322, 2323, 2328;—נִשָּׂ֗א (1 Sam. x. 3), Ox. 1, 5, 6, 8;—וְנַעַבְרָ֗ה (xiv. 6), Ox. 1, 5, 6, 8;—ע֗וֹד (xxviii. 15), Ox. 5, 6, 10, 15;—וַיֹּ֗אמֶר (2 Sam. xv. 2), Ox. 12, 92, 2322;—בֵּ֗ית (1 Ki. v. 17), Ox. 6, 7, 10; Bomb. 2;—עֹמְדִ֗ים (xii. 6; 2 Chr. x. 6), Ox. 5, 6,

---

[26] וְלִהַבְדִּ֔יל is found in Ox. 5, 21, 35; Harl. 1528; Or. 1379; Add. 4709; &c. I give ample MS. authority here, because this is the example which has misled writers on the accents from Qimchi's time (עץ סופר, p. לב) downwards. Finding the word falsely accented in their texts, and contrasting it with לְהַבְדִּיל, ver. 14, they jumped to the conclusion that Métheg was the cause of Little Zaqeph, *without considering the numberless instances in which Métheg (even when it occurs twice in the word) exercises no such influence.*

[27] As the accentuation is wrong in only *one word*, I have not thought it worth while to quote the passages at length. The student will doubtless look them up for himself, and observe how the sense requires the correction in each case. The testimony of more Codd. might have been given had it been necessary.

7, 8;—הָעֲלִיָּה (1 Ki. xvii. 19), Ox. 7; Par. 30, 89; K. 182;—אֵלָיו (xxi. 4), Ox. 1, 6, 13, 15;—הָאֲנָשִׁים (2 Ki. x. 24), Ox. 1, 76, 2322, 2323;—עֹמֵד (1 Chr. xxi. 16), Ox. 4, 9, 11; Erf. 3;—עֻזִּיָּהוּ (2 Chr. xxvi. 18), Ox. 4, 9, 12, 15;—לִדְרֹשׁ (xxxii. 31), Ox. 1, 9, 11; Erf. 3;—and לְמַהֵר (xxxiv. 3), Ox. 4, 5, 9, 11. Baer has already corrected Gen. i. 11; xvii. 19; Ezek. xliii. 7; xlvii. 8; Qoh. ix. 9; Esth. vii. 8; Dan. vii. 19 [28].

The same mistake shews itself, but not so frequently, in the change of *Pashṭa* into Zaqeph, with R'bhîa and Pashṭa preceding. So we must correct צְרוּעָה (1 Ki. xi. 26), with Ox. 1, 7, 10; Erf. 2;—וּבְיַד הַמֶּלֶךְ (2 Ki. xi. 17), Ox. 5, 8, 10, 12;—and מִכָּל־חַטֹּאתָו (Ezek. xviii. 21), Ox. 1, 7; Erf. 2, 3.

2. Another frequent source of error is the confusion between Azla and Pashṭa in Zaqeph's clause [29]. The student need never scruple to put the one for the other, where a change is necessary, e. g. בָּחַר (Deut. xxxii. 50); אֲבָל (1 Ki. xii. 11); נָקֵל (Is. xlix. 6); וְלִבִּי (Qoh. vii. 25). Compare the corrections, p. 79, note 11.

3. The blunders of Van der Hooght's text, copied without scruple by Theile, Hahn, and J. D'Allemand (whose texts are unfortunately in common use with students), are often under this head most provoking. Thus Zaqeph is substituted for Gersháyim, and vice versa! מִן־הַיּוֹם (Num. xv. 23) for מִן־הַיּוֹם; and see other instances in Is. xii. 4; Ezek. xxiii. 43; xxiv. 27; xl. 49; Neh. v. 9; 2 Chr. xvi. 1; xxxv. 15. In Josh. xi. 8, Gersháyim is *repeated* (the second time for R'bhîa)! In Judg. xiii. 8ᵇ and 2 Chr. xxv. 23ᵇ, it divides Zaqeph's (for R'bhîa's) clause! And in Jer. i. 1ᵇ, Ṭiphcha (instead of Pashṭa) is made to divide Zaqeph's clause! These are specimens of the egregious mistakes which, once introduced into a text regarded as standard, have been preserved with religious care by subsequent editors, who have not taken the trouble of consulting the far more correct and reliable text (founded on a careful collation of MSS.), brought out soon after Van der Hooght's, by a much more competent scholar, J. H. Michaelis.

---

[28] Luzzatto pointed out the errors in most of the above passages, Torath emeth, p. 63 ff.; but was not able always to adduce MS. authority for his emendations. No other writer on the accents—Spitzner, Ewald, &c.—had been at the pains of tracing out and drawing attention to these manifest mistakes.

[29] So Ginsburg, in his edition of the Massora, constantly confounds them.

CHAPTER VIII.

S'GÔLTA.

THIS accent must, on musical grounds, be always preceded by its foretone, Zarqa[1].

It cannot therefore stand on the *first* word of the verse. When due there (according to the notions of the accentuators), it gives place to Shalshéleth (p. 17). Yet there are only seven words, in which this substitution takes place: וַיִּתְמַהְמָהּ׀ (Gen. xix. 16); וַיֹּאמֶר׀ (xxiv. 12); וַיְמָאֵן׀ (xxxix. 8); וַיִּשְׁחָט׀ (Lev. viii. 23); וְנִבְהֲלוּ׀ (Is. xiii. 8); וַיֹּאמֶר׀ (Am. i. 2); וַאֲמַר־לֵהּ׀ (Ezra v. 15)[2].

Why, one naturally asks, a special sign for just these few (mostly unimportant) instances? There was no *necessity* for its introduction at all. For if we examine the passages, and compare the rules (p. 73) for the interchange of S'gôlta and Zaqeph, we shall see that *Zaqeph might have stood in every case*. When, instead of employing Zaqeph, the accentuators chose to introduce a new accent, it must have been because they designed to attach a *special meaning* to the passages in question,—to which they sought to draw attention by a peculiar melody and a peculiar sign[3]. That meaning has, however, as in other similar cases, been lost. Not that the loss is a serious one. For we may be sure that we should have had some fanciful Midrash explanation, which we can well afford to dispense with[4].

---

[1] It is also invariably followed by Athnach,—another proof (if further proof were needed) of its *dependence* on Athnach. In Job i. 8 and Ezra vii. 13 Athnach is wanting; but here S'gôlta has been wrongly placed, and must be changed into Athnach (see Baer's notes).

[2] See Mas. to Lev. viii. 23.

[3] No other explanation seems possible. For note the strange selection! *Three* out of the seven words are forms of אמר, and how often does this verb stand at the beginning of the verse! Note too that *emphatic* words in this position,—as וְקִדַּשְׁתּוֹ (Lev. xxi. 8); וְהִקְהַלְתָּ (Deut. xi. 28),—which, if a special accent was to be employed, had a claim to be marked by it, are passed over! There seems also something fanciful in the very *number* of the passages selected, four from the Tora, two from the Prophets, and one from the K'thubhim,—making up the sacred number seven!

[4] Such as is given in the Midrash לקח טוב on Gen. xxxix. 8: וַיְמָאֵן מיאון אחר מיאון הרבה פעמים, דכתיב בסמך ובשלשלת; or such as I found assigned to Jehuda Hasîd in Zalman the punctator's treatise on the accents (Par. 5), where, speaking of Shalshéleth, he says: בכל מקום שהיא בא מרבר הענין ממלאך בסירוש או במדרש, בשמו רבינו יהודה חסיר, i. e. there is a reference to an angel (!) either direct or implied.

I have only one point of interest to mention in connection with this accent. The Mas. to Lev. viii. 15 runs thus[5]: יֵ״א זוגין מן תרין בענין קדמא רביע תני׳ זקף וסי׳ הַסּוֹבֵב (Gen. ii. 11) הַסּוֹבֵב (ii. 13) וַיִּשְׁחָט (Lev. viii. 15) וַיִּשְׁחָט וכו׳ (viii. 23) (i. e. eleven groups of two words each in the same section, the first with R'bhia, the second with Zaqeph, &c.). N.B. The Shalshéleth in Lev. viii. 23 is here put under the general category of *Zaqeph*. We see then that the Massoretes well understood, not only that S'gôlta is the representative of Zaqeph, but that Shalshéleth, which takes the place of S'gôlta, is equally so[6]. I have already (p. 71) drawn attention to the importance of this rubric. How is it that no writer on the accents has taken notice of it?

When there are only *two* words in S'gôlta's clause, Zarqa necessarily comes on the first, וַיֹּאמֶר הָאָדָם (Gen. ii. 23).

When the clause consists of *three* or *more* words, the following cases will occur. (Here we have only to substitute Zarqa for Pashṭa, and we have a mere repetition of the rules already laid down for the division of Zaqeph's clause):

I. The main dichotomy may be on the *first* word before S'gôlta, and will then be always marked by Zarqa: וַיַּעַשׂ וְהִנֵּה יְהוָה נִצָּב עָלָיו וַיֹּאמַר (Gen. i. 7); אֱלֹהִים אֶת־הָרָקִיעַ (xxviii. 13).

II. The main dichotomy may come on the *second* word,

1. And will be still generally marked by Zarqa, e. g. הַנְּפִלִים וְאָכַל פְּרִי בְהֶמְתְּךָ וּפְרִי (Gen. vi. 4); הָיוּ בָאָרֶץ בַּיָּמִים הָהֵם אַדְמָתְךָ עַד הִשָּׁמְדָךְ (Deut. xxviii. 51).

2. But R'bhia is admissible *if one, or both, of the following words be long* (Zarqa then coming on the first word), e. g. הַמַּלְאָךְ הַגֹּאֵל אֹתִי מִכָּל־רָע יְבָרֵךְ אֶת־הַנְּעָרִים (Gen. xlviii. 16); הַשֹּׁלֵחַ בַּיָּם צִירִים וּבִכְלֵי־גֹמֶא עַל־פְּנֵי־מַיִם (Is. xviii. 2). See also Ex. xxxvi. 2; Num. xxi. 5; xxiii. 3; Deut. i. 41; iv. 39; Jer. iii. 25; xviii. 21; xxxi. 8, 9.

---

[5] Comp. אכלה ואכלה, § 227.

[6] Ginsburg, ט, § 234, copying from a false text (when correct texts without number were available), or himself introducing an unwarrantable correction, has pointed וַיִּשְׁחָט, in direct opposition to the Mas. he gives directly after, § 236! Even were Zaqeph due, it must be Great Zaqeph.

III. The main dichotomy may be on the *third* word.

1. R'bhîa is usually employed to mark it, and is very common (Zarqa following on the first or second word): הַעִידֹ֣תִי בָכֶ֡ם (Deut. iv. 26); הַיּ֨וֹם אֶת־הַשָּׁמַ֜יִם וְאֶת־הָאָ֗רֶץ כִּֽי־אָבֹ֤ד תֹּֽאבֵדוּן֙ מַהֵ֔ר (Is. liii. 12). לָכֵ֞ן אֲחַלֶּק־ל֣וֹ בָרַבִּ֗ים וְאֶת־עֲצוּמִים֙ יְחַלֵּ֣ק שָׁלָ֔ל

2. Zarqa occurs (like Pashṭa before Zaqeph), but is comparatively rare, כִּ֣י לֹ֤א מוּעָף֙ לַאֲשֶׁ֣ר מוּצָ֣ק לָ֔הּ (Is. viii. 23); see Gen. iii. 14; Ex. xxviii. 27; Deut. xii. 1; Am. ix. 14; Neh. ix. 32.

So it is only occasionally that Zarqa marks the *minor* dichotomy on the third word, under the following heads.

IV. When the main dichotomy is on the *fourth* word or *further*, it is always marked by R'bhîa [7].

1. The minor dichotomy may be on the first, second, or third word, and is necessarily marked by Zarqa, e. g. זָכ֞וֹר אֶת־י֤וֹם הַשַּׁבָּת֙ לְקַדְּשׁ֔וֹ שֵׁ֤שֶׁת יָמִים֙ תַּֽעֲבֹ֔ד וְעָשִׂ֖יתָ כָּל־מְלַאכְתֶּֽךָ (Ex. xx. 8, 9); י֗וֹם אֲשֶׁ֨ר עָמַ֜דְתָּ לִפְנֵ֨י יְהוָ֤ה אֱלֹהֶ֨יךָ֙ בְּחֹרֵ֔ב (Deut. iv. 10); וַיֹּ֣אמְר֔וּ מָ֚ה הָֽאָשָׁם֙ אֲשֶׁ֣ר נָשִׁ֣יב ל֔וֹ (1 Sam. vi. 4).

2. There may be *two* minor dichotomies. Here R'bhîa has to be *repeated* (as before Zaqeph), e. g. וַיֹּ֣אמֶר הַכֹּהֵ֗ן חֶ֣רֶב גָּלְיָ֣ת הַפְּלִשְׁתִּ֡י אֲשֶׁר־הִכִּ֣יתָ ׀ בְּעֵ֪מֶק הָאֵלָ֟ה הִנֵּה־הִ֞יא לוּטָ֣ה בַשִּׂמְלָה֮ אַחֲרֵ֣י הָאֵפוֹד֒ (1 Sam. xxi. 10); and so in Ex. xx. 3–5 [8]; Deut. v. 7–9 [8]; 1 Ki. ix. 9; Dan. iii. 15; v. 23; 2 Chr. vii. 22.—Or, Pashṭa comes instead of the second R'bhîa (under the same conditions as with Zaqeph, pp. 78, 79): וַיֹּ֣אמֶר הָעָ֞ם אֶל־שָׁא֗וּל הֲֽיוֹנָתָ֤ן ׀ יָמוּת֙ אֲשֶׁ֣ר עָ֠שָׂה הַיְשׁוּעָ֨ה הַגְּדוֹלָ֣ה הַזֹּאת֮ בְּיִשְׂרָאֵל֒ (1 Sam. xiv. 45). Comp. Deut. xii. 18; Josh. xviii. 14; 2 Sam. iii. 8; 1 Ki. xii. 10; xviii. 21.

---

[7] Marked falsely with Zaqeph in our texts, 1 Sam. xi. 11; 2 Chr. xiv. 7.

[8] According to טעם העליון. Ex. xx. 2 and Deut. v. 6 must not be included in S'gôlta's clause, but pointed with the *single* accentuation (as in many Codd. and by Heidenheim in his edition of עין הקורא). The dichotomy marked with Zaqeph, as in our texts, is impossible.

Where, however, Pashṭa would come *close* to Zarqa—i. e. adjoining it, or with only one word between—it is changed into Zarqa (of course only on musical grounds), and Zarqa appears *repeated*[9]: וַיְהִי ׀ בַּחֲצִ֓י הַלַּ֗יְלָה וַיהוָה֙ הִכָּ֣ה כָל־בְּכוֹר֮ בְּאֶ֣רֶץ מִצְרַ֗יִם (Ex. xii. 29); וַיָּ֥קָם דָּוִד֮ וַיָּבֹ֒א אֶל־הַמָּקוֹם֮ אֲשֶׁ֣ר חָנָה־שָׁ֣ם שָׁא֒וּל (1 Sam. xxvi. 5). Comp. Gen. xlii. 21; 2 Ki. i. 6; vii. 13; Is. xx. 2; xlv. 14; Jer. xxi. 4; Job i. 5; &c.[10]

3. There is only one passage in which *three* minor dichotomies occur[11], and for this isolated case a peculiar accentuation was fixed,—*three* Zarqas follow one another: וַיְדַבֵּ֣ר אֵלָ֗יו כֹּֽה־אָמַ֣ר יְהוָ֡ה יַ֠עַן אֲשֶׁר־שָׁלַ֣חְתָּ מַלְאָכִים֮ לִדְרֹשׁ֒ בְּבַ֣עַל זְב֗וּב אֱלֹהֵ֣י עֶקְר֔וֹן (2 Ki. i. 16). The regular accentuation would have been מַלְאָכִים֮ לִדְרֹשׁ֒, as in similar cases under Zaqeph. Verse 6 might have been accented in the same way.

Servi of S'gôlta.

S'gôlta may have (like Zaqeph) one or two servi, both 'Illûys (Mishp. hat. 32), or, as we term them, Munachs. See examples above.

Corrigenda.

It has been already mentioned that in Job i. 8, and Ezra vii. 13, S'gôlta must be changed into Athnach. For the former passage, *all Codd.* (as far as I have observed) are right; for the latter, *not a single one!*[12] Even Ben-Asher's famous Codex at Aleppo is wrong.

S'gôlta stands on the wrong word in Josh. x. 28 and 2 Chr. vii. 5. Point the former וַיַּכֶּ֣הָ לְפִי־חֶ֗רֶב וְאֶת־מַלְכָּהּ֙ הֶחֱרִ֣ם אוֹתָ֔ם וגו׳, with almost all Codd.; and the latter וַיִּזְבַּ֣ח הַמֶּ֗לֶךְ שְׁלֹמֹה֙ אֶת־זֶ֣בַח הַבָּקָ֔ר וגו׳, with Ox. 1, 4, 9; Erf. 1, 3; &c.

---

[9] Comp. the change of Great R'bhîa into Ṣinnor (Zarqa), under similar circumstances, in the accentuation of the three Books, p. 56.—But Zarqa cannot be repeated, unless R'bhîa precedes. Hence גַּם (1 Sam. ii. 15) must be changed into גַּ֥ם or גַּ֛ם, with various Codd., although Ben-Bil. (Mishp. hat. 7ᵇ) supports it. On Is. xlv. 1, see Notes at end.

[10] In Lev. xvii. 5; Josh. xxii. 5; 2 Chr. xxiii. 18, Maqqeph has fallen out after אֲשֶׁר, and in 2 Chr. xxxv. 24 after עַל. In 2 Ki. iv. 13 we must point R'bhîa for the first Zarqa, וַיֹּ֥אמֶר ל֛וֹ אֱמָר־נָ֣א אֵלֶ֗יהָ (so Ox. 31, 68; De R. 2).

[11] With Zaqeph (as we have seen) there are many such instances. The reason of the difference is that Zaqeph constantly divides Athnach's clause *near* to Athnach, whereas S'gôlta's proper place is *at a distance* from Athnach, with a shorter clause between it and the beginning of the verse.

[12] Baer indeed names one Codex, but the Athnach there is due to a second, and apparently quite modern, hand.

CHAPTER IX.

TIPHCHA.

TIPHCHA's word often stands alone, as בְּרֵאשִׁית (Gen. i. 1).

When there are *two* words (and no more) in the clause, the servus will precede, as וַיְהִי־עֶרֶב וַיְהִי־בֹקֶר (i. 5); יְהִי רָקִיעַ (i. 6); but T'bhîr is sometimes found, when Tiphcha's word is *long*, e. g. 1 Ki. ii. 46; Jer. xxxiv. 5. (Comp. p. 75; but there is no *rule* here, as in the case of Zaqeph.)

When there are *three* or *more* words in the clause, we find, *mutatis mutandis*, the rules for the division of Zaqeph's clause again carried out:

I. The main dichotomy may come on the *first* word before Tiphcha, and will then be regularly marked by T'bhîr, e. g. וַיַּרְא אֱלֹהִים אֶת־הָאוֹר ׀ וַיַּפֵּל יְהוָֹה אֱלֹהִים (Gen. i. 4); תַּרְדֵּמָה עַל־הָאָדָם (ii. 21).

II. The main dichotomy may come on the *second* word,

1. And will still be generally marked by T'bhîr, e. g. וָאִירָא אִם־אֶמְצָא בִסְדֹם חֲמִשִּׁים צַדִּיקִם (iii. 10); כִּי־עֵירֹם אָנֹכִי (xviii. 26); וַיִּבֶן יְהוָֹה אֱלֹהִים ׀ אֶת־הַצֵּלָע אֲשֶׁר־לָקַח מִן־הָאָדָם (ii. 22).

2. But *R'bhía* is admissible—as before Zaqeph—*if one of the following words be long*. (The intermediate word will then be always marked with T'bhîr[1].) Thus: יֹאכַל גּוֹיִם צָרָיו וַיַּחְתְּרוּ הָאֲנָשִׁים לְהָשִׁיב (Num. xxiv. 8); וְעַצְמֹתֵיהֶם יְגָרֵם וַיִּסְעוּ בְנֵי־יִשְׂרָאֵל וַיָּבֹאוּ אֶל־עָרֵיהֶם ׀ אֶל־הַיַּבָּשָׁה (Jon. i. 13); (Josh. ix. 17).

---

[1] Texts must therefore be corrected in Ex. xxx. 7; Lev. iv. 4; &c. In Job i. 1, I point with Ox. 4, 5, 7, 9, &c., אִישׁ הָיָה בְאֶרֶץ־עוּץ (see Norzi).

III. When the main dichotomy comes on the *third* word, or further, it is always marked by R'bhîa. Here the several cases we have had before repeat themselves:

1. There may be *only one* minor dichotomy, which is due on the first or second word. This dichotomy will be marked with T'bhîr: וַיַּשְׁכֵּם לָבָן בַּבֹּקֶר וַיְנַשֵּׁק לְבָנָיו וְלִבְנוֹתָיו (Gen. xxxii. 1); וַהֲקִמֹתִי אֶת־בְּרִיתִי בֵּינִי וּבֵינֶךָ וּבֵין זַרְעֲךָ אַחֲרֶיךָ לְדֹרֹתָם (xvii. 7); כִּי לֹא אֱלֹהִים הֵמָּה כִּי אִם־מַעֲשֵׂה יְדֵי־אָדָם עֵץ וָאָבֶן (Is. xxxvii. 19).

2. There may be *more than one* minor dichotomy. All such cases necessitate the *repetition* of R'bhîa; the same rule being followed as before Zaqeph and S'gôlta, that the second R'bhîa be changed into Pashṭa, unless at least three words intervene[2]. T'bhîr will still mark the last of the minor dichotomies on the first or second word.

Thus R'bhîa is *repeated* in Jer. xxviii. 14: כִּי כֹה־אָמַר יְהוָה צְבָאוֹת אֱלֹהֵי יִשְׂרָאֵל עֹל בַּרְזֶל נָתַתִּי עַל־צַוַּאר כָּל־הַגּוֹיִם הָאֵלֶּה לַעֲבֹד אֶת־נְבֻכַדְנֶאצַּר מֶלֶךְ־בָּבֶל. And so in Josh. xiii. 30; Jer. xxix. 14; Ezek. xiii. 18; Qoh. v. 17; and a few other instances.

On the other hand, it is changed into Pashṭa, in Is. xxxvi. 1: וַיְהִי בְּאַרְבַּע עֶשְׂרֵה שָׁנָה לַמֶּלֶךְ חִזְקִיָּהוּ עָלָה סַנְחֵרִיב מֶלֶךְ־אַשּׁוּר עַל כָּל־עָרֵי יְהוּדָה הַבְּצֻרוֹת. Comp. Deut. xx. 20[b]; xxviii. 14; Josh. x. 11; 2 Chr. xvi. 9; &c.

Pashṭa cannot, however, (on musical grounds), stand in close proximity to T'bhîr. There must be at least *two* words between[3].

---

[2] Even with three words intervening there is, as far as I have observed, only one instance of R'bhîa, Jer. xxix. 14. Comp. p. 78 note.

[3] In Num. vii. 87; Judg. xvi. 23; and 2 Chr. xviii. 23 there is only *one* word between. The Maqqeph before T'bhîr must be dropped, with various Codd.— Once, Deut. xxvi. 2, the transformation takes place *with two words intervening*. But here, Ox. 21, 51; Add. 9404 have rightly Pashṭa, instead of the first T'bhîr. In 1 Ki. v. 20 there is a misprint. For בְּנֵי read בָּנַי. In xxi. 16 we may point לָרֶדֶת with Ox. 1, 5, 6, 8, &c.

If this is not the case, Pashṭa is itself changed into T'bhîr, and the latter accent appears *repeated*[4]. (The case is exactly parallel to the change of Pashṭa into Zarqa, in S'gôlta's clause, see p. 88.) E.g. וַיֹּאמֶר בְּרַב רִכְבִּי הִנֶּנּוּ וְעָלִינוּ אֶל־הַמָּקוֹם אֲשֶׁר־אָמַר יְהוָה (Num. xiv. 40); אֲנִי עָלִיתִי מְרוֹם הָרִים (Is. xxxvii. 24). Such instances are sufficiently numerous. Comp. Gen. viii. 17; Ex. iii. 1; Deut. iii. 27; iv. 38; vi. 10; viii. 2; 1 Sam. xx. 21; xxi. 3; &c.

3. In a few passages, *three* R'bhias are due, but the second—owing to there not being in any case a sufficient interval between it and the first—is always changed to Pashṭa, e.g. וַיִּגְּשׁוּ יְהוּדָה וַיַּעַל עַל־גֹּזְזֵי צֹאנוֹ הוּא וְחִירָה רֵעֵהוּ הָעֲדֻלָּמִי (Gen. xxxviii. 12). The other examples are Ex. xxxvi. 3; Josh. vii. 19[5]; 1 Sam. xxvii. 5[5]; 2 Ki. v. 13[5]; xxiii. 12[5]; Jer. li. 64[5]; Dan. ii. 47; Ezra vi. 12; 1 Chr. xxvi. 26.

Servi of Ṭiphcha.

I. *One* servus is always Mer'kha, וַיֹּאמֶר אֱלֹהִים (Gen. i. 3). In eight instances Mer'kha appears, in Palestinian texts, in the *same word* with Ṭiphcha[6]: בְּכֹל־מוֹשְׁבֹתֵיכֶם (Lev. xxiii. 21); כָּל־הֶהָרוֹתֶיהָ (2 Ki. xv. 16); מִכָּל־תּוֹעֲבֹתֵיכֶם (Jer. viii. 18); וּמִכָּל־גִּלּוּלֵיכֶם (Ezek. xxxvi. 25); מַבְלִיגִיתִי (xliv. 6); שֶׁהֵם (Cant. vi. 5); וּבְזִבְיָתָךְ (Dan. v. 17); לְמִבָּרִאשׁוֹנָה (1 Chr. xv. 13). In most of the above cases, the object seems to have been to provide a fuller melody for the *long* words, by the substitution of an accent for Métheg[7]. In שֶׁהֵם the servus marks the first syllable as properly distinct, comp. שֶׁהֵם (Lam. iv. 9); שֶׁאֵין (Ps. cxlvi. 3).

II. The following (fourteen) are the only instances in which Ṭiphcha has *two* servi[8],—the first Darga and the second Double Mer'kha: אֲשֶׁר יַיִן, וַיָּבֵא לוֹ יַיִן (Gen. xxvii. 25); לָמָּה עָשָׂה בָּהּ (Ex. v. 15); וַיִּקְרָא לָהּ נֹבַח (xxxii.); הֲלוֹא טוֹב לָנוּ (Num. xiv. 3); לֹא צִוָּה (Lev. x. 1);

---

[4] It is clear that the change in question can only take place *when R'bhîa precedes*. Hence texts are incorrect in Josh. xx. 4 (point וְדִבֵּר), and Baer in his note to Qoh. vi. 2.

[5] See Corrigenda. Even Ben-Bil. (Mishp. hat. 35) is quite wrong, in the list he gives of these passages.

[6] These instances are fixed by the Mas. to Lev. xxiii. 21.

[7] But the Oriental text (to judge from Cod. Bab.) made no change. At Jer. viii. 18, the Massora and sign are Palestinian (see Strack's note).

[8] See the Mas. to Num. xxxii. 42 and Dikd. hat., § 22.

וַיַּחֲנוּ אֵלֶּה נֹכַח־אֵלֶּה (1 Ki. x. 3; 2 Chr. ix. 2); אֲשֶׁר לֹא הִגִּיד (42); נֶעֱוֵיתִי לוֹ בָא (xx. 29); (Ezek. xiv. 4); וַיְהִי רִיב וּמָדוֹן (Hab. i. 3); הֲלוֹא זֶה אוּד (Zech. iii. 2); וְדִי לָא יָדַע (Ezra vii. 25); וַיְהִי לֵב לָעָם (Neh. iii. 38); וַיָּנַח לוֹ אֱלֹהָיו (2 Chr. xx. 30).

The double Mer'kha here, as the servus Darga shews, is a weakened form of T'bhir[9], though what reasons led to its introduction it is vain to conjecture. The fancies that influenced the Palestinian accentuators have not been handed down to us. It is clear that in every case T'bhir might have stood, or Maqqeph been employed. The Oriental system (see Cod. Bab.) rightly rejected this irregular and unmeaning accentuation.

Corrigenda.

In Tiphcha's clause—as in Zaqeph's (p. 83)—we find instances of Zaqeph where R'bhia should have stood. Thus we must point:

כָּבוֹד (Josh. vii. 19), with Ox. 1, 5, 6, 7; Bomb. 2;—וַיֹּאמֶר לוֹ (Judg. xiii. 11), Ox. 10, 15, 83, 84; Bomb. 2;—מָקוֹם (1 Sam. xxvii. 5), Ox. 6, 7, 8, 15; Bomb. 2;—הַשִּׁלְחָן (1 Ki. vii. 48), all Codd. that I have examined;—גָּדוֹל (2 Ki. v. 13), Ox. 1, 5, 7, 8; Bomb. 2;—אֲשֶׁר עָשָׂה מְנַשֶּׁה (xxiii. 12), Ox. 7, 8, 10, 2323;—[10] הַכְּלִי (Jer. xviii. 4), Ox. 1, 9; Erf. 1, 2;—הָרָעָה (li. 64), Ox. 5, 2323, 2324, 2331. If the student will examine these passages for himself, he will see how necessary the correction is in each case.

Obs.—It is hoped that the rules for marking the dichotomy in the clauses thus far considered have appeared to the reader precise and clear. We have had a first group of accents—with similar rules—formed by Silluq and Athnach; and a second, consisting of Zaqeph, S'gôlta, and Ṭiphcha. We pass on now to the third group, embracing R'bhîa, Pashṭa, T'bhîr, and Zarqa. A leading characteristic of this group is the *much greater variety* in the accents employed for the necessary dichotomical divisions. We shall in consequence have to notice many merely *musical* variations. With this group, the formal rules for the dichotomy come to an end.

---

[9] Comp. p. 25. Hence in our texts, R'bhia stands in Ezek. xiv. 4[b], in accordance with III. 1. But it is better to point with Zaqeph, as Ox. 6, 12, 13, 14, &c., do.

[10] In the same clause read בַּחֹמֶר for בַּחֹמָר (see Norzi).

CHAPTER X.

R'BHÎA.

R'BHÎA's word stands often *alone*, as: וְהָאָרֶץ (Gen. i. 2).

When there are *two* words (and no more) in the clause, the servus is commonly employed, as in וַיֹּאמֶר אֱלֹהִים (i. 9); פָּרוּ וּרְבוּ (i. 22); but if R'bhia's word is *long*, Géresh (i. e. Gersháyim)[1] may appear: וְהִשְׁמַדְתִּי אֶת־בָּמֹתֵיכֶם (Lev. xxvi. 30).

The other examples are Gen. x. 14 (1 Chr. i. 12); Lev. xviii. 17; Deut. xxxiv. 11; Ezek. xiii. 21; xxvii. 29; 2 Chr. iv. 20. The accentuators have chosen instances, in which Gersháyim's word is long as well.

On L'garmeh, with two words in the clause, see chap. XIII.

When there are *three* or *more* words in the clause, the following cases will occur:

I. The main dichotomy may be on the *first* word before R'bhia, and is usually marked by *Géresh*: וַיֹּאמֶר לָהֶם אֱלֹהִים (Gen. i. 28); וַיַּעַשׂ אֱלֹהִים אֶת־חַיַּת הָאָרֶץ לְמִינָהּ (i. 25); וַיַּעַן אֶחָד מֵהַנְּעָרִים וַיֹּאמֶר (1 Sam. xvi. 18).

With only *three* words in the clause, a servus may come: וַיֹּאמֶר לוֹ יְהוָֹה (Gen. iv. 15); אֲנִי עָנִיתִי וַאֲשׁוּרֶנּוּ (Hos. xiv. 9).

This variation in the melody seems due to the *lighter* character of R'bhia. With such an accent, the absence of the cadence, due from the dichotomy, would not be so much felt. We have indeed already seen—under Zaqeph, S'gôlta, and even Athnach—that with only *three* words, there was not the same necessity for marking the dichotomy. But these cases differed from ours in that some compensation was made for the failure of the cadence by the presence of the minor Disjunctive—Pashta, Zarqa, and Tiphcha, respectively—in the *third* word. With the still lighter accents, that have yet to be considered, the cadence regularly fails.

What is here fixed for the *main* dichotomy, holds equally good for the *minor*. The same remark applies to the rules that follow.

---

[1] It is understood that when, in this and the following chapters, I speak of Géresh, I include Gersháyim.

II. The main dichotomy may be on the *second* word, and is still marked by Géresh: אַשְׁרֶיךָ יִשְׂרָאֵל מִי כָמוֹךָ (Deut. xxxiii. 29); וַיַּעַל לוֹט מִצּוֹעַר וַיֵּשֶׁב בָּהָר (Gen. xix. 30).

When there are only *three* words in the clause, L'garmeh may take the place of Géresh, thus affording a variety in the melody [2]. It is particularly common with small words, as כִּי, אֶת, אֲשֶׁר, כֹּל; but is not confined to them, e.g. יְהֹוָה ׀ אֱלֹהֵי הַשָּׁמַיִם (Gen. xxiv. 7); הָרִאשֹׁנוֹת ׀ מָה הֵנָּה (Is. xli. 22).

In three passages, where both R'bhia's word and that preceding are *long*, we find the fuller melody of Great T'lisha followed by Géresh: כָּל־קָרְבָּנָם לְכָל־מִנְחָתָם וּלְכָל־חַטָּאתָם (Num. xviii. 9); and so in Deut. xxv. 19 (minor dichotomy) and Jer. xxix. 14. The case is parallel to what we have observed under Athnach, Zaqeph, &c. But the cadence is too heavy for R'bhia and generally fails.

III. The main dichotomy may be on the *third* word. Here the melody varies between Géresh and Great T'lisha.

1. Géresh, followed by L'garmeh, when the minor dichotomy is on the second word, or by two servi (see above), when it is on the first, e.g. חָלִלָה לְּךָ מֵעֲשֹׂת ׀ כַּדָּבָר הַזֶּה (Gen. xviii. 25); וַיֹּאמֶר יְהוּדָה לְתָמָר כַּלָּתוֹ שְׁבִי אַלְמָנָה בֵית־אָבִיךְ (Gen. xxxviii. 11). Comp. i. 29; xxvi. 18; xxix. 2; l. 24ᵇ; Ex. iv. 18 [3].

2. Great T'lisha, with Géresh to mark the minor dichotomy on the first or second word, e.g. וְאָמַרְתָּ אֵלָיו הִשָּׁמֵר וְהַשְׁקֵט (Is. vii. 4); וַיֹּאמֶר אֵלָיו חַי־יְהֹוָה כִּי־יָשָׁר אַתָּה אַל־תִּירָא (1 Sam. xxix. 6). Comp. 2 Sam. vii. 8; Jer. xxvi. 19; xxxiv. 3ᵇ; Ezra ix. 12.

Pazer is found in the place of T'lisha, in וַאֲמַרְתֶּם זֶבַח־פֶּסַח הוּא לַיהֹוָה (Ex. xii. 27), and in Jer. xxxix. 16 [4].

---

[2] In Ex. xxvi. 2, 8 and xxxvi. 9, 15, these accents interchange in the *same* expression. Comp. also Num. xvi. 17, 18.

[3] Drop L'garmeh in Josh. i. 4; Ezek. xvii. 9, with Codd.

[4] Both here, and in the instances given IV. 2, Pazer is out of order, for it is properly followed by Great or Little T'lisha.

IV. The main dichotomy may be on the *fourth* word. Géresh, Great T'lîsha, and Pazer are all employed to mark it.

1. Géresh, with L'garmeh (occasionally repeated) to mark the minor dichotomy (or dichotomies) between it and R'bhîa, e. g. וֵאלֹהֵ֣י אֲבִיכֶ֤ם אֶ֨מֶשׁ ׀ אָמַ֧ר אֵלַ֛י לֵאמֹ֕ר (Gen. xxxi. 29); וַיִּשְׂא֣וּ בְנֵֽי־יִשְׂרָאֵ֣ל אֶת־עֵינֵיהֶ֗ם וְהִנֵּ֤ה מִצְרַ֨יִם ׀ נֹסֵ֣עַ אַחֲרֵיהֶ֔ם (Ex. xiv. 10); אֱמֹ֨ר אֲלֵיהֶ֜ם חַי־אָ֣נִי ׀ נְאֻ֣ם ׀ אֲדֹנָ֣י יְהוִ֗ה (Ezek. xxxiii. 11). Comp. Lev. xiii. 52; Josh. xxiv. 13; Jer. xxix. 32; xliv. 26[b]; xlvi. 28[b]; Jon. i. 3[b].

L'garmeh is not, however, available to mark the minor dichotomy, when due on the *first* word[5]. Hence we have R'bhîa with *three* servi in וַיָּ֨שָׁב מֵאַחֲרָ֜יו וַיִּקַּ֣ח אֶת־צֶ֤מֶד הַבָּקָר֙ וַיִּזְבָּחֵ֔הוּ (1 Ki. xix. 21), and in 2 Sam. xxi. 2[b]; 2 Ki. xx. 3 (Is. xxxviii. 3); Qoh. iv. 8[6]. But this accentuation is so anomalous, that I do not hesitate to correct it in the few passages in which it occurs, although it is found in most Codd., and recognised by the grammarians. See Corrigenda.

2. Great T'lîsha, with Géresh for the minor dichotomy, and occasionally L'garmeh as well, where a second minor dichotomy has to be marked: אַבֵּ֣ד תְּאַבְּד֗וּן אֶֽת־כָּל־הַמְּקֹמ֞וֹת אֲשֶׁ֣ר עָֽבְדוּ־שָׁ֣ם הַגּוֹיִ֗ם (Deut. xii. 2); וַיִּשְׁלַ֣ח אַבְשָׁל֗וֹם אֶת־אֲחִיתֹ֣פֶל (2 Sam. xv. 12); פַּרְשֶׁ֣גֶן אִגַּרְתָּ֗א דִּֽי־שְׁלַ֣ח תַּתְּנַ֣י ׀ הַגִּילֹנִ֤י יוֹעֵץ֙ דָּוִ֔ד פַּחַ֣ת עֲבַֽר־נַהֲרָ֗ה (Ezra v. 6). It is unnecessary to give further examples. We have here merely a musical variation of the cases under 1.

We note that Géresh cannot be employed to mark the minor dichotomy on the *first* word, because we should then have the two T'lîshas brought together, which is contrary to (musical) rule. A change in the accentuation becomes here necessary, see 3 below.

In a few instances, Pazer takes the place of Great T'lîsha, under

---

[5] L'garmeh on the first word is reserved for a particular purpose, see chapter on L'garmeh, p. 119.

[6] There are two other instances where Géresh marks a *minor* dichotomy, Num. iv. 14 and Is. v. 25.

this head, e.g. וַיִּשְׁמְע֡וּ כִּֽי־פָקַ֨ד יְהוָ֜ה אֶת־בְּנֵ֣י יִשְׂרָאֵ֗ל (Ex. iv. 31). The others are Gen. xxxii. 33; Deut. xxii. 6; 1 Sam. xx. 2; Jer. xxviii. 14; xxxviii. 7; Esth. vii. 9; Dan. v. 23; Ezra vi. 9 (minor dichotomy).

3. From the love of musical variation exhibited in the divisions just considered, we might have expected to find Pazer employed to mark the main dichotomy, with Great T'lîsha and Géresh for the minor dichotomies, as in וְשָׁ֣ם הָי֣וּ לְפָנִ֡ים נֹתְנִים֩ אֶת־הַמִּנְחָ֨ה הַלְּבוֹנָ֜ה וְהַכֵּלִ֗ים (Neh. xiii. 5). But such instances are quite uncommon [7]. The proper use of Pazer on the fourth word is to provide the means of marking the minor dichotomy on the *first* word, which means fail, as we have seen, under 1 and 2. The accent employed is always Géresh, e.g. וַיֹּ֣אמֶר הֲכִי֩ קָרָ֨א שְׁמ֜וֹ יַעֲקֹ֗ב (Gen. xxvii. 36); וַיִּשְׁלַ֣ח דָּוִ֡ד אֶת־יוֹאָב֩ וְאֶת־עֲבָדָ֨יו עִמּ֜וֹ הָלֹ֣ךְ וְקָרָ֡אתָ בְאָזְנֵ֨י יְרוּשָׁלַ֜͏ִם (2 Sam. xi. 1); וְאֶת־כָּל־יִשְׂרָאֵ֗ל לֵאמֹ֔ר (Jer. ii. 2); and so often.

V. With the main dichotomy on the *fifth* word or further, Pazer becomes the regular dividing accent.

The following are the only variations I have noticed:

Great T'lîsha may appear on the fifth word, with Géresh to mark the minor dichotomy on the third or fourth word, e.g. וַיֹּ֣אמֶר שָׁא֡וּל הַשְׁמִיע֣וּ אֶל־בְּבָ֗ל (1 Sam. xxviii. 15); צַר־לִ֣י מְאֹ֗ד וּפְלִשְׁתִּ֞ים נִלְחָמִ֥ים בִּ֣י בְּמָק֞וֹם אֲשֶׁ֣ר יִֽהְיֶה־שָּׁ֗ם (Jer. l. 29); רַבִּ֗ים כָּל־דֹּרְכֵ֣י קֶ֔שֶׁת חֲנ֥וּ עָלֶ֛יהָ סָבִ֖יב אֲדֹנִ֥י הַמֶּ֖לֶךְ (2 Sam. xv. 21).

Other variations are uncommon. Great T'lîsha occurs on the sixth word in Lev. xiii. 59; Deut. xiii. 6; Josh. xix. 47[8]; 1 Sam. xvii. 25; comp. Ezra iii. 8[b];—and Géresh on the fifth word in 1 Ki. xiv. 21; xvi. 7; Qoh. vi. 2. None of these variations occasion any difficulty.

Otherwise, Pazer is the accent employed,—*repeated* according to the requirements of the dichotomy, or for the sake of distinct

---

[7] The other examples are Is. lxvi. 20; Ezek. xliv. 25; 1 Chr. v. 24; vii. 2. In three of these, Pazer marks a minor dichotomy.

[8] Point here וַיַּפּוּ־אוֹתָהּ, with Maqqeph (Ox. 8, Erf. 2, Bomb. 1). Otherwise we should have the one solitary example of Great T'lîsha on the *seventh* word.

enunciation of details. The division of the portion of the clause between the last Pazer and R'bhîa will be according to the rules laid down above, which are (as has been stated) equally applicable to the minor as to the main dichotomy..

Examples of *one* Pazer are common, e.g. וְהֶעָרִים יֶהֱרֹסוּ וְכָל־חֶלְקָה טוֹבָה יַשְׁלִיכוּ אִישׁ־אַבְנוֹ וּמִלְאוּהָ (2 Ki. iii. 25); וּבָאוּ וְנָתְנוּ אִישׁ כִּסְאוֹ פֶּתַח ׀ שַׁעֲרֵי יְרוּשָׁלַםִ (Jer. i. 15); and Ex. vii. 19; 1 Ki. xvi. 7; Jer. xiii. 13; xxxv. 14; &c.

Two Pazers are also met with occasionally, as in וַיֹּאמֶר . אַבְנֵר אֶל־דָּוִד אָקוּמָה ׀ וְאֵלֵכָה וְאֶקְבְּצָה אֶל־אֲדֹנִי הַמֶּלֶךְ אֶת־כָּל־יִשְׂרָאֵל וְשָׁבָה אֶל־גְּדַלְיָהוּ בֶן־אֲחִיקָם בֶּן־שָׁפָן (2 Sam. iii. 21); אֲשֶׁר הִפְקִיד מֶלֶךְ־בָּבֶל בְּעָרֵי יְהוּדָה (Jer. xl. 5); and Deut. v. 8; 2 Sam. xxiv. 13ᵇ; Jer. xvii. 25; 2 Chr. xxiv. 5.

Three Pazers are found in Dan. iii. 15; 1 Chr. v. 24; xxv. 3, 4;—*four* in Josh. viii. 33; Dan. iii. 3; v. 12;—and *five* in 1 Chr. xvi. 5.

These eight instances are all I have noticed, in which Pashṭa is repeated more than once in R'bhîa's clause. In no case was the repetition necessary, for the accentuation might have been easily arranged otherwise. I confess, it looks to me as if there were something fanciful in the introduction of these instances, for (if I am not mistaken) there is the same number, *eight*, of similar instances in Pashṭa's and T'bhir's clauses[9].

Servi of R'bhîa.

I. *One* servus is always Munach, וַיֹּאמֶר אֱלֹהִים (Gen. i. 9).
In five cases[10] it is found in the *same word* with R'bhîa: [11] אַל־תֵּעָצְבוּ

---

[9] In Syriac the same accent is constantly *repeated* any number of times to mark successive details (see Bar-Hebræus, Phillips' ed., p. 43). Here we have a *rule*, which the few examples that occur of Pazer repeated for the same purpose do not justify us in laying down for the Hebrew.

[10] Fixed by the Massora to Gen. xlv. 5. In our texts it occurs falsely in 2 Ki. xxi. 7; Ezek. xiii. 21; xxxv. 12; xxxvi. 11.

[11] The idea seems to have been to draw attention to the distinction between this form and אַל־תֵּעָצְבוּ (Neh. viii. 10). Care was to be taken to read here tēāṣ'vû, not tūṅṣēvû.

(Gen. xlv. 5); [12] וְאֶסְעֲרֵם (Zech. vii. 14); אָֽנָּא (Ex. xxxii. 31); אֵילוֹ (Qoh. iv. 10); and בֵּלְטְשַׁאצַּר (Dan. i. 7). We can understand its introduction in the three last cases, the object being to indicate a *compound word*.

II. With *two* servi, the first is Darga and the second Munach, e.g. וְהִנֵּה רִבְקָה יֹצֵאת (Gen. xxiv. 15) [13].

III. For *three* servi, we have Munach, Darga, and Munach. The few instances that occur are probably all to be corrected. See below.

Corrigenda.

The following are the cases of Géresh on the fourth word with servi following, referred to p. 95, which I propose to correct as follows:

וְנָתְנוּ עָלָיו אֶת־כָּל־כֵּלָיו אֲשֶׁר יְשָׁרְתוּ־עָלָיו בָּהֶם (Num. iv. 14), with Ox. 3, 6, 10; Erf. 1, 4.

וְהַגִּבְעֹנִים לֹא מִבְּנֵי יִשְׂרָאֵל הֵמָּה (2 Sam. xxi. 2), with Ox. 1, 7, 13, 16, &c.

וַיָּשָׁב מֵאַחֲרָיו וַיִּקַּח אֶת־צֶמֶד־הַבָּקָר וַיִּזְבָּחֵהוּ (1 Ki. xix. 21), with Ox. 76; K. 403; De R. 305. Other Codd., as Ox. 32; Harl. 1528; Add. 4709; Or. 2091; De R. 226, have Zaqeph instead of R'bhîa, when the pointing of the clause will be וַיָּשָׁב מֵאַחֲרָיו וַיִּקַּח אֶת־צֶמֶד הַבָּקָר וַיִּזְבָּחֵהוּ.

זְכָר־נָא אֵת אֲשֶׁר הִתְהַלַּכְתִּי לְפָנֶיךָ (2 Ki. xx. 3; Is. xxxviii. 3), with Ox. 7, 13, 75; Jabl., &c.

חָרָה אַף־יְהוָֹה בְּעַמּוֹ וַיֵּט־יָדוֹ עָלָיו וַיַּכֵּהוּ (Is. v. 25), with Ox. 5, 9, 13, 17, 75.

יֵשׁ אֶחָד וְאֵין שֵׁנִי גַּם־בֵּן וָאָח אֵין־לוֹ (Qoh. iv. 8), with Ox. 1, 4, 6; Erf. 2, 3.

---

[12] Perhaps to mark the peculiar grammatical form.

[13] Codd. have here constantly two Munachs—an error against which Ben-Bil. expressly warns in Mishp. hat. 26—and so our texts in Josh. xiv. 6; Jer. xxx. 11; Dan. iii. 15, &c.

CHAPTER XI.

PASHṬA, T'BHÎR, AND ZARQA.

THESE three accents may be taken together, as the rules for the division of the clauses governed by them are identical.

Our investigation is further much simplified in that these rules are adopted, with little change, from those for R'bhîa's clause. The same accents (with the exception of L'garmeh, which is rarely employed) are in use to mark the necessary divisions.

It is to be noted that we are now approaching the limits of the musical division. The tendency to employ a *lighter melody* is, in consequence, observable. This tendency, which began to shew itself under R'bhîa, becomes more marked in the clauses we are about to consider; and still more so with the accents, to be examined in the next chapter, which close the musical scale.

We proceed to the analysis of the clauses governed by Pashṭa [1], T'bhîr, and Zarqa.

When there are *two* words (and no more) in the clause, the first is marked with a servus, as וְהָיוּ לִמְאוֹרֹת (Gen. i. 15); וַיַּעַשׂ אֱלֹהִים (i. 7); וַיַּרְא אֱלֹהִים (i. 4).

Géresh is however admissible, when the latter of the two words is *long* and the interval between the tone-syllables considerable, as in וְעָשָׂה אֶת־חַטָּאתוֹ (Lev. ix. 7); וְיִשְׁמְרוּ אֶת־כָּל־צוּרָתוֹ (Ezek. xliii. 11). But the punctators seldom availed themselves of this variation. I have noticed it, besides, only in Ex. xxxviii. 23; 2 Sam. iii. 25; Jer. xxx. 16; Ezek. xi. 18; xliv. 4; and Dan. i. 12 [2]. (Comp. the few similar examples before R'bhîa, p. 93. The number seems to be the same, viz. *eight*.)

When there are *three* or *more* words in the clause, we have to consider, as before, the various cases that may occur:

---

[1] Pashṭa appears, as we have seen, p. 19, under two forms, Pashṭa proper and Y'thîbh; but, as the latter *always stands alone*, it does not come under consideration in the rules that follow. For this accent, see p. 106.

[2] Baer's pointing וַיַּעַן הָאִישׁ (Zech. i. 10) cannot stand, any more than וּכְחַפֵּי־אִישׁ נְדוּדִים (Hos. vi. 9), with R'bhîa.

I. The main dichotomy may be due on the word immediately preceding. Here we should expect it to be marked (as before R'bhîa) by Géresh. But this is rarely the case. Generally, *transformation takes place, the servi of Géresh remaining.* In other words, the rhythmical cadence at the close of the clause is, with these lighter accents, purposely omitted, e. g. הָעֵד הֵעִד בָּ֜נוּ הָאִישׁ֘ לֵאמֹר (Gen. xliii. 3); וַיֵּךְ אֹתָם֘ מֶ֜לֶךְ בָּבֶל וַיְמִיתֵם (2 Ki. xxv. 21); הַעִדֹ֜תִי בָכֶם הַיּוֹם֘ (Deut. xxx. 19).

That the dichotomy is *due*, in all such cases, in the first word, is clear not only from the rules for the same, but from the comparison of such identical expressions as 2 Ki. xxi. 3[b] (R'bhîa) and 2 Chr. xxxiii. 3[b] (Pashṭa); 1 Ki. xxii. 35 (Ṭiphcha) and 2 Chr. xviii. 34 (T'bhîr); and Josh. viii. 18 (R'bhîa) and xi. 6 (Zarqa). Indeed, in the next chapter we shall find this dichotomy, although in abeyance, exercising an influence on the accents preceding.

It is only when the closing word of the clause is *long* (see above) that Géresh appears, e. g. אֲנִ֞י שָׁלַח אֶת־כָּל־מַגֵּפֹתַי֘ וַיְהִ֞י אִישׁ (Ex. ix. 14); וַיְדַבֵּ֞ר אֶל־קֹרַח וְאֶל־כָּל־עֲדָתוֹ֘ (1 Sam. i. 1); אֶחָ֞ד מִן־הָרָמָתַיִם (Num. xvi. 5). But even here it more generally fails [3].

II. The main dichotomy may be due on the *second* word,

1. And is commonly marked (as before R'bhîa) with Géresh, e. g. וַיָּבֵ֜א קַיִן מִפְּרִי יִקָּו֜וּ הַמַּיִם מִתַּחַת הַשָּׁמַיִם (Gen. i. 9); וְהִנֵּ֜ה יְהוָה נִצָּב עָלָיו֘ (xxviii. 13); הָאֲדָמָה (iv. 3).

2. But where the clause contains only *three* words, we often find the lighter melody of a *servus*, e. g. דִּרְשׁ֖וּ מֵעַל־סֵפֶר יְהוָה נֶ֖פֶשׁ וְהוּא נַעֲנֶה (Is. xxxiv. 16); וּמַ֖שׁ חֲצִי הָהָר (Zech. xiv. 4); (Is. liii. 7) [4].

3. Less frequent than 1 or 2, but not uncommon, is the musical variation of Great T'lîsha. Here Géresh should properly

---

[3] The other examples I have noticed are : before Pashṭa, Ex. xxxi. 6; xxxviii. 17; 1 Sam. xv. 18; Is. xxv. 6; Jer. xix. 13[b] (corr.);—before T'bhîr, Gen. xxxvi. 18; Num. xxxii. 2; Josh. iii. 17; 1 Ki. i. 10;—and before Zarqa, 2 Chr. xviii. 5.

[4] Codd., as we might expect, often vary. Thus we have וַיַּ֖עַן and וַיַּ֗עַן (Zech. iv. 6); וְיָצָ֖א and וְיָצָ֗א (xiv. 2); פְּתָחֶ֖יךָ and פְּתָחֶ֗יךָ (2 Chr. vi. 41); &c.

come on the first word (see the examples under R'bhîa), but has been, according to rule, transformed[5]: פֶּן־יֶחֱרֶה אַף־יְהוָֹה אֱלֹהֶיךָ (Deut. vi. 15); וַיַּעֲבֹר יְהוֹשֻׁעַ וְכָל־יִשְׂרָאֵל עִמּוֹ (Josh. x. 29); שָׁמַעְתִּי אֶת־תְּפִלָּתְךָ וְאֶת־תְּחִנָּתְךָ (1 Ki. ix. 3)[6].

In five passages, Gen. v. 29; Lev. x. 4; 2 Ki. xvii. 13; Ezek. xlviii. 10; Zeph. ii. 15 (see Mas. to Gen. v. 29), Géresh and T'lîsha are found together in the same word,—an intimation that ancient authorities *differed* as to the chanting. The later Massoretes, unable to decide which was right, directed that *both* accents should be chanted (הקורא יטעים הגרש קדם התלישא), Géresh first, as being the more common. And this chanting is observed in the present day.

It is to be noticed that the rules already laid down and those which follow, apply equally to the *minor* dichotomy, when the main dichotomy divides the clause earlier than in the several cases given.

III. With the main dichotomy on the *third* word, Géresh and Great T'lîsha—more rarely Pazer—are employed to mark it (as also with R'bhîa).

1. But Great T'lîsha becomes now the more common,—the minor dichotomy, if due on the second word, being marked by Géresh[7]; or, if on the first word, by Géresh transformed[8]; e. g. with Pashṭa: וַיֵּשְׁבוּ וַיָּבֹאוּ אֶל־עֵין מִשְׁפָּט לְמַעַן (Gen. xiv. 7); תֵּדְעוּ וְתַאֲמִינוּ לִי וְתָבִינוּ (Is. xliii. 10).

---

[5] Moreover—according to the analogy of Zaqeph on the second word before Athnach or Silluq, R'bhîa on the second word before Zaqeph, &c.—one or other of the words following T'lîsha should be *long*. But the *necessity* for this condition fails, with the transformation of Géresh and the consequent disappearance of the full rhythmical cadence. Hence we find two short words in 1 Sam. xxx. 12; Is. xxix. 4, before Pashṭa; Jon. ii. 3, before T'bhîr; and Deut. iii. 19, before Zarqa.

[6] The careless mistakes in 2 Ki. xvi. 7 and Neh. ix. 37[b] must be corrected and Azla put for Great T'lîsha, with Codd.

[7] It is not often that Géresh fails when due in the second word; yet after the analogy of II. 2, a servus may come, as in Num. xix. 10 and Josh. ii. 3, before Pashṭa;—Gen. xlii. 30 and Deut. xxii. 29, before T'bhîr;—and Num. xxx. 9; Josh. xxiii. 16, before Zarqa.

[8] In two instances, Lev. v. 12 and Num. xiv. 29, where Pashṭa's word is *long*, Géresh remains.

For T'bhîr, see Gen. xix. 20; Jer. xiii. 9;—for Zarqa, Gen. xix. 19; Josh. x. 24[9].

The (musical) variations under this head are—

(a) The fanciful transposition of T'lîsha and Géresh[10], e.g. וְאִם־תֵּרָאָה עוֹד בַּבֶּגֶד אוֹ־בַשְּׁתִי אוֹ־בָעֵרֶב (Lev. xiii. 57). The other examples are 2 Chr. xxxv. 12, with Pashṭa;—Gen. xiii. 1; Deut. xxvi. 12; Josh. xxiii. 4; Am. viii. 13; Ezra v. 3, with T'bhîr;—and Neh. iii. 15, with Zarqa.

(β) The substitution of Pazer for Great T'lîsha, Géresh remaining, as in עַל־כֵּן אֲבַכֶּה בִּבְכִי יַעְזֵר (Is. xvi. 9). Comp. Dan. ii. 28; 1 Chr. xxvii. 25; 2 Chr. iii. 3, before Pashṭa;—Gen. x. 13 (1 Chr. i. 11); 1 Sam. xxx. 14; 2 Ki. viii. 29 (2 Chr. xxii. 6); Qoh. viii. 11[b]; 1 Chr. xxiv. 4, before T'bhîr;—and 2 Chr. xxxv. 7, before Zarqa. (In Neh. xii. 36; xiii. 15, Pazer marks a minor dichotomy[11].)

2. Examples of Géresh are: וַיֹּאמֶר לוֹ אֱלֹהִים אֲנִי אֵל שַׁדַּי (Gen. xxxv. 11); וַתִּקַּח רִצְפָּה בַת־אַיָּה אֶת־הַשַּׂק וַתַּטֵּהוּ לָהּ אֶל־הַצּוּר (2 Sam. xxi. 10). Comp. for T'bhîr, Gen. xxxiv. 13; Lev. xiii. 37; and for Zarqa, Ex. xxix. 21; 1 Ki. iii. 6. (For the instances in which the minor dichotomy is due on the *first* word, comp. R'bhîa, III. 1[12].)

3. Pazer also, followed by Great T'lîsha to mark the minor dichotomy on the second word, is quite regular, e.g. וּבָאוּ עָלֶיהָ וַיְצַו הַמֶּלֶךְ אֶת־יוֹאָב וְאֶת־ (Ezek. xxiii. 24); הֹצֶן רֶכֶב וְגַלְגַּל אֲבִישַׁי וְאֶת־אִתַּי (2 Sam. xviii. 5). So before T'bhîr, Num. xxix. 18; Josh. ii. 1[b]; and before Zarqa, Gen. xxxvi. 6; Jer. xxxvi. 14. Such examples are, however, much less frequent than those under 1 and 2.

---

[9] For the rest of the chapter, I think it sufficient to give in full the examples with Pashṭa, as those with T'bhîr and Zarqa present no difference.

[10] Of course their relative disjunctive value becomes changed, with the change of position.

[11] Pazer is out of order in these instances, because it is properly followed by Great or Little T'lîsha.

[12] Neh. v. 18 must be corrected שׁוֹר אֶחָד צֹאן שֵׁשׁ־בְּרֻרוֹת וְצִפֳּרִים, as the minor dichotomy is on the first word. Harl. 5506 and Par. 102 have Munach for Great T'lîsha.

IV. With the main dichotomy on the *fourth* word, Great T'lîsha and Pazer are employed to mark it. Géresh is seldom available.

1. Great T'lîsha, when the minor dichotomy (marked with Géresh) is on the second or third word, e. g. וַאֲמַרְתֶּ֣ אֲלֵיהֶ֗ם לְכ֣וּ וְהִכִּיתֶ֔ם (Jer. xvii. 20); שִׁמְע֞וּ דְבַר־יְהוָ֗ה מַלְכֵ֣י יְהוּדָ֔ה (Judg. xxi. 10); וְחָרָ֨ה אַפִּ֤י בוֹ֙ בַיּ֣וֹם־ אֶת־יוֹשְׁבֵ֖י יָבֵ֥שׁ גִּלְעָֽד (Deut. xxxi. 17). הַה֗וּא וַעֲזַבְתִּ֞ים וְהִסְתַּרְתִּ֨י פָנַ֥י מֵהֶם֙ For T'bhîr, comp. Num. xviii. 7; Is. lxvi. 19; and for Zarqa, Deut. xxxi. 21; Jer. xlix. 19.

The variations under this head are as before:
(a) The transposition of T'lîsha and Géresh, in וַתּוֹצֵ֨א הָאָ֜רֶץ דֶּ֠שֶׁא עֵ֣שֶׂב מַזְרִ֤יעַ זֶ֙רַע֙ (Gen. i. 12); and Lev. iv. 7; 1 Ki. xvi. 21; Ezek. iii. 15; Dan. ix. 26; Ezra viii. 17[b]; all before Pashṭa[13].
(β) The substitution of Pazer for T'lîsha, Géresh remaining, in Lev. xiii. 58; Josh. xviii. 28, before Pashṭa;—and in Num. xviii. 17; Jer. xxxviii. 25; xliv. 18; Esth. i. 17; 2 Chr. xx. 26, before T'bhîr[14].

2. Pazer also may come, followed by Great T'lîsha, to mark the minor dichotomy on the second or third word, e. g. הַסֻּפִּ֡ים וְהַחֲלוֹנִ֣ים הָאֲטֻמ֣וֹת וְהָאַתִּיקִ֣ים ׀ סָבִ֗יב אַ֣ף כִּ֞י (Ezek. xli. 16); אַרְבַּ֣עַת שְׁפָטַ֣י ׀ הָרָעִ֗ים חֶ֚רֶב וְרָעָ֣ב וְחַיָּ֣ה רָעָ֔ה (xiv. 21); וַיֹּ֡אמֶר קַח־נָ֠א אֶת־בִּנְךָ֙ אֶת־יְחִֽידְךָ֤ אֲשֶׁר־אָהַ֙בְתָּ֙ (Gen. xxii. 2). Comp. Josh. vi. 23; 2 Ki. xvi. 10; Ezek. xxxvii. 25; and for T'bhîr's clause, Gen. vii. 2; xlv. 23; 2 Sam. iii. 29. I have noticed no example in Zarqa's clause.

But Pazer's proper function in the fourth word is to mark the main dichotomy, when the minor dichotomy—represented by Géresh transformed [15]—is due on the *first* word. (Great T'lîsha

---

[13] The minor dichotomies are so pointed in Pashṭa's clause, 1 Sam. xvii. 51; and in T'bhîr's, Gen. xxi. 14.

[14] In 1 Ki. xix. 11, where Pazer marks a minor dichotomy, Géresh must come on the second word, with many Codd.

[15] In Lev. xx. 4, where Pashṭa's word is *long*, Géresh is found; and so in 1 Ki. x. 5, with Pazer on the fifth word. Contrast the division in R'bhîa's clause, where Géresh *always stands*.

cannot be used, because it would come immediately before Little T'lisha,—a juxtaposition which, as we have seen, is not allowed.) E. g. וְאַתָּ֨ה אַל־תִּירָ֜א עַבְדִּ֤י יַעֲקֹב֙ נְאֻם־יְהוָ֔ה (Jer. xxx. 10); וַיֹּ֡אמֶר אֶת־אֱלֹהַ֞י אֲשֶׁר־עָשִׂ֨יתִי֙ לְקַחְתֶּ֔ם וְאֶת־הַכֹּהֵ֖ן (Judg. xviii. 24); and so in Gen. xlviii. 15; Ex. v. 14; &c., before Pashṭa; and in 2 Ki. xxiii. 29; Is. liv. 17; &c., before T'bhîr [16]. Here again examples with Zarqa fail.

EXCEPTIONS.—Géresh cannot properly appear on the *fourth* word, except by transposition (see I. *a* above) or by the introduction of L'garmeh [17] to mark the minor dichotomy. Such instances, therefore, as כִּֽי־אָמַ֞ר עַבְדְּךָ֣ אֶחְבְּשָׁה־לִּ֤י הַחֲמוֹר֙ וְאֶרְכַּ֣ב עָלֶ֔יהָ (2 Sam. xix. 27), must either be regarded as exceptional and altogether anomalous, or we must be prepared to correct them (like the similar instances in R'bhîa's clause, p. 98) with the help of Codd. The latter is (I doubt not) the proper course. For instance, in the passage just given, I propose to point אֶחְבְּשָׁה־לִּ֤י הַחֲמוֹר֙, with Add. 15451; Harl. 5722; De R. 554, &c. By the simple insertion of Maqqeph between the first word and T'bhîr in Josh. xxi. 11, and between the second and third words in Judg. xx. 34 and 1 Ki. v. 25, these passages are reduced to order. In Jer. xxxviii. 16 I have found Pazer—and in Num. iii. 39; 1 Sam. xviii. 5; 2 Sam. xiv. 30; and 2 Chr. ix. 25, R'bhîa—for Géresh. These are the only passages which (as far as I have observed) need correction. I have not thought it necessary to cite, for the several instances, the authority on which the correction is made. It is enough that the student should understand that the anomaly which they exhibit admits of being removed, and that so the rules above laid down are confirmed. It is only from this latter point of view that the emendations made are of any consequence [18].

V. With the main dichotomy on the *fifth* word or further, Pazer is (as in R'bhîa's clause) the regular dividing accent.

---

[16] In the lists Ezek. xliii. 11; Dan. iii. 2; Neh. xi. 7; and 2 Chr. xvii. 8, Pazer (marking a minor dichotomy) comes on the *third* word, because of two servi in the first.

[17] Lev. x. 6; xxi. 10; and Ruth i. 2, are the only examples of this division.

[18] There are besides, the passages in which Géresh marks a *minor* dichotomy, and which must be corrected in the same way. Thus Maqqeph will come between the first word and T'bhîr in 1 Ki. ix. 11; between the first and second words in Deut. xx. 14 and 2 Sam. xviii. 29 (where לְשַׁלַּ֖ח must at the same time have its accent changed to Azla); and between the second and third words in Josh. xxi. 6 and Dan. x. 11. Pazer will take the place of Géresh in 1 Sam. xvii. 23, and Great T'lisha that of Little T'lisha in Esth. vi. 13.

PASHṬA, T'BHÎR, AND ZARQA.   105

As before R'bhia, Great T'lisha may stand on the fifth word, with Géresh to mark the minor dichotomy on the third word, e. g. וַיִּתְקַבְּצוּ אֵלָיו כָּל־אִישׁ מָצוֹק וְכָל־אִישׁ אֲשֶׁר־לוֹ נֹשֶׁא (1 Sam. xxii. 2). Comp. for Pashṭa, Ex. ii. 14; 1 Ki. xiv. 21;—for T'bhîr, Num. ix. 1; Is. xxxvi. 22;—and for Zarqa, Zech. xiv. 4; Ezra v. 17 [19].

Géresh cannot come on the fifth word,—as L'garmeh altogether fails for the minor dichotomy,—except indeed, as in Deut. xvii. 5, through *transposition*. Three passages need in consequence correction, Ex. v. 8; 2 Ki. v. 1 [20]; and 2 Chr. xxii. 11[b]; in all of which I point with various Codd., Great for Little T'lisha.

In all other instances Pazer is employed,—*repeated* if necessary, according to the requirements of the dichotomy, or for the sake of distinct enunciation of details.

Examples of *one* Pazer are common enough: גַּם כָּל־הָאָדָם אֲשֶׁר נָתַן־לוֹ הָאֱלֹהִים עֹשֶׁר וּנְכָסִים וְהִשְׁלִיטוֹ לֶאֱכֹל מִמֶּנּוּ (Qoh. v. 18); וַיִּירְשׁוּ בָּתִּים מְלֵאִים־כָּל־טוּב בֹּרוֹת חֲצוּבִים (Neh. ix. 25); וְאַתָּה הַפְקֵד אֶת־הַלְוִיִּם עַל־ כְּרָמִים וְזֵיתִים מִשְׁכַּן הָעֵדֻת וְעַל כָּל־כֵּלָיו (Num. i. 50). Other examples in Pashṭa's clause are 2 Ki. ix. 26; Esth. iii. 13; 2 Chr. xxxv. 18[b];—in T'bhîr's, 1 Sam. xvii. 40; 1 Ki. ix. 26; Ezek. xxii. 30;—and in Zarqa's, 2 Ki. xxiii. 4; Ezek. xlviii. 21; 2 Chr. xxxii. 15.

Two Pazers are also not uncommon, e. g. עַתָּה הִנֵּה בָטַחְתָּ וַיְמַהֲרוּ (2 Ki. xviii. 21); לָךְ עַל־מִשְׁעֶנֶת הַקָּנֶה הָרָצוּץ הַזֶּה וַיַּשְׁלִימוּ וַיֵּצְאוּ אַנְשֵׁי־הָעִיר לִקְרַאת־יִשְׂרָאֵל לַמִּלְחָמָה הוּא וְכָל־עַמּוֹ (Josh. viii. 14). Comp. for Pashṭa, Ezek. xxi. 3; Dan. iii. 5; Neh. i. 6;—and for T'bhîr, Num. ix. 5; 1 Chr. xii. 40; 2 Chr. xxiii. 1. Two Pazers are not found in Zarqa's clause.

---

[19] Deut. xx. 14; Josh. xxi. 6; 1 Ki. ix. 11; and Dan. x. 11;—as corrected, see previous note,—come under this head. In 1 Sam. xvii. 51 Great T'lisha appears on the sixth word; but it is better to point with R'bhia instead (so Ox. 16; Add. 9398, 11657). We thus avoid having Great T'lisha both before and after Géresh.

[20] In this passage, a double change is necessary. No doubt Great T'lisha in the first word is to be made Little T'lisha, with Ox. 7, 13, 20, 24, &c., וַנִּגְּעֶךָ. The two T'lishas constantly interchange in Codd.

Three Pazers are found in Dan. iii. 7; Ezra viii. 16; Neh. viii. 4; xi. 7; xii. 41; xiii. 15; 1 Chr. iii. 24; xxviii. 1;—*four* in Josh. vii. 24; Ezek. xliii. 11; Dan. iii. 2; 1 Chr. xv. 24;—*five* in Neh. xii. 36; 2 Chr. xvii. 8;—*six* in Neh. viii. 7;—and *eight* in 1 Chr. xv. 18.

Eight of these sixteen examples are in Pashṭa's clause, and eight in T'bhîr's. They are mostly instances where details have to be given of names, &c. In all, the multiplication of the Pazers might have been avoided, if the accentuators had been so minded. Comp. the remark under R'bhîa, p. 97. The examples (it will be observed) occur almost all in the later Books.

On Y'thîbh in the place of Pashṭa.

The substitution is entirely on musical grounds. In the chanting of Pashṭa's word, an *anacrusis* or *appoggiatura* was needed, which it was not possible to introduce, when the tone came on the *first letter* and no servus preceded[21]. In such cases the melody of Pashṭa underwent a change, represented by Y'thîbh (see p. 19), e.g. אַף כִּי־אָמַר אֱלֹהִים (Gen. iii. 1); אֵלֶּה תּוֹלְדֹת נֹחַ (vi. 9).—When the servus preceded, as in וְהָאָרֶץ הָיְתָה תֹהוּ (i. 2); וַיִּקַּח מִשָּׁם אֶבֶן (1 Sam. xvii. 49), the *appoggiatura* (or a substitute for it) was provided.

As the sign for M'huppakh is the same as that for Y'thîbh, there would be occasionally uncertainty as to which accent was intended. The cases are those in which the word, requiring the one or other of these accents, comes between R'bhîa and the Pashṭa which serves as foretone to Zaqeph. Here M'huppakh is, of course, as common as possible. But Y'thîbh is sometimes due, as the representative of R'bhîa repeated (according to the rule, p. 78, 2), e.g. וַיֹּאמֶר יְהוָֹה אֵלַי שֶׁקֶר הַנְּבִיאִים נִבְּאִים בִּשְׁמִי (Jer. xiv. 14), where, however, many Codd. (and our texts) point M'huppakh. To obviate confusion in these cases, and others which might arise from the ignorance or carelessness of punctators[22], the Massoretes drew up a list of the

---

[21] According to Ben-Asher, vocal Sh'va sufficed for the auxiliary note, שְׁמַיִם חוֹבְרוֹת אִישׁ (Ezek. i. 11); but not apparently in Ben-Naphtali's view, who pointed שָׁמַיִם with Y'thîbh. (This punctuation is found in our texts, Ezek. xli. 24.)

[22] As 2 Ki. x. 30, corrected p. 79, note 11.

passages in which, according to their judgment, the word immediately preceding Pashṭa was to be pointed with *Y'thîbh* [23], viz. אִ֚ן (Lev. v. 2); אֶ֚ת (Deut. i. 4; Is. v. 24); בָּ֚ל (Is. xxx. 32; Ezra ix. 4); שֶׁ֚קֶר (Jer. xiv. 14); אִ֚ישׁ (xvi. 12; xxii. 30); and יְ֚דַ (Dan. ii. 10; vii. 27; Ezra vi. 8). In all other cases, M'huppakh was to be chanted [24].

Servi of Pashṭa, T'bhîr, and Zarqa [25].

The chief difference is in the servi immediately preceding these accents. The other servi—when there are two or more—follow the same general rules.

I. One servus.

1. **Pashṭa** has sometimes M'huppakh, sometimes Mer'kha.

a. M'huppakh, when one or more syllables intervene between the servus and the tone-syllable of Pashṭa's word (vocal Sh'va and furtive Pathach being allowed to count as syllables), e. g. הִנֵּה־נָ֥א הוֹאַ֙לְתִּי֙ (Gen. xviii. 31); שְׁלֹ֥שׁ סְאִ֙ים֙ (xviii. 6); לִשְׁלֹ֥חַ יָ֙ד֙ (Esth. iii. 6).

In a few forms, compounded with שֶׁ, M'huppakh appears in the *same word* with Pashṭa, שֶׁ֙אֲהֲבָ֔ה (Cant. i. 7). Comp. i. 12; iii. 4; Qoh. i. 7; vii. 10 [26]. The object is to indicate a compound word [27].

β. Mer'kha, when no syllable intervenes, e. g. הָיְתָ֥ה תֹ֙הוּ֙ (Gen. i. 2); יָדַ֥ע שׁ֙וֹר֙ (Is. i. 3). But if Paseq comes between the words, M'huppakh will stand, יֹ֥ום ׀ יֹ֙ום֙ (Is. lviii. 2) [28].

---

[23] טעמא לאחור (Mas. to Dan. ii. 10), i. e. 'with the accent put backwards,' in reference to the position of Y'thîbh.

[24] So far the list answers a certain purpose. But in itself it is a poor one, and has been but little regarded by punctators or editors. In only three instances is Y'thîbh really required.

[25] These servi, owing to the fine musical distinctions and the many exceptions, give more trouble than all the other servi put together. The Orientals and Ben-Naphtali had more simple rules.

As before, I cannot undertake to enumerate the many errors of our texts. The student, as he comes across them, may correct them according to the following rules, which are firmly established.

[26] See Norzi on Cant. i. 7.

[27] So the Mas. requires M'huppakh in אֲסַרְחַדֹּ֛ן (Ezra iv. 2), a compound of two words, which are kept distinct in ordinary texts.

[28] As Baer has rightly pointed. And so we must correct Jer. xii. 5 and 1 Chr. viii. 38 (ix. 44 is right). The Mas. to Deut. viii. 15 (which gives the instances where Paseq comes between two nouns, the first of which has M'huppakh and the second Pashṭa) is very defective. Beside the above instances, Ezek. xlvii. 16 and Ruth iv. 11 are wanting.

2. **T'bhîr** has sometimes Darga, sometimes Mer'kha.

a. Darga, when two or more syllables intervene between the servus and T'bhîr (vocal Sh'va generally and furtive Pathach counting as above), e. g. וַיִּקְרָא הָאָדָם (Gen. iii. 20); כִּי־נַחַשׁ יְנַחֵשׁ (xliv. 15); וְכִי תִזְבְּחוּ (Lev. xix. 5); נָתַתִּי לָךְ (Gen. xlviii. 22); מַדּוּעַ קִוֵּיתִי (Is. v. 4).

β. Mer'kha, when only one syllable, or none at all, intervenes: וַיִּקְרָא שָׁם, נַעֲשֶׂה אָדָם (Gen. i. 26); וְהָיָה לָּךְ (vi. 21); וַיִּבֶן נֹחַ (viii. 20); (xiii. 4)[29].

Exceptions.—The simple vocal Sh'va which follows a vowel, whether short or long, was not counted of sufficient length to constitute a syllable. Hence we find Mer'kha appointed for all such cases as אֲשֶׁר פְּקָדַי, פָּרוּ וְרָבוּ (Gen. i. 28); הַנְּבִאִים בִּשְׁמִי (Jer. xxiii. 25); (Num. xxvi. 64); וְאִם־לֹא תֵלְכִי (Judg. iv. 8); וְשִׂלַּמְתִּי שִׁמְרוֹן (Mic. i. 6). The explanation seems to be that the pronunciation of the Sh'va in these cases was less distinctly heard than when it comes at the beginning of a word, or at the beginning of a syllable after silent Sh'va[30].

---

[29] The Mas. to Ex. xxi. 35 lays it down that there are thirteen exceptions in which Darga comes, where Mer'kha is due. (We must strike out the words וזגין מתחלפין, with which Jacob ben-Chayyim has headed the list. They make nonsense, and have come from confusion with the Mas. to Lev. xi. 12.) The list is most correctly given in Dikd. hat., § 19: הָיוּ (Gen. xviii. 18); יִפֹּל (Ex. xxi. 35); לוֹ (Lev. vii. 33); אֲשֶׁר (Deut. xiv. 10; Is. xix. 25); גִּין (Josh. viii. 9, 12); מְאוֹת (1 Sam. xxx. 17); יָרַע (2 Sam. xx. 6); כְּשֹׁד (Hos. x. 14); תִּמְצָא (Qoh. ix. 10); חָפֵץ (2 Chr. xviii. 33); לֹא (xxx. 3). It is clear to my mind that we have in these exceptions (and those which follow) merely the errors of some model Codex, for the *same words in the same connection* are at one time pointed according to rule, at another against it. Comp. Lev. xi. 12 (אֲשֶׁר) with Deut. xiv. 10, and 1 Ki. xxii. 34 (חָפֵץ) with 2 Chr. xviii. 33.

[30] Heidenheim (Mishp. hat. 27ᵇ) and Baer (Dikd. hat., p. 13 note) maintain indeed the Sh'va in the above cases—even when the vowel is long—to be *quiescent;* and cite Ben-Asher, Chayyug, Aben-Ezra, and others as of the same view. But that these early grammarians were only driven to adopt their view from the supposed exigencies of the accentuation is clear from the punctuation of certain MSS. lately brought from Yemen,—provided with a peculiar system of superlinear vocalization, not yet familiar to scholars,—*which invariably mark the Sh'va after a long vowel as vocal.* (See, e. g. Pl. LIV of the Palæographical Society's publications, Oriental series, and the accompanying description.) The sign used is a bar over the letter, thus—I drop the peculiar vocalization—אֲשֶׁר יָצְאוּ (Num. xxxiii. 1, in the Plate), the Mer'kha, it will be observed, still retained. We thus see that there were Jewish authorities, which did not accept Ben-Asher's view, just as Qimchi (Mikhlol, 152ᵇ) emancipated himself from the error of his predecessors.

But when Paseq follows, Darga always stands: הִמּוֹל ׀ יִמּוֹל (Gen. xvii. 13); מִיּוֹם ׀ לְיוֹם (Esth. iii. 7); &c.

Obs.—Mer'kha, if no other servus precedes, is sometimes found in the *same word* with T'bhîr. The rule is as follows:—When a *long* vowel, with Métheg and simple Sh'va following, immediately precedes T'bhîr, Mer'kha takes the place of the Métheg, e. g. יָרַד (Deut. xiii. 10); אֶת־יֹשְׁבֵי (xiii. 16); בְּבִירְתָּא (Ezra vi. 2); וְאֶצְאָה (2 Chr. i. 10)[31]. But when a vowel or half-vowel (compound Sh'va) intervenes, Métheg remains, as in אָהֳלִיבָמָה (Gen. xxxvi. 18); וְרָחֲצוּ (Ex. xxx. 19)[32].

Ben-Naphtali and the Orientals (as may be seen in Ḉod. Bab.) did not follow this rule, which really seems to have no *raison d'être*. Indeed, although adopted by grammarians, it was but little observed in practice.

3. **Zarqa** has Munach (properly 'Illuy), e. g. וַיְבָרֶךְ אֹתָם (Gen. i. 28); וַיִּקְרְבוּ יְמֵי־יִשְׂרָאֵל (xlvii. 29)[33]. אֲשֶׁמִים ׀ אֲנַחְנוּ (xlii. 21);

II. Two SERVI. The first will be Munach, if on the *first letter*,— if on any other, Azla[34]; the second will be according to Rule I.

---

[31] Ben-Bil. (MS.) lays down the rule in the following terms: התביר אם שרתו משרת אחד בתינתו לא יהיה כי אם מרכא, ואשר מוקיקו להיות עמו מרכא בתינתו לשרתו הם ב׳ תנאים, האחד הוא שיהיה קורם האות שתחתיו התביר אות שתחתיו שבא או שוכן או מניע, והשני הוא שיהיה קורם האות שתחתיו שבא אחד מן ג׳ המלכים אֶה אוֹ אִי, כגון וַיִּצְאָ֛וּ, יִשְׁתָּרֶ֛גוּ, הַתְּפֻוֹנֶ֛נָּה, בר מן אחד שיש עם אות המרכא נקורה מלמטה, והוא בְּגִירְתָּא דבעורא. No one else (as far as I have seen) has given the rule correctly. Heidenheim (Mishp. hat. 26ᵇ) has copied the false text of Moses the punctator. The rubrics in Ginsb. Mas. מ, § 239 ff., are a complete muddle.

[32] Three exceptions are indeed named (Dikd. hat., § 20): נַתְעַלִי (Ezek. xxxvi. 3); אַל־תִּלָּחֲמוּ (2 Chr. xiii. 12); עַל־הַפְּחָגִים (xxxi. 9). But doubtless Métheg and Mer'kha have been here confounded (in Codd. they are often quite alike), just as Ben-Bil. (Mishp. hat. 29ᵇ) and others have confounded them in אִם־קָטִירוֹ ׀ וְאִם־הֲעוֹרְדִי (Cant. ii. 7), where Mer'kha, following Darga, is impossible.

[33] In ten passages, according to the Mas., Mer'kha comes instead of Munach: אֹפֶר (Ex. vi. 6); אַח־רֹאשׁ (xxx. 12); בְּכֹל (2 Sam. vii. 7; 1 Chr. xvii. 6); שׁוּר (1 Ki. i. 19, 25); וְחָצִי (1 Chr. v. 18); וִיעֲלִי (xiv. 11); נִסְפָּה (xxi. 12); and נֶגֶד (Ruth iv. 4). See Dikd. hat., § 21 end. (There has apparently been some confusion, in the punctuation of these words, with the rule for Zarqa's servi under II. Perhaps some of my readers, who have occupied themselves with the accentuation, have occasionally made, as I have found myself making, the same mistake.) Many authorities omit either 1 Chr. xvii. 6, or 1 Ki. i. 25, thus leaving one example exceptional, and another (with the same words) regular. Comp. note 29.

[34] The principle of this variation has been explained under Y'thîbh, p. 106. Here also, when another servus (Little T'lisha) precedes, Azla will stand even on the first letter.

1. **Pashṭa.** שָׂא נָא עֵינֶיךָ (Gen. xiii. 14); לֵיל שִׁמֻּרִים הוּא (Ex. xii. 42); יְצַו יְהֹוָה אִתְּךָ (Deut. xxviii. 8); וַיַּעֲבֵר אֱלֹהִים רוּחַ (Gen. viii. 1)[35].

In seven instances, Azla takes the place of Métheg in the *same word* with M'huppakh (or Mer'kha): וּבְאַחֵיכֶם (Lev. xxv. 46); כָּל־הָעֵדָה (Num. xx. 1); הַמַּאֲכָלְךָ (Deut. viii. 16). Comp. Ezek. xliii. 11; Dan. iii. 2; Ezra vii. 24; 2 Chr. xxxv. 25[36]. Once Munach comes[37] with the first letter, שֶׁהֵם (Lam. iv. 9).—Ben-Naphtali and the Orientals had no such instances, nor in the similar cases that follow.

2. **T'bhir.** זֶה יִהְיֶה לְךָ (Num. xviii. 9); וְהָבָל הֵבִיא גַם־הוּא (Gen. iv. 4); וַיַּחֲלֹק עֲלֵיהֶם ׀ לַיְלָה (xiv. 15)[38].

In six instances, Azla takes (in some texts) the place of Métheg in the *same word* with Darga or Mer'kha[39]: וַיֹּאמְרוּ (Is. xxx. 16); עַד־עֵרָה (xxxii. 15); וְאִפְּלְטָה (Job i. 15, 16, &c.); בְּנֵי־קוֹלָיָה (Neh. xi. 7); וְיוֹחָנָן (1 Chr. iii. 24); וַאֲרַנְיָהוּ (2 Chr. xvii. 8).

3. **Zarqa.** וַיֹּאמֶר מִי שָׂם פֶּה (Ex. iv. 11); שֵׁשֶׁת יָמִים תַּעֲבֹד (xx. 9); מֹשֶׁה לְפַרְעֹה (viii. 5)[40].

But here a curious musical change may take place. If Métheg occurs in Zarqa's word, or Paseq precedes, Mer'kha comes instead of Munach, between Azla and Zarqa, e. g. וַיָּבֹא יַעֲקֹב מִן־הַשָּׂדֶה (Gen. xxx. 16); וְזָבְדַנִי אֱלֹהִים ׀ אֹתִי (xxx. 20)[41]. Ben-Naphtali, and—to judge from Cod. Bab.—the Orientals, made no distinction of this kind.

---

[35] Once (Dikd. haṭ., § 23) Munach is said to come instead of Azla, בְּיוֹם אַרְבָּעָה עָשָׂר (Esth. ix. 15). And so our texts. But most Codd. point regularly.

[36] See Mas. to Lev. xxv. 46; and for Deut. viii. 16, Mishp. haṭ. 25.

[37] See Mas. parva סעמים ב׳ בתרי, viz. here and Cant. vi. 5 (with Ṭiphcha).

[38] One exception is named (Dikd. haṭ., § 19): כִּי אֵין לַעֲמוֹד (Ezra ix. 15) for אֵין, and so our texts. Evidently a *lapsus calami*.

[39] There is no Mas. here, and the double accentuation fails very generally for some of the instances in Codd. In support of it, see Baer's note to Is. xxxii. 15.

[40] In two passages, 2 Ki. viii. 5 and 2 Chr. vi. 32, Mer'kha is said to occur for Munach in the *first* word (Dikd. haṭ., p. 23). Maqqeph (which is marked in our texts) has fallen out, and then Métheg been taken for Mer'kha.

Ewald, p. 224, gives a string of passages (copied from Spitzner) in which Munach is put for Azla, when the tone is *not* on the first letter. But *they are all false examples,* and do not appear in correct texts!

[41] The exceptions under this head given by grammarians (e. g. Dikd. haṭ., § 21) are that (1) Mer'kha occurs four times, Deut. xix. 5; 2 Sam. iv. 8; v. 11 (1 Chr. xiv. 1), *without either Métheg or Paseq;* (2) Munach three times, Josh. xviii. 14; Dan. vi. 13; Neh. viii. 15, *before Métheg;* and (3) Munach twice, Gen. xxxvii. 22

PASHTA, T'BHÎR, AND ZARQA. 111

In three instances, Azla takes the place of Métheg in the *same word* with Mer'kha: וְאֶל־אִיתָמָר ׀ (Lev. x. 12); אִם־יִצְאוּ בְנוֹת־שִׁילוֹ (Judg. xxi. 21); לָאוֹצָרוֹת ׀ (Neh. xii. 44)[42].

III. THREE SERVI. The first is Little T'lisha, the second Azla, and the third as under II, e. g. בְּרִית מֶלַח עוֹלָם הוּא (Num. xviii. 19); וַיֹּאמֶר יְהוָה אֱלֹהִים ׀ אֶל־הַנָּחָשׁ (Gen. xxxiii. 16); בַּיּוֹם הַהוּא עָשׂוּ וַיָּשָׁב (iii. 14).

It is to be noted that three or more servi are entirely due to the transformation of Géresh in the first word,—i. e. allowing the corrections made p. 104. Not unfrequently, Paseq is employed to mark the dichotomy due on this word.

IV. FOUR or MORE SERVI. All preceding Little T'lisha will be Munachs, e. g. וַיַּרְעֵם יְהוָה בְּקוֹל־גָּדוֹל בַּיּוֹם הַהוּא עַל־פְּלִשְׁתִּים (1 Sam. vii. 10); הֲלוֹא כִבְנֵי כֻשִׁיִּים אַתֶּם לִי (Amos ix. 7); בַּהֲדֹף יְהוָה אֱלֹהֶיךָ אֹתָם ׀ מִלְּפָנֶיךָ (Deut. ix. 4).

T'bhir and Zarqa are not found with more than *four* servi; Pashṭa has *five* in Josh. xix. 51; 1 Sam. vii. 10; Ezek. xxi. 3; and 2 Chr. ii. 3; and once, 2 Ki. xviii. 14, *six*. But such long clauses as those last named are generally avoided by the employment of Pazer or Great T'lisha in subordination to the last servus, see next chap., p. 118.

---

and 2 Ki. iv. 13, *before Paseq*. But how unreliable such lists are may be seen from their all omitting Num. xxx. 15, which is fixed by a standard Massoretic rubric to Gen. xxx. 16. Even the Massora is quite wrong in a rubric, cited briefly in Mishp. hat. 16ᵇ and Ginsb. Mas. ט, § 229, but which I found given at length in Ox. 2325 to Deut. xix. 5: כל דאתי ורקא עם געיא במרכא גּמֹ דאתין בלא 'געיא והם במרכא וסים, then follow the seven instances under 1 and 2, i. e. those under 2 are all *without Métheg!*

[42] See Mas. to Lev. x. 12, or Dikd. hat., p. 23.

CHAPTER XII.

GÉRESH, PAZER, AND GREAT T'LÎSHA.

I TAKE these three accents together, not only because of their frequent interchange, but because they all serve the same purpose of marking the divisions in the clauses governed by R'bhîa, Pashṭa, &c.

GÉRESH. This accent appears under two forms, Géresh proper, and Double Géresh or Gersháyim[1]. Neither admits of repetition.

Géresh is used when the tone is on the *penultimate*, e. g. וַיֹּאמֶר (Gen. xix. 2), מַדּוּעַ (Judg. xi. 7); or *when Azla precedes*, as in וַיֹּאמֶר אֱלֹהִים (Gen. vi. 13);—Gershayim, when the tone is on the *ultimate*, and Azla does *not* precede, e. g. וַיִּשְׁמָעוּ (iii. 8); קַח בְּיָדְךָ (Jer. xliii. 9); עֵץ פְּרִי (i. 11)[2].

Géresh and Gershayim may stand without a servus. Or Géresh may have from one to five servi[3], but Gershayim can only have one.

1. One servus (*a*) is Munach, when on the *first* letter of the word, תַּחַת הַנְּחֹשֶׁת (Is. lx. 17). This is the only servus Gershayim can take.

(β) When not on the first letter, the servus is Azla: שְׁנַיִם שְׁנַיִם (Gen. vii. 9); וַיִּקַּח תֶּרַח (xi. 31); חֲלִילָה לּוֹ (xviii. 25).

2. Two servi. The first is Little T'lisha, and the second Azla (even on the first letter): וַיֹּאמֶר אֵלָיו הָאֱלֹהִים (xx. 6); וַיֹּאמֶר לָהּ בֹּעַז (Ruth ii. 14).

3. Three or more servi. All before Little T'lisha are Munachs. Three servi are common, four much less so, and five rare[4].

---

[1] Both were high notes,—the double stroke (we may suppose) with a *fuller* intonation than the single.

[2] Our texts have, of course, their mistakes. Thus Gershayim is falsely placed in Josh. vi. 23; 1 Sam. xxvi. 19; 2 Ki. ix. 10; &c.

[3] It will be observed that the servi are the same, as the second, third, &c., before Pashṭa, T'bhîr, and Zarqa. The reason is that the *servi of Géresh remained*, after the transformation of Géresh in the first word before the accents named.

[4] The examples I have noted with *five* servi are Judg. xi. 17; 1 Ki. xxi. 2; Jer. iii. 1; viii. 1; xxxvi. 6; Ezek. xlvii. 18; Dan. i. 4. In Jer. viii. 1 our texts have falsely *six* servi, (see Mishp. hat. 10.)

Obs.—Azla may take the place of light Métheg[5] in the *same word* with Géresh (only of course not on the *first* letter), when no other servus precedes[6], e. g. וְנָתַתִּי (Gen. xlviii. 4); וַיֹּאמְרוּ (Ex. xvi. 15); וְהָיְתָה (Is. xxviii. 4); וּבָתִּים (Deut. vi. 11); כָּל־הֶעָרִים (Josh. xxi. 38).

Exceptions are: (a) Forms like וַתַּעֲבֹר (2 Ki. xiv. 9) and בֶּן־אֲעָשָׂה (Jer. xix. 12). Comp. the failure of Munach with the same forms in Zaqeph's word, p. 81. (β) When R'bhîa follows[7], e. g. וַיֹּאמְרוּ הָבָה (Gen. xi. 4) and וְהָיְתָה חֶבֶל הַיָּם (Zeph. ii. 6). Yet if Great T'lîsha precedes, Azla takes the place of Métheg, even before R'bhîa, comp. Lev. xiv. 51; Deut. vii. 13; xxv. 19; &c.[8]

PAZER appears under two forms,—the same in disjunctive value[9],—Great and Little Pazer, see p. 21.

Little Pazer, or Pazer (as it is simply called), is of frequent occurrence, indeed is indispensable for the proper division of the clauses governed by R'bhîa, Pashṭa, &c. It may be repeated (as we have seen) as often as is judged necessary. Once, 1 Chr. xv. 18, it occurs eight times in succession.

---

[5] Not of heavy Métheg. Hence כָּל־הַמַּחֲלָה (Ex. xv. 26). Comp. p. 80, note 16. These fine distinctions have not been noticed by accentuologists. The instances in our texts in which Azla is omitted, or falsely introduced, are hardly worth recording.

[6] The Mas. fin. 33ᵃ names four passages,—Josh. viii. 25; 1 Ki. xii. 24; 1 Chr. xv. 18; xxviii. 11,—in which Azla stands for Métheg, *although Little T'lîsha precedes.* (Great T'lîsha might have stood, and then all would have been regular.)

[7] See Mas. to 1 Sam. xi. 9 and Zeph. ii. 6.

[8] Little T'lîsha has always Azla after it, and as the melody of the two T'lîshas must have been similar, it is not surprising to find the same tendency on the part of Great T'lîsha.

[9] حكمهم واحد فى القطع (Ox. 2512). Great Pazer had no doubt a fuller and stronger *melody*, הרעמתו גדולה (De R. 1262).

It will be found that Pazer alone, or the last of a series, has generally in musical sequence Great or Little T'lîsha after it. Most of the examples to the contrary have been already given in chaps. X and XI, to which are to be added Ex. xxxiv. 4; Jer. xxxviii. 12; Esth. vi. 13; and the instances in which L'garmeh takes the place of Great T'lîsha (p. 118), Gen. xxviii. 9; 1 Sam. xiv. 3, 47; 2 Sam. xiii. 32; 2 Ki. xviii. 17; Jer. xl. 11; and Ezek. ix. 2. Sometimes we can correct our texts, as שְׁתֵּי (Josh. iv. 8); גְּנֵי (xxii. 9, 31); שְׁנֵי (Judg. vii. 25).

Little Pazer may stand alone, or may have from one to six servi, all of which will be Munachs[10]. One, two, and three servi are very common, four less so, and five or six quite rare[11]. Examples may be seen in Gen. i. 21; xxi. 14; xxxvi. 6; Num. iii. 4; &c.

Great Pazer, or Qarne Phara (as it is commonly called), occurs only sixteen times[12], and in every instance Little Pazer might be substituted for it. The object of its introduction seems to have been to draw attention to something which seemed to the accentuators *noteworthy* in the verse in which it occurs[13]. Thus in Num. xxxv. 5 to the *measurement* laid down (which has indeed perplexed commentators to the present day); in 2 Sam. iv. 2 to the *defective reading* (לְאִישׁ־בֹּשֶׁת has fallen out); in Jer. xiii. 13 to the remarkable explanation of the *symbol*, verse 12 (comp. the similar example in Neh. v. 13); &c. All mere trifling! nor need we be surprised if we cannot, in some instances, trace the fancy which led to the employment of this peculiar sign. Some punctators dispensed with it altogether[14]. Unlike Little Pazer, it does not admit of repetition.

Great Pazer never stands *alone*, but is always preceded by at least two servi, the first of which is Munach, and the second Galgal. It may have as many as six servi, all of which, except the last, will be Munachs[15].

---

[10] Once the servus occurs in the *same word* with Pazer, אֲנָ֡א (Gen. l. 17). Texts have it falsely in וְהַלְוִיִּ֡ם (Neh. xii. 41).

[11] *Five* servi I have noticed only in 1 Ki. vi. 1, and *six* only in Jer. xxxv. 15.

[12] Fixed by the Mas. to Ezek. xlviii. 21, viz. Num. xxxv. 5; Josh. xix. 51; 2 Sam. iv. 2; 2 Ki. x. 5; Jer. xiii. 13; xxxviii. 25; Ezek. xlviii. 21; Esth. vii. 9; Ezra vi. 9; Neh. i. 6; v. 13; xiii. 5, 15; 1 Chr. xxviii. 1; 2 Chr. xxiv. 5; xxxv. 7. Eight times before R'bhia, and eight times before Pashṭa and its sister-accents. (On the number *eight* in connection with these accents and Pazer, see p. 97.)

[13] Comp. Man. du Lect., p. 92 above: מעם אלו הפסורים הגדולים אמרו לפי שיש בפסוקים אלה חוזק ביותר וננבהין יותר מדאי, לכך נעשו פזרי גדולים, i.e. 'because there is in these verses a greater weight, and they are to be made more than usually prominent, for this reason Great Pazers were appointed.'

[14] So the Codex known as Sinai: ולא נקד קרני פרה בכל הסיני (Ginsb. Mas. ח, § 665).

[15] It has *five* servi in Josh. xix. 51; 1 Chr. xxviii. 1; and *six* in Ezek. xlviii. 21; Ezra vi. 9; (see Man. du Lect., p. 91.) The Mas. to Ezek. l. c. has a notice that it has twice *seven* servi. For the correction, see Baer's note on the passage.

GREAT T'LÎSHA, like Géresh and Pazer, marks the division in clauses governed by R'bhîa, Pashṭa, &c. It cannot be repeated [16]; nor can Great and Little T'lîsha come together without a disjunctive between [17].

Great T'lîsha may stand alone, or may have from one to five servi, all of which will be Munachs. One or two servi are very common, three less so, and four or five quite rare [18].

N. B. Great and Little T'lîsha, as being similar in melody, are constantly interchanged in Codd., particularly where the former is subordinated to Géresh or the servus that takes the place of Géresh, p. 116 ff. In such cases the one or the other may stand, e. g. יֹאכַל or יֹאכֵל (Lev. vii. 18); וַיִּשְׁלַח or וַיִּשְׁלָח (2 Sam. v. 11); יְהוּא or יֵהוּא (2 Ki. x. 25); שַׂמְתָּ or שַׂמְתָּ (Jer. xxxii. 20); וַיֵּצֵא or וַיֵּצֵא (xli. 6); &c. Of a different class are the mistakes in our texts [19]: אֶרֶץ (Gen. xxiii. 15); נֵזֶר (Lev. xxi. 12); יִשָּׂאוּ (Josh. vi. 4); וְאֶת־עַבְדֵיכֶם (1 Sam. viii. 16); לְבָרֵךְ (1 Ki. i. 47); וַיַּשְׁכֵּם (2 Ki. vi. 15); בִּלְאָדָן (2 Ki. xx. 12; Is. xxxix. 1); כָּל־הַדָּבָר (Jer. xlii. 4); מִלְחַמְתָּם (Ezek. xxxii. 27); נְדַבְרַיָּא (Dan. iii. 3); קַרְנָא (iii. 7); פְּסַנְתֵּרִין (iii. 15); הַבָּאִים (Ezra viii. 35); סַמִּים (2 Chr. xiii. 11) [20]; with the particles also, לֹא, כִּי, אֲשֶׁר (Ex. ix. 24; 1 Sam. ii. 24; Jer. xxix. 10; Ezek. iii. 5);—all contrary to the rules for the consecution of the servi, or for the logical (syntactical) division of the clause. Doubtless, it is the frequent interchange of these two accents,

---

[16] As in ordinary texts falsely, Deut. v. 14.

[17] One example occurs, 2 Sam. xiv. 32, which is doubtless to be corrected, although supported by the testimony of Codd. and of grammarians like Ben-Bil. 9ᵃ, and his copyists, Chayyug, p. 129, and Man. du Lect., p. 82. It is a mistake, like the two Zarqas (1 Sam. ii. 15), also defended by Ben-Bil., and like S'gôlta (Ezra vii. 13), which has the support of all Codd. without exception, and yet which so conservative an editor as Baer has found it necessary to reject. The simplest correction is found in Ox. 8, Erf. 3, Bomb. 1, וְאִשְׁלְחָה אֶחָד אֶל־הַמֶּלֶךְ לֵאמֹר, whereby the Little T'lîsha is cancelled.

Ben-Bil. (Mishp. hat. 35ᵇ) lays down a strange rule, which Baer has adopted in his note to Gen. vii. 7, that Great T'lîsha is not allowed after Zaqeph, unless the latter has Pashṭa preceding. Such a rule, if it existed, would admit of no conceivable explanation. But it *does not exist*, see Ex. x. 14; Deut. xii. 8; 1 Ki. xvii. 20; xxii. 14; Ruth iv. 14.

[18] *Four* I have noticed only in Judg. xviii. 7; 2 Sam. viii. 10; Neh. iv. 1; vi. 1; and *five* only in Jer. xli. 1; Ezek. xlvii. 12.

[19] All of which admit of correction by the help of Codd.

[20] Correct here also וּבְעָרָב with Maqqeph. Texts have R'bhîa!

and the loose way in which Little T'lisha is often subordinated to Géresh, where Great T'lisha might have stood[21], that has led to the mistaken notion that Little T'lisha has sometimes a *disjunctive* value. Comp. p. 26, 5[22].

The three accents we have just considered mark the *last* musical and interpunctional divisions. The consequence is that the dichotomy generally fails in their clauses, the utmost that is done to mark it being the occasional introduction of the slight pause made by Paseq: קַח מַטְּךָ וּנְטֵה־יָדְךָ֡ עַל־מֵימֵ֣י מִצְרַ֗יִם (Deut. xxxi. 17); וְאָמַ֗ר וְחָרָ֨ה אַפִּ֤י ב֙וֹ בַּיּ֣וֹם־הַה֔וּא (Ex. vii. 19); וַיְדַבֵּ֣ר אַחְאָ֣ב אֶל־נָב֣וֹת ׀ (Mal. i. 6); אָ֣ב אָ֤נִי אַיֵּ֣ה כְבוֹדִ֗י (1 Ki. xxi. 2); לֵאמֹ֑ר ׀ תְּנָה־לִּ֤י אֶת־כַּרְמְךָ֙ וַתִּשָּׂ֨א אֹתִ֤י ר֙וּחַ ׀ בֵּ֣ין־ (Num. xxxii. 29); וּבֵין־רְאוּבֵ֣ן ׀ אִתְּכֶ֔ם הָאָ֖רֶץ וּבֵ֥ין הַשָּׁמָ֑יִם (Ezek. viii. 3).

This is particularly the case with Pazer and Great T'lisha; but with Géresh, the established musical sequence, of which we had so many examples in the chapters treating of R'bhîa, Pashṭa, &c., has been utilized, so as to make Pazer and Great T'lisha serve as dividers of its clause,—Great T'lisha on the first or second word, Pazer on the third word or further[23],—e. g. וַיְמַ֡ן יְהוָֽה־אֱלֹהִ֣ים ׀ קִֽיקָיוֹן֩ וַיַּ֨עַל ׀ מֵעַ֣ל לְיוֹנָ֗ה (Jon. iv. 6; instead of וַיִּזְבְּח֣וּ בַיּוֹם־הַה֗וּא זְבָחִ֣ים גְּדוֹלִ֔ים); (וַיְמַ֤ן יְהוָֽה־אֱלֹהִים֙ קִֽיקָיוֹן֒ וְאָמַרְתָּ֞ לֶהָרִ֗ים (Neh. xii. 43; instead of בַּיּ֥וֹם הַה֖וּא); וַיִּשְׂמָ֑חוּ וְלַגְּבָע֣וֹת לָאֲפִיקִ֣ים וְלַגֵּאָי֑וֹת ׀ כֹּה־אָמַ֣ר ׀ אֲדֹנָ֣י יְהוִ֗ה (Ezek. xxxvi. 6; instead of וְאָמַרְתָּ֞ לֶהָרִ֤ים וְלַגְּבָעוֹת֙); וַתַּסְתִּירֵ֔הוּ יְהוֹשַׁבְעַת֩ בַּת־הַמֶּ֨לֶךְ יְהוֹרָ֜ם אֵ֣שֶׁת ׀ יְהוֹיָדָ֣ע הַכֹּהֵן֒ וְגוֹ' (2 Chr.

---

[21] See, for instance, Gen. i. 25; Judg. x. 6; 2 Sam. xv. 2; 2 Ki. xxiv. 2; Is. xxvii. 1; Jer. iii. 1; viii. 1; Ezek. ix. 6; xliv. 5; Mal. i. 6.

[22] The Mas. to 1 Sam. xii. 3 numbers eight passages, in which Little T'lisha is followed by Paseq,—a proof, if any were needed, that it cannot really serve as a disjunctive.

[23] Pazer rarely comes on the *second* word, as in Ex. xxxiv. 4 (comp. p. 113, note 9).

xxii. 11; Pazers instead of Munachs). Comp. Gen. xvii. 8; Num. iii. 38; xix. 13; 1 Sam. xvii. 39; 2 Sam. ix. 10; xx. 3; 1 Ki. ii. 33^b; viii. 20^b; Jer. xxxv. 15; Qoh. vi. 2 [24].

The distinctness and emphasis, which it might be required to note, were thus secured for Géresh's clause; although it must be allowed that the division fails at times where we should have expected to find it [25].

Writers on the accents have found here a confusion, which has much perplexed them. For, in the division of clauses governed by R'bhîa, Pashṭa, &c., Pazer constantly marks the main dichotomy, with Great T'lîsha following for the first, and Géresh for the second of the minor dichotomies (Géresh therefore marking the *smallest* of the dichotomies); whereas here, in the same clauses, *Géresh marks the main dichotomy*, and has Pazer and Great T'lîsha subordinated to it. The explanation (as it seems to me) is that the *musical pause* in the case of these several minor disjunctives was so *slight*, that they readily lent themselves to this variation in their (relative) interpunctional value [26]. Something similar occurs in our own system of interpunction. The logical pause with the *comma* is always slight; and sometimes one comma is subordinated to another, sometimes to a colon, semicolon, &c., farther on in the clause.

This subordination was carried out still further. Géresh (as we have seen) does not always maintain its position. When due on the first word before Pashṭa, T'bhîr, or Zarqa, it is almost invariably transformed to a servus (p. 100). What is observable is that Great T'lîsha and Pazer are often found *subordinated to this servus* (which stands for Géresh), just as if Géresh itself were

---

[24] Sometimes, when there are only *two* words in Géresh's clause, the first is, for the sake of emphasis or distinctness, pointed with Great T'lîsha, as in Gen. vi. 19; Ex. xxx. 31 (corrected p. 60); 1 Ki. xiii. 33; 2 Chr. iii. 2.

[25] A corresponding division in Great T'lîsha's clause, with Pazer to mark the dichotomy, is very rare. I have noted only the following instances: Gen. viii. 22; Lev. xx. 17; 1 Ki. vi. 1 (point מִצְרַיִם with Codd.); Esth. iii. 13; Ezra iii. 9; 2 Chr. xxxi. 2.

[26] Of course the accentuators might have adopted another course. They might have introduced new musical notes or phrases, with corresponding signs; but this would have complicated the system, without any appreciable advantage. Practically little or no inconvenience or confusion has resulted from the simpler course, which they preferred to adopt, although theoretically it must be pronounced irregular.

present [27], e. g. סׄוּרוּ נָ֠א אֶל־בֵּ֨ית עַבְדְּכֶם֙ וְלִ֔ינוּ (Gen. xix. 2);
וְשַׂמְתִּ֣י מָק֠וֹם לְעַמִּ֨י לְיִשְׂרָאֵ֤ל וּנְטַעְתִּיו֙ (2 Sam. vii. 10; 1 Chr. xvii. 9);
וַתִּשְׁבְּנָה הֶעָ֠רִים אֲשֶׁ֨ר לָקְחוּ־פְלִשְׁתִּ֤ים מֵאֵת֙ יִשְׂרָאֵ֔ל (1 Sam. vii. 14);
וַיִּבָּדֵ֣ל אַהֲרֹ֠ן לְהַקְדִּישׁוֹ֙ קֹ֣דֶשׁ קָֽדָשִׁ֔ים לְיִשְׂרָאֵל֒ (1 Chr. xxiii. 13). Comp. for T'bhîr's clause, Ex. xxviii. 30[b]; Lev. i. 11; Deut. vi. 22; Josh. xi. 7;—and for Zarqa's, Judg. vii. 20; 2 Sam. iv. 8; Neh. viii. 17.

EXCEPTIONS.—Instead of Great T'lîsha, L'garmeh is occasionally employed to mark the division in Géresh's clause. The Mas. to Jer. iv. 19 notes eleven passages, in which this accent is subordinated to (משרת)[28] Géresh, at the second word from it, viz. Gen. xxviii. 9; 1 Sam. xiv. 3, 47; 2 Sam. xiii. 32; 2 Ki. xviii. 17; Jer. iv. 19; xxxviii. 11; xl. 11; Ezek. ix. 2; Hag. ii. 12; and 2 Chr. xxvi. 15. Once, Is. xxxvi. 2, it is subordinated to Géresh transformed. The accentuators must have designed by this exceptional accentuation to signalize these passages as deserving of special notice or special emphasis. The reader may be left to trace for himself these Massoretic fancies, which (it so happens) are for the most part sufficiently obvious. The most notable instance is 2 Ki. xviii. 17[29], on which see notes at end.

---

[27] Comp. in the poetical system (טעמי אמ״ת, p. 61) L'garmeh and Pazer subordinated to the servus that stands for D'chî.

[28] The expression is hardly correct (although the term ܡܫܡܫܐ is similarly used in Syriac, comp. Bar-Zu'bî, ed. Martin, p. 4). Ox. 2322 and Jequthiel to Gen. xxviii. 9 have סמוך instead.

[29] Where our texts have falsely Little T'lîsha with Paseq, for L'garmeh.

CHAPTER XIII.

L'GARMEH [1].

I. L'GARMEH's proper place is in R'bhîa's clause [2].

1. It marks the dichotomy there, and admits of repetition, as we saw in the chapter on R'bhîa, §§ II, III, IV.

2. It stands in the place of Paseq, when this latter sign is due before R'bhîa [3]. Thus וַיֹּ֣אמֶר ׀ לֹא (Gen. xviii. 15); מִיָּמִים֨ ׀ הַבְּכ֨וֹר ׀ נָדָ֑ב (1 Sam. ii. 19); אָבִ֨י ׀ אָבִ֜י (2 Ki. xiii. 14); יָמִ֨ימָה (Num. iii. 2) are all instances of *Paseq;* but the corresponding examples, וַיֹּ֨אמֶר ׀ לֹא (Josh. v. 14); מִיָּמִ֨ים ׀ יָמִ֜ימָה (Judg. xi. 40); אָבִ֨י ׀ אָבִ֜י (2 Ki. ii. 12); and הַבְּכ֨וֹר ׀ אַמְנ֜וֹן (1 Chr. iii. 1), all *L'garmehs* [4].

The object of the change was simply musical. The rules for Paseq will shew that it could only have stood when R'bhîa's clause consists of *two* words, or has *Géresh on the second word*. But here L'garmeh was musically admissible, and was preferred to the simpler melody of Munach-Paseq.

For us indeed the change made has no meaning. For we cannot appreciate the musical distinction, and even the *signs* are, in the Palestinian system, by some strange oversight, *the same* (see p. 22).

---

[1] To prevent mistakes in the chanting, some punctators marked in the margin of their texts לֹ֨, against the instances in which L'garmeh is due (so Ox. 15, 70, 71; Add. 21161; De R. 2; &c.); and Ginsburg has thought it worth while to fill up page after page of his great work with these marginal notes. But they are *no Massora!* And what is one to say to them, when they are not even correctly given!!

[2] Comp. Ben-Bil. (Mishp. hat. 7ᵇ): כל לגרמי׳ שבמקרא באים לפני רביע, לבד במקומות מעוטים.

[3] The Massora and grammarians allow but one exception in favour of Paseq: כֹּה־אָמַ֣ר הָאֵ֣ל ׀ יְהֹוָ֗ה (Is. xlii. 5). So Ox. 4 in the Mas. marg. to this passage, לית פסק סמוך לרביע, i. e. 'the only instance of Paseq immediately followed by R'bhia,' and so Ben-Bil. l.c. The fancy seems to have been to make this passage agree with Ps. lxxxv. 9, where Paseq with the same words must stand.

[4] A list of these L'garmehs will be found after the Paseq-list, p. 129.

II. The following are the only examples in which L'garmeh occurs, without R'bhîa following:

Before Pashṭa, Lev. x. 6; xxi. 10; Ruth i. 2;[5] and before Géresh (or Géresh transformed), the passages cited p. 118[6]. In these few anomalous cases, it comes where Great T'lîsha might have stood. The grounds for the change have been indicated, l. c.

SERVI OF L'GARMEH.

L'garmeh may stand alone, or may have one or two servi.

One servus is Mer'kha, הִנֵּה מִצְרַיִם (Ex. xiv. 10).

Two servi. The first is Azla and the second Mer'kha[7]: וְאֵינֶנּוּ חָסֵר לְנַפְשׁוֹ (Qoh. vi. 2); וְשֶׁבַע עֶשְׂרֵה שָׁנָה (1 Ki. xiv. 21; 2 Chr. xii. 13). These are, I believe, the only instances[8]. So there are only two passages in the three Books in which L'garmeh has *two* servi (טעמי אמ"ת, p. 94).

CHAPTER XIV.

PASEQ.

WE come to the *final* touch, applied to the system we have been so long considering. After the verse had been arranged musically, according to the rules above laid down, two or more words might be left joined by the accents, which it might nevertheless seem desirable, for the sake of effect in the reading, to separate by a slight pause. The sign Paseq—a short perpendicular line, like a bar—was placed between the words for that purpose. The meaning of the term פָּסֵק, 'cutting off,' =

---

[5] See Mas. parva to Lev. xxi. 10, and Mishp. hat. 34[b].

[6] Ben-Bil. indeed (Mishp. hat. 34[a]) makes L'garmeh come before Pazer, citing as examples Dan. iii. 2 and Neh. viii. 7. But these are instances of Paseq. (Yet Heidenheim does not correct this manifest error.)

[7] So the Massora requires, see Norzi on 2 Chr. xii. 13 and Ginsb. ט, § 230. The authorities quoted by Baer (in his note on Qoh. vi. 2) for *two Mer'khas* must therefore be rejected.

[8] The two other passages, cited in Mishp. hat. 23[b]—1 Sam. xxvii. 1 and Ezek. viii. 6—are in most Codd. pointed as in printed texts.

'separating,' indicates its function. This sign had no proper musical value, and was therefore not numbered among the accents.

There is only one exception to the general meaning of the sign, and that is when it is associated with Munach, to constitute the independent musical accent, known as L'garmeh. The inventive faculty of the accentuators was certainly here at fault.

In the case of Shalshéleth, Paseq is apparently joined to a *disjunctive* accent. In reality it has been introduced in imitation of the Great Shalshéleth of the three Books, where it has its proper meaning. Unnecessary it is, and fails in many Codd. See p. 18 above[1].

This sign was subject to certain general rules in its application; but before proceeding to investigate these rules, we must ascertain *where it is really due* in the text.

Modern writers on the accents have been quite content to take the printed text as a guide, without being aware how incorrect it is. I have noted more than *sixty* instances in which Paseq fails in Van der Hooght's edition, to say nothing of the passages in which it is falsely introduced.—The printed lists are our only other authority for the Paseqs, but they too are not to be trusted. That given in Bomb. 2 (*Massora finalis*, letter פ) and copied in Buxtorf's Rabbinical Bible (ditto, pp. 60, 61) is disfigured by a mass of L'garmehs, has many omissions, and often marks Paseq falsely in the passages cited. Ginsburg's list, I. p. 647 ff., is equally faulty, frequently offending against the Massora itself and the readings of all respectable Codd. Baer's lists, as far as they go, are of course far more correct, but even they are not altogether reliable.

I was thus driven to draw up a list for myself, and succeeded, after some trouble, in bringing together the necessary materials. Several Codd. exist, which enumerate the Paseqs for the whole of the text, quoting the passages in which they occur[2]. Others do the same for particular Books[3]. Whilst a third class have the Paseqs marked in the margin by the abbreviation פס or פ[4]. By the comparison

---

[1] It is surprising to find Prof. Graetz, in an article on Paseq (in his Monatschrift for Sept. 1882, pp. 394–5), placing it after Pashṭa and T'bhir! Other extraordinary mistakes are found in the same article.

[2] They are the Aleppo Cod. (see Preface, p. x); the St. Petersburg Cod. B 19ᵃ (dated A.D. 1009); Add. 15251; and Modena xxvi. By far the most correct of these is the St. Petersburg list, for a copy of which I am indebted to Dr. Harkavy.

[3] As Add. 21161, Ar. Or. 16, Or. 2628; Ox. 2438; De R. 196; and Simson's חבור הקונים.

[4] Add. 21161; Ox. 15, 70, 71; K. 154; and De R. 2. Cod. Bab. is also to some extent useful.

of these several sources, I have been able to compile what I believe to be a correct list of the Paseqs, according to the Massora and the ideas of the old punctators. It will be found at the end of the present chapter, and will, of course, be adopted for the rules that follow.

I divide the Paseqs into two classes, the ordinary Paseq, which may precede *any* disjunctive accent, and separates *two* words that are kept together by the accents; and the extra-ordinary Paseq (*Paseq dichotomicum*), which is *confined to certain accents* (named below), and appears where *three* or more words are conjoined [5].

I. The ordinary Paseqs may be subdivided into

1. *Paseq distinctivum*, which comes between two words, that are to be distinguished as to *sense*, e. g. וַיֹּאמֶר ׀ לֹא (Gen. xviii. 15) [6], in contrast to וַיֹּאמֶר לוֹ ;—כָּלָה ׀ עָשֹׂוּ (xviii. 21), כָּלָה not to be made (as the ordinary construction would make it) *accusative;*—חָצוֹר ׀ חֲדַתָּה (Josh. xv. 25), to be treated as two *distinct* names, like חָצוֹר ׀ רָמָה (Neh. xi. 33), and the instances in Josh. xv. 55; xix. 7; Ezek. xlvii. 16.

This Paseq is further found in a few cases of *specification*, where attention is to be drawn to details, as נָטְפוּ ׀ וּשְׁחֵלֶת (Ex. xxx. 34) and אֲרָיוֹת ׀ בָּקָר (1 Ki. vii. 29) [7]. It is necessary in Neh. ii. 13 and 1 Chr. xxvii. 12 to insure correctness of reading; and in וְיָשֵׂם ׀ פָּנָיו (Dan. xi. 17, 18) it seems meant as a *nota bene* to the reader to distinguish these instances from וְיָשֵׂב פָּנָיו (ver. 19).

2. *Paseq emphaticum*, e. g. יְהוָֹה ׀ יְהוָֹה ׀ יִמְלֹךְ (Ex. xv. 18);

---

[5] We have here a proof that Paseq was the *latest* of the signs, for its presence depends on the other (accentual) signs having been fixed. I mention this, because some scholars (as Graetz) have supposed that its use preceded that of the accents.

[6] Cf. Judg. xii. 5; 1 Sam. ii. 16 (Q'ri); 1 Ki. ii. 30; xi. 22. Yet וַיֹּאמְרוּ לֹא (Gen. xix. 2; 1 Sam. viii. 19) is not so distinguished from וַיֹּאמְרוּ לוֹ (Judg. xviii. 19; Esth. vi. 13).

[7] The other examples are Josh. viii. 33; Ezra vii. 17; Neh. xii. 44; and the names in 1 Chr. i. 24; viii. 38 (ix. 44); and xv. 18. This Paseq, once introduced, might evidently have been multiplied to any extent, but seems to have been intended only in the few instances given.

חֶרְפַּת ׀ (Deut. vi. 4); הַיוֹנָתָן ׀ יָמוּת (1 Sam. xiv. 45); אֶחָד
אֲדֹנָי (Is. xxxvii. 24); עַל־הַדָּם ׀ תֹּאכֵלוּ (Ezek. xxxiii. 25);
כַּצֵּל ׀ יָמֵינוּ (1 Chr. xxix. 15).

The examples under this head are sufficiently numerous, indeed so much so, that we may regard this emphatic use as the chief object of the ordinary Paseq.

In a few cases this Paseq is introduced—to insure emphatic pronunciation—between the Divine names. The most notable instance of the kind occurs in Josh. xxii. 22; but this belongs under II. 2. The other examples are הָאָדוֹן ׀ יְהוָה (Ex. xxiii. 17; xxxiv. 23); הָאֵל ׀ יְהוָה (Is. xlii. 5); הָאֱלֹהִים ׀ יְהוָה (2 Chr. xxx. 19).

3. *Paseq homonymicum.* Where a word is *repeated*, in the same or a similar form, Paseq not unfrequently appears between. (This use of Paseq is closely related to that last given.) E. g. אַבְרָהָם ׀ אַבְרָהָם (Gen. xxii. 11); אָמֵן ׀ אָמֵן (Num. v. 22); הִמּוֹל ׀ יִמּוֹל (Gen. xvii. 13); שַׁקֵּץ ׀ תְּשַׁקְּצֶנּוּ (Deut. vii. 26); הַשֹּׁמֵעַ ׀ יִשְׁמָע (Ezek. iii. 27); עָמֹק ׀ עָמֹק מִי יִמְצָאֶנּוּ (Qoh. vii. 24).

We must not, however, suppose that we have here to do with a *rule*. The accentuators found a certain emphasis in the expressions quoted, which they marked with Paseq, but in the majority of similar instances they omitted the sign. A particular emphasis is no doubt lacking in most cases[a], yet they might have introduced it, on their own principle, in many other passages, as כִּי־גֵאֹה גָּאָה (Ex. xv. 1);

---

[a] Thus, we could understand the failure of Paseq, in the case of numerals, שִׁבְעָה שִׁבְעָה (Gen. vii. 2); שְׁנַיִם שְׁנַיִם (vii. 9), &c.,—of distributives generally, as בַּבֹּקֶר בַּבֹּקֶר (2 Ki. xvii. 29); גּוֹי גּוֹי (2 Ki. xvii. 29); עֵדֶר עֵדֶר (Gen. xxxii. 17); אִישׁ אִישׁ (Lev. xvii. 3); בַּבֹּקֶר בַּבֹּקֶר (Ex. xvi. 21), &c.,—and of current expressions like מְאֹד מְאֹד (Gen. vii. 19); פָּנִים אֶל־פָּנִים (Gen. xxxii. 31), עַיִן בְּעַיִן (Deut. xix. 21); כְּעֶצֶם מְעַט (Ex. xxiii. 30); &c. But instances like these account only very partially for the omission of the sign. For instance, it rarely comes between the inf. abs. and the finite verb, מוֹת תָּמוּת, &c.; although the very object of this construction is to give strength and emphasis to the expression. Sometimes perhaps we may account for its absence, by supposing that the words were meant to be pronounced with animation and rapidity, as סָרוּ סָרוּ (Is. li 11); סֹלּוּ־סֹלּוּ (lvii. 14).

הַמוֹנִים הֲמוֹנִים (Joel iv. 14); רָזִי־לִי רָזִי־לִי (Is. xxiv. 16); שַׁבַּת שַׁבָּתוֹן (xxxi. 15); &c. They have been very particular in placing it (twenty-six times) wherever סָבִיב ׀ סָבִיב occurs in Ezekiel (viii. 10; xxxvii. 2; xl. 5; &c.), so that more than one third of the examples they give consists of these instances. On the other hand they intentionally omitted it in מֹשֶׁה מֹשֶׁה (Ex. iii. 4), and the Midrash gives the reason: 'With Moses the prophetic gift *never ceased*' (לֹא פָסֵק)[9]!

4. *Paseq euphonicum* is introduced, in a few cases, for the sake of distinct pronunciation, *when one word ends and the next begins with the same letter:* גַּן ׀ נָעוּל (Cant. iv. 12); אֲנָשִׁים ׀ מְעַט (Neh. ii. 12); בַּרְזֶל ׀ לָרֹב (1 Chr. xxii. 3); and once with cognate letters, נָחָשׁ ׀ שָׂרָף (Deut. viii. 15)[10].

The other instances are Judg. i. 7; 1 Chr. ii. 25; xxii. 5; xxix. 11; 2 Chr. xx. 1; xxxiv. 12. But this small number of examples shews that *the failure of Paseq is the rule*[11], as in בַּשָּׁמַיִם מִמַּעַל (Deut. iv. 39; Josh. ii. 11); עֵשָׂו בִּשְׂדֵה (Deut. xi. 15); שְׁמַע עַבְדְּךָ (1 Sam. xxiii. 11); לֹא־תֹאכַל לֶחֶם (1 Ki. xiii. 17); &c. The student may find for himself as many examples as he pleases.

N. B. כִּי ׀ יָרֵאָה (Gen. xviii. 15) does not come under this head, for כִּי is constantly followed by Yôd, e. g. כִּי יָרֵא (xix. 30); nor יְהֹוָה ׀ יִמְלֹךְ (Ex. xv. 18); (אֲדֹנָי) ׀ יָרֵאָה (xxii. 14); הֵילִילוּ ׀ וְזַעֲקוּ (Jer. xlviii. 20). These are all instances of *Paseq emphaticum*.

II. The extraordinary Paseq—or *Paseq dichotomicum*, as it will be more convenient to call it—was due to the circumstance that the accentual system failed to provide the necessary signs for marking the dichotomy, in clauses governed by certain of the minor disjunctive accents. Paseq was then (occasionally) employed in place of the missing disjunctive sign. Thus—

---

[9] See Midrash rabba on Exodus, sect. 2, towards end (quoted by Levy, Neuhebr. W. B., s. v. פסק), or Norzi ad loc.

[10] In Berakhoth 15ᵇ below, the careful pronunciation of such words is insisted on; but no hint is given that Paseq sometimes comes between, to insure it.—This sign was, of course, unknown in the Talmudic time.

[11] The notion that the separation by Paseq takes place, when other letters, as two different labials, or (as Graetz supposes) Mem and Aleph (!), come together, is thus clearly shewn to have no foundation.—If the *same* letters are generally not separated by Paseq, a fortiori *dissimilar* ones would not be.

(1) On the *first* word before Pashṭa, T'bhîr, and Zarqa (see p. 100): וַיִּקְרָ֣א אֱלֹהִ֤ים ׀ לָאוֹר֙ (Gen. i. 5; comp. וַיִּקְרָ֨א אֱלֹהִ֤ים לָֽרָקִ֨יעַ, verse 8, with the dichotomy *marked* by T'bhîr); בְּהַדָּ֣ף יְהוָ֣ה ׀ אֱלֹהֶ֤יךָ אֹתָם֙ ׀ מִלְּפָנֶ֔יךָ (Deut. ix. 4).

In a few instances, this Paseq represents a *minor* dichotomy as well: Josh. xix. 51; Judg. xx. 25; 1 Sam. xxiv. 11 (comp. xxvi. 23); Jer. li. 37; 1 Chr. xxi. 15.—In 2 Ki. xviii. 14 it occurs thrice.

(2) On *any word* before Géresh, Pazer, or Great T'lîsha, because these accents have regularly no subordinate disjunctive. For the same reason, Paseq is not unfrequently *repeated*. E.g. וַיְדַבֵּ֣ר אַחְאָ֣ב אֶל־נָב֣וֹת ׀ לֵאמֹ֣ר ׀ תְּנָה־לִּ֣י אֶֽת־כַּרְמְךָ֡ (1 Ki. xxi. 2); הֲתָב֣וֹא לְךָ֣ שֶֽׁבַע־שָׁנִ֣ים ׀ רָעָב֣ ׀ בְּאַרְצֶ֗ךָ (2 Sam. xxiv. 13); בְּהָנִ֣יחַ יְהוָ֣ה אֱלֹהֶ֣יךָ ׀ לְךָ֡ (Deut. xxv. 19).

EXCEPTIONS.—Before the other disjunctive accents, Silluq, Athnach, Zaqeph, &c., there was no necessity for Paseq, as a subordinate disjunctive was always available to mark the dichotomy[12]. The only exception is in the case of S'gôlta, in the following passages: Gen. xxvi. 28; Ex. xxxv. 35; Deut. ix. 21; 1 Sam. xi. 7; Jer. xliv. 25; 1 Chr. xxi. 12. Here Paseq takes the place of *Zarqa*,—another proof to my mind of its late introduction, for its appearance is doubtless due to the false notion, which prevailed at least from Ben-Asher's time downwards, that S'gôlta is to be regarded as a kind of appendage to Zarqa (see p. 17). Like Zarqa therefore it might have Paseq before it.

In deciding whether the dichotomy should be marked or not, the accentuators were guided by the same general principles as in the use of the ordinary Paseq. (It is only under the first head that a necessary difference exists, and that an extension must be given to the meaning of the term used.) Thus we have:

1. *Paseq distinctivum*, marking details, indicating a slight logical pause, easing the reading of a long syntactical clause, &c. Comp. the examples given above, and Gen. i. 21 (Ezek. xlvii. 9);

---

[12] Comp. קָד֣וֹשׁ (Is. vi. 3) and עֲבָדַ֣י (lxv. 13 *bis*).

Ex. xx. 4; 1 Sam. vii. 14; 1 Ki. xiii. 11; Jer. xxxv. 15; Ezek. xlv. 1; Ezra vi. 9; Neh. viii. 17, &c.[13]

It is particularly employed to separate the Divine Name (in any of its forms) from the word following. In such cases the Divine Name *directly precedes* one of the accents we are considering[14]. With any of the other disjunctive accents, it would in such a position be necessarily marked off by the dichotomy.—A half of the examples of *Paseq distinctivum* are of this class. Comp. Gen. i. 5, 10, 27; ii. 21, 22; iii. 14; &c.

2. *Paseq emphaticum*, in Deut. xvi. 16; 1 Sam. xii. 3; Jer. xii. 5; xlix. 37; Ezek. xiv. 21; xxxvi. 5; &c.

But care must be taken to note the context. Graetz has asked, Why has אֲבִיהֶם ׀ לָהֶם וַיִּתֵּן in 2 Chr. xxi. 3 Paseq, and in Job xlii. 15 no Paseq? Answer, Because of the marked contrast in the former passage between the first and second halves of the verse—a contrast which fails in the latter.

3. *Paseq homonymicum*, in the following (eight) instances: Num. xvii. 28; Josh. viii. 33; 2 Sam. xiv. 26; Jer. xv. 12; Ezek. xlvii. 12 and xlviii. 21 (not xlv. 7); 2 Chr. xxi. 19; xxx. 10.

4. *Paseq euphonicum*, in Ex. xx. 4 (second example); Num. xxxii. 33; Is. vi. 2; lxv. 13; Jer. li. 37 (*bis*); Hos. ix. 1; 2 Chr. xxxv. 18; &c.

5. *Paseq euphemisticum*. The object of this Paseq was to separate the Divine Name from a word, which it seemed unseemly to associate with it. We found no example of this Paseq between *two* words, and the only instances of it in our present division are: אָדָם ׀ אֱלֹהִים בָּרָא אֲשֶׁר (Deut. iv. 32); רוּחַ

---

[13] This Paseq is (as stated) used with more freedom than when only two words have to be taken into account. Thus it appears, at first sight, strange that וַיַּשְׁכֵּם ׀ אַבְרָהָם בַּבֹּקֶר (Gen. xxi. 14) should be marked with Paseq (Moses' rising, Ex. xxxiv. 4, is not so signalized). The explanation seems to be that just before, xix. 27, and just after, xxii. 3, this expression has the dichotomy, and so it is introduced here. In 2 Ki. xxv. 4, the pause made by the Paseq may indicate the missing verb, יִבְרְחוּ (Jer. lii. 7). In Gen. xxxvii. 22 and 2 Ki. iv. 13 the anomalous servus (p. 110, note 41) may intimate that some punctators dispensed with the Paseq, which certainly appears *de trop*.

[14] When it is the *second* word, e.g. Gen. i. 25; Deut. ix. 4; Is. viii. 7, Paseq almost always fails.

וַיָּ֣קָם יְהוָ֣ה ׀ אֱלֹהִ֣ים ׀ רָעָ֑ה (1 Sam. xviii. 10; xix. 9) and שָׂטָ֣ן ׀ יְהוָ֣ה ׀ שָׂטָ֑ן (1 Ki. xi. 14)[15]. This Paseq is more common in the three Books.

But, as in the case of the ordinary Paseq, the *failure* of the sign is more conspicuous than its presence. It is constantly wanting where it might have marked a necessary *distinction*, or *emphasis;* and where two like words, or like letters coming together require it[16]. Writers on the accents, from Ben-Asher to Ewald, have not troubled themselves at all about this strange lack of consistency in the use of Paseq, although it stands in such marked contrast to the precision in the employment of the accentual signs. This circumstance seems again to point to a (comparatively) late introduction of the sign.—The same want of system is seen in the three Books, comp. טעמי אמ״ת, p. 97.

List of Paseqs[17].

(In making use of this list, the student must be careful to distinguish the *L'garmehs* of the text, see pp. 119, 120.)

Gen. (29) i. 5, 10, 21, 27; ii. 21, 22; iii. 14; xii. 17; xiv. 15 (עֲלֵיהֶ֣ם ׀); xvii. 13; xviii. 15 (*ter*, כִּ֣י ׀ יְרֵאָ֑ה), 21; xxi. 14, 17; xxii. 11, 14; xxvi. 28; xxx. 8, 20; xxxvii. 22; xxxix. 10; xlii. 13, 21, 22; xliii. 11; xlvi. 2 (*bis*).

Ex. (14) xiii. 18 (אֱלֹהִ֣ים ׀); xiv. 21; xv. 18; xvi. 5; xvii. 6, 15; xx. 4 (*bis*); xxiii. 17; xxx. 34; xxxiv. 6 (*bis*), 23; xxxv. 35.

Lev. (8) v. 12; x. 3, 6, 12; xi. 32, 35; xiii. 45; xxiii. 20.

Num. (22)[18] iii. 2, 38 (אֹֽהֶל־מוֹעֵ֣ד ׀); v. 22; vi. 20, 25, 26; ix. 10; xi. 25, 26 (*bis*); xv. 31; xvi. 7 (*bis*); xvii. 21, 28; xxi. 1; xxii. 20; xxx. 13 (אֹתָ֣ם ׀); xxxii. 29, 33; xxxv. 16.

Deut. (22) iii. 20; iv. 32; v. 8 (*bis*, as in Ex. xx. 4); vi. 4, 22; vii. 1, 26 (*bis*); viii. 15; ix. 4, 21; xvi. 16; xvii. 8; xxii. 6; xxv. 19; xxvii. 9; xxviii. 12, 20, 25, 68; xxix. 12 (הַיּ֣וֹם ׀).

---

[15] Some punctators on this principle mark נָשִׂ֣יא ׀ אֱלֹהִ֣ים ׀ אַ֑תָּה (Gen. xxiii. 6). So De R. 7, 266; Bomb. 1 and 2. See Norzi and Ginsb. iii. p. 54.

[16] So also after the Divine Name, as in Gen. iv. 15ᵇ; viii. 1ᵇ; xi. 8; Ex. xxxiii. 11; Is. liv. 17ᵇ; 1 Chr. xxviii. 4; &c. Sometimes individual punctators introduce the Paseq in such instances.

[17] I have put in brackets the Paseqs (61) that fail in Van der Hooght's text.

The *totals* of the Paseqs for the several Books I have taken from the St. Pet. Cod. Other lists supply the same partially. These numbers supply a useful means of control, so that it is rarely necessary to take account of the variations that occur in Codd.

[18] The lists give 22 as the total, but furnish only 21. I have no doubt that the missing example is וַיָּ֣מָת נָדָ֣ב וַאֲבִיה֑וּא ׀ לִפְנֵ֣י יְהוָ֑ה (iii. 4). Paseq is found here in many Codd., Ox. 19, 22, 23, 26, &c., also in Bomb. 1; and is marked in the margin פס, in Erf. 1; De R. 2, 7.

Josh. (22) i. 15; ii. 19 (בֵּיתְךָ ׀); viii. 33 (*ter*); xi. 20; xiv. 10 (יְהוָֹה ׀ אוֹתִי); xv. 7, 25, 55; xix. 7 (עָ֑י ׀), 11, 51 (*ter*); xxii. 22 (*quater*), 31 (הַיּוֹם ׀), 32; xxiv. 32.

Judg. (9) i. 7; ii. 18; xi. 17 (*bis*, אֱדוֹם ׀); xii. 5 (וַיֹּאמֶר ׀ לֹא); xviii. 2; xx. 25 (*bis*, לִקְרָאתָם ׀), 35.

1 Sam. (32)[19] i. 3 (מִיָּמִים ׀ יָמִימָה); ii. 16, 19; iii. 9 (לֵךְ ׀), 10; v. 9 (יַד־יְהוָֹה ׀); vii. 14; ix. 10, 16, 24 (הָעָם ׀); xi. 7; xii. 3; xiv. 3 (כֹּהֵן ׀ יְהוָֹה), 36 (פְּלִשְׁתִּים ׀), 45 (הֲיוֹנָתָן ׀), 47; xvii. 40; xviii. 10 (*ter*); xix. 9; xx. 12, 21 (קָחֶנּוּ ׀); xxiv. 11 (*bis*); xxv. 14, 25, 31, 36; xxvi. 7, 23; xxviii. 12 (אֶל־שָׁאוּל ׀).

2 Sam. (11) ii. 1; iii. 12, 21; vii. 24; xiv. 26, 32; xx. 3; xxiv. 3, 13 (*bis*), 16.

1 Ki. (25)[19] i. 36, 45 (הַנָּבִיא ׀); ii. 30; vii. 24, 25 (*bis*, פָּנִים ׀ יָמָּה), 29, 35 (עָגֹל ׀); viii. 65; xi. 14, 22, 36; xii. 16 (*bis*, אֶת־הַמֶּלֶךְ ׀), 32 (*bis*); xiii. 4, 11; xviii. 12; xix. 7; xx. 25, 30; xxi. 2 (*bis*, לֵאמֹר ׀); xxii. 8.

2 Ki. (17) iii. 16; iv. 13, 19; vii. 1; x. 5, 6; xii. 22; xiii. 14; xviii. 14 (*ter*); xix. 4, 16, 23 (חֵרַפְתָּ ׀); xxiv. 2; xxv. 4, 17.

Is. (27)[20] iii. 7; iv. 5; v. 19; vi. 2 (עֹמְדִים ׀), 3; x. 14; xi. 11 (אֲדֹנָי ׀); xxi. 2 (*bis*); xxii. 13; xxiv. 3 (*bis*); xxv. 7; xxvi. 3; xxxi. 4; xxxvii. 4, 17, 24; xl. 28; xlii. 5; lvii. 19; lviii. 2 (יוֹם ׀ יוֹם)[21]; lxiii. 7; lxv. 13; lxvi. 19, 20 (*bis*).

Jer. (30) i. 13; iv. 1, 19[22]; vi. 11, 14; vii. 9; viii. 11; ix. 2; xi. 5; xii. 5; xv. 12; xvii. 25; xxi. 7; xxiii. 6; xxxi. 40; xxxii. 44; xxxiii. 16; xxxiv. 1; xxxv. 15 (*bis*); xli. 10; xliv. 25; xlviii. 20; xlix. 24 (וְרָטַט ׀), 37; l. 14, 29; li. 2, 37 (*bis*, בְּבֶל ׀).

Ezek. (24)[23] iii. 27 (*bis*); vii. 11 (הֶחָמָס ׀); viii. 3; xiv. 21; xxi. 3; xxvi. 16; xxxiii. 25 (עַל־הַדָּם ׀); xxxiv. 8; xxxv. 12; xxxvi. 5; xxxix. 11; xli. 16; xlv. 1; xlvii. 9, 12 (*bis*), 16, 17; xlviii. 1 (חֶתְלֹן ׀), 21 (*ter*), 35. And, as the Massora adds, כֹּל סָבִיב ׀ סָבִיב דכותהון.

Minor Prophets (8). Hos. ix. 1 (יִשְׂרָאֵל ׀), 4 (לַיהוָֹה ׀); Zeph. iii. 15; Hag. i. 12; ii. 4, 20; Zech. xi. 12; xiv. 2[24].

---

[19] The number fixed by the St. Pet. list for Samuel is 43; and for Kings, 42.

[20] By a *lapsus calami* on the part of the copyist, the St. Pet. Cod. gives the total as 13!

[21] This example fails in all lists, although fixed by the Mas. to Gen. xxix. 10.

[22] The second מֵעַי ׀ is with Paseq; the first with L'garmeh, p. 118.

[23] There has been again a mistake on the part of the copyist of the St. Pet. Cod., for while he gives the total as 23, the list contains 24.

[24] Baer gives besides Zech. iii. 2; iv. 7, on the authority of the Mas. parva Erf. ms. But this Codex is elsewhere wrong, in fixing the Paseqs, e. g. in 1 Sam. viii. 19; 2 Ki. iii. 25. Some few texts indeed also give these examples in Zech., but they are not found in any list.

Five Megillôth. Cant. (8) i. 13, 14 ('וְהַכֹּפֶר); ii. 7, 13 ('וְהַגְּפָנִים); iii.
5, 11 ('צְאֶנָה); iv. 12ᵃ; viii. 4;—Ruth iv. 11;—Lam. (8) i. 15, 16;
ii. 1, 5, 6, 7 ('אֲדֹנָי), 8; v. 21;—Qoh. (2) i. 6; vii. 24;—Esth. (14)
iii. 7; ix. 7–9, 27 (bis, 'הַיְּהוּדִים); x. 1 ('אֲחַשְׁוֵרֹשׁ).
Dan. (9) iii. 2; iv. 20; v. 12 ('מְפַשַּׁר), 23; ix. 18, 19 (bis); xi. 17,
18 ('וְיִשָּׁם).
Ezra (5)²⁴ vi. 9 (ter, 'יוֹם בְּיוֹם); vii. 17 ('תּוֹרִין); x. 9.
Neh. (12) ii. 12, 13; viii. 6, 7 (bis), 9, 17 ('הַשַּׁבִּי), 18; xi. 33 ('חָצוֹר);
xii. 44 ('לָאוֹצָרוֹת); xiii. 15 (bis).
1 Chr. (28)²⁵ i. 24 ('שֵׁם); ii. 25; viii. 38; ix. 20, 44; xii. 18, 20, 40;
xiii. 6; xv. 18; xvii. 22; xxi. 3 ('עַל־עַמּוֹ), 12 (bis), 15 (bis); xxii.
3, 5; xxiv. 6; xxvii. 1 (bis)²⁶, 12 ('לַבֵּן יְמִינִי); xxviii. 1 ('וּמִקְנֶה);
xxix. 2, 11, 15 ('פָּצֵל), 21, 23.
2 Chr. (29) i. 11 ('אֱלֹהִים); ii. 9; iv. 3, 4 (bis, 'פָּנִים יָמָּה); x. 16; xii.
6, 7; xiii. 12; xvi. 8 ('לְחַיִל); xviii. 7; xix. 10; xx. 1, 8, 22; xxi.
3, 18, 19; xxiv. 11 ('לְיוֹם); xxvi. 17; xxx. 10, 19, 21; xxxiii. 14;
xxxiv. 12; xxxv. 18, 21 (bis), 25.

I add a list of the L'garmehs, which take the place of Paseq before
R'bhia (p. 119)²⁷. The rules for their occurrence will be the same
as those for the *ordinary* Paseq, given above²⁸.

Gen. iii. 15; xvii. 14; xxiii. 6; xxix. 9ᵇ; xlv. 5; Ex. xxx. 13; Num.
vii. 13ᵇ, 19ᵇ, &c.; x. 29, 35ᵇ; xx. 21; Deut. i. 33ᵇ; v. 4, 22ᵇ; xxxii. 39;
Josh. v. 14; ix. 12; Judg. xi. 40; xvi. 2; xviii. 7ᵇ; xx. 28²⁹, 31ᵇ; xxi.
19, 22²⁹; 1 Sam. ix. 9, 12ᵇ; xvi. 5, 7ᵇ; xx. 25; xxvi. 16ᵇ; 2 Sam. xii. 23;
xv. 20, 30²⁹; 1 Ki. vi. 29; vii. 23ᵇ; xix. 4ᵇ; 2 Ki. ii. 12; v. 22; xvii. 36;
xxv. 16; Is. ix. 16; xix. 16ᵇ; xxi. 8ᵇ; xxii. 2, 11; xlix. 21ᵇ; Jer. xx. 4;
l. 34; lii. 20; Ezek. xxiv. 17; xxxv. 12; Zech. i. 8²⁹; vi. 15²⁹; xiv. 12ᵇ;
Cant. iv. 14; viii. 14; Ruth i. 13; iii. 3, 13; Qoh. ix. 3; Dan. iv. 15ᵇ;
Neh. ii. 12; 1 Chr. iii. 1ᵇ; xxviii. 10; 2 Chr. iv. 2ᵇ; xxi. 19.

---

²⁴ The number for Ezra and Neh. varies between 15 and 17. Some lists (as
St. Pet., Aleppo, and Modena) reject the first example in Neh. viii. 7; and all
omit xii. 44, although the Mas. to Lev. x. 12 requires it. Note what Ben-Asher
says (Dikd. hat., p. 23), וּמִקְצָת הַסּוֹפְרִים הָרִאשׁוֹנִים קוֹרִים לָאוֹצָרוֹת לַתְּרוּמוֹת.
And so the old Codd. Add. 21161 and Erf. 3 point.

²⁵ The number fixed in the St. Pet. list for Chronicles is 57.

²⁶ The lists omit the second Paseq of Van der Hooght's text.

²⁷ Perhaps some additional instances may be found, which I have overlooked.
I have purposely omitted Josh. xv. 18 (comp. Judg. i. 14); Is. vii. 25 (although
marked in Baer's text); Dan. xi. 6 (with various Codd.); and 2 Chr. xviii. 3 (do.).

²⁸ Attention may be drawn to Judg. xvi. 2; 1 Sam. xvi. 7; and 2 Chr. xxi. 19,
where L'garmeh seems to indicate the defective grammatical construction, as
Paseq in 2 Ki. xxv. 2.

²⁹ Many texts omit.

APPENDIX I.

NOTES ON SOME DIFFICULT OR OTHERWISE NOTEWORTHY PASSAGES.

(A.V. stands for Authorized Version; R.V. for Revised Version; and Prob. for *Probebibel*, the German revision of Luther's translation.)

Gen. xx. 13. וַיְהִי כַּאֲשֶׁר הִתְעוּ אֹתִי אֱלֹהִים מִבֵּית אָבִי וגו'. The R'bhia here—the greatest disjunctive in S'gôlta's clause—is due to the over-scrupulousness of the early accentuators, who shrank from associating the Sacred Name with a Verb signifying 'to cause to *err!*' What monstrous interpretations were the result may be seen in Targ. Onq. and Sopherim iv. 6[1]. The proper accentuation is וַיְהִי כַּאֲשֶׁר־הִתְעוּ אֹתִי ׀ אֱלֹהִים מִבֵּית אָבִי, found, more or less correctly given, in various Codd.[2]

xxxv. 22. We have here a *double* accentuation,—the one with Silluq at יִשְׂרָאֵל, answering to the number of verses (154) in the Parasha and further indicated by פ (פתוחה) following,—the other with Athnach at ישראל, adopted by the Occidentals, that Reuben's abominable act might be slurred over in the chanting as rapidly as possible[3]. The Orientals kept to the single accentuation with *two* verses (see Baer's Five Megillôth, p. v, and Ginsb. Mas. i. p. 592), which must have been the original.

Ex. xx. 3-17 and Deut. v. 7-18. The Orientals and Occidentals differed also in the pointing of the Decalogue. The former had the single accentuation (known as טעם העליון) according to the commandments[4]. This was no doubt the original, for the verses of the Parasha in each case are reckoned accordingly (72 and 118). On the other

---

[1] The Jerus. Talm. (Megilla 13ᵃ) and Jerus. Targ. try to get over the fancied difficulty by treating אֱלֹהִים as חוֹל (*profunus*); but this explanation did not meet with acceptance, as the accents shew. Some commentators indeed adopted it and sought to accommodate it to the recognised accentuation, by taking אֱלֹהִים מִבֵּית אָבִי as 'the (false) gods of my father's house!' So Bekhor Shor, and the author of the old Commentary known as ג"י (quoted in מנחת שי *ad loc.*).

[2] Ox. 1, 5, 34, 2437; Add. 15250, Harl. 1528; Berl. 4; Leipz. 1.

[3] On the same ground the Mishna (Megilla 25ᵃ) directs: נקרא ולא מתרגם, 'to be read without Targum.'

[4] See Pinsker, Einleitung, p. 48 ff.

hand, the Palestinians introduced a second division (טעם התחתון), breaking up the longer verses (3–6, 8–11), and bringing together the shorter ones (13–16); with the view of easing and equalizing the reading [5].

xxv. 34 (xxxvii. 20). One of the five passages in the Tora, named in the Talmud (Yoma 52ᵃ) and Mas. to Deut. xxxi. 16, as אֵין לָהֶם הַכְרֵעַ, 'about (the accentual division of) which no decision had been arrived at.' The question was whether מְשֻׁקָּדִים is to be taken with what precedes, or what follows (see Rashi). The LXX translate one way, the Targums another. The Massoretic text agrees with the latter.

xxxii. 1ᵇ. זֶה׀ מֹשֶׁה הָאִישׁ. The traditional construction supposes a transposition, 'This man Moses.' See LXX, Vulg., Pesh.—Similarly הַמָּקוֹם comes *after* the nom. pr., Ezra viii. 17.

xxxiii. 19. וְקָרָאתִי בְשֵׁם יְהֹוָה. According to the accents, 'And I will proclaim Jehovah by name.' Comp. xxxiv. 6 and R.V. xxxiv. 5 marg.

Num. xxxvi. 5. בֵּן, with Zaqeph (although no Codex so); comp. xxvii. 7. בֵּן is made by the accents a particle, as in verse 10ᵇ: so the LXX οὕτως. In the same way כִּי, Is. iii. 24ᵇ, is treated in most texts as a particle.

Deut. v. 19. קוֹל גָּדוֹל וְלֹא יָסָף, kept together by the accents, in accordance with the strange rendering found in the Talmud (Sota 10ᵇ, Sanhedrin 17ᵃ), Targums, and Pesh., 'With a loud voice, that did not cease,' i.e. without intermission [7]. See Rashi.

xxvi. 5. אֲרַמִּי אֹבֵד אָבִי cannot be rendered, according to the accents, 'An Aramæan, ready to perish, was my father,' for that would require the Pashṭa at אֹבֵד; but must be taken to mean, with Targ., Midrash [8], Vulg., and Rashi, 'An Aramæan (Laban) sought to destroy my father.' Aben-Ezra, Rashbam, Qimchi, and modern scholars generally, reject the accentuation. Yet Heidenheim, in his commentary מודע לבינה, defends it, and Baer (in a letter to me) agrees!

---

[5] But this division seems not to have come into general use. At least, the public reading has long been according to the longer verses.

The terms עליון and החתון have reference to the position of the accents,—the longer verses shewing a large proportion of accents placed *above* the words, whereas in the shorter verses the accents *below* the words greatly preponderate. Comp. the expressions טעמא מליעיל and מלרע in the Mas. to Gen. xxiii. 3.

[6] A technical phrase not understood by Hupfeld, Stud. u. Krit., 1837, p. 852, or Dillmann, Herzog's Encycl. ii. p. 392.

[7] יסף taken in the sense of אסף (Niphal). The same meaning was assigned to the word in Gen. xxxviii. 26 and Num. xi. 25.

[8] Siphre and לקח טוב.

xxxii. 5. שִׁחֵת לוֹ לֹא. Accents must remain, as both Targums, LXX, and Pesh. shew. We must then translate, 'They corrupted (injured) *Him* not.' Jerome, Aben-Ezra, and of course moderns, rightly break loose from the accents.

Josh. iv. 3. הָכֵן שְׁתֵּים־עֶשְׂרֵה אֲבָנִים. Kept together by the accents. The inf. constr. (fixed by Mas. *ad loc.*) must not be confounded—as by Targ., Qim., R. V., &c.—with inf. abs. הָכֵן (iii. 17), and joined, contrary to the accents, with the words preceding. Comp. Knobel and Keil.

vi. 10^b. Accents support Driver's view, Heb. Tenses, p. 161, Obs. Parallel is 2 Sam. x. 5^b (1 Chr. xix. 5).

Judg. vi. 24. Some Codd.—as Ox. 13, 2324; Harl. 5773; Erf. 2—and the Soncino ed., point וַיִּקְרָא־לוֹ יְהוָה שָׁלוֹם, and this is no doubt correct[9]; except that, according to the Paseq rules, we ought to have יְהוָה ׀ שָׁלוֹם, comp. Ex. xvii. 15; Ezek. xlviii. 35.

xii. 4^b. According to the accents (note the two Zaqephs) we must render:

'Fugitives of Ephraim are ye!
Gilead (his place) is in the midst of Ephraim, in the midst of Manasseh.'

Comp. Ewald, Gesch. ii. p. 455.

xiv. 15 end. The accentuation requires us to take הֲלֹא as הֲלֹם, 'hither.' So Targ. and Tanchum. If the punctators had regarded הֲלֹא as interrogative, they must have pointed: הֲלֹא יְרֵשֵׁנוּ קְרָאתֶם לָנוּ. Some few Codd. (see De R. Var. Lect.) *read* הֲלֹם, but this is contrary to the Mas. (Frensdorff, p. 251)[10].

xv. 19^b. עַל־כֵּן ׀ קָרָא שְׁמָהּ עֵין הַקּוֹרֵא אֲשֶׁר בַּלֶּחִי. A false accentuation, due to a false rendering,—to be traced in LXX, Vulg., and Pesh.,—which takes לֶחִי here, as in the early part of the verse, in the sense of 'jaw-bone.'

xvi. 28^b. אַחַת.—וְאִנָּקְמָה נְקַם־אַחַת מִשְּׁתֵי עֵינַי מִפְּלִשְׁתִּים. is made by the accents emphatic; Samson asks for vengeance for *one* of his eyes. The reward for the other was to be in the world to come! This explanation—although not accepted by Targ., LXX, Vulg., and many modern scholars—is found in Talmud[11], Midrash[11], Rashi, Qim., and

---

[9] This too is what is meant in Midrash rabba on Leviticus, Par. 9.

[10] There is an interesting marginal note in the old Reuchlin Cod. of the Prophets (K. 154): פליג׳, בקריות של סוראי הלם כתיב וקרי הלא, לנהרדעי כת׳ הלא וק׳ הלם. The Schools at Sura and Neharda'a belonged to the general category of Orientals (מדנחאי).

[11] See Jerusalem Talmud, Sota, cap. 1, § 8; and Midrash rabba on Numbers, Par. 9.

APPENDIX I. 133

adopted by our best modern commentator, Bertheau. It seems indeed the only possible one, with the text as it is.

2 Sam. v. 6ᵇ. The accentuation is in accordance with Targ., LXX, and Vulg., which make the subj. of the second לֵאמֹר 'the blind and the lame,' who are represented as making themselves responsible for the safety of the city against David's attacks.

xi. 25 end. The message sent is the important part of the verse. Hence it commands the main division (comp. p. 35 β). וַחֲזָקֵהוּ, as of minor importance, is joined on to the latter part of the speech.

xv. 34. Note the mispunctuation of our texts, וְאִם־הָעִיר תָּשׁוּב וְאָמַרְתָּ לְאַבְשָׁלוֹם עַבְדְּךָ אֲנִי הַמֶּלֶךְ אֶהְיֶה וגו׳, which can only mean: 'And thou shalt say to Absalom thy servant: I will be the king, &c.'! Correct עַבְדְּךָ אֲנִי הַמֶּלֶךְ, with Ox. 1, 10, 12, 13, &c.

xx. 18 end. וְכֵן הֵתַמּוּ, made by accents a part of the מָשָׁל, 'And so they will certainly attain their end.' Perf. of assurance, like הֵסִירָךְ, v. 6 (see above). If the accentuators had meant to express the meaning adopted by Vulg., Qim., and moderns, they must have pointed לֵאמֹר with R'bhia instead of Zaqeph.

1 Ki. vi. 1. The emphasis is thrown on the *second* of the dates named. (Just so in Ezek. xl. 1.) But point מִצְרַיִם, Great T'lisha, with Ox. 7, 76, 2326; Harl. 5710; &c.

xviii. 42ᵇ, 46. The accents dwell on the pictorial features. Hence the division is not as with us.

2 Ki. iii. 25. עַד־הִשְׁאִיר אֲבָנֶיהָ בַּקִּיר חֲרָשֶׂת. The false accentuation here is due to the mistaken notion, found in Targ., Verss., Rashi, &c., that חֲרָשֶׂת is an *appellative:* 'They left the stones thereof in the wall' (broken to pieces, like) 'a mass of sherds.' Even the vocalization, קִיר with the article, seems occasioned by this strange explanation. Qimchi was apparently the first to see that קִיר חֲרָשֶׂת is *nom. pr.*, as in Is. xvi. 7.

x. 15. וַיֹּאמֶר יְהוֹנָדָב יֵשׁ וָיֵשׁ. Rabb. comm., one and all, take יֵשׁ וָיֵשׁ together. Their explanation is כפל לחזק. With the rendering usually adopted—found in LXX and Vulg.—the accents must have been quite otherwise.

xviii. 17. וַיִּשְׁלַח מֶלֶךְ־אַשּׁוּר אֶת־תַּרְתָּן וְאֶת־רַב־סָרִיס וְאֶת־רַב־שָׁקֵה מִן־לָכִישׁ. Why the irregular L'garmeh (p. 118) in Géresh's clause? Because the accentuators designed a special warning for the reader. Only Rab-shakeh's name was to be associated with Lachish. Tartan and Rab-saris, as they are not named in Is. xxxvi. 2, were supposed to have come later, at the head of the second embassy (xix. 9). But that was sent from Libnah, *not from Lachish* (xix. 8) [12]. Their names

---

[12] Comp. Seder 'Olam, cap. 23, quoted by Rashi and Qimchi.

therefore were carefully separated from Lachish by the special disjunctive L'garmeh, whilst Rab-shakeh's was joined to it in the regular way. A notable specimen of Massoretic exegesis, the connection of which with the accentuation seems to have escaped every one's notice.

Is. i. 5. Targ., Abu'l-walîd (*Opuscules*, p. cv), and Aben-Ezra join עוֹד with the words following, and this pointing is found in some Codd.,—as Bab.; Ox. 23, 78,—עַל־מֶה תֻכּוּ עוֹד תּוֹסִיפוּ סָרָה. But unquestionably the *textus rec.* is right.

i. 9. Here also כִּמְעָט כִּסְדֹם הָיִינוּ are taken together, in Berakhoth 19ᵃ, and by Targ., Abu'l-walîd (l. c.), Rashi, and even Cheyne,—against the better sense, the unvarying accentuation, and the Massora (כִּמְעָט בְּ).

i. 13. קְטֹרֶת תּוֹעֵבָה הִיא לִי, 'incense of abomination is it to me.' So Targ., Rashi, Ewald, &c. The disregard of the accents, found in LXX, Vulg., and some Rabb. comm., shews itself also in A.V. and R.V.

v. 24. Cod. Bab. has וַחֲשַׁשׁ לֶהָבָה יִרְפֶּה, making לֶהָבָה acc. loci. Even with our pointing, it may be so rendered, see p. 46, 3. It is quite unnecessary, with Ewald, Hitzig, and Ges. Lex., to translate *foenum flammae*, i. e. *flagrans*.

viii. 14ᵇ. No commentator, ancient or modern, seems to have noticed that the accentuation here is untenable. It has been due to a false interpretation, found in Targ. and Rashi, which takes לְפַח וּלְמוֹקֵשׁ as *in apposition* to לִשְׁנֵי בָתֵּי יִשְׂרָאֵל, 'To the two houses of Israel, who set themselves as a gin and a snare' &c. If we would pay any regard to the sense, we must point: וּלְאֶבֶן נֶגֶף וּלְצוּר מִכְשׁוֹל לִשְׁנֵי בָתֵּי יִשְׂרָאֵל.

viii. 23. The marked emphasis resting on the words וְהָאַחֲרוֹן הִכְבִּיד has led to the main pause of the verse being placed there. What follows, דֶּרֶךְ הַיָּם וְגו׳, may be treated as Zusatz (see p. 57), 'by the way of the sea, &c.' Comp. Ewald. It is not necessary to suppose, with Luzzatto, that the Athnach is due to the Haggadic paraphrase of Targ.

ix. 5ᵇ. וַיִּקְרָא שְׁמוֹ פֶּלֶא יוֹעֵץ, an abnormal accentuation,—the object being to mark not only the Name, but in a special and emphatic manner the *separation* of פֶּלֶא from יוֹעֵץ, 'Wonder,—Counsellor[13].'

---

[13] Which Cheyne and others have not seen; or, if they have, ought, in all fairness, to have pointed out.

May I (without offence) remark that one learned professor after another has got out of his depth in trying to explain the accentual and grammatical peculiarities of the few words quoted? (1) Caspari (Micha, p. 223) makes of the Pashṭa a Qadma,

APPENDIX I.

The regular accent for this purpose would have been [1] פֶּלֶא. (On the general division of the half-verse, see p. 49, 1.)

xvii. 5. בְּאֱסֹף קָצִיר קָמָה. Most commentators neglect the accents, which however are duly regarded in LXX and Pesh.; קָצִיר being taken in the same sense as in verse 11.

xix. 9. שָׂרִיקוֹת, adjective outside the rest of the clause, see p. 53, 3 a. Not to be rendered as Delitzsch proposes.

xx. 4. The Athnach fixes the limit to the comparison made with Isaiah, for certainly he did not go חָשׂוּף שֵׁת.

xxiii. 7 b. According to the accents must be translated: 'Whose feet were wont to carry her, from days of old, from her first beginning, to sojourn afar off.' The version of Rabbinical commentators and most moderns would require: מִימֵי־קֶדֶם בַּדְמָתָהּ.

xxv. 1. יְהוָֹה אֱלֹהַי אַתָּה. 'Jehovah, *my God* art Thou!' Emphasis.

xxviii. 28. The R. V. pays attention to the accentuation. Not so the bulk of modern commentators.

xxix. 16 a. Not understood,—as ancient Verss. and Jewish comm. down to Luzzatto shew. Hence the false accentuation: כַּחֹמֶר הַיֹּצֵר.

xxx. 7 b. In Ox. 4, 74, 78; Add. 11657, we have the pointing רָהַב הֵם שָׁבֶת, which suits the rendering: 'Rahab! they are a sitting still.'

xxx. 21. Accents make the last words *a part of the speech*. So Targ., LXX, Vulg., Pesh., and Qim., against Aben-Ezra and moderns.

xxx. 32. No commentator (as far as I have observed) has seen that for the ordinary rendering to stand, we must have R'bhia at מוּסָדָה; but this we cannot introduce, because the Massora (see p. 107) has fixed Y'thibh for כָּל. Vulg. and Prob. pay regard to the accentuation.

xxxiii. 23. A case of parallelism with addition (p. 39). Jewish commentators refer the whole verse to Assyria. Had they referred,

---

and will give a reason for it! (2) Delitzsch proposes an impossible accentuation, וַיִּקְרָא שְׁמוֹ פֶּלֶא יוֹעֵץ אֵל גִּבּוֹר וגו', Géresh before and after T'lisha! (3) Kautzsch (Ges. Gr., § 93, Anm. 1. D), disregarding the accentuation—as though vowels and accents were not from the same source—would have us believe on the authority of Dikd. hat., § 36, that פֶּלֶא is in *st. constr.*; yet if he had looked on a few pages to § 72 of the same work, he would have found this notion plainly contradicted, as indeed it must have been sooner or later, for it is in direct opposition to the Mas. to Lev. xxii. 23. One would not have expected to find an antiquated error, due to the first groping after grammatical rules, revived by a German professor in the present day!

with many modern commentators, the first part of the verse to Jerusalem and the second to Assyria, Athnach could not have failed at נֵס. As it is, the helpless hulk falls a ready prey.

xxxvi. 2. See note, 2 Ki. xviii. 17.

xxxviii. 13ª. How are we to account for the accentuation? Gesenius and those who have followed him, down to Cheyne, say: 'From the exigencies of rhythm,'—a notion which Jewish writers would have passed by as שִׁבּוּשׁ. With the rendering which these scholars propose we should have had שִׁוִּיתִי עַד־בֹּקֶר כָּאֲרִי וגו׳; comp. xl. 3 and a hundred other passages. The accents are no doubt to be traced to the same source as the false version of Targum: 'I roared as a lion, till the morning.' Comp. also Sa'adia [14].

xlv. 1. According to Rashi on Megilla 12ª, the anomalous accentuation (Zarqa without S'gôlta following [15]) was meant to draw attention to the traditional דרש, found in the text of the Talmud, l. c.: 'Was then Cyrus משיח? Nay! the Holy One said to the Messiah, I complain to thee concerning Cyrus, &c.' [16] Such crotchets of Jewish learning we may well put on one side, and point regularly (with our ordinary text and many Codd.) לְכוֹרֶשׁ. Only then we shall require R'bhîa, instead of the first Zarqâ [17], כֹּה־אָמַר יְהֹוָה לִמְשִׁיחוֹ לְכוֹרֶשׁ.

xlv. 24ᵇ. An alternative punctuation is found in Ox. 2421; Add. 21161; Hm. 9: עָדָיו יָבוֹא וְיֵבֹשׁ, which is an improvement, but contrary to the Mas. Lev. xi. 34. With the ordinary pointing, וְיֵבֹשׁ must be taken as = בַּכְּלִמָּה, ver. 16ᵇ.

lvi. 9. The ridiculous accentuation of this verse can only be rendered in one way. See Rashi, Qimchi, &c.

lxvi. 5ᵇ. For the meaning of the accents, see Rashi, Aben-Ezra, or Rosenmüller.—The Vulg. and most moderns (see e. g. Delitzsch) rightly disregard them.

lxvi. 12. Strange that no commentator before Luzzatto should

---

[14] Sa'adia's text is to be read: وساورت الاسد فى زئاره الى الغداة , 'And I was like the lion in his roaring, until the morning.' So Or. 1474, 2211. No sense can be made of the Ox. text, as edited by Paulus.

[15] Cf. Baer's text and the Mas. parva found in many Codd. (Ox. 69, 2323; Erf. 1, &c.) ל׳ ורקא בלא סגולה, or ל׳ רביע אחר ורקא.

[16] So Sa'adia: كورش (regarding) عن المسيح قال الله كذى. The title משיח, applied to no other heathen king, was counted too great a one for Cyrus. Hence some other interpretation had to be found; and Cyrus' name, in comparison, slurred over.

[17] With Harl. 5498, Add. 9398, 9399; Par. 4, &c.

have found any difficulty in the accentuation [18]: 'Behold, I extend to her, as a peaceful river and as an overflowing stream, the glory of the Gentiles,' &c. Did the accentuators miss the art. in כְּנָהָר and consider that something else was intended than by the כְּנַהַר שָׁלוֹם of xlviii. 18?

Jer. xxxii. 9ᵇ. שִׁבְעָה שְׁקָלִים וַעֲשָׂרָה הַכָּסֶף. On the division here, which has completely baffled commentators, see Rule, p. 42 above.

Ezek. i. 11. וּפְנֵיהֶם וְכַנְפֵיהֶם פְּרֻדוֹת מִלְמָעְלָה,—another instance of the Rule just quoted.

iii. 20. הוּא יָמוּת to be made, as accents indicate, a relative clause. (So Abendana, Ewald, Hitzig, and Prob.) In *b* the logical division is neglected, that the emphasis may come on the first words: '*Because thou hast not warned him, in his iniquity he shall die.*'

iv. 6. Punctators sometimes shew the same differences of opinion as commentators. In this verse, Ox. 17; Harl. 5498; and Par. 4, have Athnach at אַרְבָּעִים יוֹם. And so in vii. 13ᵇ, Ox. 17, 69, and Bab. have בַּעֲוֹנוֹ or בְּעֲוֹנוֹ;—in xv. 2 Bab. has מִכָּל־עֵץ הַזְּמוֹרָה, with LXX, Vulg., and Ewald;—in xviii. 30ᵇ, Ox. 1, 6, 7; Erf. 1, 3, have וְלֹא־יִהְיֶה לָכֶם לְמִכְשׁוֹל עָוֹן; and in xxxi. 15 most Codd. have הֶאֱבַלְתִּי. Such examples might be greatly multiplied.

vi. 10. וְיָדְעוּ כִּי־אֲנִי יְהֹוָה וגו׳. Note the emphasis thrown by Athnach on the Divine Name. 'And they shall know that *I Jehovah* have not spoken in vain,' &c. If the student has any doubt on the point, let him turn to such parallel passages as xxii. 22ᵇ; xxxv. 12; xxxvii. 14ᵇ; Num. xiv. 14; Jer. ii. 19.

xxi. 3ᵇ. Render, 'Behold, I kindle in thee a fire, and it shall devour in thee every green tree and every dry tree, without being quenched [19],—inflaming flame (that it will be).' The last words are in apposition to the latent subject in אֹכְלָה, and come in, as such, with marked effect, at the close of the clause. Comp. Jer. ii. 23ᵇ. The ordinary rendering would require Zaqeph, or at least R'bhia, on יָבֵשׁ.

xxv. 9ᵇ. Accents, 'the glory of the land of Beth-jeshimoth,' &c., and so Pesh. renders; but this cannot be correct. Yet I have not found צְבִי אֶרֶץ, which is what we require, in any Codex.

xl. 1. The stress is laid on the *second* of the dates named (comp. above, 1 Ki. vi. 1). The destruction of the old city is emphasized, in contrast to the revelation of the new one, in the verse following.

xliv. 22ᵇ. On the Zaqeph in אַלְמָנָה see Comm.

---

[18] It is traceable in LXX, Vulg., Arab. (Polygl.), and Cod. Ambros. (Syr.), but not in Targ., Pesh., or Rabb. Comm.

[19] Driver, Heb. Tenses, § 162.

Mic. ii. 4b. לְשׁוֹבֵב שָׂדֵינוּ יְחַלֵּק. Accents evidently treat שׁוֹבֵב as inf., with LXX, Rashi, Qim., and even some modern authorities. For the rendering usually adopted, 'rebellious, reprobate,' we need Tiphcha on לְשׁוֹבֵב, and this is found in some Codd., as Ox. 6, 7; Add. 4708, Or. 1474.

iv. 10b. וּבָאתָ עַד־בָּבֶל שָׁם תִּנָּצֵלִי. We expect Zaqeph at בָּבֶל (comp. modern interpunction). But a fine antithesis is established by the accentuation: 'Thou shalt come to Babylon, there to be *delivered*.' Babylon was the last place in the world where deliverance could have been anticipated.

Hab. i. 3. וַיְהִי רִיב וּמָדוֹן יִשָּׂא. Almost all modern commentators neglect the accentuation, although this is one of the passages in which the Massoretes have been very particular in fixing it (see p. 92). רִיב וּמָדוֹן make a common subject to יִשָּׂא (Ges. Heb. Gr., § 148. 2).

ii. 18. The Athnach simply represents a pause for effect, such as we might make in reading the verse. Rabbinical commentators, however, see in it the main logical pause, and begin the second half of the verse by repeating מָה הוֹעִיל, 'What profit is there in all these, that &c.?'

iii. 3, 9, 13. The extraordinary rendering assigned to סֶלָה, = לְעוֹלָם, in Talm., Targ., &c., suffices to account for the false accentuation, most conspicuous in verse 9.

Hag. ii. 16. מִהְיוֹתָם, 'Since they (those days) were,' *subordinated*, as בְּיָמָיו, &c., p. 48, 5.

Cant. viii. 6b. Most Codd. have רִשְׁפֵּי as our texts (see Rashi on the accentuation). But the modern rendering, 'Its flashes are flashes of fire, a flame of Jah,' is much more effective, and has also the support of Codd., Ox. 6, 2437; Add. 15282, Harl. 5506, &c., thus: רְשָׁפֶיהָ רִשְׁפֵּי אֵשׁ שַׁלְהֶבֶתְיָה.

Qoh. ii. 3b. Almost all modern commentators silently transfer Athnach to בְּסִכְלוּת. The accentuation on the other hand will give the meaning: 'And my heart was to guide me in wisdom, and was (at the same time) to lay hold on folly [20].' This rendering, with its oxymoron of *insipiens sapientia*, is far more telling than the tame construction adopted, as more regular, by moderns.

ii. 16. The weight of meaning comes on the first clause. Hence the Athnach.

viii. 10a. The A. V., with the old Verss. and Rabb. comm. generally, respects the accents; but R. V. and most moderns follow Aben-Ezra, and quite disregard them.

---

[20] On the inf. with לְ, as continuing the part. construction, see Driver, Heb. Tenses, § 206.

APPENDIX I.

viii. 11. אֲשֶׁר אֵין־נַעֲשָׂה פִתְגָם מַעֲשֵׂה הָרָעָה מְהֵרָה וגו׳. Ewald and Hengstenberg try to do justice to the accentuation; but, with the rendering usually adopted by both ancients and moderns, we must point, אֲשֶׁר אֵין־נַעֲשָׂה פִתְגָם מַעֲשֵׂה הָרָעָה מְהֵרָה, with Ox. 20, 36; Add. 9399, Or. 2696; De R. 10; (comp. similar examples, p. 51 above)[21].

ix. 10. Codd., e.g. Ox. 13, 17, 26, 34, give us the option of joining בְּכֹחֲךָ עֲשֵׂה, 'do it with thy might,' as Targ., LXX, Vulg., A.V., R.V., &c.

xi. 8. The last words, כָּל־שֶׁבָּא הָבֶל, are properly logically distinct, but have been joined on to the clause preceding, from their supposed close connection with it in sense: 'Let him remember the days of darkness, that they will be many, (that) all that cometh (after the present life) is vanity.'

Esth. ix. 31. The Athnach is better transferred to הַפֻּרִים, as Targ., Vulg., and Rabb. comm. render. See also Bertheau. This pointing is found in Add. 4709 and Hm. 19.

1 Chr. vi. 46ᵃ. There is a fatal omission here, which Jewish commentators do not fail to notice, and which the accents are meant to indicate: מִמִּשְׁפַּחַת הַמַּטֶּה is supposed to stand for מִמִּשְׁפַּחַת מַטֵּה אֶפְרַיִם (comp. Josh. xxi. 5)[22].

ix. 17ᵇ. וַאֲחֵיהֶם is contrary both to the Mas. (which requires וַאֲחִיהֶם)[23] and the accentuation. Yet no commentator makes any remark. Vulg. *frater eorum* and Pesh. are right. The reading וַאֲחֵיהֶם has necessarily led to the pointing of our texts, which we must correct with Codd., וַאֲחִיהֶם שַׁלּוּם הָרֹאשׁ.

2 Chr. xxiv. 14. Translators and commentators follow LXX and Vulg. in the rendering of הָעָלוֹת, but the latter have not a syllable to say about this rendering being contrary to the accents. The accents indeed represent the uniform Jewish tradition that an instrument or vessel of some kind is meant [24]. A tradition of this kind introduced into the Massoretic text deserves at least notice.

---

[21] Luzzatto (Kerem Chemed ix. 7) saw that this pointing was necessary, but found no MS. to support it. Delitzsch, in his remark on the accentuation, has not seen that the Zaqeph extends its influence to Athnach, which makes his explanation inadmissible.

[22] It is considered that וּמִמַּחֲצִית־דָן (Josh. l. c.) may be dispensed with, because Dan is not named—but included in Ephraim—vers. 51–54.

[23] See Frensdorff, p. 9, and אכלה ואכלה, § 17.

[24] The word is derived by Abu'l-walīd (Lex. s. v.) from the Hiphil form. The notion—found in Pseudo-Rashi, and marg. of A.V. and R.V.—that it is the pl. of עֱלִי (Prov. xxvii. 22), 'pestles,' cannot be entertained, for the article is out of place here, and the meaning quite inappropriate.

2 Chr. xxx. 18, 19. Not only LXX, Vulg., and Pesh., but Jewish tradition from very early times, as in the Middôth of R. Eli'ezer, § 11 [25], made these verses run into one another. By the abrupt break in the middle of the prayer, the Massoretes seem to have designed (*more suo*, when employing an anomalous accentuation) to draw special attention to the prayer itself,—a prayer without a parallel, the meaning of which extended far beyond the occasion that called it forth.

The following notes relate to passages of less importance:

Josh. ii. 5. R'bhîa has been falsely introduced. Point וַיְהִי הַשַּׁעַר לִסְגּוֹר בַּחֹשֶׁךְ, with Ox. 2436; Harl. 5683, 5773, Or. 2091; &c.: 'And the gate was about to close at dusk.'

Judg. iv. 21[b]. וְהוּא־נִרְדָּם וַיָּעַף וַיָּמֹת, with Ox. 19; Add. 4709, 9398, Or. 2696; &c. Comp. p. 33, note. For the Qames in נִרְדָּם, see Norzi.

1 Ki. vii. 6[b]. Better וְעַמֻּדִים וָעָב עַל־פְּנֵיהֶם, with Ox. 13; Hm. 3, 11; as Vulg. and Thenius render.

vii. 36[b]. If we are to make any sense, we must point כְּמַעַר־אִישׁ וְלֹיוֹת סָבִיב, with Ox. 1, 72, 2329; Harl. 5722; &c.—a double Zusatz, see R. V. The words were not understood by Jewish scholars, who derive מער from the post-biblical עָרָה (Piel), 'to join.' Hence the false accentuation of our texts.

2 Ki. xxii. 14 (2 Chr. xxxiv. 22). Point חֻלְדָּה הַנְּבִיאָה אֵשֶׁת שַׁלֻּם בֶּן־תִּקְוָה בֶּן־חַרְחַס שֹׁמֵר הַבְּגָדִים, with Vi. 5; K. 172. Printed texts and Codd. generally make Charchas, not Shallum, 'keeper of the robes.'

Is. xxviii. 16[b]. אֶבֶן בֹּחַן פִּנַּת יִקְרַת מוּסָד מוּסָּד, with Ox. 1, 9, 69; Erf. 2; &c. R'bhîa is necessary for the sense.

xxxv. 1[b]. Better וְתָגֵל עֲרָבָה וְתִפְרַח בַּחֲבַצָּלֶת, with Bab.; Ox. 13; Erf. 1, 3.

xl. 13. Here also it is better to accent מִי־תִכֵּן אֶת־רוּחַ יְהֹוָה, with Bab.; Ox. 5, 82; Erf. 2; &c.; and so avoid the mistake of Targ., Sa'adia, and Qim., who render: 'Who hath prepared the spirit? Jehovah.'

---

[25] The tradition was followed by Sa'adia, Qim., Pseudo-Rashi, and the author of the Comm. on Chron. edited by Kirchheim. If we except the doubtful paraphrase of the Targum, Aben-Ezra (e. g. in Sachoth, p. 73[b]) was the first to propose an independent construction for ver. 18, by supplying אלה after בעד. He owns that he stands alone. And he hardly found a follower till Gesenius in his Thesaurus, p. 706, proposed the same explanation.

Jer. li. 58. Again the better pointing is חֹמוֹת בָּבֶל הָרְחָבָה עַרְעֵר, תִּתְעַרְעָר, with Ox. 70, 72, 76; Erf. 1; &c.: 'The broad wall of Babel shall be razed to the ground.' Comp. Ewald, § 318ᵃ.

Ezek. xlv. 21ᵇ. חַג שְׁבֻעוֹת יָמִים מַצּוֹת יֵאָכֵל. Note the st. constr. in חַג.

Amos vi. 6. The accentuation of our texts הַשֹּׁתִים בְּמִזְרְקֵי יַיִן corresponds to Targ., and the notion of Rabb. comm. (see Baur's note) that the st. constr. stands here for st. abs.! But Bab.; Ox. 70, 76; Erf. 3; &c., point regularly הַשֹּׁתִים בְּמִזְרְקֵי־יַיִן.

Cant. i. 3. Point שֶׁמֶן תּוּרַק שְׁמֶךָ. So Ox. 15, 19, 51; Erf. 1, 2, 4; and the Verss.

Qoh. i. 5ᵇ. Targ., Verss., Rashi, Aben-Ezra, all render as if they had before them וְאֶל־מְקוֹמוֹ שׁוֹאֵף, which is beyond doubt the true accentuation, and is found in Ox. 12, 26; Add. 4709, 21160; &c.

Dan. ix. 25. R'bhîa and Géresh must clearly change places, thus: וְתֵדַע וְתַשְׂכֵּל מִן־מֹצָא דָבָר לְהָשִׁיב וגו'. Ox. 97; Add. 15250; De R. 518, have R'bhîa, but only Ox. 97, Géresh right.

Ezra x. 14. The same correction is necessary: יַעַמְדוּ־נָא שָׂרֵינוּ לְכָל־הַקָּהָל וְכֹל אֲשֶׁר בְּעָרֵינוּ הֹשִׁיב וגו'. But here Codd. are all wrong. Only Par. 31; De R. 737; and Hm. 16, have R'bhîa right.

1 Chr. iii. 17. Jewish tradition, LXX, Vulg., and A.V. make אַסִּר a *nom. proprium*. We must then point וּבְנֵי יְכָנְיָה אַסִּר, with Ox. 6, 71, 72; Add. 9399; &c.

iv. 19. A similar correction is needed here: וּבְנֵי אֵשֶׁת הוֹדִיָּה אֲחוֹת נַחַם אֲבִי קְעִילָה הַגַּרְמִי. But this I have found only in De R. 552 (old) and 775.

2 Chr. iv. 9ᵇ. For the sense it is necessary to point: וּדְלָתוֹת לָעֲזָרָה, with Harl. 1528, Add. 15252; Ber. 32.

NOTE.—My readers may perhaps have noticed in the foregoing remarks that the Targum, and no less Rabbinical commentaries, do not always agree with the accentuation. We see that from early times a certain liberty was claimed in rendering and expounding the text. The accents, although respected and generally followed, were not regarded—notwithstanding particular assertions, as those of Aben-Ezra, to the contrary[26]—as of final authority. With respect to the Targums, we may bear in mind that the most important ones are of *Oriental* origin, which circumstance may account for some at least of the variations.

---

[26] Comp. Luzzatto, Prolegomeni, p. 187 ff.

APPENDIX II.

ON THE SUPERLINEAR [SO-CALLED BABYLONIAN] SYSTEM OF ACCENTUATION.

The researches of a Qaraite Jew, Abraham Firkowitsch, in the synagogues of the Crimea, brought to light, about fifty years ago, some Hebrew MSS. marked with a peculiar system of punctuation, previously quite unknown to scholars[1]. The characteristic of this system, as regards the position of the signs, is that they are almost all *above* the words (i.e. above the line from which the words depend). To the term '*superlinear*' therefore as describing it, no exception can be taken; whereas 'Babylonian,' as we shall afterwards see, is a misnomer.

The accentual notation found in these MSS. (as compared with the Palestinian) is as follows:

1. Silluq remains unchanged . . . . דָּבָֽר׃
2. Athnach is the same, but is placed *above* the word . . דָּ֑בָר
3. S'gôlta is represented by a mutilated Shîn, the initial of שָׂרַי (p. 17) . . . . דָּבָ֒ר

---

[1] For a description of the MSS. containing this punctuation, see Cat. of Heb. MSS. in the Imperial Library at St. Petersburg, Nos. 132, 133, and B 3. (Ox. 64 is a fragment of 132, although not so described in the Ox. Cat.) Of the three MSS. named by far the most important is B 3, which contains in a state of perfect preservation the whole of the later Prophets. It was photo-lithographed in 1876, at the expense of the late Emperor of Russia, and so placed at the service of scholars. The text of this Codex—known as *Codex Babylonicus*—is all we need to form a correct idea of the system we are about to consider. I may, however, add that there is in the St. Petersburg Library a fourth MS., not yet catalogued (but labelled as Tschufut-Kale 8ᵃ), containing Job xxxv. 10 to end of the book. (A specimen of some verses of this Codex is prefixed to Baer's edition of Job.) Till these MSS. were discovered, the only notice of the existence of a superlinear system of punctuation was contained in the following epigraph to a MS. of the Pent. with Targ. in De Rossi's Library (dated 1311), no. 12: תרגום זה נעתק מספר אשר הובא מארץ בבל והיה מנוקד למעלה בנקוד ארץ אשור, והסכו ר' נחן ברבי מכיר בר' מנחם מאנקונא בר' שמואל בר' מכיר ממדינת אוויירי בר' שלםה הוא אשר נדע קרן המחלוצץ בארץ מגנצא בשם המבורך בר' מנחם בר' צדוק הנקדן, והגיהו ונסחו לנקור סברני (comp. Zunz, Zur Geschichte u. Literatur, p. 110).

APPENDIX II. 143

    Shalshéleth has the figure of a hanging 'chain' (p. 17), followed by the sign for S'gôlta [2] . . . .   דָּבָ֓ר

4. Great and Little Zaqeph are not distinguished. The sign is the initial letter of זָקֵף [3] . . . .   דָּבָ֔ר

5. Ṭiphcha before Athnach is Athnach inverted . .   דָּבָ֖ר
Ṭiphcha before Silluq is the Palestinian sign, or the initial of וְהִי (p. 18) [4] . . . . .   דָּבָ֖ר

6. R'bhîa is represented by the initial of חָזֵר [5] . .   דָּבָ֗ר

7. Zarqa. The initial letter could not be used, because it was appropriated to Zaqeph. So apparently the name צִנּוֹרִי (p. 19) was taken, and the *second* letter chosen as the sign [6] . . . . .   דָּבָ֮ר

8. Pashṭa and Y'thîbh are not distinguished. The common sign is the initial of יְתִיב (p. 20). For the peculiar form of the sign, see (in Cod. Bab.) Is. xix. 25 marg.   דָּבָ֚ר
Where Pashṭa is repeated, a simpler form is given to the second sign, and it is made recumbent . .   דָּבָ֙ר

9. T'bhîr, represented by the initial letter . . .   דָּבָ֛ר

10. Géresh and Gersháyim have one sign, the initial of טֶרֶם (p. 20) . . . .   דָּבָ֜ר

11. L'garmeh. The sign is the initial of נֶגֶד (p. 22) . .   דָּבָ֣ר
Pazer and Great T'lîsha fail.

---

[2] This accent is described in the Mas. to Is. xiii. 8 as זרקא מסלסלא,—which should rather have been שרי מסלסלא. But Zarqa, according to the fancy of the later Massoretes, threw S'gôlta into the shade (see p. 17).

[3] In Cod. Bab. (Mas. to Jer. xiv. 18) we find the strange name אוקומי, 'set upright,' used for Zaqeph. Comp. Ginsb. Mas. iii. p. 364, § 19.

[4] In the text of Job this sign is regularly used; in Cod. Bab. but very rarely, except in the first page, Is. i. 4, 8, 9, &c.

[5] This name for R'bhîa occurs in a list at the end of Sepher Hariqma, p. 239, and in a manuscript list before me. Certainly no name could be more appropriate, for the frequent 'recurrence' of this accent is a main characteristic of the system. In Or. 1473, I found the initial of רביע used, דָּבָ֗ר.

[6] So in the Mas. magna to Num. i. 20, the סימן for the names of five out of the twelve tribes is either the *second* or the *third* letter; and in Arabic, the sign for نُسْخَة is خ, the *third* letter.—The Dagesh in the case before us was retained, to distinguish the sign from that used for L'garmeh, no. 11.

The *servi* employed—Munach, M'huppakh, Mer'kha, Darga, Azla, and Little T'lîsha—are the same as in the Palestinian system.

The originators of this system seem to have taken note of the weak points of (what I must assume for the present was) the older system, and to have applied a suitable correction. Thus the sign for L'garmeh cannot now be mistaken for Munach-Paseq; and Pashṭa can no longer be confounded with Azla, nor Y'thîbh with M'huppakh. *Simplicity* was also evidently aimed at by the employment of a *single* sign respectively for Zaqeph, Pashṭa, and Géresh; and by dispensing with the unmeaning accent, Great Pazer (and Galgal). But it was a mistake to reject Little Pazer and Great T'lisha, which are (generally speaking) needed for the division of the clauses in which they occur. R'bhîa, which takes their place in this system, does not answer the purpose.

Before proceeding to the special rules for this system of accentuation, there is a question *in limine*, that requires to be answered. Was this superlinear accentuation, with its equally peculiar vocalization, *identical with the Oriental mode of punctuation?* Such (as far as I have noticed) is the view of all scholars, who have expressed an opinion on the subject. But this is a mistake, which, though excusable, is none the less a serious one. The notation in use among the Orientals (מדנחאי) was beyond question the same as that of the Occidentals (מערבאי), differing only occasionally in its application. How otherwise are we to explain the Oriental reading of [7] וַתַּעְגַּב סגול (Ezek. xxiii. 5)? The superlinear system *has no S'gôl*, and writes this word (as Cod. Bab. shews) וְתֶּעְגָּב (וַתַּעְגַּב). We learn from this example that the Massoretes, in giving the חלופי מדנחאי, quoted a text constructed on the same system as the Palestinian. Can indeed (I would ask) a single Massoretic rubric be found, which *alludes to the peculiarities of the superlinear system?* and yet the differences of this system are far more important than most of those which are given under the name of the Orientals. The system was in short for the Palestinian Massoretes non-existent.—Moreover, what Gaon, what grammarian (Rabbinical or Qaraite), what Jewish writer, of the East or West, can be named who mentions *a different mode of punctuation* as in use among the Orientals[8]? Has their silence no meaning?

---

[7] See Baer's edition of Ezekiel, p. 110, and Ginsb. Mas. i. p. 596, and iii. p. 32.

[8] Where reference is made, as it often is, by Jewish authorities, to the הלופין between the two great Schools of the East and West, it is in such terms as we might apply to the remains that have come down to us. I have given two instances, p. 6, note 14, and here is a third, clearer still, as late as the 12th century, from the חלוק הקראים והרבנים of Elia ben-Abraham (quoted by Pinsker, Liqq. Qad., p. 102): ועוד ראו חלופי מערבאי ומדנחאי בתורה, זה אומר בכה וזה אומר בכה, מה שילמוד זה חסר ילמוד זה מלא, ומה שילמוד זה מלא ילמוד זה

APPENDIX II. 145

Especially important is this negative testimony as furnished by Sa'adia's writings. Here was a Gaon, at the head of one of the chief Oriental Academies—a scholar, who was in the habit of going into the minutest details of any subject which he handled—(who lived too *after* the date of the introduction of the system we are considering[9]), and yet who knows positively nothing of any Oriental differences answering to the differences of the superlinear punctuation. For instance, in chap. ii. § 2 of his commentary on Jeṣira[10], he enumerates the seven vowels, including S'gôl, and in iv. § 3 he lays down the vocalization of the article in הֶהָרִים, as with S'gôl, and of the final guttural in forms like לִשְׁמֹעַ, as with Pathach; yet does not add (as according to modern scholars he ought to have done) that the Orientals had no S'gôl, and that they pointed הַהָרִים with Pathach and לִשְׁמֹעַ without Pathach. What is observable is that in the very section last quoted he mentions *other* differences of pronunciation between the Orientals and Occidentals.—The conclusion is that the Oriental system of vocalization had no such distinguishing peculiarities as the superlinear, in other words was identical with the Palestinian; and what is true of the vocalization, must have held equally good for the accentuation[11].

חסר, מה שילמור וה חיבה אחת ילמור וה שתי חיבות, מה שילמור וה במסורה במסרת) ילמר זה בטעם, וכן מסורת הרבה אחר למערבאי ואחר למדנחאי. (lege). I may add the undesigned testimony of R. Petachiah, who visited Bagdad, circa 1180, and who refers to the נקוד in use among the Jews of that region (Benisch's ed., p. 15), but makes no allusion to any different notation, which yet, had it existed, must have struck him, a Western Jew, as something very remarkable and deserving of being chronicled in his narrative.—Moreover, copies of MSS. have been brought from China, and published by the 'Society for promoting Christianity among the Jews,' which, from the epigraphs, are clearly of *Persian* origin, but which have the ordinary punctuation. We may conclude that in Persia, as in other parts of the East, this was the prevalent system.

[9] Cod. Bab. was written in the year 916, and Sa'adia was called to Sura (when thirty-six years of age) in 928.

[10] I quote from the Ox. Cod.

[11] We now see the unfortunate mistake that has been made in naming this newly discovered system *Babylonian* (= Oriental). The mistake is not, however, altogether of modern origin. For it is but fair to state that this system is recognised as 'Oriental' in some of the Tschufut-Kale Bible Codd. (48, 87, 103, 116), e.g. Cod. 87, 1 Sam. xxv. 3, Mas. למדנ כלבו כת בלבי קרין; and 2 Sam. xiii. 21, Mas. למערב והסלך דוד ששע את כל־הדברים האלה כת וכן קר

ולמדנח שלע כל־הדברים האלה כת וכן קר

and Cod. 116, Ps. cxxxvii. 5, אֶשְׁפָּחֵךְ, note, למדנח אשכחת כת אשכחני קר. (I am indebted for these extracts to Prof. Strack of Berlin, who very kindly placed at my disposal the notes he had taken from the various Tschufut-Kale MSS.) The

In what light then are we to regard this superlinear punctuation? It stands outside the system common to the Oriental and Occidental Schools, and would seem to have been an attempt to simplify and introduce regularity into the older system. The influence of the Arabic is evident in the vocalization, and perhaps also in the accentuation, where *initial letters* represent the accents, just as in Arabic they stand for Teshdîd, Medda, &c.

Such an attempt, even if more successful than it actually was, could hardly have been looked on with favour by the heads of Schools in the East, and by other scholars, who may have become acquainted with it; for it must have seemed to them very like a tampering with sacred things,—the punctuation being referred at least to the authority of Ezra. Hence we may explain their silence with regard to it. The inventors of the system themselves shrank from applying their new-fangled signs to the Sacred Name יהוה (אדני), which is either marked with the older Qāmeṣ-sign יְהוָה (as in 132, 133), or not marked at all (as in Cod. Bab. and Tschufut-Kale 8ᵃ)[12]. A proof of the inferior esteem in which this system was held is that in Yemen, where it was in use in a modified and much simpler form, the Sacred text, when associated with Targum or Forms of prayer, has generally the Palestinian signs, and only the latter the superlinear[13].

That this system is of *Oriental origin* may indeed be taken for granted from its exhibiting, as in Cod. Bab., the readings peculiar to the Orientals. It was *an* Oriental, but not *the* Oriental, system.

The relation in which it stood to the Palestinian (which was one and the same with the Oriental) is indicated by the vowels and accents of this last-named system being constantly found in the MSS. with superlinear punctuation. This phenomenon receives its ready explanation, if we suppose the superlinear punctuation to have been an offshoot from the Oriental,—in which case it naturally remained under the influence of the system from which it was derived, and by which it must have been always overshadowed. I shall aim, in the following remarks, at shewing that the relation thus indicated really

---

writers of these notices were doubtless in the same position as modern scholars. They had no other texts with Oriental readings, and naturally concluded that the texts which contained such readings, exhibited also the Oriental mode of punctuation.—It is different with the name 'Assyrian,' adopted by some scholars, on the authority of the epigraph, quoted in note 1. But can we trust the unsupported testimony of a single copyist? Is it likely that an Italian Jew, of the 14th century, should have known the *origin* of this system, when scribes living in the East were ignorant of it? The statements contained in the epigraphs to Jewish texts have always to be received *cum grano*.

[12] Later punctators indeed, as those of the Yemen Codd. of the 14th and 15th centuries in the British Museum, were less particular.

[13] A specimen of Bible text with Targum is given in Pl. XCI of the Palæographical Society's Publications (Oriental Series). Oxford Scholars may also compare the Siddurs (1145 and 2498) in the Bodleian Library.

existed. Of course I shall confine myself to the accentuation ; but we may rest satisfied that if so important a part of the punctuation was *derived*, the whole system was no less so.

It is time now to turn to *the peculiarities* of this system (as far as the accents are concerned). And of these by far the most striking is *the frequent recurrence of R'bhîa*, in season and out of season. This accent is found subordinated not only to S'gôlta, Zaqeph, and Ṭiphcha (as in our system), but to all the disjunctives in turn (except L'garmeh), even to Géresh and a second R'bhîa ! Indeed the originators of this system went out of their way to bring in this favourite accent, as may be seen in Is. x. 24 ; Jer. xiii. 11 ; xxxvi. 6 ; &c. In the case of the other disjunctives, the variations from the Palestinian usage (mistakes having been corrected) are unimportant. Géresh and L'garmeh are found more freely used (with the exception that L'garmeh is not repeated) before R'bhîa ; L'garmeh and Paseq frequently interchange, &c. But these are minor matters. The *general conformity* of the two texts—when allowance has been made for the abnormal use of R'bhîa [14]—has not been sufficiently noticed by scholars [15]. But the key found, all is perfectly simple.

---

[14] Thus, with this allowance made, all the main rules for the sequence of the accents given in the previous pages—as for the position of Athnach in the verse; the substitution of Zaqeph for Ṭiphcha before Silluq or Athnach, pp. 62 and 69; the subordination of S'gôlta and Zaqeph to Athnach, p. 70; of R'bhîa and Pashṭa to Zaqeph, p. 77 f. ; &c.—are carried out.

[15] Who, for instance, would suppose, from reading Pinsker's 'Einleitung in das Babylonisch-Hebräische Punctationssystem,' that there was this general conformity? Prof. Strack indeed remarks (Zeitsch. für Luth. Theol. 1877, p. 31) : 'Die Accente werden im *Codex Babylonicus* nach ziemlich denselben Regeln gesetzt, welche für unsere Bibelhandschriften gelten. Man hat nur wenige Besonderheiten des babylonischen Systems stetz im Gedächtniss zu behalten, um im Stande zu sein, die meisten tiberianisch interpungirten Verse umzuaccentuiren.' But though he mentions, in the note, that R'bhîa takes the place of a second Zaqeph, and may occur as many as seven times in the same half-verse, he has failed to see that the singular rules for the introduction of R'bhîa are the main cause of the peculiarities to which he refers. He was, however, on the right track in adding (p. 32) : 'Dies ist ein neuer Beweis dafür, dass das babylonische System sich nicht selbständig gebildet hat.' It is a pity that the learned Professor did not pursue his investigations further. But he was doubtless hampered by the notion held by him, in common with other scholars (see his article on the Massora, Herzog's Encyclop. ix. p. 393), that the Babylonian system of punctuation was one and the same with the superlinear,—a notion which he has supplemented by the hypothesis (l. c.): ' Dass ursprünglich warscheinlich nur *ein* System existirte, welchem das übliche, tiberiensische, in bezug auf Stellung und Form der Zeichen näher gestanden haben dürfte als das babylonische.' I give these views of Dr. S., though only partially agreeing with my own, because he is the only scholar, beside Pinsker, who has carefully considered the subject of the superlinear accentuation.

APPENDIX II.

The following rules will shew how it is that R'bhia is of such frequent occurrence:

1. Pazer and Great T'lisha are wanting; and Géresh is confined to R'bhia's clause, and even there is not admitted if L'garmeh follows. And *instead of these accents*—i. e. of Pazer and Great T'lisha; of Géresh in the clauses of Pashṭa, Zarqa, and T'bhir; and of Géresh in R'bhia's clause, when L'garmeh follows—*R'bhia is used;* or if two of them come together, R'bhia, preceded by Géresh (or less frequently L'garmeh), may be employed. It is these changes that occasion the most frequent variations in the accentuation.

2. The repetition of Zaqeph is not allowed. If due a second or third time (according to our texts), *R'bhia appears instead.*

3. *R'bhia is not transformed* (as in the Palestinian system, see p. 90, 2) in Ṭiphcha's clause.

The result of the above variations is that many clauses are *overburdened with R'bhias*. The question suggests itself, Could such a system have ever been practically in use for chanting?

Let us next notice how these rules are carried out; and we shall see clearly that we have to do with a *derived*—not, as is generally supposed, an original and independent—system.

a. Of course, when R'bhia takes the place of Pazer, Great T'lisha, or Géresh, the servi (if any) should be made to conform to the change of accent. But what do we find? *The original servi* (as I shall call them) *constantly left standing*. Thus, those of Pazer, כִּֽי־בָ֞ה אָמַ֣ר־יְהוָ֗ה אֵלַ֔י (Is. xxxi. 4); of T'lisha, וְשִׁבְעִ֣ים אִ֣ישׁ מִזִּקְנֵ֣י בֵֽית־יִשְׂרָאֵ֗ל (Ezek. viii. 11); and more conspicuously of Géresh, יוֹצִ֗יאוּ אֶת־עַצְמ֣וֹת מַלְכֵֽי־יְהוּדָ֣ה וְאֶת־ עַצְמ֨וֹת־שָׂרָ֜יו וְאֶת־עַצְמ֣וֹת הַכֹּהֲנִ֗ים (Jer. viii. 1). And yet R'bhia, when standing in its own right, has its servi in agreement with the Palestinian system, as in Is. v. 25; xi. 2; xxx. 6; &c.

β. So when Géresh stands for Pazer, Great T'lisha, or Pashṭa, *the servi of these accents remain*, e. g. of Pazer, אִם־לֹ֤א יַ֙עַן֙ הֱיוֹת־צֹאנִ֣י לָבַ֗ז (Ezek. xxxiv. 8); of T'lisha, כִּ֣י כַאֲשֶׁ֣ר הַשָּׁמַ֤יִם הַחֲדָשִׁ֗ים (Is. lxvi. 22); of Pashṭa, לֹא־יִשָּׂ֨א ג֤וֹי אֶל־גּוֹי֙ (Is. ii. 4). But Géresh, when originally due, has its regular and well-known servi, as may be seen everywhere in the text, e. g. Jer. iii. 1 (five servi)[16].

γ. The rule for the transformation of a second and third Zaqeph is regularly carried out[17]. Thus, בְּקוּנָ֨ה כַמּוֹכֵ֜ר כַּמַּלְוֶה֙ כַּלֹּוֶ֔ה כַּנֹּשֶׁ֖ה כַּאֲשֶׁ֥ר נֹשֶׁ֖א בֽוֹ (Is. xxiv. 2) becomes כַּקּוֹנֶ֨ה כַּמּוֹכֵ֜ר כַּמַּלְוֶ֣ה כַּלֹּוֶ֗ה כַּנֹּשֶׁ֛ה כַּאֲשֶׁ֥ר נֹשֶׁ֖א בֽוֹ׃

---

[16] Note in connection with Géresh, וַיִּקַּ֣ח עֶֽבֶד־מֶ֠לֶךְ אֶת־הָאֲנָשִׁ֗ים (Jer. xxxviii. 11), where וַיִּקַּ֣ח has evidently been taken from the Palestinian text, without any recognition of the value of L'garmeh (p. 118).

[17] The original accentuation sometimes shews itself through the disguise that has been thrown over it, as in Jer. xxviii. 11; xxxi. 23; xliv. 2; Ezek. xxiv. 27;

APPENDIX II. 149

Here also we see that we have to do with a *derived* system; for where Zaqeph (with two words in its clause) has Pashṭa preceding, as in the example just quoted, R'bhîa takes Géresh before it, but where Zaqeph has a servus, as מִמִּדְבָּר בָּא (Is. xxi. 1), R'bhîa retains the servus. Now for Zaqeph there is a fixed rule, see p. 75; but there is no corresponding rule for R'bhîa in this system [18].

Observe also what confusion is the result of this transformation of Zaqeph. There may be a R'bhîa subordinated to it,—as in Is. lxii. 4; Jer. iii. 16; Ezek. xx. 28[b],—but instead of this R'bhîa being transformed to Géresh (or L'garmeh), as the sense requires, when R'bhîa has taken the place of Zaqeph, it is allowed to remain! In short, as with the servi above, the transformation has been only half carried out.

δ. This system accepts the principle of the transformation of R'bhîa in Zaqeph's clause; for where Pashṭa stands in our text, according to the rule pp. 78–9, it has also Pashṭa [19]. In the few instances also in Cod. Bab.,—Is. xx. 2; xlv. 14; Jer. xxi. 4; xxxvi. 32,—in which a second R'bhîa is due before S'gôlta, transformation has taken place, although not to Zarqa, as in our texts (see p. 88), but to L'garmeh. [The query is, whether Zarqa was not originally intended; comp. the similarity of the two signs, p. 143.] So far the Palestinian practice has been followed. But the inconsistency that runs through the whole system again shews itself. The rule for the transformation of R'bhîa has not, and could not have, been carried out *generally*, or the main characteristic of the system (p. 147) would have disappeared. Hence two or more R'bhîas in immediate sequence are as common as can be. Even in Ṭiphcha's clause the second R'bhîa stands, e. g. וַתֹּאמֶר בְּרָב רִכְבִּי אֲנִי עָלִיתִי מְרוֹם הָרִים (Is. xxxvii. 24), where we have רִכְבִּי (see the rule and examples, p. 91). In Ezek. xl. 42 we find R'bhîa transformed in the first half of the verse before Zaqeph, but *not* transformed in the second half before Ṭiphcha.

It is unnecessary to go into further details. We may conclude, with absolute certainty, from the instances cited, that the Palestinian punctuation was before the originators of this superlinear system [20]. Their

---

and Deut. ix. 5[b] (Ox. 64), where, through an oversight, the second Zaqeph *has been left standing*. In Jer. xix. 15; xxv. 30; xxxv. 17, the second Zaqeph has been transformed, but *not the third*.

[18] Another indication is that where our text has קָמֵץ בּוּקֵק, and the Zaqeph is changed into R'bhîa, Qāmeṣ still remains, as in Jer. ii. 19; Ezek. vii. 12; Hos. iii. 4.

[19] Or, by some strange mistake,—as in Is. xxxviii. 3; Jer. v. 19[b]; xliii. 10,— *T'bhîr*. That Pashṭa, however, is the proper sign is clear from the servus M'huppach preceding.

[20] I believe that it would be equally easy to shew that the superlinear *vocalization*, which, as a system, is far more complete and coherent, still presupposes the Palestinian as a basis.

APPENDIX II.

attempt, however, to modify and improve upon it must, as far at least as the accents are concerned, be pronounced a failure, and for us quite worthless. Inconsequent and contradictory, this new system is a mere travesty of the Palestinian. Even the simplicity apparently aimed at by the constant introduction of R'bhîa leads only to confusion, by destroying the fine lines of distinction established for the sense by the older system.—I do not, of course, mean to deny the proper value attaching to Codd. with this peculiar notation, which consists in their furnishing Oriental readings, *quantum valeant*, not to be found elsewhere,—among which are accentual variations that are sometimes not without interest.

I have already mentioned that the superlinear system is found in a modified and much simpler form in MSS. that have been lately brought from Yemen. But these MSS. will not detain us. The *accentuation*, so far as it is superlinear [21], is in all cases *very incomplete*. Sometimes it is confined to Silluq and Athnach [22]. At others, Zaqeph is found as well (often with a strange admixture of Palestinian signs) [23]. It need hardly be added that I have found these MSS. of no service to me in my investigations.

One point, which has escaped the notice of scholars, I may mention in conclusion. These Yemen MSS. do not exhibit the Oriental readings. We have in them the *Palestinian* text, with a superlinear punctuation.

---

[21] In Or. 1467, 2363, we find the confusing arrangement of the Palestinian accentuation with the superlinear vocalization. See Pl. LIV of the Palæographical Society's Publications, Oriental Series (Or. 1467 is, however, incorrectly described there as of Babylonian or Persian origin).

[22] As in Or. 1469, 2373, 2374.

[23] In Or. 2366, 2368, 2703, 2704.

INDEX I. SUBJECTS.

(The numbers refer to the pages; n stands for note.)

Accents, musical signs 1; division of, according to musical value, 13, 14; mark the sense 2; interpunctional value relative 58; explanation of irregularities 3, 32 ff; anomalies due to fancies of accentuators 33, 67, 73, 85, 92, 114, 118, 130, 136, 140; accentual signs not known to Talmud 5; falsely assigned to Ezra 5; probable date of introduction 4 ff; number, names, and notation 10, 15 ff; disjunctive and conjunctive 9; kings and servi 9; prepositive and postpositive 12.

Adverbial expressions, at head of clause 47, 48; separated from the noun they qualify 54.

Athnach 16; marks main dichotomy of verse 29, 61 ff; rules for dichotomy of its own clause 69 ff; servi 73.

Azla 25; servus to Pashṭa, T'bhîr, and Zarqa 110, Géresh 112, and L'garmeh 120; in same word with Géresh 113.

Babylonian system of punctuation 142 ff; falsely so called 145; derived from Palestinian 147 ff.

Ben-Asher and Ben-Naphtali, differences between 82 n, 107 n, 109, 110 (*bis*).

Cantillation, practised in early times 1; variation in 63.

Clauses, appended 37, 38; participial 54; procemial 34 ff; relative 54; supplemental 32; verbal 49, 50.

Conjunctions 52.

Correlative expressions 55.

Darga 25; servus to R'bhîa 98, T'bhîr 108, and Ṭiphcha 91.

Dichotomy, meaning of 29; origin of 30; rules for 31 ff; continuous 29; main and minor 29; syntactical 44 ff.

Emphasis 32 ff.

Galgal 26; servus to Great Pazer 114.

Géresh (Gershâyim) 20, 112; marks dichotomy in clauses of R'bhîa 93 ff, Pashṭa, T'bhîr, and Zarqa 100 ff; transformed 100; transposed 102, 103; in same word with Great T'lîsha 101; servi 112.

Interjections 52.

L'garmeh 22, 119; marks dichotomy in R'bhîa's clause 94 f; rarely in other clauses 120; takes place of Paseq before R'bhîa 119; repeated 95; servi 120.

Massora corrected 27 n, 81 n (*quater*), 107 n, 111 n.

Mây'la 26; in same word with Silluq 67, and Athnach 73.

Mer'kha 24; servus to Silluq 67, Ṭiphcha 91, Pashṭa 107, T'bhîr 108, Zarqa 110, and L'garmeh 120; in same word with Ṭiphcha 91, and T'bhîr 109; Double Mer'kha 25; servus to Ṭiphcha 91.

M'huppakh or Mahpakh 24; servus to Pashṭa 107, in same word 107.

Munach 22; servus to Athnach 73, Zaqeph 80, S'gôlta 88, R'bhîa 97, 98, Pashṭa and T'bhîr 109, 111, Zarqa 109 (*bis*), 111, Géresh 112, Pazer 114, and Great T'lîsha 115; in same word with Athnach 73, Zaqeph 80, and R'bhîa 97.

Musical changes 72, 75, 78, 80, 88, 90, 92, 93, 95, 99, 100, 102, 106, 110, 119.

Nominal predicate at head of clause 51.

Nouns, in apposition 53; joined by *Vav* 53; adjective separated from substantive 53.

Object at head of clause 46.

Orientals and Occidentals, differences between 6, 63 n, 67 n, 73 n, 91 n, 92, 109, 110 (*bis*), 130 (*bis*), 144 n.

Parallelism 38; with and without addition 39; progressive 40.
Parenthesis, rules for marking 42.
Paseq, rules for 122 ff; constantly fails 123, 124, 127; list of Paseqs 127-9.
Pashṭa 19; foretone to Zaqeph 75; marks dichotomy in clauses of Zaqeph 76 ff, S'gôlta 87, and Tiphcha 90; repeated 79; rules for dichotomy of its clause 100 ff; confounded with Azla 84; servi 107 f.
Pazer, Great and Little 21, 113, 114; mark dichotomy in clauses of R'bhia 94 ff, Pashṭa, T'bhîr, and Zarqa 101 ff, Géresh 116, and (rarely) Great T'lîsha 117 n; servi 114. Little Pazer repeated 97, 105, 106.
Prepositions 47, 54, 55.

Qadma 25; name falsely used 82 n.

R'bhia 18; marks dichotomy in clauses of Zaqeph 76 ff, S'gôlta 86 f, Tiphcha 89 f; repeated 78, 87, 90; rules for dichotomy of its clause 93 ff; servi 97.
Rhythmical cadence 62, 77, 93, 100.

Servi, two in same word 110 (*bis*), 111.
S'gôlta 16; represents Zaqeph 71; marks dichotomy in Athnach's clause 70; rules for dichotomy of its own clause 86 ff; servi 88.
Shalshéleth 17, 25; stands for S'gôlta 85; why introduced 85.
Silluq 16; rules for dichotomy of its clause 61 ff; servus 67.
Specification, rules for marking 40 ff.
Status constructus 55; genitive relation in Chaldee 55 n.
Subject at head of clause 45, 46.

T'bhîr 20; marks dichotomy in Tiphcha's clause 89 f; repeated 91; rules for dichotomy of its clause 100 ff; servi 107 ff.

Ṭiphcha 18; foretone to Silluq 61, and Athnach 69; in same word with ditto 67, 73; marks dichotomy in clauses of ditto 61 ff, 69 f; rules for dichotomy of its own clause 89 ff; servi 91.
T'lîsha, Great 21, 115; marks dichotomy in clauses of R'bhia 94 ff, Pashṭa, T'bhîr, and Zarqa 100 ff, and Géresh 116; servi 115. Great and Little T'lîsha, frequent interchange of 115.
T'lîsha, Little 22, 26; servus to Pashṭa, T'bhîr, and Zarqa 111, and Géresh 112; always followed by Azla 113 n.
Transformation, varieties of—Géresh transformed to servus 100; Pashṭa to Zarqa 88, and T'bhîr 91; R'bhia to Pashṭa 78, 87, 90.

Verbs, two in same construction 56; one introductory to other 56; inf. and fin. 56; verbal clauses 49, 50.
Verses, division of text into 27, 28; length of 61.
Vocative 48, 49 n.

Word *long*, technical meaning of 62 n.

Y'thîbh 20, 106.

Zaqeph 18; Great Zaqeph 83; Little Zaqeph, marks dichotomy in clauses of Silluq 62 ff, and Athnach 69 f; repeated 65, 66, 70; falsely introduced 67, 74, 83, 84, 92; rules for dichotomy of its clause 76 ff; servi 80; Munach and M'thîga in Zaqeph's word 80-82.
Zarqa 19; foretone to S'gôlta 85; marks dichotomy in S'gôlta's clause 86 f; repeated 88; rules for dichotomy of its clause 100 ff; servi 107 ff.
Zarqa-lists explained 15 n.
Zusatz 45, 47, 48, 57; Double Zusatz 45, 48, 57.

INDEX II. HEBREW TECHNICAL TERMS.

21. אופן ועגלה	24. מאריך	19. צנורי
143 n. אוקומי	20. מוכרת	17. קבלה
25. אול ואתי	22 n. מיושב	25 n. קרמא ואולא
25. אשל	9. מלכים	21. קרני פרה
23. גלגל	25. משכן	17. רודף לורקא
18. דחי	25, 82 n. מקל	17 n. רתק (רתוק)
26. דחויה	24 n. מקיף	23. שופר גדול
82 n. דרבן	17 n. מעיר	23. ש׳ הולך
131. הכרע	17 n. מרעים	23. ש׳ ישר
82 n. המוה	9. משרתים	22. ש׳ מונח
25. תרין חוטרין	81. מתיגה	23. ש׳ מכרבל
143. חור	22. נגרא	22 n. ש׳ מעמד
131 n. טעם העליון	9. נגינות	23. ש׳ עלוי
131 n. טעם התחתון	26. נטויה	25. שישלא
18. טרחא	16. סחפא	17. שרי
20. טרס	17 n. סלסלה	26 (bis). תלישא קטנה
17 n, 20. טרסא	26. עגולה	21. תרסא
26. ירח בן יומו	2 n. פיסוק טעמים	

INDEX III. SCRIPTURE PASSAGES.

GENESIS		EXODUS		NUMBERS	
1. 1	32	2. 5	50	4. 6	60
11	57	3. 12	35	5. 19	60
16	37	10. 9	40	20. 13	35
18	83 n	12. 23	35	25. 15	60
21	33	20. 2	87 n	28. 19	41
6. 9	35 n, 42	3–17	130	30. 8	67
19	117 n	24. 4	34	36. 5	131
7. 13	41	25. 22	34		
8. 22	117 n	34	131	DEUTERONOMY	
12. 8	41 n	27. 19	41	2. 10	46
13. 10	57 n	30. 31	60	3. 11	35
14. 13	50	32. 1	131	4. 40	57
20. 13	130	33. 19	131	5. 6	87 n
25. 20	41	34. 31	54	7–18	130
30. 7	51	35. 23	41	19	131
34. 28	41			9. 28	42
35. 10	33	LEVITICUS		11. 6	41
22	130	13. 4	60	22. 29	67
37. 2	35 n	16. 2	41	26. 5	131
19	60	18. 18	47	15	58
42. 33	56 n	21. 22	42	28. 52	57
36	40				

28. 56 50
32. 5 132

Joshua
1. 4 .... 94 n
   7 83
2. 5 140
4. 3 132
   6 59
6. 10 132
  21 41
7. 19 92
10. 28 88
11. 8 84

Judges
2. 1 83
4. 5 51
  21 .... 33 n, 140
5. 12 67
6. 21 37
  24 132
9. 46 68
11. 39 33
12. 4 132
13. 8 .... 66 n
  11 92
14. 15 132
15. 19 132
16. 9 67
  26 60
  28 132
20. 27, 28 .... 43 n

1 Samuel
2. 15 .... 88 n
3. 3 43
10. 3 83
  22 59
11. 5 74
  11 .... 87 n
14. 6 83
  41 68
25. 43 59
27. 5 92
28. 15 83

2 Samuel
5. 6 133
10. 5 132
11. 25 133
14. 32 .... 115 n
15. 2 83
  34 133
17. 3 67
18. 7 59
  29 .... 104 n
19. 27 104
  33 60

20. 18 133
21. 4 50
22. 2 ff 63
  28 68

1 Kings
5. 17 83
6. 1 133
  7 60
7. 6 140
  7 42
  36 .... 42, 140
  48 92
10. 12 59
11. 26 84
12. 6 83
14. 22 67
17. 19 84
  24 60
18. 42 133
  46 133
19. 11 .... 103 n
21. 4 84
22. 8 32

2 Kings
3. 25 133
5. 1 105
  13 92
10. 5 41
  15 133
  24 84
11. 17 84
16. 7 .... 101 n
18. 17 133
20. 11 59
22. 14 140
23. 12 92
24. 15 59
25. 4 .... 126 n

Isaiah
1. 5 134
  9 134
  13 134
2. 20 57
3. 24 42
5. 24 134
7. 3 68
8. 14 134
  23 134
9. 5 134
  6 (corr.) .... 41 n
15. 7 40
17. 5 135
19. 7 40
  9 135
20. 4 135

22. 6 68
23. 7 135
24. 16 36
25. 1 135
28. 6 74
  16 .... 33, 140
  28 135
29. 5 39
  15 50
  16 135
30. 7 135
  21 135
  32 135
  33 .... 42 n
33. 22 39
  23 135
35. 1 140
36. 2 136
  9 53
37. 26 50
38. 13 136
40. 2 50
  13 140
41. 3 54
42. 16 39
  24 .... 32, 50
44. 12 40
45. 1 136
  24 136
48. 22 32
49. 21 41
53. 10 34
54. 1 39
  15 32
56. 9 136
59. 21 36
63. 13 .... 57 n
64. 3 40
66. 5 136
  12 136
  19 41

Jeremiah
1. 1 84
2. 23 35
15. 18 74
18. 4 92
24. 3 33
27. 9 .... 76 n
29. 18 68
32. 9 137
  29 59
41. 3 41
  11 60
42. 14 40
43. 12 59
46. 18 68
50. 5 60
51. 55 68

INDEX III. SCRIPTURE PASSAGES.

51. 58 141
    64 92

Ezekiel
1. 11 137
3. 20 137
4. 6 137
6. 9 137
7. 13 137
8. 5 68
14. 4 .... 92 n
    7 40
15. 2 137
16. 45 .... 40 n
18. 21 84
    30 137
21. 3 137
25. 9 137
27. 27 41
31. 15 137
39. 13 35
40. 1 137
44. 22 137
45. 11 .... 42, 59
    21 141
    14 74
    21 42

Hosea
1. 6 36
4. 10 68
9. 8 59

Joel
4. 7 .... 76 n

Amos
1. 3 42
4. 2 36
    10 40
5. 27 68
6. 2 40
    6 141

Obadiah
11 40

Jonah
1. 8 60

Micah
2. 4 138
4. 10 138

Habakkuk
1. 3 138
2. 4 46
    18 138
3. 3, 9 138

Haggai
2. 16 138

Zechariah
2. 2 59
10. 5 60

Job
1. 1 .... 89 n
    8 88
    21 34
2. 4 68

Canticle
1. 3 141
8. 6 138

Qohéleth
1. 5 141
2. 3 138
    16 138
3. 17 42
7. 2 35
8. 10 138
    11 139
9. 4 74
    10 139
11. 3 74
    8 139

Esther
2. 12 43
9. 26 41
    28 60
    31 139

Daniel
3. 16 50
5. 15 50
6. 4 33
9. 25 141
12. 2 60

Ezra
4. 17 41
6. 8 .... 79 n
7. 13 88
8. 35 115
10. 14 141

Nehemiah
5. 18 .... 102 n
9. 37 .... 101 n

1 Chronicles
3. 17 141
4. 19 141
5. 21 .... 80 n
6. 34 42
    46 139
7. 3 68
9. 17 139
11. 31 74
12. 25 74
16. 8 ff 63
21. 16 84
28. 4 59

2 Chronicles
2. 13 34
4. 9 141
7. 5 88
10. 6 83
13. 11 115
14. 7 .... 87 n
22. 11 74
24. 14 139
26. 18 84
28. 10 46
    13 46
30. 18, 19 140
32. 31 84
33. 19 68
34. 3 84
    4 74

THE END.

BY THE SAME AUTHOR,

טעמי אמ״ת. *A Treatise on the Accentuation of the Three so-called Poetical Books of the Old Testament, Psálms, Proverbs, and Job.* With an Appendix containing the Treatise, assigned to R. Jehuda ben-Bil'am, on the same subject, in the original Arabic. 1881. Paper covers, 5s.

Extracts from notices and reviews.

'A more lucid or masterly exposition of a complicated subject could scarcely be imagined. . . . It is enough to say that Dr. Wickes' treatise will be indispensable to all who would read aright the accentuation of the three books, and to express our hope that he may one day supplement it by another devoted to that of the remaining twenty-one.' (Prof. Driver, in *Academy*, May 20, 1882.)

'Dr. Wickes' book will take its place beside the best Hebrew grammars, and no advanced student of the poetical books will find himself able to dispense with its guidance.' (Dr. Neubauer, in *Athenæum*, Feb. 25, 1882.)

'Speciell über die Accentuation der poetischen Bücher handelt William Wickes in einer ganz vorzüglichen, auf der gründlichsten Vorbereitung beruhenden Arbeit.' (Prof. Siegfried, in *Theologischer Jahresbericht* for 1881.)

'Eximius libellus.' (Prof. Delitzsch, in Preface to *Daniel*, p. iii.)

'Il Dr. Wickes col suo bel libro ha reso un vero servigio alla filologia ebraica, e quale pochi altri forse avrebbero reso con ugual paziente costanza di ricerche.' (Prof. Guidi, of Rome, in *Bollettino Italiano degli studii orientali*, 1882.)

OXFORD: AT THE CLARENDON PRESS.
LONDON: HENRY FROWDE,
OXFORD UNIVERSITY PRESS WAREHOUSE, AMEN CORNER, E.C.

March, 1887.

Clarendon Press, Oxford

A SELECTION OF

BOOKS

PUBLISHED FOR THE UNIVERSITY BY

HENRY FROWDE,

AT THE OXFORD UNIVERSITY PRESS WAREHOUSE,
AMEN CORNER, LONDON.

ALSO TO BE HAD AT THE
CLARENDON PRESS DEPOSITORY, OXFORD.

[*Every book is bound in cloth, unless otherwise described.*]

LEXICONS, GRAMMARS, ORIENTAL WORKS, &c.

ANGLO-SAXON.—*An Anglo-Saxon Dictionary*, based on the MS. Collections of the late Joseph Bosworth, D.D., Professor of Anglo-Saxon, Oxford. Edited and enlarged by Prof. T. N. Toller, M.A. (To be completed in four parts.) Parts I and II. A—HWISTLIAN. 4to. 15*s*. each.

CHINESE.—*A Handbook of the Chinese Language.* By James Summers. 1863. 8vo. half bound, 1*l*. 8*s*.

—— *A Record of Buddhistic Kingdoms*, by the Chinese Monk FÂ-HIEN. Translated and annotated by James Legge, M.A., LL.D. Crown 4to. cloth back, 10*s*. 6*d*.

ENGLISH.—*A New English Dictionary, on Historical Principles:* founded mainly on the materials collected by the Philological Society. Edited by James A. H. Murray, LL.D., with the assistance of many Scholars and men of Science. Part I. A—ANT. Part II. ANT—BATTEN. Imperial 4to. 12*s*. 6*d*. each.

—— *An Etymological Dictionary of the English Language.* By W. W. Skeat, M.A. *Second Edition.* 1884. 4to. 2*l*. 4*s*.

——Supplement to the First Edition of the above. 4to. 2*s*. 6*d*.

—— *A Concise Etymological Dictionary of the English Language.* By W. W. Skeat, M.A. *Second Edition.* 1885. Crown 8vo. 5*s*. 6*d*.

GREEK.—*A Greek-English Lexicon*, by Henry George Liddell, D.D., and Robert Scott, D.D. Seventh Edition, Revised and Augmented throughout. 1883. 4to. 1*l.* 16*s.*

—— *A Greek-English Lexicon*, abridged from Liddell and Scott's 4to. edition, chiefly for the use of Schools. Twenty-first Edition. 1884. Square 12mo. 7*s.* 6*d.*

—— *A copious Greek-English Vocabulary*, compiled from the best authorities. 1850. 24mo. 3*s.*

—— *A Practical Introduction to Greek Accentuation*, by H. W. Chandler, M.A. Second Edition. 1881. 8vo. 10*s.* 6*d.*

HEBREW.—*The Book of Hebrew Roots*, by Abu 'l-Walîd Marwân ibn Janâh, otherwise called Rabbî Yônâh. Now first edited, with an Appendix, by Ad. Neubauer. 1875. 4to. 2*l.* 7*s.* 6*d.*

—— *A Treatise on the use of the Tenses in Hebrew.* By S. R. Driver, D.D. Second Edition. 1881. Extra fcap. 8vo. 7*s.* 6*d.*

—— *Hebrew Accentuation of Psalms, Proverbs, and Job.* By William Wickes, D.D. 1881. Demy 8vo. stiff covers, 5*s.*

ICELANDIC.—*An Icelandic-English Dictionary*, based on the MS. collections of the late Richard Cleasby. Enlarged and completed by G. Vigfússon, M.A. With an Introduction, and Life of Richard Cleasby, by G. Webbe Dasent, D.C.L. 1874. 4to. 3*l.* 7*s.*

—— *A List of English Words the Etymology of which is illustrated by comparison with Icelandic.* Prepared in the form of an APPENDIX to the above. By W. W. Skeat, M.A. 1876. stitched, 2*s.*

—— *An Icelandic Primer*, with Grammar, Notes, and Glossary. By Henry Sweet, M.A. Extra fcap. 8vo. 3*s.* 6*d.*

—— *An Icelandic Prose Reader*, with Notes, Grammar and Glossary, by Dr. Gudbrand Vigfússon and F. York Powell, M.A. 1879. Extra fcap. 8vo. 10*s.* 6*d.*

LATIN.—*A Latin Dictionary*, founded on Andrews' edition of Freund's Latin Dictionary, revised, enlarged, and in great part rewritten by Charlton T. Lewis, Ph.D., and Charles Short, LL.D. 1879. 4to. 1*l.* 5*s.*

MELANESIAN.—*The Melanesian Languages.* By R. H. Codrington, D.D., of the Melanesian Mission. 8vo. 18*s.*

SANSKRIT.—*A Practical Grammar of the Sanskrit Language*, arranged with reference to the Classical Languages of Europe, for the use of English Students, by Sir M. Monier-Williams, M.A. Fourth Edition. 8vo. 15*s.*

—— *A Sanskrit-English Dictionary*, Etymologically and Philologically arranged, with special reference to Greek, Latin, German, Anglo-Saxon, English, and other cognate Indo-European Languages. By Sir M. Monier-Williams, M.A. 1872. 4to. 4*l.* 14*s.* 6*d.*

SANSKRIT.—*Nalopákhyánam.* Story of Nala, an Episode of the Mahá-Bhárata: the Sanskrit text, with a copious Vocabulary, and an improved version of Dean Milman's Translation, by Sir M. Monier-Williams, M.A. Second Edition, Revised and Improved. 1879. 8vo. 15*s.*

—— *Sakuntalā.* A Sanskrit Drama, in Seven Acts. Edited by Sir M. Monier-Williams, M.A. Second Edition, 1876. 8vo. 21*s.*

SYRIAC.—*Thesaurus Syriacus:* collegerunt Quatremère, Bernstein, Lorsbach, Arnoldi, Agrell, Field, Roediger: edidit R. Payne Smith, S.T.P. Fasc. I-VI. 1868-83. sm. fol. each, 1*l.* 1*s.* Fasc. VII. 1*l.* 11*s.* 6*d.*
Vol. I, containing Fasc. I-V, sm. fol. 5*l.* 5*s.*

—— *The Book of Kalīlah and Dimnah.* Translated from Arabic into Syriac. Edited by W. Wright, LL.D. 1884. 8vo. 21*s.*

GREEK CLASSICS, &c.

Aristophanes: A Complete Concordance to the Comedies and Fragments. By Henry Dunbar, M.D. 4to. 1*l.* 1*s.*

Aristotle: The Politics, with Introduction, Notes, etc., by W. L. Newman, M.A., Fellow of Balliol College, Oxford. Vols. I. and II. *Nearly ready.*

Aristotle: The Politics, translated into English, with Introduction, Marginal Analysis, Notes, and Indices, by B. Jowett, M.A. Medium 8vo. 2 vols. 21*s.*

Catalogus Codicum Graecorum Sinaiticorum. Scripsit V. Gardthausen Lipsiensis. With six pages of Facsimiles. 8vo. *linen,* 25*s.*

Heracliti Ephesii Reliquiae. Recensuit I. Bywater, M.A. Appendicis loco additae sunt Diogenis Laertii Vita Heracliti, Particulae Hippocratei De Diaeta Libri Primi, Epistolae Heracliteae. 1877. 8vo. 6*s.*

Herculanensium Voluminum Partes II. 1824. 8vo. 10*s.*

Fragmenta Herculanensia. A Descriptive Catalogue of the Oxford copies of the Herculanean Rolls, together with the texts of several papyri, accompanied by facsimiles. Edited by Walter Scott, M.A., Fellow of Merton College, Oxford. Royal 8vo. *cloth,* 21*s.*

Homer: A Complete Concordance to the Odyssey and Hymns of Homer; to which is added a Concordance to the Parallel Passages in the Iliad, Odyssey, and Hymns. By Henry Dunbar, M.D. 1880. 4to. 1*l.* 1*s.*

—— *Scholia Graeca in Iliadem.* Edited by Professor W. Dindorf, after a new collation of the Venetian MSS. by D. B. Monro, M.A., Provost of Oriel College. 4 vols. 8vo. 2*l.* 10*s.* Vols. V and VI. *In the Press.*

—— *Scholia Graeca in Odysseam.* Edidit Guil. Dindorfius. Tomi II. 1855. 8vo. 15*s.* 6*d.*

Plato : Apology, with a revised Text and English Notes, and a Digest of Platonic Idioms, by James Riddell, M.A. 1878. 8vo. 8s. 6d.

—— *Philebus*, with a revised Text and English Notes, by Edward Poste, M.A. 1860. 8vo. 7s. 6d.

—— *Sophistes and Politicus*, with a revised Text and English Notes, by L. Campbell, M.A. 1867. 8vo. 18s.

—— *Theaetetus*, with a revised Text and English Notes. by L. Campbell, M.A. Second Edition. 8vo. 10s. 6d.

—— *The Dialogues*, translated into English, with Analyses and Introductions, by B. Jowett, M.A. A new Edition in 5 volumes, medium 8vo. 1875. 3l. 10s.

—— *The Republic*, translated into English, with an Analysis and Introduction, by B. Jowett, M.A. Medium 8vo. 12s. 6d.

Thucydides : Translated into English, with Introduction, Marginal Analysis, Notes, and Indices. By B. Jowett, M.A. 2 vols. 1881. Medium 8vo. 1l. 12s.

THE HOLY SCRIPTURES, &c.

STUDIA BIBLICA.—Essays in Biblical Archæology and Criticism, and kindred subjects. By Members of the University of Oxford. 8vo. 10s. 6d.

ENGLISH.—*The Holy Bible in the earliest English Versions*, made from the Latin Vulgate by John Wycliffe and his followers : edited by the Rev. J. Forshall and Sir F. Madden. 4 vols. 1850. Royal 4to. 3l. 3s.

[Also reprinted from the above, with Introduction and Glossary by W. W. Skeat, M.A.

—— *The Books of Job, Psalms, Proverbs, Ecclesiastes, and the Song of Solomon :* according to the Wycliffite Version made by Nicholas de Hereford, about A.D. 1381, and Revised by John Purvey, about A.D. 1388. Extra fcap. 8vo. 3s. 6d.

—— *The New Testament in English,* according to the Version by John Wycliffe, about A.D. 1380, and Revised by John Purvey, about A.D. 1388. Extra fcap. 8vo. 6s.]

ENGLISH.—*The Holy Bible:* an exact reprint, page for page, of the Authorised Version published in the year 1611. Demy 4to. half bound, 1*l.* 1*s.*

—— *The Psalter, or Psalms of David, and certain Canticles,* with a Translation and Exposition in English, by Richard Rolle of Hampole. Edited by H. R. Bramley, M.A., Fellow of S. M. Magdalen College, Oxford. With an Introduction and Glossary. Demy 8vo. 1*l.* 1*s.*

—— *Lectures on Ecclesiastes.* Delivered in Westminster Abbey by the Very Rev. George Granville Bradley, D.D., Dean of Westminster. Crown 8vo. 4*s.* 6*d.*

GOTHIC.—*The Gospel of St. Mark in Gothic,* according to the translation made by Wulfila in the Fourth Century. Edited with a Grammatical Introduction and Glossarial Index by W. W. Skeat, M.A. Extra fcap. 8vo. 4*s.*

GREEK.—*Vetus Testamentum* ex Versione Septuaginta Interpretum secundum exemplar Vaticanum Romae editum. Accedit potior varietas Codicis Alexandrini. Tomi III. Editio Altera. 18mo. 18*s.*

—— *Origenis Hexaplorum* quae supersunt; sive, Veterum Interpretum Graecorum in totum Vetus Testamentum Fragmenta. Edidit Fridericus Field, A.M. 2 vols. 1875. 4to. 5*l.* 5*s.*

—— *The Book of Wisdom:* the Greek Text, the Latin Vulgate, and the Authorised English Version; with an Introduction, Critical Apparatus, and a Commentary. By William J. Deane, M.A. Small 4to. 12*s.* 6*d.*

—— *Novum Testamentum Graece.* Antiquissimorum Codicum Textus in ordine parallelo dispositi. Accedit collatio Codicis Sinaitici. Edidit E. H. Hansell, S.T.B. Tomi III. 1864. 8vo. half morocco. Price reduced to 24*s.*

—— *Novum Testamentum Graece.* Accedunt parallela S. Scripturae loca, etc. Edidit Carolus Lloyd, S.T.P.R. 18mo. 3*s.*

On writing paper, with wide margin, 10*s.*

—— *Novum Testamentum Graece* juxta Exemplar Millianum. 18mo. 2*s.* 6*d.* On writing paper, with wide margin, 9*s.*

—— *Evangelia Sacra Graece.* Fcap. 8vo. limp, 1*s.* 6*d.*

—— *The Greek Testament*, with the Readings adopted by the Revisers of the Authorised Version:—

    (1) Pica type, with Marginal References. Demy 8vo. 10*s.* 6*d.*
    (2) Long Primer type. Fcap. 8vo. 4*s.* 6*d.*
    (3) The same, on writing paper, with wide margin, 15*s.*

—— *The Parallel New Testament,* Greek and English; being the Authorised Version, 1611; the Revised Version, 1881; and the Greek Text followed in the Revised Version. 8vo. 12*s.* 6*d.*

The Revised Version is the joint property of the Universities of Oxford and Cambridge.

GREEK.—*Canon Muratorianus:* the earliest Catalogue of the Books of the New Testament. Edited with Notes and a Facsimile of the MS. in the Ambrosian Library at Milan, by S. P. Tregelles, LL.D. 1867. 4to. 10s. 6d.

—— *Outlines of Textual Criticism applied to the New Testament.* By C. E. Hammond, M.A. Fourth Edition. Extra fcap. 8vo. 3s. 6d.

HEBREW, etc.—*The Psalms in Hebrew without points.* 1879. Crown 8vo. 3s. 6d.

—— *A Commentary on the Book of Proverbs.* Attributed to Abraham Ibn Ezra. Edited from a MS. in the Bodleian Library by S. R. Driver, M.A. Crown 8vo. paper covers, 3s. 6d.

—— *The Book of Tobit.* A Chaldee Text, from a unique MS. in the Bodleian Library; with other Rabbinical Texts, English Translations, and the Itala. Edited by Ad. Neubauer, M.A. 1878. Crown 8vo. 6s.

—— *Horae Hebraicae et Talmudicae,* a J. Lightfoot. A new Edition, by R. Gandell, M.A. 4 vols. 1859. 8vo. 1l. 1s.

LATIN.—*Libri Psalmorum* Versio antiqua Latina, cum Paraphrasi Anglo-Saxonica. Edidit B. Thorpe, F.A.S. 1835. 8vo. 10s. 6d.

—— *Old-Latin Biblical Texts: No. I.* The Gospel according to St. Matthew from the St. Germain MS. (g_1). Edited with Introduction and Appendices by John Wordsworth, D.D. Small 4to., stiff covers, 6s.

—— *Old-Latin Biblical Texts: No. II.* Portions of the Gospels according to St. Mark and St. Matthew, from the Bobbio MS. (k), &c. Edited by John Wordsworth, D.D., W. Sanday, M.A., D.D., and H. J. White, M.A. Small 4to., stiff covers, 21s.

OLD-FRENCH.—*Libri Psalmorum* Versio antiqua Gallica e Cod. MS. in Bibl. Bodleiana adservato, una cum Versione Metrica aliisque Monumentis pervetustis. Nunc primum descripsit et edidit Franciscus Michel, Phil. Doc. 1860. 8vo. 10s. 6d.

FATHERS OF THE CHURCH, &c.

St. Athanasius: Historical Writings, according to the Benedictine Text. With an Introduction by William Bright, D.D. 1881. Crown 8vo. 10s. 6d.

—— *Orations against the Arians.* With an Account of his Life by William Bright, D.D. 1873. Crown 8vo. 9s.

St. Augustine: Select Anti-Pelagian Treatises, and the Acts of the Second Council of Orange. With an Introduction by William Bright, D.D. Crown 8vo. 9s.

Canons of the First Four General Councils of Nicaea, Constantinople, Ephesus, and Chalcedon. 1877. Crown 8vo. 2s. 6d.

—— *Notes on the Canons of the First Four General Councils.* By William Bright, D.D. 1882. Crown 8vo. 5s. 6d.

Cyrilli Archiepiscopi Alexandrini in XII Prophetas. Edidit P. E. Pusey, A.M. Tomi II. 1868. 8vo. cloth, 2l. 2s.

—— *in D. Joannis Evangelium.* Accedunt Fragmenta varia necnon Tractatus ad Tiberium Diaconum duo. Edidit post Aubertum P. E. Pusey, A.M. Tomi III. 1872. 8vo. 2l. 5s.

—— *Commentarii in Lucae Evangelium* quae supersunt Syriace. E MSS. apud Mus. Britan. edidit R. Payne Smith, A.M. 1858. 4to. 1l. 2s.

—— Translated by R. Payne Smith, M.A. 2 vols. 1859. 8vo. 14s.

Ephraemi Syri, Rabulae Episcopi Edesseni, Balaei, aliorumque Opera Selecta. E Codd. Syriacis MSS. in Museo Britannico et Bibliotheca Bodleiana asservatis primus edidit J. J. Overbeck. 1865. 8vo. 1l. 1s.

Eusebius' Ecclesiastical History, according to the text of Burton, with an Introduction by William Bright, D.D. 1881. Crown 8vo. 8s. 6d.

Irenaeus: The Third Book of St. Irenaeus, Bishop of Lyons, against Heresies. With short Notes and a Glossary by H. Deane, B.D. 1874. Crown 8vo. 5s. 6d.

Patrum Apostolicorum, S. Clementis Romani, S. Ignatii, S. Polycarpi, quae supersunt. Edidit Guil. Jacobson, S.T.P.R. Tomi II. Fourth Edition, 1863. 8vo. 1l. 1s.

Socrates' Ecclesiastical History, according to the Text of Hussey, with an Introduction by William Bright, D.D. 1878. Crown 8vo. 7s. 6d.

ECCLESIASTICAL HISTORY, BIOGRAPHY, &c.

Ancient Liturgy of the Church of England, according to the uses of Sarum, York, Hereford, and Bangor, and the Roman Liturgy arranged in parallel columns, with preface and notes. By William Maskell, M.A. Third Edition. 1882. 8vo. 15s.

Baedae Historia Ecclesiastica. Edited, with English Notes, by G. H. Moberly, M.A. 1881. Crown 8vo. 10s. 6d.

Bright (W.). Chapters of Early English Church History.
1878. 8vo. 12s.

Burnet's History of the Reformation of the Church of England.
A new Edition. Carefully revised, and the Records collated with the originals, by N. Pocock, M.A. . 7 vols. 1865. 8vo. *Price reduced to* 1l. 10s.

Councils and Ecclesiastical Documents relating to Great Britain and Ireland. Edited, after Spelman and Wilkins, by A. W. Haddan, B.D., and W. Stubbs, M.A. Vols. I. and III. 1869-71. Medium 8vo. each 1l. 1s.

> Vol. II. Part I. 1873. Medium 8vo. 10s. 6d.
>
> Vol. II. Part II. 1878. Church of Ireland; Memorials of St. Patrick. Stiff covers, 3s. 6d.

Hamilton (John, Archbishop of St. Andrews), The Catechism of. Edited, with Introduction and Glossary, by Thomas Graves Law. With a Preface by the Right Hon. W. E. Gladstone. 8vo. 12s. 6d.

Hammond (C. E.). Liturgies, Eastern and Western. Edited, with Introduction, Notes, and Liturgical Glossary. 1878. Crown 8vo. 10s. 6d.

> An Appendix to the above. 1879. Crown 8vo. paper covers, 1s. 6d.

John, Bishop of Ephesus. The Third Part of his Ecclesiastical History. [In Syriac.] Now first edited by William Cureton, M.A. 1853. 4to. 1l. 12s.

—— Translated by R. Payne Smith, M.A. 1860. 8vo. 10s.

Leofric Missal, The, as used in the Cathedral of Exeter during the Episcopate of its first Bishop, A.D. 1050-1072; together with some Account of the Red Book of Derby, the Missal of Robert of Jumièges, and a few other early MS. Service Books of the English Church. Edited, with Introduction and Notes, by F. E. Warren, B.D. 4to. half morocco, 35s.

Monumenta Ritualia Ecclesiae Anglicanae. The occasional Offices of the Church of England according to the old use of Salisbury, the Prymer in English, and other prayers and forms, with dissertations and notes. By William Maskell, M.A. Second Edition. 1882. 3 vols. 8vo. 2l. 10s.

Records of the Reformation. The Divorce, 1527-1533. Mostly now for the first time printed from MSS. in the British Museum and other libraries. Collected and arranged by N. Pocock, M.A. 1870. 2 vols. 8vo. 1l. 16s.

Shirley (W. W.). Some Account of the Church in the Apostolic Age. Second Edition, 1874. Fcap. 8vo. 3s. 6d.

Stubbs (W.). Registrum Sacrum Anglicanum. An attempt to exhibit the course of Episcopal Succession in England. 1858. Small 4to. 8s. 6d.

Warren (F. E.). Liturgy and Ritual of the Celtic Church. 1881. 8vo. 14s.

ENGLISH THEOLOGY.

Bampton Lectures, 1886. *The Christian Platonists of Alexandria.* By Charles Bigg, D.D. 8vo. 10s. 6d.

Butler's Works, with an Index to the Analogy. 2 vols. 1874. 8vo. 11s.

Also separately,

Sermons, 5s. 6d.   *Analogy of Religion*, 5s. 6d

Greswell's Harmonia Evangelica. Fifth Edition. 8vo. 1855. 9s. 6d.

Heurtley's Harmonia Symbolica: Creeds of the Western Church. 1858. 8vo. 6s. 6d.

Homilies appointed to be read in Churches. Edited by J. Griffiths, M.A. 1859. 8vo. 7s. 6d.

Hooker's Works, with his life by Walton, arranged by John Keble, M.A. Sixth Edition, 1874. 3 vols. 8vo. 1l. 11s. 6d.

—— the text as arranged by John Keble, M.A. 2 vols. 1875. 8vo. 11s.

Jewel's Works. Edited by R. W. Jelf, D.D. 8 vols. 1848. 8vo. 1l. 10s.

Pearson's Exposition of the Creed. Revised and corrected by E. Burton, D.D. Sixth Edition, 1877. 8vo. 10s. 6d.

Waterland's Review of the Doctrine of the Eucharist, with a Preface by the late Bishop of London. Crown 8vo. 6s. 6d.

—— *Works*, with Life, by Bp. Van Mildert. A new Edition, with copious Indexes. 6 vols. 1856. 8vo. 2l. 11s.

Wheatly's Illustration of the Book of Common Prayer. A new Edition, 1846. 8vo. 5s.

Wyclif. A Catalogue of the Original Works of John Wyclif, by W. W. Shirley, D.D. 1865. 8vo. 3s. 6d.

—— *Select English Works.* By T. Arnold, M.A. 3 vols. 1869-1871. 8vo. 1l. 1s.

—— *Trialogus.* With the Supplement now first edited. By Gotthard Lechler. 1869. 8vo. 7s.

HISTORICAL AND DOCUMENTARY WORKS.

British Barrows, a Record of the Examination of Sepulchral
Mounds in various parts of England. By William Greenwell, M.A., F.S.A.
Together with Description of Figures of Skulls, General Remarks on Prehistoric Crania, and an Appendix by George Rolleston, M.D., F.R.S. 1877.
Medium 8vo. 25*s*.

Britton. A Treatise upon the Common Law of England,
composed by order of King Edward I. The French Text carefully revised,
with an English Translation, Introduction, and Notes, by F. M. Nichols, M.A.
2 vols. 1865. Royal 8vo. 1*l*. 16*s*.

Clarendon's History of the Rebellion and Civil Wars in
England. 7 vols. 1839. 18mo. 1*l*. 1*s*.

Clarendon's History of the Rebellion and Civil Wars in
England. Also his Life, written by himself, in which is included a Continuation of his History of the Grand Rebellion. With copious Indexes.
In one volume, royal 8vo. 1842. 1*l*. 2*s*.

Clinton's Epitome of the Fasti Hellenici. 1851. 8vo. 6*s*. 6*d*.

—— *Epitome of the Fasti Romani.* 1854. 8vo. 7*s*.

Corpvs Poeticvm Boreale. The Poetry of the Old Northern
Tongue, from the Earliest Times to the Thirteenth Century. Edited, classified, and translated, with Introduction, Excursus, and Notes, by Gudbrand
Vigfússon, M.A., and F. York Powell, M.A. 2 vols. 1883. 8vo. 42*s*.

Freeman (E. A.). History of the Norman Conquest of England; its Causes and Results. In Six Volumes. 8vo. 5*l*. 9*s*. 6*d*.

—— *The Reign of William Rufus and the Accession of*
Henry the First. 2 vols. 8vo. 1*l*. 16*s*.

Gascoigne's Theological Dictionary ("Liber Veritatum"):
Selected Passages, illustrating the condition of Church and State, 1403-1458.
With an Introduction by James E. Thorold Rogers, M.A. Small 4to.
10*s*. 6*d*.

Magna Carta, a careful Reprint. Edited by W. Stubbs, D.D.
1879. 4to. stitched, 1*s*.

Passio et Miracula Beati Olaui. Edited from a Twelfth-
Century MS. in the Library of Corpus Christi College, Oxford, with an
Introduction and Notes, by Frederick Metcalfe, M.A. Small 4to. stiff
covers, 6*s*.

Protests of the Lords, including those which have been expunged, from 1624 to 1874; with Historical Introductions. Edited by James E. Thorold Rogers, M.A. 1875. 3 vols. 8vo. 2*l.* 2*s.*

Rogers (J. E. T.). History of Agriculture and Prices in England, A.D. 1259–1793.

    Vols. I and II (1259–1400). 1866. 8vo. 2*l.* 2*s.*

    Vols. III and IV (1401–1582). 1882. 8vo. 2*l.* 10*s.*

Saxon Chronicles (Two of the) parallel, with Supplementary Extracts from the Others. Edited, with Introduction, Notes, and a Glossarial Index, by J. Earle, M.A. 1865. 8vo. 16*s.*

Stubbs (W., D.D.). Seventeen Lectures on the Study of Medieval and Modern History, &c., delivered at Oxford 1867–1884. Demy 8vo. half-bound, 10*s.* 6*d.*

Sturlunga Saga, including the Islendinga Saga of Lawman Sturla Thordsson and other works. Edited by Dr. Gudbrand Vigfússon. In 2 vols. 1878. 8vo. 2*l.* 2*s.*

York Plays. The Plays performed by the Crafts or Mysteries of York on the day of Corpus Christi in the 14th, 15th, and 16th centuries. Now first printed from the unique MS. in the Library of Lord Ashburnham. Edited with Introduction and Glossary by Lucy Toulmin Smith. 8vo. 21*s.*

Statutes made for the University of Oxford, and for the Colleges and Halls therein, by the University of Oxford Commissioners. 1882. 8vo. 12*s.* 6*d.*

Statuta Universitatis Oxoniensis. 1886. 8vo. 5*s.*

The Examination Statutes for the Degrees of B.A., B. Mus., B.C.L., and B.M. Revised to Hilary Term, 1887. 8vo. sewed, 1*s.*

The Student's Handbook to the University and Colleges of Oxford. Extra fcap. 8vo. 2*s.* 6*d.*

The Oxford University Calendar for the year 1887. Crown 8vo. 4*s.* 6*d.*

    The present Edition includes all Class Lists and other University distinctions for the seven years ending with 1886.

    Also, supplementary to the above, price 5s. (pp. 606),

The Honours Register of the University of Oxford. A complete Record of University Honours, Officers, Distinctions, and Class Lists; of the Heads of Colleges, &c., &c., from the Thirteenth Century to 1883.

MATHEMATICS, PHYSICAL SCIENCE, &c.

Acland (H. W., M.D., F.R.S.). Synopsis of the Pathological Series in the Oxford Museum. 1867. 8vo. 2s. 6d.

De Bary (Dr. A.). Comparative Anatomy of the Vegetative Organs of the Phanerogams and Ferns. Translated and Annotated by F. O. Bower, M.A., F.L.S., and D. H. Scott, M.A., Ph.D., F.L.S. With 241 woodcuts and an Index. Royal 8vo., half morocco, 1l. 2s. 6d.

Goebel (Dr. K.). Outlines of Classification and Special Morphology of Plants. A New Edition of Sachs' Text Book of Botany, Book II. English Translation by H. E. F. Garnsey, M.A. Revised by I. Bayley Balfour, M.A., M.D., F.R.S. With 407 Woodcuts. Royal 8vo. half Morocco, 21s.

Lectures on the Physiology of Plants. By Julius Sachs. Translated by H. Marshall Ward, M.A. With 445 Woodcuts. Royal 8vo. *Just ready.*

Müller (J.). On certain Variations in the Vocal Organs of the Passeres that have hitherto escaped notice. Translated by F. J. Bell, B.A., and edited, with an Appendix, by A. H. Garrod, M.A., F.R.S. With Plates. 1878. 4to. paper covers, 7s. 6d.

Price (Bartholomew, M.A., F.R.S.). Treatise on Infinitesimal Calculus.

Vol. I. Differential Calculus. Second Edition. 8vo. 14s. 6d.

Vol. II. Integral Calculus, Calculus of Variations, and Differential Equations. Second Edition, 1865. 8vo. 18s.

Vol. III. Statics, including Attractions; Dynamics of a Material Particle. Second Edition, 1868. 8vo. 16s.

Vol. IV. Dynamics of Material Systems; together with a chapter on Theoretical Dynamics, by W. F. Donkin, M.A., F.R.S. 1862. 8vo. 16s.

Pritchard (C., D.D., F.R.S.). Uranometria Nova Oxoniensis. A Photometric determination of the magnitudes of all Stars visible to the naked eye, from the Pole to ten degrees south of the Equator. 1885. Royal 8vo. 8s. 6d.

—— *Astronomical Observations* made at the University Observatory, Oxford, under the direction of C. Pritchard, D.D. No. 1. 1878. Royal 8vo. paper covers, 3s. 6d.

Rigaud's Correspondence of Scientific Men of the 17th Century, with Table of Contents by A. de Morgan, and Index by the Rev. J. Rigaud, M.A. 2 vols. 1841–1862. 8vo. 18s. 6d.

Rolleston (George, M.D., F.R.S.). Scientific Papers and Addresses. Arranged and Edited by William Turner, M.B., F.R.S. With a Biographical Sketch by Edward Tylor, F.R.S. With Portrait, Plates, and Woodcuts. 2 vols. 8vo. 1l. 4s.

Westwood (J. O., M.A., F.R.S.). Thesaurus Entomologicus Hopeianus, or a Description of the rarest Insects in the Collection given to the University by the Rev. William Hope. With 40 Plates. 1874. Small folio, half morocco, 7l. 10s.

The Sacred Books of the East.

TRANSLATED BY VARIOUS ORIENTAL SCHOLARS, AND EDITED BY
F. MAX MÜLLER.

[Demy 8vo. cloth.]

Vol. I. The Upanishads. Translated by F. Max Müller. Part I. The *Kh*ândogya-upanishad, The Talavakâra-upanishad, The Aitareya-âra*n*yaka, The Kaushîtaki-brâhma*n*a-upanishad, and The Vâ*g*asaneyi-sa*m*hitâ-upanishad. 10s. 6d.

Vol. II. The Sacred Laws of the Âryas, as taught in the Schools of Âpastamba, Gautama, Vâsish*th*a, and Baudhâyana. Translated by Prof. Georg Bühler. Part I. Âpastamba and Gautama. 10s. 6d.

Vol. III. The Sacred Books of China. The Texts of Confucianism. Translated by James Legge. Part I. The Shû King, The Religious portions of the Shih King, and The Hsiâo King. 12s. 6d.

Vol. IV. The Zend-Avesta. Translated by James Darmesteter. Part I. The Vendîdâd. 10s. 6d.

Vol. V. The Pahlavi Texts. Translated by E. W. West. Part I. The Bundahi*s*, Bahman Ya*s*t, and Shâyast lâ-shâyast. 12s. 6d.

Vols. VI and IX. The Qur'ân. Parts I and II. Translated by E. H. Palmer. 21s.

Vol. VII. The Institutes of Vish*n*u. Translated by Julius Jolly. 10s. 6d.

Vol. VIII. The Bhagavadgîtâ, with The Sanatsu*g*âtîya, and The Anugîtâ. Translated by Kâshinâth Trimbak Telang. 10s. 6d.

Vol. X. The Dhammapada, translated from Pâli by F. Max Müller; and The Sutta-Nipâta, translated from Pâli by V. Fausböll; being Canonical Books of the Buddhists. 10s. 6d.

Vol. XI. Buddhist Suttas. Translated from Pâli by T. W. Rhys Davids. 1. The Mahâparinibbâna Suttanta; 2. The Dhamma-*k*akkappavattana Sutta; 3. The Tevi*gg*a Suttanta; 4. The Akankheyya Sutta; 5. The *K*etokhila Sutta; 6. The Mahâ-sudassana Suttanta; 7. The Sabbâsava Sutta. 10s. 6d.

Vol. XII. The Satapatha-Brâhma*n*a, according to the Text of the Mâdhyandina School. Translated by Julius Eggeling. Part I. Books I and II. 12s. 6d.

Vol. XIII. Vinaya Texts. Translated from the Pâli by T. W. Rhys Davids and Hermann Oldenberg. Part I. The Pâtimokkha. The Mahâvagga, I–IV. 10s. 6d.

Vol. XIV. The Sacred Laws of the Âryas, as taught in the Schools of Apastamba, Gautama, Vâsish*th*a and Baudhâyana. Translated by Georg Bühler. Part II. Vâsish*th*a and Baudhâyana. 10s. 6d.

Vol. XV. The Upanishads. Translated by F. Max Müller. Part II. The Ka*th*a-upanishad, The Mu*nd*aka-upanishad, The Taittirîyaka-upanishad, The B*ri*hadâra*ny*aka-upanishad, The *S*veta*s*vatara-upanishad, The Pra*sn*a-upanishad, and The Maitrâya*n*a-Brâhma*n*a-upanishad. 10s. 6d.

Vol. XVI. The Sacred Books of China. The Texts of Confucianism. Translated by James Legge. Part II. The Yî King. 10s. 6d.

Vol. XVII. Vinaya Texts. Translated from the Pâli by T. W. Rhys Davids and Hermann Oldenberg. Part II. The Mahâvagga, V–X. The *K*ullavagga, I–III. 10s. 6d.

Vol. XVIII. Pahlavi Texts. Translated by E. W. West. Part II. The Dâ*d*istân-î Dînîk and The Epistles of Mânû*sk*îhar. 12s. 6d.

Vol. XIX. The Fo-sho-hing-tsan-king. A Life of Buddha by A*s*vaghosha Bodhisattva, translated from Sanskrit into Chinese by Dharmaraksha, A.D. 420, and from Chinese into English by Samuel Beal. 10s. 6d.

Vol. XX. Vinaya Texts. Translated from the Pâli by T. W. Rhys Davids and Hermann Oldenberg. Part III. The *K*ullavagga, IV–XII. 10s. 6d.

Vol. XXI. The Saddharma-pu*nd*arîka; or, the Lotus of the True Law. Translated by H. Kern. 12s. 6d.

Vol. XXII. *G*aina-Sûtras. Translated from Prâkrit by Hermann Jacobi. Part I. The Â*k*ârâṅga-Sûtra. The Kalpa-Sûtra. 10s. 6d.

Vol. XXIII. The Zend-Avesta. Translated by James Darmesteter. Part II. The Sîrôzahs, Ya*s*ts, and Nyâyi*s*. 10s. 6d.

Vol. XXIV. Pahlavi Texts. Translated by E. W. West. Part III. Dînâ-î Maînôg-î Khirad, *S*îkand-gûmânîk, and Sad-Dar. 10s. 6d.

Second Series.

Vol. XXV. Manu. Translated by Georg Bühler. 21s.

Vol. XXVI. The Satapatha-Brâhmana. Translated by Julius Eggeling. Part II. 12s. 6d.

Vols. XXVII and XXVIII. The Sacred Books of China.
The Texts of Confucianism. Translated by James Legge. Parts III and IV. The Lî Kî, or Collection of Treatises on the Rules of Propriety, or Ceremonial Usages. 25s.

Vols. XXIX and XXX. The Grihya-Sûtras, Rules of Vedic Domestic Ceremonies. Translated by Hermann Oldenberg.

Part I (Vol. XXIX), 12s. 6d. *Just Published.*
Part II (Vol. XXX). *In the Press.*

The following Volumes are in the Press:—

Vol. XXXI. The Zend-Avesta. Part III. The Yasna, Visparad, Âfrînagân, and Gâhs. Translated by the Rev. L. H. Mills. *Just ready.*

Vol. XXXII. Vedic Hymns. Translated by F. Max Müller. Part I.

Vol. XXXIII. Nârada, and some Minor Law-books. Translated by Julius Jolly. [*Preparing.*]

Vol. XXXIV. The Vedânta-Sûtras, with Sankara's Commentary. Translated by G. Thibaut. [*Preparing.*]

*** *The Second Series will consist of Twenty-Four Volumes.*

Clarendon Press Series

I. ENGLISH, &c.

A First Reading Book. By Marie Eichens of Berlin; and edited by Anne J. Clough. Extra fcap. 8vo. stiff covers, 4*d*.

Oxford Reading Book, Part I. For Little Children. Extra fcap. 8vo. stiff covers, 6*d*.

Oxford Reading Book, Part II. For Junior Classes. Extra fcap. 8vo. stiff covers, 6*d*.

An Elementary English Grammar and Exercise Book. By O. W. Tancock, M.A. Second Edition. Extra fcap. 8vo. 1*s*. 6*d*.

An English Grammar and Reading Book, for Lower Forms in Classical Schools. By O. W. Tancock, M.A. Fourth Edition. Extra fcap. 8vo. 3*s*. 6*d*.

Typical Selections from the best English Writers, with Introductory Notices. Second Edition. In 2 vols. Extra fcap. 8vo. 3*s*. 6*d*. each.
Vol. I. Latimer to Berkeley.   Vol. II. Pope to Macaulay.

Shairp (J. C., LL.D.). Aspects of Poetry; being Lectures delivered at Oxford. Crown 8vo. 10*s*. 6*d*.

A Book for the Beginner in Anglo-Saxon. By John Earle, M.A. Third Edition. Extra fcap. 8vo. 2*s*. 6*d*.

An Anglo-Saxon Reader. In Prose and Verse. With Grammatical Introduction, Notes, and Glossary. By Henry Sweet, M.A. Fourth Edition, Revised and Enlarged. Extra fcap. 8vo. 8*s*. 6*d*.

A Second Anglo-Saxon Reader. By the same Author. Extra fcap. 8vo. *Nearly ready.*

An Anglo-Saxon Primer, with Grammar, Notes, and Glossary. By the same Author. Second Edition. Extra fcap. 8vo. 2*s*. 6*d*.

Old English Reading Primers; edited by Henry Sweet, M.A.
 I. Selected Homilies of Ælfric. Extra fcap. 8vo., stiff covers, 1*s*. 6*d*.
 II. Extracts from Alfred's Orosius. Extra fcap. 8vo., stiff covers, 1*s*. 6*d*.

First Middle English Primer, with Grammar and Glossary. By the same Author. Extra fcap. 8vo. 2*s*.

Second Middle English Primer. Extracts from Chaucer, with Grammar and Glossary. By the same Author. Extra fcap. 8vo. 2*s*.

Principles of English Etymology. First Series. By W. W. Skeat, Litt.D. Crown 8vo. *Nearly ready.*

The Philology of the English Tongue. By J. Earle, M.A.
Third Edition. Extra fcap. 8vo. 7s. 6d.

An Icelandic Primer, with Grammar, Notes, and Glossary.
By the same Author. Extra fcap. 8vo. 3s. 6d.

An Icelandic Prose Reader, with Notes, Grammar, and Glossary.
By G. Vigfússon, M.A., and F. York Powell, M.A. Ext. fcap. 8vo. 10s. 6d.

A Handbook of Phonetics, including a Popular Exposition of
the Principles of Spelling Reform. By H. Sweet, M.A. Extra fcap. 8vo. 4s. 6d.

Elementarbuch des Gesprochenen Englisch. Grammatik,
Texte und Glossar. Von Henry Sweet. Extra fcap. 8vo., stiff covers, 2s. 6d.

The Ormulum; with the Notes and Glossary of Dr. R. M.
White. Edited by R. Holt, M.A. 1878. 2 vols. Extra fcap. 8vo. 21s.

Specimens of Early English. A New and Revised Edition.
With Introduction, Notes, and Glossarial Index. By R. Morris, LL.D., and W. W. Skeat, M.A.
> Part I. From Old English Homilies to King Horn (A.D. 1150 to A.D. 1300).
> Second Edition. Extra fcap. 8vo. 9s.
> Part II. From Robert of Gloucester to Gower (A.D. 1298 to A.D. 1393).
> Second Edition. Extra fcap. 8vo. 7s. 6d.

Specimens of English Literature, from the 'Ploughmans
Crede' to the 'Shepheardes Calender' (A.D. 1394 to A.D. 1579). With Introduction, Notes, and Glossarial Index. By W. W. Skeat, M.A. Extra fcap. 8vo. 7s. 6d.

The Vision of William concerning Piers the Plowman, in three
Parallel Texts; together with *Richard the Redeless*. By William Langland (about 1362–1399 A.D.). Edited from numerous Manuscripts, with Preface, Notes, and a Glossary, by W. W. Skeat, Litt.D. 2 vols. 8vo. 31s. 6d.

The Vision of William concerning Piers the Plowman, by
William Langland. Edited, with Notes, by W. W. Skeat, M.A. Third Edition. Extra fcap. 8vo. 4s. 6d.

Chaucer. I. *The Prologue to the Canterbury Tales;* the
Knightes Tale; The Nonne Prestes Tale. Edited by R. Morris, Editor of Specimens of Early English, &c., &c. Extra fcap. 8vo. 2s. 6d.

—— II. *The Prioresses Tale; Sir Thopas;* The Monkes
Tale; The Clerkes Tale; The Squieres Tale, &c. Edited by W. W. Skeat, M.A. Second Edition. Extra fcap. 8vo. 4s. 6d.

—— III. *The Tale of the Man of Lawe;* The Pardoneres
Tale; The Second Nonnes Tale; The Chanouns Yemannes Tale. By the same Editor. Second Edition. Extra fcap. 8vo. 4s. 6d.

Gamelyn, The Tale of. Edited with Notes, Glossary, &c., by
W. W. Skeat, M.A. Extra fcap. 8vo. Stiff covers, 1s. 6d.

Minot (Laurence). Poems. Edited, with Introduction and
Notes, by Joseph Hall, M.A. Extra fcap. 8vo. *Nearly ready.*

Spenser's Faery Queene. Books I and II. Designed chiefly for the use of Schools. With Introduction, Notes, and Glossary. By G. W. Kitchin, D.D. Extra fcap. 8vo. 2s. 6d. each.

Hooker. Ecclesiastical Polity, Book I. Edited by R. W. Church, M.A. Second Edition. Extra fcap. 8vo. 2s.

OLD ENGLISH DRAMA.

The Pilgrimage to Parnassus with *The Two Parts of the Return from Parnassus.* Three Comedies performed in St. John's College, Cambridge, A.D. MDXCVII–MDCI. Edited from MSS. by the Rev. W. D. Macray, M.A., F.S.A. Medium 8vo. Bevelled Boards, Gilt top, 8s. 6d.

Marlowe and Greene. Marlowe's Tragical History of Dr. Faustus, and *Greene's Honourable History of Friar Bacon and Friar Bungay.* Edited by A. W. Ward, M.A. *New and Enlarged Edition.* Extra fcap. 8vo. 6s.

Marlowe. Edward II. With Introduction, Notes, &c. By O. W. Tancock, M.A. Extra fcap. 8vo. 3s.

SHAKESPEARE.

Shakespeare. Select Plays. Edited by W. G. Clark, M.A., and W. Aldis Wright, M.A. Extra fcap. 8vo. stiff covers.

- The Merchant of Venice. 1s.
- Richard the Second. 1s. 6d.
- Macbeth. 1s. 6d.
- Hamlet. 2s.

Edited by W. Aldis Wright, M.A.

- The Tempest. 1s. 6d.
- As You Like It. 1s. 6d.
- Julius Cæsar. 2s.
- Richard the Third. 2s. 6d.
- King Lear. 1s. 6d.
- Midsummer Night's Dream. 1s. 6d.
- Coriolanus. 2s. 6d.
- Henry the Fifth. 2s.
- Twelfth Night. 1s. 6d.
- King John. 1s. 6d.

Shakespeare as a Dramatic Artist; a popular Illustration of the Principles of Scientific Criticism. By R. G. Moulton, M.A. Crown 8vo. 5s.

Bacon. I. *Advancement of Learning.* Edited by W. Aldis Wright, M.A. Second Edition. Extra fcap. 8vo. 4s. 6d.

—— II. *The Essays.* With Introduction and Notes. By S. H. Reynolds, M.A., late Fellow of Brasenose College. *In Preparation.*

Milton. I. *Areopagitica.* With Introduction and Notes. By John W. Hales, M.A. Third Edition. Extra fcap. 8vo. 3s.

—— II. *Poems.* Edited by R. C. Browne, M.A. 2 vols. Fifth Edition. Extra fcap. 8vo. 6s. 6d. Sold separately, Vol. I. 4s.; Vol. II. 3s.

In paper covers:—
Lycidas, 3d.   L'Allegro, 3d.   Il Penseroso, 4d.   Comus, 6d.
Samson Agonistes, 6d.

—— III. *Samson Agonistes.* Edited with Introduction and Notes by John Churton Collins. Extra fcap. 8vo. stiff covers, 1s.

Bunyan. I. *The Pilgrim's Progress, Grace Abounding, Relation of the Imprisonment of Mr. John Bunyan.* Edited, with Biographical Introduction and Notes, by E. Venables, M.A. 1879. Extra fcap. 8vo. 5s. In ornamental Parchment, 6s.

—— II. *Holy War, &c.* Edited by E. Venables, M.A. In the Press.

Clarendon. *History of the Rebellion.* Book VI. Edited by T. Arnold, M.A. Extra fcap. 8vo. 4s. 6d.

Dryden. *Select Poems.* Stanzas on the Death of Oliver Cromwell; Astræa Redux; Annus Mirabilis; Absalom and Achitophel; Religio Laici; The Hind and the Panther. Edited by W. D. Christie, M.A. Second Edition. Extra fcap. 8vo. 3s. 6d.

Locke's Conduct of the Understanding. Edited, with Introduction, Notes, &c., by T. Fowler, M.A. Second Edition. Extra fcap. 8vo. 2s.

Addison. *Selections from Papers in the Spectator.* With Notes. By T. Arnold, M.A. Extra fcap. 8vo. 4s. 6d. In ornamental Parchment, 6s.

Steele. *Selections from the Tatler, Spectator, and Guardian.* Edited by Austin Dobson. Extra fcap. 8vo. 4s. 6d. In white Parchment, 7s. 6d.

Pope. With Introduction and Notes. By Mark Pattison, B.D.

—— I. *Essay on Man.* Extra fcap. 8vo. 1s. 6d.

—— II. *Satires and Epistles.* Extra fcap. 8vo. 2s.

Parnell. *The Hermit.* Paper covers, 2d.

Gray. *Selected Poems.* Edited by Edmund Gosse. Extra fcap. 8vo. Stiff covers, 1s. 6d. In white Parchment, 3s.

—— *Elegy and Ode on Eton College.* Paper covers, 2d.

Goldsmith. *The Deserted Village.* Paper covers, 2d.

Johnson. I. *Rasselas; Lives of Dryden and Pope.* Edited by Alfred Milnes, M.A. (London). Extra fcap. 8vo. 4s. 6d., or *Lives of Dryden and Pope* only, stiff covers, 2s. 6d.

—— II. *Vanity of Human Wishes.* With Notes, by E. J. Payne, M.A. Paper covers, 4d.

Boswell's Life of Johnson. *With the Journal of a Tour to the Hebrides.* Edited, with copious Notes, Appendices, and Index, by G. Birkbeck Hill, D.C.L., Pembroke College. With Portraits and Facsimiles. 6 vols. Medium 8vo. *Nearly ready.*

Cowper. Edited, with Life, Introductions, and Notes, by H. T. Griffith, B.A.

—— I. *The Didactic Poems of* 1782, with Selections from the Minor Pieces, A.D. 1779–1783. Extra fcap. 8vo. 3s.

—— II. *The Task, with Tirocinium,* and Selections from the Minor Poems, A.D. 1784–1799. Second Edition. Extra fcap. 8vo. 3s.

Burke. *Select Works.* Edited, with Introduction and Notes, by E. J. Payne, M.A.

—— I. *Thoughts on the Present Discontents; the two Speeches on America.* Second Edition. Extra fcap. 8vo. 4s. 6d.

—— II. *Reflections on the French Revolution.* Second Edition. Extra fcap. 8vo. 5s.

—— III. *Four Letters on the Proposals for Peace with the* Regicide Directory of France. Second Edition. Extra fcap. 8vo. 5s.

Keats. *Hyperion*, Book I. With Notes by W. T. Arnold, B.A. Paper covers, 4d.

Byron. *Childe Harold.* Edited, with Introduction and Notes, by H. F. Tozer, M.A. Extra fcap. 8vo. 3s. 6d. In white Parchment, 5s.

Scott. *Lay of the Last Minstrel.* Edited with Preface and Notes by W. Minto, M.A. With Map. Extra fcap. 8vo. Stiff covers, 2s. Ornamental Parchment, 3s. 6d.

—— *Lay of the Last Minstrel.* Introduction and Canto I., with Preface and Notes, by the same Editor. 6d.

II. LATIN.

Rudimenta Latina. Comprising Accidence, and Exercises of a very Elementary Character, for the use of Beginners. By John Barrow Allen, M.A. Extra fcap. 8vo. 2s.

An Elementary Latin Grammar. By the same Author. Forty-second Thousand. Extra fcap. 8vo. 2s. 6d.

A First Latin Exercise Book. By the same Author. Fourth Edition. Extra fcap. 8vo. 2s. 6d.

A Second Latin Exercise Book. By the same Author. Extra fcap. 8vo. 3s. 6d.

Reddenda Minora, or Easy Passages, Latin and Greek, for Unseen Translation. For the use of Lower Forms. Composed and selected by C. S. Jerram, M.A. Extra fcap. 8vo. 1s. 6d.

Anglice Reddenda, or Easy Extracts, Latin and Greek, for Unseen Translation. By C. S. Jerram, M.A. Third Edition, Revised and Enlarged. Extra fcap. 8vo. 2s. 6d.

Anglice Reddenda. Second Series. By the same Author. Extra fcap. 8vo. 3s. *Just Published.*

Passages for Translation into Latin. For the use of Passmen and others. Selected by J. Y. Sargent, M.A. Fifth Edition. Extra fcap. 8vo. 2s. 6d.

Exercises in Latin Prose Composition; with Introduction, Notes and Passages of Graduated Difficulty for Translation into Latin. By G. G. Ramsay, M.A., LL.D. Second Edition. Extra fcap. 8vo. 4s. 6d.

Hints and Helps for Latin Elegiacs. By H. Lee-Warner, M.A. Extra fcap. 8vo. 3s. 6d.

First Latin Reader. By T. J. Nunns, M.A. Third Edition. Extra fcap. 8vo. 2s.

Caesar. The Commentaries (for Schools). With Notes and Maps. By Charles E. Moberly, M.A.
    Part I. *The Gallic War.* Second Edition. Extra fcap. 8vo. 4s. 6d.
    Part II. *The Civil War.* Extra fcap. 8vo. 3s. 6d.
    The Civil War. Book I. Second Edition. Extra fcap. 8vo. 2s.

Cicero. Speeches against Catilina. By E. A. Upcott, M.A., Assistant Master in Wellington College. *In the Press.*

Cicero. Selection of interesting and descriptive passages. With Notes. By Henry Walford, M.A. In three Parts. Extra fcap. 8vo. 4s. 6d.
    Each Part separately, limp, 1s. 6d.
    Part I. Anecdotes from Grecian and Roman History. Third Edition.
    Part II. Omens and Dreams: Beauties of Nature. Third Edition.
    Part III. Rome's Rule of her Provinces. Third Edition.

Cicero. De Senectute. Edited, with Introduction and Notes, by L. Huxley, M.A. Extra fcap. 8vo. 2s.
    Or separately, Text and Introduction, 1s. Notes 1s.

Cicero. Selected Letters (for Schools). With Notes. By the late C. E. Prichard, M.A., and E. R. Bernard, M.A. Second Edition. Extra fcap. 8vo. 3s.

Cicero. Select Orations (for Schools). In Verrem I. De Imperio Gn. Pompeii. Pro Archia. Philippica IX. With Introduction and Notes by J. R. King, M.A. Second Edition. Extra fcap. 8vo. 2s. 6d.

Cornelius Nepos. With Notes. By Oscar Browning, M.A. Second Edition. Extra fcap. 8vo. 2s. 6d.

Horace. Selected Odes. With Notes for the use of a Fifth Form. By E. C. Wickham, M.A. In two Parts. Extra fcap. 8vo. *cloth*, 2s.
    Or separately, Part I. Text, 1s. Part II. Notes, 1s.

Livy. Selections (for Schools). With Notes and Maps. By H. Lee-Warner, M.A. Extra fcap. 8vo. In Parts, limp, each 1s. 6d.
    Part I. The Caudine Disaster. Part II. Hannibal's Campaign in Italy. Part III. The Macedonian War.

Livy. Books V–VII. With Introduction and Notes. By A. R. Cluer, B.A. Second Edition. Revised by P. E. Matheson, M.A. Extra fcap. 8vo. (In one or two vols.) 5s.

Livy. Books XXI, XXII, and XXIII. With Introduction and Notes. By M. T. Tatham, M.A. Extra fcap. 8vo. 4s. 6d.

Ovid. Selections for the use of Schools. With Introductions and Notes, and an Appendix on the Roman Calendar. By W. Ramsay, M.A. Edited by G. G. Ramsay, M.A. Third Edition. Extra fcap. 8vo. 5s. 6d.

Ovid. Tristia. Book I. The Text revised, with an Introduction and Notes. By S. G. Owen, B.A. Extra fcap. 8vo. 3s. 6d.

Plautus. Captivi. Edited by W. M. Lindsay, M.A. Extra fcap. 8vo. *In the Press.*

Plautus. The Trinummus. With Notes and Introductions. Intended for the Higher Forms of Public Schools. By C. E. Freeman, M.A., and A. Sloman, M.A. Extra fcap. 8vo. 3s.

Pliny. Selected Letters (for Schools). With Notes. By the late C. E. Prichard, M.A., and E. R. Bernard, M.A. Extra fcap. 8vo. 3s.

Sallust. With Introduction and Notes. By W. W. Capes, M.A. Extra fcap. 8vo. 4s. 6d.

Tacitus. The Annals. Books I–IV. Edited, with Introduction and Notes for the use of Schools and Junior Students, by H. Furneaux, M.A. Extra fcap. 8vo. 5s.

Terence. Andria. With Notes and Introductions. By C. E. Freeman, M.A., and A. Sloman, M.A. Extra fcap. 8vo. 3s.

—— ***Adelphi.*** With Notes and Introductions. Intended for the Higher Forms of Public Schools. By A. Sloman, M.A. Extra fcap. 8vo. 3s.

Tibullus and Propertius. Selections. Edited by G. G. Ramsay, M.A. Extra fcap. 8vo. (In one or two vols.) 6s. *Just Published.*

Virgil. With Introduction and Notes. By T. L. Papillon, M.A. Two vols. Crown 8vo. 10s. 6d. The Text separately, 4s. 6d.

Virgil. The Eclogues. Edited by C. S. Jerram, M.A. In two Parts. Crown 8vo. *Nearly ready.*

Catulli Veronensis Liber. Iterum recognovit, apparatum criticum prolegomena appendices addidit, Robinson Ellis, A.M. 1878. Demy 8vo. 16s.

—— ***A Commentary on Catullus.*** By Robinson Ellis, M.A. 1876. Demy 8vo. 16s.

Catulli Veronensis Carmina Selecta, secundum recognitionem Robinson Ellis, A.M. Extra fcap. 8vo. 3s. 6d.

Cicero de Oratore. With Introduction and Notes. By A. S. Wilkins, M.A.
    Book I. 1879. 8vo. 6s.   Book II. 1881. 8vo. 5s.

—— ***Philippic Orations.*** With Notes. By J. R. King, M.A. Second Edition. 1879. 8vo. 10s. 6d.

Cicero. Select Letters. With English Introductions, Notes, and Appendices. By Albert Watson, M.A. Third Edition. Demy 8vo. 18s.

—— *Select Letters.* Text. By the same Editor. Second Edition. Extra fcap. 8vo. 4s.

—— *pro Cluentio.* With Introduction and Notes. By W. Ramsay, M.A. Edited by G. G. Ramsay, M.A. 2nd Ed. Ext. fcap. 8vo. 3s. 6d.

Horace. With a Commentary. Volume I. The Odes, Carmen Seculare, and Epodes. By Edward C. Wickham, M.A. Second Edition. 1877. Demy 8vo. 12s.

—— A reprint of the above, in a size suitable for the use of Schools. Extra fcap. 8vo. 6s. (May also be had in two parts.)

Livy, Book I. With Introduction, Historical Examination, and Notes. By J. R. Seeley, M.A. Second Edition. 1881. 8vo. 6s.

Ovid. P. Ovidii Nasonis Ibis. Ex Novis Codicibus edidit, Scholia Vetera Commentarium cum Prolegomenis Appendice Indice addidit, R. Ellis, A.M. 8vo. 10s. 6d.

Persius. The Satires. With a Translation and Commentary. By John Conington, M.A. Edited by Henry Nettleship, M.A. Second Edition. 1874. 8vo. 7s. 6d.

Juvenal. XIII Satires. Edited, with Introduction and Notes, by C. H. Pearson, M.A., and Herbert A. Strong, M.A., LL.D., Professor of Latin in Liverpool University College, Victoria University. In two Parts. Crown 8vo. Complete, 6s. *Just Published.*

Also separately, Part I. Introduction, Text, etc., 3s. Part II. Notes, 3s. 6d.

Tacitus. The Annals. Books I–VI. Edited, with Introduction and Notes, by H. Furneaux, M.A. 8vo. 18s.

Nettleship (H., M.A.). Lectures and Essays on Subjects connected with Latin Scholarship and Literature. Crown 8vo. 7s. 6d.

—— *The Roman Satura:* its original form in connection with its literary development. 8vo. sewed, 1s.

—— *Ancient Lives of Vergil.* With an Essay on the Poems of Vergil, in connection with his Life and Times. 8vo. sewed, 2s.

Papillon (T. L., M.A.). A Manual of Comparative Philology. Third Edition, Revised and Corrected. 1882. Crown 8vo. 6s.

Pinder (North, M.A.). Selections from the less known Latin Poets. 1869. 8vo. 15s.

Sellar (W. Y., M.A.). Roman Poets of the Augustan Age. VIRGIL. New Edition. 1883. Crown 8vo. 9s.

—— *Roman Poets of the Republic.* New Edition, Revised and Enlarged. 1881. 8vo. 14s.

Wordsworth (J., M.A.). Fragments and Specimens of Early Latin. With Introductions and Notes. 1874. 8vo. 18s.

III. GREEK.

A Greek Primer, for the use of beginners in that Language.
By the Right Rev. Charles Wordsworth, D.C.L. Seventh Edition. Extra fcap. 8vo. 1s. 6d.

Easy Greek Reader. By Evelyn Abbott, M.A. In two Parts. Extra fcap. 8vo. 3s.
 The Text and Notes may be had separately, 1s. 6d. each.

Graecae Grammaticae Rudimenta in usum Scholarum. Auctore Carolo Wordsworth, D.C.L. Nineteenth Edition, 1882. 12mo. 4s.

A Greek-English Lexicon, abridged from Liddell and Scott's 4to. edition, chiefly for the use of Schools. Twenty-first Edition. 1884. Square 12mo. 7s. 6d.

Greek Verbs, Irregular and Defective; their forms, meaning, and quantity; embracing all the Tenses used by Greek writers, with references to the passages in which they are found. By W. Veitch. Fourth Edition. Crown 8vo. 10s. 6d.

The Elements of Greek Accentuation (for Schools): abridged from his larger work by H. W. Chandler, M.A. Extra fcap. 8vo. 2s. 6d.

A SERIES OF GRADUATED GREEK READERS:—

First Greek Reader. By W. G. Rushbrooke, M.L. Second Edition. Extra fcap. 8vo. 2s. 6d.

Second Greek Reader. By A. M. Bell, M.A. Extra fcap. 8vo. 3s. 6d.

Fourth Greek Reader; being Specimens of Greek Dialects. With Introductions, etc. By W. W. Merry, M.A. Extra fcap. 8vo. 4s. 6d.

Fifth Greek Reader. Selections from Greek Epic and Dramatic Poetry, with Introductions and Notes. By Evelyn Abbott, M.A. Extra fcap. 8vo. 4s. 6d.

The Golden Treasury of Ancient Greek Poetry: being a Collection of the finest passages in the Greek Classic Poets, with Introductory Notices and Notes. By R. S. Wright, M.A. Extra fcap. 8vo. 8s. 6d.

A Golden Treasury of Greek Prose, being a Collection of the finest passages in the principal Greek Prose Writers, with Introductory Notices and Notes. By R. S. Wright, M.A., and J. E. L. Shadwell, M.A. Extra fcap. 8vo. 4s. 6d.

Aeschylus. Prometheus Bound (for Schools). With Introduction and Notes, by A. O. Prickard, M.A. Second Edition. Extra fcap. 8vo. 2s.

—— *Agamemnon.* With Introduction and Notes, by Arthur Sidgwick, M.A. Second Edition. Extra fcap. 8vo. 3s.

—— *Choephoroi.* With Introduction and Notes by the same Editor. Extra fcap. 8vo. 3s.

Aristophanes. In Single Plays. Edited, with English Notes, Introductions, &c., by W. W. Merry, M.A. Extra fcap. 8vo.
    I. The Clouds, Second Edition, 2*s.*
    II. The Acharnians, 2*s.*   III. The Frogs, 2*s.*

Cebes. Tabula. With Introduction and Notes. By C. S. Jerram, M.A. Extra fcap. 8vo. 2*s.* 6*d.*

Demosthenes. Olynthiacs and Philippics. Edited by Evelyn Abbott, M.A. Extra fcap. 8vo. In two Parts. *In the Press.*

Euripides. Alcestis (for Schools). By C. S. Jerram, M.A. Extra fcap. 8vo. 2*s.* 6*d.*

—— *Helena.* Edited, with Introduction, Notes, etc., for Upper and Middle Forms. By C. S. Jerram, M.A. Extra fcap. 8vo. 3*s.*

—— *Iphigenia in Tauris.* Edited, with Introduction, Notes, etc., for Upper and Middle Forms. By C. S. Jerram, M.A. Extra fcap. 8vo. cloth, 3*s.*

—— *Medea.* By C. B. Heberden, M.A. In two Parts. Extra fcap. 8vo. 2*s.*
    Or separately, Part I. Introduction and Text, 1*s.*
    Part II. Notes and Appendices, 1*s.*

Herodotus, Selections from. Edited, with Introduction, Notes, and a Map, by W. W. Merry, M.A. Extra fcap. 8vo. 2*s.* 6*d.*

Homer. Odyssey, Books I–XII (for Schools). By W. W. Merry, M.A. Twenty-seventh Thousand. Extra fcap. 8vo. 4*s.* 6*d.*
    Book II, separately, 1*s.* 6*d.*

—— *Odyssey,* Books XIII–XXIV (for Schools). By the same Editor. Second Edition. Extra fcap. 8vo. 5*s.*

—— *Iliad,* Book I (for Schools). By D. B. Monro, M.A. Second Edition. Extra fcap. 8vo. 2*s.*

—— *Iliad,* Books I–XII (for Schools). With an Introduction, a brief Homeric Grammar, and Notes. By D. B. Monro, M.A. Second Edition. Extra fcap. 8vo. 6*s.*

—— *Iliad,* Books VI and XXI. With Introduction and Notes. By Herbert Hailstone, M.A. Extra fcap. 8vo. 1*s.* 6*d.* each.

Lucian. Vera Historia (for Schools). By C. S. Jerram, M.A. Second Edition. Extra fcap. 8vo. 1*s.* 6*d.*

Plato. Selections from the Dialogues [including the whole of the *Apology* and *Crito*]. With Introduction and Notes by John Purves, M.A., and a Preface by the Rev. B. Jowett, M.A. Extra fcap. 8vo. 6*s.* 6*d.*

Sophocles. For the use of Schools. Edited with Introductions and English Notes. By Lewis Campbell, M.A., and Evelyn Abbott, M.A. *New and Revised Edition.* 2 Vols. Extra fcap. 8vo. 10s. 6d.

Sold separately, Vol. I, Text, 4s. 6d.; Vol. II, Explanatory Notes, 6s.

Sophocles. In Single Plays, with English Notes, &c. By Lewis Campbell, M.A., and Evelyn Abbott, M.A. Extra fcap. 8vo. limp.

Oedipus Tyrannus, Philoctetes. New and Revised Edition, 2s. each.
Oedipus Coloneus, Antigone, 1s. 9d. each.
Ajax, Electra, Trachiniae, 2s. each.

—— *Oedipus Rex:* Dindorf's Text, with Notes by the present Bishop of St. David's. Extra fcap. 8vo. limp, 1s. 6d.

Theocritus (for Schools). With Notes. By H. Kynaston, D.D. (late Snow). Third Edition. Extra fcap. 8vo. 4s. 6d.

Xenophon. Easy Selections (for Junior Classes). With a Vocabulary, Notes, and Map. By J. S. Phillpotts, B.C.L., and C. S. Jerram, M.A. Third Edition. Extra fcap. 8vo. 3s. 6d.

—— *Selections* (for Schools). With Notes and Maps. By J. S. Phillpotts, B.C.L. Fourth Edition. Extra fcap. 8vo. 3s. 6d.

—— *Anabasis,* Book I. Edited for the use of Junior Classes and Private Students. With Introduction, Notes, etc. By J. Marshall, M.A., Rector of the Royal High School, Edinburgh. Extra fcap. 8vo. 2s. 6d.

—— *Anabasis,* Book II. With Notes and Map. By C. S. Jerram, M.A. Extra fcap. 8vo. 2s.

—— *Cyropaedia,* Books IV and V. With Introduction and Notes by C. Bigg, D.D. Extra fcap. 8vo. 2s. 6d.

Aristotle's Politics. By W. L. Newman, M.A. [*In the Press.*]

Aristotelian Studies. I. On the Structure of the Seventh Book of the Nicomachean Ethics. By J. C. Wilson, M.A. 8vo. stiff, 5s.

Aristotelis Ethica Nicomachea, ex recensione Immanuelis Bekkeri. Crown 8vo. 5s.

Demosthenes and Aeschines. The Orations of Demosthenes and Æschines on the Crown. With Introductory Essays and Notes. By G. A. Simcox, M.A., and W. H. Simcox, M.A. 1872. 8vo. 12s.

Head (Barclay V.). Historia Numorum: A Manual of Greek Numismatics. Royal 8vo. half-bound. 2l. 2s. *Just Published.*

Hicks (E. L., M.A.). A Manual of Greek Historical Inscriptions. Demy 8vo. 10s. 6d.

Homer. Odyssey, Books I–XII. Edited with English Notes, Appendices, etc. By W. W. Merry, M.A., and the late James Riddell, M.A. 1886. Second Edition. Demy 8vo. 16*s*.

Homer. A Grammar of the Homeric Dialect. By D. B. Monro, M.A. Demy 8vo. 10*s*. 6*d*.

Sophocles. The Plays and Fragments. With English Notes and Introductions, by Lewis Campbell, M.A. 2 vols.

    Vol. I. Oedipus Tyrannus. Oedipus Coloneus. Antigone. 8vo. 16*s*.

    Vol. II. Ajax. Electra. Trachiniae. Philoctetes. Fragments. 8vo. 16*s*.

IV. FRENCH AND ITALIAN.

Brachet's Etymological Dictionary of the French Language, with a Preface on the Principles of French Etymology. Translated into English by G. W. Kitchin, D.D. Third Edition. Crown 8vo. 7*s*. 6*d*.

—— *Historical Grammar of the French Language.* Translated into English by G. W. Kitchin, D.D. Fourth Edition. Extra fcap. 8vo. 3*s*. 6*d*.

Works by GEORGE SAINTSBURY, M.A.

Primer of French Literature. Extra fcap. 8vo. 2*s*.

Short History of French Literature. Crown 8vo. 10*s*. 6*d*.

Specimens of French Literature, from Villon to Hugo. Crown 8vo. 9*s*.

MASTERPIECES OF THE FRENCH DRAMA.

Corneille's Horace. Edited, with Introduction and Notes, by George Saintsbury, M.A. Extra fcap. 8vo. 2*s*. 6*d*.

Molière's Les Précieuses Ridicules. Edited, with Introduction and Notes, by Andrew Lang, M.A. Extra fcap. 8vo. 1*s*. 6*d*.

Racine's Esther. Edited, with Introduction and Notes, by George Saintsbury, M.A. Extra fcap. 8vo. 2*s*.

Beaumarchais' Le Barbier de Séville. Edited, with Introduction and Notes, by Austin Dobson. Extra fcap. 8vo. 2*s*. 6*d*.

Voltaire's Mérope. Edited, with Introduction and Notes, by George Saintsbury. Extra fcap. 8vo. cloth, 2*s*.

Musset's On ne badine pas avec l'Amour, and *Fantasio.* Edited, with Prolegomena, Notes, etc., by Walter Herries Pollock. Extra fcap. 8vo. 2*s*.

    The above six Plays may be had in ornamental case, and bound in Imitation Parchment, price 12*s*. 6*d*.

Sainte-Beuve. Selections from the Causeries du Lundi. Edited by George Saintsbury. Extra fcap. 8vo. 2*s.*

Quinet's Lettres à sa Mère. Selected and edited by George Saintsbury. Extra fcap. 8vo. 2*s.*

Gautier, Théophile. Scenes of Travel. Selected and Edited by George Saintsbury. Extra fcap. 8vo. 2*s.*

L'Éloquence de la Chaire et de la Tribune Françaises. Edited by Paul Blouët, B.A. (Univ. Gallic.). Vol. I. French Sacred Oratory. Extra fcap. 8vo. 2*s.* 6*d.*

Edited by GUSTAVE MASSON, B.A.

Corneille's Cinna. With Notes, Glossary, etc. Extra fcap. 8vo. *cloth*, 2*s.* Stiff covers, 1*s.* 6*d.*

Louis XIV and his Contemporaries; as described in Extracts from the best Memoirs of the Seventeenth Century. With English Notes, Genealogical Tables, &c. Extra fcap. 8vo. 2*s.* 6*d.*

Maistre, Xavier de. Voyage autour de ma Chambre. Ourika, by *Madame de Duras;* Le Vieux Tailleur, by *MM. Erckmann-Chatrian;* La Veillée de Vincennes, by *Alfred de Vigny;* Les Jumeaux de l'Hôtel Corneille, by *Edmond About;* Mésaventures d'un Écolier, by *Rodolphe Töpffer.* Third Edition, Revised and Corrected. Extra fcap. 8vo. 2*s.* 6*d.*

Molière's Les Fourberies de Scapin, and *Racine's Athalie.* With Voltaire's Life of Molière. Extra fcap. 8vo. 2*s.* 6*d.*

Molière's Les Fourberies de Scapin. With Voltaire's Life of Molière. Extra fcap. 8vo. stiff covers, 1*s.* 6*d.*

Molière's Les Femmes Savantes. With Notes, Glossary, etc. Extra fcap. 8vo. *cloth,* 2*s.* Stiff covers, 1*s.* 6*d.*

Racine's Andromaque, and *Corneille's Le Menteur.* With Louis Racine's Life of his Father. Extra fcap. 8vo. 2*s.* 6*d.*

Regnard's Le Joueur, and *Brueys and Palaprat's Le Grondeur.* Extra fcap. 8vo. 2*s.* 6*d.*

Sévigné, Madame de, and her chief Contemporaries, Selections from the Correspondence of. Intended more especially for Girls' Schools. Extra fcap. 8vo. 3*s.*

Dante. Selections from the Inferno. With Introduction and Notes. By H. B. Cotterill, B.A. Extra fcap. 8vo. 4*s.* 6*d.*

Tasso. La Gerusalemme Liberata. Cantos i, ii. With Introduction and Notes. By the same Editor. Extra fcap. 8vo. 2*s.* 6*d.*

V. GERMAN.

Scherer (W.). A History of German Literature. Translated from the Third German Edition by Mrs. F. Conybeare. Edited by F. Max Müller. 2 vols. 8vo. 21*s.*

Max Müller. The German Classics, from the Fourth to the Nineteenth Century. With Biographical Notices, Translations into Modern German, and Notes. By F. Max Müller, M.A. A New Edition, Revised, Enlarged, and Adapted to Wilhelm Scherer's 'History of German Literature,' by F. Lichtenstein. 2 vols. crown 8vo. 21*s.*

GERMAN COURSE. By HERMANN LANGE.

The Germans at Home; a Practical Introduction to German Conversation, with an Appendix containing the Essentials of German Grammar. Second Edition. 8vo. 2*s.* 6*d.*

The German Manual; a German Grammar, Reading Book, and a Handbook of German Conversation. 8vo. 7*s.* 6*d*

Grammar of the German Language. 8vo. 3*s.* 6*d.*

German Composition; A Theoretical and Practical Guide to the Art of Translating English Prose into German. 8vo. 4*s.* 6*d.*

Lessing's Laokoon. With Introduction, English Notes, etc. By A Hamann, Phil. Doc., M.A. Extra fcap. 8vo. 4*s.* 6*d.*

Schiller's Wilhelm Tell. Translated into English Verse by E. Massie, M.A. Extra fcap. 8vo. 5*s.*

Also, Edited by C. A. BUCHHEIM, Phil. Doc.

Becker's Friedrich der Grosse. Extra fcap. 8vo. *In the Press.*

Goethe's Egmont. With a Life of Goethe, &c. Third Edition. Extra fcap. 8vo. 3*s.*

—— *Iphigenie auf Tauris.* A Drama. With a Critical Introduction and Notes. Second Edition. Extra fcap. 8vo. 3*s.*

Heine's Prosa, being Selections from his Prose Works. With English Notes, etc. Extra fcap. 8vo. 4*s.* 6*d.*

Heine's Harzreise. With Life of Heine, Descriptive Sketch of the Harz, and Index. Extra fcap. 8vo. paper covers, 1*s.* 6*d.*; cloth, 2*s.* 6*d.*

Lessing's Minna von Barnhelm. A Comedy. With a Life of Lessing, Critical Analysis, etc. Extra fcap. 8vo. 3*s.* 6*d.*

—— *Nathan der Weise.* With Introduction, Notes, etc. Extra fcap. 8vo. 4*s.* 6*d.*

Schiller's Historische Skizzen; Egmont's Leben und Tod, and Belagerung von Antwerpen. With a Map. Extra fcap. 8vo. 2s. 6d.

—— *Wilhelm Tell*. With a Life of Schiller; an historical and critical Introduction, Arguments, and a complete Commentary, and Map. Sixth Edition. Extra fcap. 8vo. 3s. 6d.

—— *Wilhelm Tell*. School Edition. With Map. 2s.

Modern German Reader. A Graduated Collection of Extracts in Prose and Poetry from Modern German writers:—
Part I. With English Notes, a Grammatical Appendix, and a complete Vocabulary. Fourth Edition. Extra fcap. 8vo. 2s. 6d.
Part II. With English Notes and an Index. Extra fcap. 8vo. 2s. 6d.

Niebuhr's Griechische Heroen-Geschichten. Tales of Greek Heroes. Edited with English Notes and a Vocabulary, by Emma S. Buchheim. School Edition. Extra fcap. 8vo., *cloth*, 2s. *Stiff covers*, 1s. 6d.

VI. MATHEMATICS, PHYSICAL SCIENCE, &c.

By LEWIS HENSLEY, M.A.

Figures made Easy: a first Arithmetic Book. Crown 8vo. 6d.

Answers to the Examples in Figures made Easy, together with two thousand additional Examples, with Answers. Crown 8vo. 1s.

The Scholar's Arithmetic: with Answers. Crown 8vo. 4s. 6d.

The Scholar's Algebra. Crown 8vo. 4s. 6d.

Aldis (W. S., M.A.). A Text-Book of Algebra. Crown 8vo. Nearly ready.

Baynes (R. E., M.A.). Lessons on Thermodynamics. 1878. Crown 8vo. 7s. 6d.

Chambers (G. F., F.R.A.S.). A Handbook of Descriptive Astronomy. Third Edition. 1877. Demy 8vo. 28s.

Clarke (Col. A. R., C.B., R.E.). Geodesy. 1880. 8vo. 12s. 6d.

Cremona (Luigi). Elements of Projective Geometry. Translated by C. Leudesdorf, M.A. 8vo. 12s. 6d.

Donkin. Acoustics. Second Edition. Crown 8vo. 7s. 6d.

Euclid Revised. Containing the Essentials of the Elements of Plane Geometry as given by Euclid in his first Six Books. Edited by R. C. J. Nixon, M.A. Crown 8vo. 7s. 6d.

Sold separately as follows,

Books I–IV. 3s. 6d.   Books I, II. 1s. 6d.
Book I. 1s.

Galton (Douglas, C.B., F.R.S.). The Construction of Healthy Dwellings. Demy 8vo. 10s. 6d.

Hamilton (Sir R. G. C.), and J. Ball. Book-keeping. New and enlarged Edition. Extra fcap. 8vo. limp cloth, 2s.
  Ruled Exercise books adapted to the above may be had, price 2s.

Harcourt (A. G. Vernon, M.A.), and H. G. Madan, M.A. Exercises in Practical Chemistry. Vol. I. Elementary Exercises. Third Edition. Crown 8vo. 9s.

Maclaren (Archibald). A System of Physical Education: Theoretical and Practical. Extra fcap. 8vo. 7s. 6d.

Madan (H. G., M.A.). Tables of Qualitative Analysis. Large 4to. paper, 4s. 6d.

Maxwell (J. Clerk, M.A., F.R.S.). A Treatise on Electricity and Magnetism. Second Edition. 2 vols. Demy 8vo. 1l. 11s. 6d.

—— *An Elementary Treatise on Electricity.* Edited by William Garnett, M.A. Demy 8vo. 7s. 6d.

Minchin (G. M., M.A.). A Treatise on Statics with Applications to Physics. Third Edition, Corrected and Enlarged. Vol. I. *Equilibrium of Coplanar Forces.* 8vo. 9s. Vol. II. *Statics.* 8vo. 16s.

—— *Uniplanar Kinematics of Solids and Fluids.* Crown 8vo. 7s. 6d.

Phillips (John, M.A., F.R.S.). Geology of Oxford and the Valley of the Thames. 1871. 8vo. 21s.

—— *Vesuvius.* 1869. Crown 8vo. 10s. 6d.

Prestwich (Joseph, M.A., F.R.S.). Geology, Chemical, Physical, and Stratigraphical. Vol. I. Chemical and Physical. Royal 8vo. 25s.

Roach (T., M.A.). Elementary Trigonometry. Crown 8vo. Nearly ready.

Rolleston's Forms of Animal Life. Illustrated by Descriptions and Drawings of Dissections. New Edition. (*Nearly ready.*)

Smyth. A Cycle of Celestial Objects. Observed, Reduced, and Discussed by Admiral W. H. Smyth, R.N. Revised, condensed, and greatly enlarged by G. F. Chambers, F.R.A.S. 1881. 8vo. *Price reduced to* 12s.

Stewart (Balfour, LL.D., F.R.S.). A Treatise on Heat, with numerous Woodcuts and Diagrams. Fourth Edition. Extra fcap. 8vo. 7s. 6d.

***Vernon-Harcourt** (L. F., M.A.)*. *A Treatise on Rivers and Canals*, relating to the Control and Improvement of Rivers, and the Design, Construction, and Development of Canals. 2 vols. (Vol. I, Text. Vol. II, Plates.) 8vo. 21*s*.

—— *Harbours and Docks;* their Physical Features, History, Construction, Equipment, and Maintenance; with Statistics as to their Commercial Development. 2 vols. 8vo. 25*s*.

***Watson** (H. W., M.A.)*. *A Treatise on the Kinetic Theory of Gases*. 1876. 8vo. 3*s*. 6*d*.

***Watson** (H. W., D. Sc., F.R.S.), and S. H. Burbury, M.A.*
I. *A Treatise on the Application of Generalised Coordinates to the Kinetics of a Material System*. 1879. 8vo. 6*s*.
II. *The Mathematical Theory of Electricity and Magnetism*. Vol. I. Electrostatics. 8vo. 10*s*. 6*d*.

***Williamson** (A. W., Phil. Doc., F.R.S.)*. *Chemistry for Students*. A new Edition, with Solutions. 1873. Extra fcap. 8vo. 8*s*. 6*d*.

VII. HISTORY.

***Bluntschli** (J. K.)*. *The Theory of the State*. By J. K. Bluntschli, late Professor of Political Sciences in the University of Heidelberg. Authorised English Translation from the Sixth German Edition. Demy 8vo. half bound, 12*s*. 6*d*.

***Finlay** (George, LL.D.)*. *A History of Greece* from its Conquest by the Romans to the present time, B.C. 146 to A.D. 1864. A new Edition, revised throughout, and in part re-written, with considerable additions, by the Author, and edited by H. F. Tozer, M.A. 7 vols. 8vo. 3*l*. 10*s*.

***Fortescue** (Sir John, Kt.)*. *The Governance of England:* otherwise called The Difference between an Absolute and a Limited Monarchy. A Revised Text. Edited, with Introduction, Notes, and Appendices, by Charles Plummer, M.A. 8vo. half bound, 12*s*. 6*d*.

***Freeman** (E.A., D.C.L.)*. *A Short History of the Norman Conquest of England*. Second Edition. Extra fcap. 8vo. 2*s*. 6*d*.

***George** (H. B., M.A.)*. *Genealogical Tables illustrative of Modern History*. Third Edition, Revised and Enlarged. Small 4to. 12*s*.

***Hodgkin** (T.)*. *Italy and her Invaders*. Illustrated with Plates and Maps. Vols. I—IV, A.D. 376–553. 8vo. 3*l*. 8*s*.

***Kitchin** (G. W., D.D.)*. *A History of France*. With numerous Maps, Plans, and Tables. In Three Volumes. *Second Edition*. Crown 8vo. each 10*s*. 6*d*.
    Vol. 1. Down to the Year 1453.
    Vol. 2. From 1453–1624.   Vol. 3. From 1624–1793.

Payne (E. J., M.A.). A History of the United States of America. In the Press.

Ranke (L. von). A History of England, principally in the Seventeenth Century. Translated by Resident Members of the University of Oxford, under the superintendence of G. W. Kitchin, D.D., and C. W. Boase, M.A. 1875. 6 vols. 8vo. 3*l*. 3*s*.

Rawlinson (George, M.A.). A Manual of Ancient History. Second Edition. Demy 8vo. 14*s*.

Rogers (J. E. Thorold, M.A.). The First Nine Years of the Bank of England. 8vo. cloth. *Just ready*.

Select Charters and other Illustrations of English Constitutional History, from the Earliest Times to the Reign of Edward I. Arranged and edited by W. Stubbs, D.D. Fifth Edition. 1883. Crown 8vo. 8*s*. 6*d*.

Stubbs (W., D.D.). The Constitutional History of England, in its Origin and Development. Library Edition. 3 vols. demy 8vo. 2*l*. 8*s*.

Also in 3 vols. crown 8vo. price 12*s*. each.

—— *Seventeen Lectures on the Study of Medieval and Modern History*, &c., delivered at Oxford 1867-1884. Demy 8vo. half-bound, 10*s*. 6*d*.

Wellesley. A Selection from the Despatches, Treaties, and other Papers of the Marquess Wellesley, K.G., during his Government of India. Edited by S. J. Owen, M.A. 1877. 8vo. 1*l*. 4*s*.

Wellington. A Selection from the Despatches, Treaties, and other Papers relating to India of Field-Marshal the Duke of Wellington, K.G. Edited by S. J. Owen, M.A. 1880. 8vo. 24*s*.

A History of British India. By S. J. Owen, M.A., Reader in Indian History in the University of Oxford. In preparation.

VIII. LAW.

Alberici Gentilis, I.C.D., I.C., De Iure Belli Libri Tres. Edidit T. E. Holland, I.C.D. 1877. Small 4to. half morocco, 21*s*.

Anson (Sir William R., Bart., D.C.L.). Principles of the English Law of Contract, and of Agency in its Relation to Contract. Fourth Edition. Demy 8vo. 10*s*. 6*d*.

—— *Law and Custom of the Constitution.* Part I. Parliament. Demy 8vo. 10*s*. 6*d*.

Bentham (Jeremy). An Introduction to the Principles of Morals and Legislation. Crown 8vo. 6*s*. 6*d*.

Digby (Kenelm E., M.A.). An Introduction to the History of the Law of Real Property. Third Edition. Demy 8vo. 10*s*. 6*d*.

Gaii Institutionum Juris Civilis Commentarii Quattuor; or, Elements of Roman Law by Gaius. With a Translation and Commentary by Edward Poste, M.A. Second Edition. 1875. 8vo. 18*s*.

Hall (W. E., M.A.). International Law. Second Ed. 8vo. 21*s.*

Holland (T. E., D.C.L.). The Elements of Jurisprudence.
Third Edition. Demy 8vo. 10*s.* 6*d.*

—— *The European Concert in the Eastern Question*, a Collection of Treaties and other Public Acts. Edited, with Introductions and Notes, by Thomas Erskine Holland, D.C.L. 8vo. 12*s.* 6*d.*

Imperatoris Iustiniani Institutionum Libri Quattuor; with Introductions, Commentary, Excursus and Translation. By J. B. Moyle, B.C.L.. M.A. 2 vols. Demy 8vo. 21*s.*

Justinian, The Institutes of, edited as a recension of the Institutes of Gaius, by Thomas Erskine Holland, D.C.L. Second Edition, 1881. Extra fcap. 8vo. 5*s.*

Justinian, Select Titles from the Digest of. By T. E. Holland, D.C.L., and C. L. Shadwell, B.C.L. 8vo. 14*s.*

Also sold in Parts, in paper covers, as follows:—
Part I. Introductory Titles. 2*s.* 6*d.*   Part II. Family Law. 1*s.*
Part III. Property Law. 2*s.* 6*d.*   Part IV. Law of Obligations (No. 1). 3*s.* 6*d.*
Part IV. Law of Obligations (No. 2). 4*s.* 6*d.*

Lex Aquilia. The Roman Law of Damage to Property: being a Commentary on the Title of the Digest 'Ad Legem Aquiliam' (ix. 2). With an Introduction to the Study of the Corpus Iuris Civilis. By Erwin Grueber, Dr. Jur., M.A. Demy 8vo. 10*s.* 6*d.*

Markby (W., D.C.L.). Elements of Law considered with reference to Principles of General Jurisprudence. Third Edition. Demy 8vo. 12*s.*6*d.*

Twiss (Sir Travers, D.C.L.). The Law of Nations considered as Independent Political Communities.
Part I. On the Rights and Duties of Nations in time of Peace. A new Edition, Revised and Enlarged. 1884. Demy 8vo. 15*s.*
Part II. On the Rights and Duties of Nations in Time of War. Second Edition Revised. 1875. Demy 8vo. 21*s.*

IX. MENTAL AND MORAL PHILOSOPHY, &c.

Bacon's Novum Organum. Edited, with English Notes, by G. W. Kitchin, D.D. 1855. 8vo. 9*s.* 6*d.*

—— Translated by G. W. Kitchin, D.D. 1855. 8vo. 9*s.* 6*d.*

Berkeley. The Works of George Berkeley, D.D., formerly Bishop of Cloyne; including many of his writings hitherto unpublished. With Prefaces, Annotations, and an Account of his Life and Philosophy, by Alexander Campbell Fraser, M.A. 4 vols. 1871. 8vo. 2*l.* 18*s.*
The *Life, Letters,* &c. 1 vol. 16*s.*

—— *Selections from.* With an Introduction and Notes. For the use of Students in the Universities. By Alexander Campbell Fraser, LL.D. Second Edition. Crown 8vo. 7*s.* 6*d.*

Fowler (*T., D.D.*). *The Elements of Deductive Logic*, designed mainly for the use of Junior Students in the Universities. Eighth Edition, with a Collection of Examples. Extra fcap. 8vo. 3s. 6d.

—— *The Elements of Inductive Logic*, designed mainly for the use of Students in the Universities. Fourth Edition. Extra fcap. 8vo. 6s.

—— *and Wilson* (*J. M., B.D.*). *The Principles of Morals* (Introductory Chapters). 8vo. *boards*, 3s. 6d.

—— *The Principles of Morals.* Part II. (Being the Body of the Work.) 8vo. 10s. 6d. *Just Published.*

Edited by T. FOWLER, D.D.

Bacon. Novum Organum. With Introduction, Notes, &c. 1878. 8vo. 14s.

Locke's Conduct of the Understanding. Second Edition. Extra fcap. 8vo. 2s.

Danson (*J. T.*). *The Wealth of Households.* Crown 8vo. 5s.

Green (*T. H., M.A.*). *Prolegomena to Ethics.* Edited by A. C. Bradley, M.A. Demy 8vo. 12s. 6d.

Hegel. The Logic of Hegel; translated from the Encyclopaedia of the Philosophical Sciences. With Prolegomena by William Wallace, M.A. 1874. 8vo. 14s.

Lotze's Logic, in Three Books; of Thought, of Investigation, and of Knowledge. English Translation; Edited by B. Bosanquet, M.A., Fellow of University College, Oxford. 8vo. *cloth,* 12s. 6d.

—— *Metaphysic,* in Three Books; Ontology, Cosmology, and Psychology. English Translation; Edited by B. Bosanquet, M.A. 8vo. *cloth,* 12s. 6d.

Martineau (*James, D.D.*). *Types of Ethical Theory.* Second Edition. 2 vols. Crown 8vo. 15s.

Rogers (*J. E. Thorold, M.A.*). *A Manual of Political Economy,* for the use of Schools. Third Edition. Extra fcap. 8vo. 4s. 6d.

Smith's Wealth of Nations. A new Edition, with Notes, by J. E. Thorold Rogers, M.A. 2 vols. 8vo. 1880. 21s.

X. ART, &c.

Head (*Barclay V.*). *Historia Numorum. A Manual of Greek* Numismatics. Royal 8vo. *half morocco,* 42s.

Hullah (*John*). *The Cultivation of the Speaking Voice.* Second Edition. Extra fcap. 8vo. 2s. 6d.

Ouseley (*Sir F. A. Gore, Bart.*). *A Treatise on Harmony.* Third Edition. 4to. 10s.

—— *A Treatise on Counterpoint, Canon, and Fugue,* based upon that of Cherubini. Second Edition. 4to. 16s.

—— *A Treatise on Musical Form and General Composition.* Second Edition. 4to. 10s.

Robinson (J. C., F.S.A.). A Critical Account of the Drawings
by Michel Angelo and Raffaello in the University Galleries, Oxford. 1870. Crown 8vo. 4s.

Ruskin (John, M.A.). A Course of Lectures on Art, delivered before the University of Oxford in Hilary Term, 1870. 8vo. 6s.

Troutbeck (J., M.A.) and R. F. Dale, M.A. A Music Primer (for Schools). Second Edition. Crown 8vo. 1s. 6d.

Tyrwhitt (R. St. J., M.A.). A Handbook of Pictorial Art. With coloured Illustrations, Photographs, and a chapter on Perspective by A. Macdonald. Second Edition. 1875. 8vo. half morocco, 18s.

Upcott (L. E., M.A.). An Introduction to Greek Sculpture. Crown 8vo. 4s. 6d.

Vaux (W. S. W., M.A.). Catalogue of the Castellani Collection of Antiquities in the University Galleries, Oxford. Crown 8vo. 1s.

The Oxford Bible for Teachers, containing supplementary HELPS TO THE STUDY OF THE BIBLE, including Summaries of the several Books, with copious Explanatory Notes and Tables illustrative of Scripture History and the characteristics of Bible Lands; with a complete Index of Subjects, a Concordance, a Dictionary of Proper Names, and a series of Maps. Prices in various sizes and bindings from 3s. to 2l. 5s.

Helps to the Study of the Bible, taken from the OXFORD BIBLE FOR TEACHERS, comprising Summaries of the several Books, with copious Explanatory Notes and Tables illustrative of Scripture History and the Characteristics of Bible Lands; with a complete Index of Subjects, a Concordance, a Dictionary of Proper Names, and a series of Maps. Crown 8vo. *cloth*, 3s. 6d.; 16mo. *cloth*, 1s.

LONDON: HENRY FROWDE,
OXFORD UNIVERSITY PRESS WAREHOUSE, AMEN CORNER,

OXFORD: CLARENDON PRESS DEPOSITORY,
116 HIGH STREET.

☞ *The* DELEGATES OF THE PRESS *invite suggestions and advice from all persons interested in education; and will be thankful for hints, &c. addressed to the* SECRETARY TO THE DELEGATES, *Clarendon Press, Oxford.*

www.ingramcontent.com/pod-product-compliance
Lightning Source LLC
Chambersburg PA
CBHW020907230426
43666CB00008B/1341